Entrepreneurial Cognition

Dean A. Shepherd • Holger Patzelt

Entrepreneurial Cognition

Exploring the Mindset of Entrepreneurs

Dean A. Shepherd
University of Notre Dame
South Bend, IN, USA

Holger Patzelt
Technical University Munich
München, Bayern, Germany

ISBN 978-3-319-71781-4   ISBN 978-3-319-71782-1 (eBook)
https://doi.org/10.1007/978-3-319-71782-1

Library of Congress Control Number: 2017961832

© The Editor(s) (if applicable) and The Author(s) 2018. This book is an open access publication.
Open Access This book is licensed under the terms of the Creative Commons Attribution 4.0 International License (http://creativecommons.org/licenses/by/4.0/), which permits use, sharing, adaptation, distribution and reproduction in any medium or format, as long as you give appropriate credit to the original author(s) and the source, provide a link to the Creative Commons license and indicate if changes were made.
The images or other third party material in this book are included in the book's Creative Commons license, unless indicated otherwise in a credit line to the material. If material is not included in the book's Creative Commons license and your intended use is not permitted by statutory regulation or exceeds the permitted use, you will need to obtain permission directly from the copyright holder.
The use of general descriptive names, registered names, trademarks, service marks, etc. in this publication does not imply, even in the absence of a specific statement, that such names are exempt from the relevant protective laws and regulations and therefore free for general use.
The publisher, the authors and the editors are safe to assume that the advice and information in this book are believed to be true and accurate at the date of publication. Neither the publisher nor the authors or the editors give a warranty, express or implied, with respect to the material contained herein or for any errors or omissions that may have been made. The publisher remains neutral with regard to jurisdictional claims in published maps and institutional affiliations.

Printed on acid-free paper

This Palgrave Macmillan imprint is published by Springer Nature
The registered company is Springer International Publishing AG
The registered company address is: Gewerbestrasse 11, 6330 Cham, Switzerland

Dean would like to dedicate this book to his daughter Meg and the rest of Diamond Dynamics Blue (for reasons stated in the preface).

Holger would like to dedicate this book to his wife Sylvia and daughter Helen.

Preface

"What do you know about softball?" asks my daughter as she hopes to convince me (Dean) to resign as assistant (and first base) coach of her softball team. I must admit I had asked myself the same question over the last two years, but I told her that perhaps I know a bit about how to think, which I believed had helped the girls and the team. In past seasons, the girls had worn their hearts on their sleeves such that one error (e.g., striking out looking) created such a negative emotional reaction (and a stream of tears) that it created a subsequent more intense negative emotion that the rest of the team caught, putting performance in a downward spiral.

I worked with the girls on how some errors are part of the game, explaining that they are a source of learning, and I gave them some tools for regulating their emotions. As with all coaches of junior sports, we (the other coaches and I) struggled at times to capture and maintain the girls' attention. We worked on mechanisms that helped them switch their attention to critical events (with some but not complete success). We worked on helping each girl find/develop her identity for the specific role she plays on the field and for the identity of the team (which sometimes created identity conflict as we asked some girls to play non-preferred positions for the good of the team). It was interesting to see how the team developed their knowledge of the game—from not knowing where to throw the ball once fielded to consciously thinking before the play where they would throw the ball if it were to come to them (given which bases were occupied by the other team) and, eventually, more automatically making the "right" play.

Sometimes the girls played like superstars, whereas other times they played horribly, and while the other coaches and I tried to stimulate the former and eliminate the latter, we never completely understood the "special sauce" of the team's motivation. However, we did find that they played better when they were more relaxed and energetic than "professional" and bored, which was stimulated by music during warm-up and a team dance just before the game started. (I would have joined in the team dance, but my daughter was already embarrassed by my being so close to the action and telling unfunny jokes all the time.)

I followed my daughter's advice and stopped coaching this season. Having coached the girls for two years, I think I was able to import some of my knowledge into helping develop their cognition (individually and collectively as a team). From them, I learned the different ways in which people think and the complexity of a team's shared cognition, and I learned that helping people regulate their emotions is not an easy task.

Fortunately, this book is not about the thinking, feelings, and actions of a girl's softball team but about the cognitions of individuals engaged in the entrepreneurial context—a topic that we (Dean and Holger) have been studying for over two decades.

University of Notre Dame South Bend, IN, USA Technical University Munich Munich, Bayern, Germany	Dean A. Shepherd Holger Patzelt

Acknowledgments

Dean and Holger would like to thank Ali Ferguson for the help in copy-editing the manuscript, Alexis Bezos and Ali Webster for their help in formatting the book, and Marcus Ballenger and Jazmine Robles from Palgrave Macmillan for their editorial support.

We would also like to thank the co-authors on the studies that directly contributed to the content of this book (roughly in order that they occur in the book): Trent Williams, Robert Baron, Anne Domurath, Dawn DeTienne, Julio DeCastro, David Deeds, Steve Bradley, Jeff McMullen, Stephanie Fernhaber, Tricia McDougall, Johan Wiklund, Evan Douglas, Mark Shanley, Dev Jennings, Willie Ocasio, Denis Grégoire, Pam Barr, Melissa Cardon, Maw Der Foo, Marcus Wolfe, Orla Byrne, Mike Haynie, Sara Thorgren, Joakim Wincent, Dan Holland, Deniz Ucbasaran, Andy Lockett, John Lyon, Rene Bakker, Young rok Choi, Denis Warnecke, Jeff Covin, Don Kuratko, Judith Behrens, Holger Ernst, Moren Levesque, Jeff Hornsby, Jennifer Bott, Nicki Breugst, Ethel Brundin, Anja Klaukien, and Rob Mitchell.

Contents

1 Introduction — 1

2 Prior Knowledge and Entrepreneurial Cognition — 7

3 Motivation and Entrepreneurial Cognition — 51

4 Attention and Entrepreneurial Cognition — 105

5 Entrepreneurial Identity — 137

6 Emotion and Entrepreneurial Cognition — 201

7 Conclusion — 259

Index — 277

List of Figures

Fig. 5.1	Optimal distinctiveness for an entrepreneuring individual's identity	144
Fig. 5.2	Micro-identities and the 'super-ordinate' identity	145
Fig. 5.3	Compartmentalization of micro-identities	148
Fig. 5.4	Integration of micro-identities	149
Fig. 5.5	Managing entrepreneurs' multiple micro-identities to maximize PWB	152
Fig. 5.6	Optimal distinctiveness and psychological well-being	153
Fig. 5.7	Managing multiple identities	154

CHAPTER 1

Introduction

How do people think? By understanding how people think, we can do a better job of explaining their actions. Both of us (the authors) were drawn to this topic in the extreme context of entrepreneurship. This context is extreme because the actions associated with entrepreneurship can have a substantial impact on the individual taking the actions, the economy, communities, the environment, and society as a whole. For example, to explain why one individual creates a venture to benefit the community (Shepherd and Williams 2014) whereas another individual creates a venture that harms the natural environment for personal gain (Shepherd et al. 2013), we need to understand people's cognitions—what happens in their minds. Not only are the outcomes of entrepreneurial actions extreme (in their impact), but the associated decision making is also extreme—extreme in uncertainty, complexity, time pressure, emotionality, and identity investment. We felt that investigating cognition under such extreme conditions afforded us the opportunity to work—and push forward—the knowledge frontier. That is, we were able to take the existing body of knowledge (from relevant literatures on cognitive science, decision making, and other aspects of psychology) and adapt it, twist it, and blend it to make a new form that would explain entrepreneurial cognition. For example, how do people make decisions in highly uncertain environments—that is, when one does not know the odds of different alternative outcomes occurring (i.e., risk), nor does one even know the possible alternative outcomes because, at this stage, they are not yet knowable? Such decisions typically need to be made quickly (e.g., before the window of opportunity closes) and require substantial investment of cognitive and emotional resources, and the impact of these decisions is highly consequential (e.g., a misstep could lead to failure).

The topic of entrepreneurial cognition has fascinated us and motivated our research over the last two decades. Although this research has resulted in publications in the top entrepreneurship, strategy, management, and psychology journals, we thought now would be a good time to pause, reflect on our work, and bring these individual pieces of the puzzle together to provide a cohesive big picture of entrepreneurial cognition. This book is the culmination of our motivation to provide this big picture.

ENTREPRENEURIAL CONTEXT AND COGNITION

The environments organizations operate within are complex and dynamic and often involve swift, significant, and discontinuous change (Hitt 2000). As such, managers must act strategically in response to these changes to maintain their firm's competitive advantage (Ireland and Hitt 1999; Pérez-Nordtvedt et al. 2008). Individuals and organizations can take advantage of opportunities arising in such dynamic environments and realize substantial gains (Eisenhardt 1989; Eisenhardt and Martin 2000; Sirmon et al. 2007). On the other hand, however, uncertainty surrounding these environmental changes' source, magnitude, and consequences can make identifying and acting upon opportunities a challenging endeavor. Why are some individuals and managers able to identify and successfully act upon opportunities in uncertain environments while others are unable to do so?

The current book proposes that an important answer to the above question emerges from the individuals' entrepreneurial mindset. Entrepreneurship scholars explore "how opportunities to bring into existence 'future' goods and services are discovered, created, an exploited, by whom, and with what consequences" (Venkataraman 1997: 120). Specifically, over that last two decades, scholars have conducted various studies with the aim to better understand the components, antecedents, and outcomes of an entrepreneurial mindset; these studies have explored how characteristics of individuals, teams, organizations, and environments facilitate or obstruct entrepreneurial thinking and action.

This book culminates the results of our research on this topic. In various studies, we have applied a cognitive lens to understand individuals' knowledge, motivation, attention, identity, and emotions in the entrepreneurial process.

First, in a series of studies we have explored the role of prior knowledge at the start of the entrepreneurial process. We assume that heterogeneity in individuals' knowledge provides an answer to one of the most important questions in entrepreneurship research: Why do some individuals recognize new business opportunities while others do not? More specifically, we ask: How do different types of knowledge trigger the recognition of different types (e.g., commercial, sustainable, health-related, international) of opportunities? How do different sources of knowledge (internal and external to the entrepreneur) influence opportunity recognition? Having identified important types and sources of knowledge, how do cognitive processes, in particular structural alignment, in conjunction with prior knowledge impact opportunity identification? In Chap. 2, we address these questions drawing on extant research from both cognitive science and entrepreneurship.

Second, beyond knowledge, motivation is an important driver of entrepreneurs' identification and subsequent exploitation of opportunities. While we acknowledge the motivational role of financial rewards for entrepreneurship and explore how financial rewards interact with prior knowledge, we note that many entrepreneurs are driven by non-financial motivation. What types of motivation other than financial can motivate (or demotivate) entrepreneurial action? What types of motivation trigger the exploitation of opportunities targeted toward sustaining nature or the communal environment and developing society as a whole? And how does one's psychological and physical health impact entrepreneurial motivation? What is the role of one's personal values in driving such motivation? And finally, what triggers the motivation to persist with entrepreneurial action in the face of obstacles (as opposed to engaging in it in the first place)? In Chap. 3 we address these questions from multiple theoretical angles to gain a comprehensive understanding of what motivates entrepreneurs to discover, exploit, and persist with new opportunities of various types.

Third, management and entrepreneurship research has highlighted the important role of attention in the entrepreneurial process. Given that attention is a limited cognitive resource, allocation to those aspects of the environment that are related to new opportunities is central to entrepreneurial action. How can managers' attention be guided in organizations to facilitate opportunity identification? How does the allocation of entrepreneurs' attention impact opportunity evaluation? What drives managers' attention to underperforming entrepreneurial projects? Finally, how does attention interfere with entrepreneurs' metacognitive processes—processes which are known to be of central importance to develop entrepreneurial cognition? In Chap. 4, we try to answer these questions and illustrate how attentional processes guide entrepreneurial cognition.

Fourth, one important topic in psychology research is to understand how individuals develop their self-identity—that is, how do they answer the question "Who am I?" This research has shown that a meaningful self-identity is central to individuals' psychological functioning and well-being. How can entrepreneurs develop such a meaningful identity that balances distinctiveness and belonging and therefore maximizes well-being? Further, how can entrepreneurs manage different micro-identities across different situations (e.g., entrepreneur and family member)? How can individuals use an entrepreneurial career to recover from traumatic events that disrupt their current work identities? And finally, in the specific case of family businesses where business-related and family-related identities highly overlap, how can entrepreneurs cope with identity conflict? In Chap. 5, we tackle these questions drawing on optimal distinctiveness theory and other theoretical streams from the identity literature.

Fifth, entrepreneurship has often been depicted as an "emotional rollercoaster" with multiple, and sometimes extreme, ups and downs, and psychologists have long established that these emotional experiences impact individuals' cognitions. How do emotions, both positive and negative, impact entrepreneurs' opportunity recognition? How do emotions, displayed by supervisors, impact employees' entrepreneurial motivation? Further, given that the failure of entrepreneurial projects is known to often cause substantial negative emotions, how do these emotions impact team members' learning and organizational commitment? And how do these effects depend on the organizational environment and individual coping behaviors and self-compassion? In Chap. 6 we explore these questions to shed more light on the role of emotions for entrepreneurial cognition.

Chapter 7 concludes the book by discussing implications for scholars and practitioners. We suggest a number of directions for future research that hopefully inspire future scholarship on individuals' and managers' abilities to identify and successfully act upon the opportunities provided by the dynamic, hypercompetitive, and uncertain business environments of today.

REFERENCES

Eisenhardt, K. M. (1989). Making fast strategic decisions in high-velocity environments. *Academy of Management Journal, 32*(3), 543–576.
Eisenhardt, K. M., & Martin, J. A. (2000). Dynamic capabilities: What are they? *Strategic Management Journal, 21*(10/11), 1105–1121.
Hitt, M. A. (2000). The new frontier: Transformation of management for the new millennium. *Organizational Dynamics, 28*(3), 7–17.
Ireland, R. D., & Hitt, M. A. (1999). Achieving and maintaining strategic competitiveness in the 21st century: The role of strategic leadership. *Academy of Management Executive, 13*(1), 43–57.
Pérez-Nordtvedt, L., Payne, G. T., Short, J. C., & Kedia, B. L. (2008). An entrainment-based model of temporal organizational fit, misfit, and performance. *Organization Science, 19*(5), 785–801.
Shepherd, D. A., & Williams, T. A. (2014). Local venturing as compassion organizing in the aftermath of a natural disaster: The role of localness and community in reducing suffering. *Journal of Management Studies, 51*(6), 952–994.
Shepherd, D. A., Patzelt, H., & Baron, R. A. (2013). "I care about nature, but…": Disengaging values in assessing opportunities that cause harm. *Academy of Management Journal, 56*(5), 1251–1273.
Sirmon, D. G., Hitt, M. A., & Ireland, R. D. (2007). Managing firm resources in dynamic environments to create value: Looking inside the black box. *Academy of Management Review, 32*(1), 273–292.
Venkataraman, S. (1997). The distinctive domain of entrepreneurship research. *Advances in Entrepreneurship, Firm Emergence and Growth, 3*(1), 119–138.

Open Access This chapter is licensed under the terms of the Creative Commons Attribution 4.0 International License (http://creativecommons.org/licenses/by/4.0/), which permits use, sharing, adaptation, distribution and reproduction in any medium or format, as long as you give appropriate credit to the original author(s) and the source, provide a link to the Creative Commons license and indicate if changes were made.

The images or other third party material in this chapter are included in the chapter's Creative Commons license, unless indicated otherwise in a credit line to the material. If material is not included in the chapter's Creative Commons license and your intended use is not permitted by statutory regulation or exceeds the permitted use, you will need to obtain permission directly from the copyright holder.

CHAPTER 2

Prior Knowledge and Entrepreneurial Cognition

The ability to identify opportunities is among the most important skills successful entrepreneurs have (Ardichvili et al. 2003), thus making this topic particularly important for entrepreneurship research. For instance, Gaglio and Katz (2001: 95) argued that "understanding the opportunity identification process represents one of the core intellectual questions for the domain of entrepreneurship." Additionally, research on the resource-based view of the firm has recently begun exploring opportunity identification as a resource that can result in competitive advantage through the process of exploitation (Alvarez and Busenitz 2001). As can be expected, researchers are rather interested in understanding why, when, and how certain individuals are able to recognize opportunities whereas other individuals either cannot or do not (Shane and Venkataraman 2000). In particular, studies have found that knowledge—"a fluid mix of framed experience, important values, contextual information, and expert insight that provides a framework for evaluating and incorporating new experiences and information" (Davenport and Prusak 1998: 4)—plays a crucial role in the entrepreneurial process. How do individuals' prior knowledge and knowledge acquired through external sources impact the opportunity-recognition process? Which type of knowledge matters for which type of opportunities? And which cognitive processes during opportunity recognition does knowledge trigger? In this chapter, we investigate the relationship between knowledge, cognitive processes, and entrepreneurs' opportunity recognition.

© The Author(s) 2018
D. A. Shepherd, H. Patzelt, *Entrepreneurial Cognition*,
https://doi.org/10.1007/978-3-319-71782-1_2

Prior Knowledge and Opportunity Recognition

Thus far, entrepreneurship research has largely taken an Austrian economics perspective centered on the notion of prior knowledge. Austrian economics scholars suggest that differing levels of prior knowledge allow some individuals to identify certain opportunities while others fail to do so (Hayek 1945; Venkataraman 1997). Prior knowledge, which denotes the unique information a person has on a particular topic, enables that person to recognize particular opportunities (Venkataraman 1997; Shane 2000). Individuals obtain prior knowledge, for example, from their education (Gimeno et al. 1997) or experience at work (Evans and Leighton 1989; Cooper et al. 1994). Prior knowledge is often gained through experiential learning, either intentionally or unintentionally, via direct experience, the experiences of others (vicarious learning), and/or second-hand experience (Huber 1991). As an example, Ed Pauls, the inventor of the NordicTrack, is a prime example of how prior knowledge facilitates opportunity recognition. A mechanical engineer passionate about cross-country skiing, Ed was often frustrated when he was not able to go skiing due to severe weather. From this frustration, he identified an opportunity and used his engineering knowledge and skills to develop an indoor cross-country ski machine.

Previous studies on cognition have argued that increased knowledge within a specific field can lead to important advantages for individuals. For example, individuals become increasingly efficient as they gain more knowledge about a task through experience—namely, they begin to focus their attention on crucial dimensions of the task, generally dimensions that contribute the most variance to decision outcomes (Choo and Trotman 1991). Additionally, those who have more knowledge seem to draw more on intuition and thus make decisions in a more automatic way as opposed to going through more mindful methodical processing (Logan 1990). Automatic processing and the resulting decisions are generally quicker than the more methodical processing.

Busenitz and Barney (1997) showed that entrepreneurs—compared to managers—tend to depend on heuristics to increase the speed of their decisions. Without these heuristics, entrepreneurs would often miss out on opportunities as the window of time to act on opportunities tends to close quickly. Furthermore, general human capital, which refers to prior knowledge gained through education, helps individuals accumulate and integrate new knowledge, which in turn opens up a wider opportunity set (Gimeno et al. 1997). Indeed, Davidsson and Honig (2003) found that the number of years of education an individual has positively influences that person's likelihood of identifying new opportunities. Applying the literature on prior knowledge to the recognition of opportunities, those with more prior knowledge (compared to those with less prior knowledge) will pay more attention to the most important aspects of the available information and will then process this information more efficiently, thus facilitating the recognition of more opportunities. Beyond their focus on key information dimensions and enhanced information-processing efficiency, knowledgeable individuals develop stronger, more, and richer connections between mental concepts (Gobbo and Chi 1986), which in turn enhance their capabilities to recognize innovative opportunities.

Researchers have also shown that prior knowledge is an important element of creativity. According to Amabile (1997: 42), relevant knowledge or expertise "can be viewed as the set of cognitive pathways that may be followed for solving a given problem or doing a given task—the problem solver's network of possible wanderings." Further, in their study on absorptive capacity, Cohen and Levinthal (1990: 130) highlighted why pertinent prior knowledge can increase the number of innovative ideas: "the prior possession of relevant knowledge and skill is what gives rise to creativity, permitting the sorts of associations and linkages that may have never been considered before." Thus, prior knowledge seems to increase individuals' ability not only to produce more opportunities but also to enhance those opportunities' level of innovativeness. For example, in one study, my (Dean) colleague and I (Shepherd and DeTienne 2005) found that more prior knowledge about customer problems leads to the recognition of a greater number of opportunities. In addition, the opportunities higher-knowledge individuals identify tend to have high levels of innovativeness. These results are in line with the arguments presented by researchers who study entrepreneurship through the lens of Austrian economics as well as with the literature on cognition. However, these results may not be applicable to other types of prior knowledge, and they may not represent a clear-cut blessing.

Studies in the expertise literature (e.g., Fiske and Taylor 1991) have shown that as individuals gain experience, their thoughts can start to become channeled in such a way that they fall into mental ruts. For instance, when an individual has prior knowledge of ways to serve the market, his or her thoughts may be channeled along known pathways. In turn, creative thought becomes more difficult and unlikely, thus making the recognition of innovative opportunities more challenging. Such mental ruts also tend to make it increasingly difficult for seasoned decision makers to identify new variables or recognize environmental change (Tversky and Kahneman 1974), and they limit individuals' ability to think "outside the box," which can make recognizing more innovative opportunities difficult. Whether this limited creativity and constrained ability to identify opportunities help or hurt firm performance seems to be determined by the task at hand in relation to the knowledge comprising the particular individual's expertise (Shanteau 1992). As such, entrepreneurship scholars who explore the connection between prior knowledge and opportunity identification must carefully differentiate between types of prior knowledge.

Both of these perspectives could be possible—namely, that prior knowledge leads people to recognize more opportunities that display themselves higher in innovativeness but that some individuals may become entrenched in mental ruts as they gain more experience. Indeed, this relationship could be curvilinear such that there is an early increase in the number and innovativeness of opportunities until a plateau is reached, which is then followed by a decline. These are just expectations, however; additional research is needed to fully understand these relationships.

Moreover, it is likely that prior knowledge and opportunity identification are related in a more complicated way than a clear-cut main-effect-only explanation. Through our more in-depth analysis, we found that the relationship between individuals' prior knowledge of customer problems and their ability to recognize an opportunity varies depending on—at least to some extent—differences in the financial reward they receive for completing the task (Shepherd and DeTienne 2005; see also Csikszentmihalyi 1975, 2000; Maheswaran and Sternthal 1990). While it is valuable to explain why certain individuals (and not others) recognize opportunities based on the prior knowledge they have, the mechanisms underlying how prior knowledge facilitates opportunity recognition remain largely unclear to date. Interestingly, a better understanding of the relationship between prior knowledge and opportunity recognition may come from focusing on specific potential opportunities, namely, those that enhance the natural and communal environments, to which we now turn.

Prior Knowledge and Opportunities That Support and Enhance Natural and Communal Environments

Known as "a source of resources and services for the utilitarian life support of humankind" (Costanza et al. 1997; Daily 1997), the *natural environment* includes the *earth*, *biodiversity*, and *ecosystems* and the phenomena that constitute the physical world (Parris and Kates 2003). Numerous individuals and groups have noted the importance of protecting the natural environment for fear of threats to the existence of many species, including humans, if the natural world is damaged. The Global Scenario Group, for example, encouraged the world's population to protect the "beauties of the earth," while others have emphasized how important it is to safeguard open green spaces and natural resources (Boston Indicators Project 2007).

Referring to the communities in which people live, the communal environment consists of a complex network of relationships between people with common history, norms, meanings, values, and identity (Etzioni 1996). Unique to communities are their specific *culture, groups,* and *places*. In case these distinguishing elements are threatened, the community faces decline and even collapse. Culture, in particular, plays a central role in the communal environment as "human beings have a right to culture—not just any culture, but to their own" (Margalit and Halbertal 2004: 529). Thus, the ability to conserve a culture as an element of the larger society enables community members to develop and secure their personal identity.

Knowledge of Natural and Communal Environments

Individuals' prior knowledge about natural and communal environments is likely to influence their ability to identify possible opportunities to protect and/or maintain those environments. Knowledge of air- and water-pollution sources in developing economies, for instance, facilitated individuals' recognition of opportunities for ovens that considerably lessen particle pollutants in households as well as opportunities for inexpensive methods to convert polluted water to drinking water (Prahalad 2007). Furthermore, knowledge about specific cultures has uncovered opportunities to sustain those cultures (Foley 2003). For example, Peredo and Chrisman (2006: 322–323) introduced:

> [community-based enterprise as] an adaptive and socially innovative response to macro-economic social, legal, and political factors with economic, social, environmental, political, and cultural fallout for already impoverished communities. The effectiveness and energy … of community reaction to these factors may be facilitated by local community culture, which taps into ancestral values, practices, and collective learning from previous community mobilizations. The energy of a local response fosters a cycle between culture and action: local culture encourages community action, but, at the same time, community action reinforces local culture and entrepreneurship.

Indeed, individuals who do not have this type of knowledge about the environment and/or culture may be too uninformed to even question whether any changes take place in these phenomena and whether such changes affect the life of human beings (Patzelt and Shepherd 2011). Thus, it is unlikely that such individuals will identify opportunities to protect natural and communal environments.

Differences in people's prior knowledge about natural and communal environments can be explained—at least partially—by variation in their education, life experiences, and cultural and social backgrounds. Individuals specializing in chemistry, for example, have the scientific knowledge needed to understand the chemical processes underlying ozone-layer damage, air pollution, and wastewater treatment. Similarly, individuals with a specialization in biology have the knowledge needed to comprehend pollution's biological impact on aquatic habitats. Moreover, individuals' social and cultural backgrounds may affect their prior knowledge and ability to identify opportunities. For instance, opportunities to maintain a threatened culture are often identified by members of that particular culture (Foley 2003).

Heterogeneity in prior knowledge can also help explain variation in how people direct their attention toward certain characteristics of natural and communal environments and thus their ability to identify opportunities that protect those environments (consistent with Shepherd and Patzelt 2011). In other words, individuals are much more likely to pay attention to sustainability opportunities that relate to their prior knowledge about a particular part of the environment (consistent with Shane 2000). For instance, while reducing greenhouse gas emissions and conserving the rain forest both counter climate change to a degree (Tilman et al. 2002), when beginning to think about opportunities to offset climate change, individuals with a background in chemistry will likely identify different opportunities than individuals with a background in biology. Chemists are more likely to focus on developing new chemicals that can substitute for greenhouse gases, whereas biologists are more likely to focus on protecting the rain forest by developing, for example, alternative materials for producing furniture so as to reduce the use of tropical woods.

Prior Knowledge of Societal Problems

Prior knowledge about societal problems often enables individuals to identify opportunities to develop economic and non-economic gains for disadvantaged people (Patzelt and Shepherd 2011). People can acquire this type of prior knowledge from a variety of sources, including education, work experience, personal experience, and social experience. Differences in prior knowledge about societal problems are likely to at least partially explain why some people and organizations pay attention to particular aspects of developing economic and non-economic gains for society, whereas others pay attention to other aspects. Identifying opportunities to assist disadvantaged others by creating economic and non-economic gains is often easier when individuals can take others' perspective and "put themselves in their shoes." By attempting to take another person's perspective, the individual tries to understand that person's thoughts by cognitively positioning him- or herself in the other person's situation to obtain information about his or her development needs. Depending on their prior knowledge of societal problems, individuals will process and use this information in different ways and will focus on different methods to develop people and society.

Entrepreneurial Knowledge: Bringing It All Together for Action

In addition to having knowledge about natural and communal environments and about societal problems, having prior *entrepreneurial* knowledge is often imperative in identifying possible opportunities. Individuals' entrepreneurial knowledge likely impacts how much their prior knowledge of natural and communal environments facilitates their identification of opportunities that protect or sustain those environments (Patzelt and Shepherd 2011). For instance, Ibrahim Abouleish—founder of the Egyptian company Sekem—realized that reduced pesticide use and the introduction of organic agricultural methods could help protect the natural environment in this country. Abouleish was able to identify this specific opportunity due to his in-depth knowledge of the pharmaceutical market, which he gained throughout his career in the pharmaceutical industry. Based on this unique knowledge, Abouleish formed the opportunity belief that organic food and herbs can be grown and commercialized in national and international food and pharmaceutical markets. Thus, Abouleish complemented his knowledge about organic agriculture with entrepreneurial knowledge in order to protect the environment, and this complementarity increased the effect of Abouleish's prior knowledge on his development of a sustainability opportunity belief (Seelos and Mair 2005; as described in Patzelt and Shepherd 2011).

Knowledge, Entrepreneurship, and Others' Health

Health plays an inarguably important role in people's lives, so it is unsurprising that scholars are interested in investigating this topic. Although there is some entrepreneurship research focusing on health (e.g., the impact a career as an entrepreneur has on people's psychological [e.g., Tetrick et al. 2000] and physical [Boyd and Gumpert 1983] well-being or research on startups in the biopharmaceutical industry that develop new drugs [e.g., Evans and Varaiya 2003; Deeds et al. 1999; Patzelt et al. 2008]), there are many opportunities left to substantially grow this research stream and thus contribute to our understanding of entrepreneurial phenomena (and, hopefully, people's lives) (Shepherd and Patzelt 2015). When we use the term "health," we are referring to both physical health ("the physiological and physical status of the body") and mental health ("the state of the mind, including basic intellectual functions") (Ware et al. 1981). Additionally, to ensure the scope of our task is feasible, we limit our discussion to *personal* health as these health-related aspects "end at the skin" and therefore have a clearly defined boundary (Ware et al. 1981).

Those who have prior knowledge about the health problems of others are likely to be the individuals who identify opportunities to improve these others' health. Many individuals personally deal with health-related problems or gain familiarity with such problems by caring for loved ones. By directly or indirectly experiencing a particular health problem, an individual not only develops a strong understanding of the specifics of the problem but also gains in-depth knowledge of existing treatments and how those treatments fall short. In turn, this knowledge can lead the individual to recognize latent demand. For instance, Han Pham was infected by bacteria from a mishap with a dirty vaccination needle. Later, while in graduate school for design, Pham recognized an opportunity stemming from her needlestick injury and developed the YellowOne Needle Cap, which is a yellow cap made of plastic. The cap turns cans for soft drink into a safe receptacle for discarded needles by preventing the needles from coming back out (www.designtoimprovlife.dk).

While individuals who directly or indirectly experience health problems may recognize an opportunity for someone, they may not have the knowledge required to personally act on the opportunity (McMullen and Shepherd 2006). Acting on an opportunity to develop a new product to overcome a health problem, for instance, might require knowledge of marketing, production, and management in the particular health sector as well as the resources to do so. Take the example from above again: Pham's invention of the YellowOne Needle Cap ultimately resulted from the design knowledge she gained in graduate school. Acting on an opportunity to overcome health problems could be an especially significant context in which individuals who create and use innovations to solve their own health problems begin a process (perhaps unintentionally) that results in the development and exploitation of the health opportunity. It appears that studies on this process could build on the concept of user innovation (Shah and Tripsas 2007; von Hippel 1988). This perspective might be useful to develop the field of health entrepreneurship.

While they have different knowledge from individuals who have directly and indirectly experienced health issues, people who have not experienced problems with their own health may also possess knowledge that leads to the identification and exploitation of health-improving opportunities. For instance, some people have a deep understanding of technologies with the potential to become health solutions, such as engineer Dean Kamien. Kamien realized that many people who live in third-world countries do not have access to clean drinking water. This lack of clean water represents a significant health problem since drinking water that is of bad quality is full of microbial pathogens. These pathogens, in particular when combined with bad sanitation and poor hygiene, contribute to more than 1.7 million deaths every year (Ashbolt 2004). Kamien's goal was, in his words, to "solve the biggest world problem" by using his inventing and engineering knowledge to develop the Slingshot. The Slingshot is a system that is portable and requires little power but purifies water to an acceptable quality for humans (www.slingshotdoc.com).

Professionals in the field of medicine have particularly comprehensive knowledge about health problems across many different people, which makes them particularly capable of identifying opportunities that may address (some of these) problems (Simmons 2002). Studying patent data from the American Medical Association, Chatterji, Fabrizio, Mitchell, and Schulman (2008: 1532) discovered that "20% of the medical device patents filed in the United States during 1990–1996" came from doctors. However, while medical doctors may be in the position to identify opportunities for someone, they may ultimately feel they lack the knowledge necessary to exploit those opportunities, thus concluding that entrepreneurial action is infeasible (we address motivational issues in Chap. 3).

Prior Knowledge and Opportunities That Alleviate Others' Suffering After a Disaster

Many situations can lead to human suffering. Natural disasters, however, are particularly frequent occurrences that cause suffering of many individuals. The International Federation of Red Cross and Red Crescent Societies reports that in 2010, 406 natural disasters (not counting, e.g., epidemics and wars) occurred throughout the world (Armstrong et al. 2011). The damages these events caused amount to more than $123 billion, and the people killed in these events amount to more than 304 million (Armstrong et al. 2011). Overall, 2010 was the year with the greatest number of people affected by natural disasters; however, the data show that natural disasters regularly lead to significant human suffering (Armstrong et al. 2011). For the individual, *suffering* involves "the experience of pain or loss that evokes a form of anguish that threatens an individual's sense of meaning about his or her personal existence" (Dutton et al. 2006: 60; see also Sutcliffe and Vogus 2003).

Many organizations step in after natural disasters to aid victims and help the affected area recover. While these organizations do help many individuals, frequently they cannot address all victims' urgent needs, so suffering continues (e.g., Schneider 1992; Van Wart and Kapucu 2011). However, my (Dean) colleague and I (Shepherd and Williams 2014; Williams and Shepherd 2016) found that in this context—namely, when there are numerous outside resources after a disaster but established organizations are ineffective at alleviating suffering—local venturing is often successful. More specifically, local ventures are very effective at recognizing opportunities to organize abundant resources (generally provided by sources that are not harmed by the disaster). These ventures are also effective in the fast delivery of resources to those in need. This type of entrepreneurial action works well since it is locally driven, rapid, and customized to the urgent needs of those suffering.

Before investigating prior knowledge's role as a resource, it is important to understand how a disaster changes other resources. Disasters considerably reduce the amount of material, or *tangible*, resources in an area, such as *infrastructure, shelter, water, food, and physical health*, thus often worsening people's suffering. Disasters can ruin people's homes, including their houses, clothing, and belongings; devastate community infrastructure; kill or injure animals; destroy businesses, including business buildings, equipment, and inventory; and injure or kill community members.

While disasters cause significant damage at the local level, especially damage to much-needed resources, several non-physical, or *intangible*, resources are crucial for compassion venturing to ease victims' suffering (Shepherd and Williams 2014). Intangible resources constitute the community's social architecture. After a disaster, community members often maintain these non-physical resources. Moreover, sometimes they try to even improve them. For instance, after the Black Saturday bushfire disaster in Australia, "localness" or "being local" was influential in driving entrepreneurial actions, and an important factor of this localness was local knowledge (Shepherd and Williams 2014).

Referring to location-specific information, local knowledge includes a community's terrain, history, social networks, community members' skills, and available resources. After Black Saturday, local knowledge played a key role in facilitating collaboration among locals (individuals and organizations). Moreover, local knowledge triggered the cooperation between locals and non-locals and enabled more rapid delivery of customized solutions that helped address the victims' suffering. Local knowledge was primarily informal and tacit as it was generally not documented and was frequently challenging to transmit to others (Shepherd and Williams 2014).

INTERNATIONAL KNOWLEDGE AND OPPORTUNITIES TO GO ABROAD

International knowledge constitutes a critical intangible resource for entrepreneurship in an international context. However, due to liabilities of newness and foreignness, it can be difficult for individuals and organizations to obtain this knowledge. Contrary to arguments based on absorptive capacity, entrepreneurial firms' management teams (TMTs) having little international experience tend to capitalize on external sources providing international knowledge, such as venture capital organizations, alliance partners, and other firms in close proximity (Domurath and Patzelt 2016; Fernhaber et al. 2009).

International entrepreneurship comprises the "discovery, enactment, evaluation, and exploitation of opportunities across national borders to create future goods and services" (Oviatt and McDougall 2005). A majority of international entrepreneurship research has focused on new ventures (Zahra and George 2002), particularly on such ventures' need to address substantial limitations stemming from their newness and smallness as a prerequisite for internationalization (Knight and Cavusgil 2004). To become international, a venture must have a competitive advantage as a basis for dealing with the added costs of foreign business operations and succeed in doing business abroad (Dunning 2000; Rugman 1981). These tasks require resources. While many firms tend to leverage resources that are tangible when they enter international markets, resources that are intangible are frequently more likely to yield competitive advantage because they are difficult for competitors to replicate (Kotha et al. 2001). Researchers have shown that international knowledge, particularly for new ventures, constitutes a crucial intangible resource for internationalizing business operations (Bloodgood et al. 1996; Carpenter et al. 2003; Reuber and Fischer 1997).

Most scholarly work on international entrepreneurship has concentrated on the international experience of entrepreneurial TMTs as the main source of international knowledge. Because prior knowledge and experience enable individuals and firms to more readily identify opportunities (Shane 2000; Wiklund and Shepherd 2003; Patzelt and Shepherd

2011; and discussed above), new ventures that have more international knowledge based on their TMTs' prior experience will recognize a larger number of opportunities in foreign markets and therefore internationalize to a greater extent than ventures without such knowledge. New ventures may further utilize their TMTs' international experience to attract alliance partners from the international business arena and thus build credibility in foreign markets. Moreover, many firms whose TMT has international experience are able to internationalize more quickly than their counterparts (Reuber and Fischer 1997). This faster internationalization facilitates such firms' integration of international considerations into their organizational structure and processes sooner, thus speeding up growth in international markets (Autio et al. 2000) and yielding higher efficiency (Oviatt et al. 1995). Moreover, earlier internationalization can lead to a higher share of foreign sales of total sales (Reuber and Fischer 1997).

While prior research on international knowledge acquired internally through TMTs' previous experience has provided important insights into new venture internationalization, scholars have failed to adequately investigate international knowledge that comes from outside new ventures. This research gap is surprising given the important role the external environment plays in new venture internationalization (e.g., Coviello 2006; Johanson and Vahlne 2003) and entrepreneurs' assessments of opportunities in foreign markets (Domurath and Patzelt 2016), especially for overcoming liabilities of newness and foreignness. Most new ventures depend on knowledge sources that are external to the organization in order to confirm they are operating effectively and to enhance their overall chance of high performance (McGrath and MacMillan 1995). Internationalizing firms are likely to have a similar reliance on outside knowledge sources to learn how to effectively enter into foreign markets (Domurath and Patzelt 2016). While the internationalization process of new ventures can be influenced by their TMTs' prior international experience, the international business environment constantly changes (Hitt et al. 1998), making the value of TMTs' experience decline over time (Anand et al. 2002) and increasing the need for outside knowledge sources.

Alliance Partners

Strategic alliances are cooperative inter-firm agreements with the purpose of creating competitive advantages for all parties involved (Das and Teng 2000). These alliances represent an important formal relationship which provides entrepreneurial ventures with access to the resources they need for growth (Baum et al. 2000). In addition to gaining access to important resources, new firms are also likely to learn from the knowledge they obtain through these partnerships (Johannisson 2000; Haeussler et al. 2012). For instance, by interacting with alliance partners, entrepreneurial firms could access business intelligence or learn about new opportunities. Indeed, as Hite (2005: 113) contended, an entrepreneurial firm's partners provide the "conduits, bridges and pathways through which the firm can find and access external opportunities and resources." Scholars have also argued that strategic alliances provide the best access to new ideas and innovation (Dyer and Singh 1998) and are an important source of tacit knowledge about markets (Anand et al. 2002); these assets are indispensable for entrepreneurial ventures' growth and survival.

Thus, strategic alliances are a key external source of knowledge for entrepreneurial ventures. Accordingly, a strategic partner's level of business operations in or engagement with foreign markets likely affects to what extent the new venture's recognized opportunity and knowledge resources are international. Previous theoretical work has suggested that there is a positive link between new ventures' development of strategic partnerships and internationalization (Coviello and Munro 1995). The transmission of international knowledge influences this association to some degree (Johanson and Vahlne 2003), with higher levels of international knowledge among alliances having a larger influence on new ventures' efforts to internationalize. Numerous studies back this notion. Through surveying new ventures, Coviello and Munro (1995) found that 64% of the ventures' initial entry into international markets and the entry mode chosen stemmed from opportunities that were revealed to them by their alliance partners as opposed to the ventures' own opportunity-identification efforts. Similarly, Chen and Chen (1998) contented that alliance partnerships lead to higher levels of direct foreign investment and that smaller firms generally depend on such partnerships when internationalizing to a greater extent than larger firms. This higher dependence on alliances is likely the result of a lack of options and decreased information for decision making among small firms. Unsurprisingly, entrepreneurial firms are typically smaller than older firms (Hanks et al. 1993). Thus, forming alliances with firms that have higher levels of international experience in addition to a strong presence in an international market can greatly aid the ventures hoping to internationalize through enhanced knowledge of the local market (Fernhaber et al. 2009; Lu and Beamish 2001).

Venture Capital Firms

Building relationships with venture capital firms is another crucial way for new ventures to grow their knowledge base for recognizing new business opportunities (Fernhaber et al. 2009). Existing research has suggested that venture capital firms often provide entrepreneurial ventures with more than just financial resources (Sapienza 1992). These firms add value to entrepreneurial ventures by providing reputations (Chang 2004), granting access to expertise in business management (Baum and Silverman 2004; Ruhnka et al. 1992), assisting the ventures in finding and recruiting qualified personnel (MacMillan et al. 1989), and helping entrepreneurs formulate an appropriate strategy for their firm (Fried et al. 1998; MacMillan et al. 1989). An additional way venture capital organizations might be valuable to entrepreneurial ventures is by sharing knowledge related to foreign market entry, which likely occurs as a result of the managerial influence venture capitalists have over the entrepreneurial firms in their portfolios.

Venture capital firms generally take an active management role in their investees (Baum and Silverman 2004; Ruhnka et al. 1992); some even believe that they contribute directly to a venture's human resources (Florin et al. 2003). High levels of involvement are rooted in the risks venture capital firms take on when financing new ventures. Moreover venture capitalists not only desire to safeguard their invested capital but also to guarantee a high return on it (Fried et al. 1998). Sometimes, a venture capital firm's investment in a new venture can lead to the replacement of individuals in certain management positions (even the founder in some cases), participation in the board of directors, and continual monitoring of the investee's performance (Carpenter et al. 2003; Fried et al. 1998). That is, because venture capital organizations own part of their investees and provide them with access to limited finance, they often have numerous possibilities to affect what strategic decisions their investees take.

An examination of the existing literature shows that venture capital has become a global practice. Venture capitalists make widespread investments outside domestic markets (Wright et al. 2005). It is likely that a new firm will be encouraged to internationalize when the venture capital firm financing it has a high level of international knowledge/expertise. Along these lines, prior studies have investigated how greater ownership among external investors results in higher rates of ventures' activities in foreign markets (George et al. 2005). We build on these studies by suggesting that venture capital firms aid in the internationalization process of entrepreneurial ventures by providing them with international knowledge. Of course, the impact of venture capital firms' knowledge in this context varies depending on the extent of their international experience (Fernhaber et al. 2009).

Proximal Firms

Research on knowledge spillovers has argued that firms can profit from other firms' knowledge through informal interactions. This research has highlighted the importance of geographic proximity to one another for effective knowledge transfer to occur (Audretsch and Feldman 1996). As Saxenian (1990: 97) explained, people "meet at trade shows, industry conferences, and the scores of seminars, talks, and social activities organized by local business organizations and trade associations. In these forums, relationships are easily formed and maintained, technical and market information is exchanged, business contacts are established, and new enterprises are conceived." A particularly good illustration of the value of knowledge spillovers can be seen in industries characterized by intense research and development (R&D). Many multinational corporations, for instance, have built their R&D labs in specific locations based on the likelihood that spillovers of knowledge occur (Feinberg and Gupta 2004). The degree to which knowledge from one firm spills over to other firms is partially determined by the presence (or lack) of the relevant industry in the firm's specific geographic area. For instance, while Silicon Valley is the most renowned area for the development of new software, other top tech regions in the United States, such as San Francisco, Boston, and Austin, also represent regions in which knowledge spillovers can advance entrepreneurial firms depending on their industry presence. The notion of knowledge spillovers is usually associated with technological knowledge; however, knowledge spillovers are likely to also occur for international knowledge (Fernhaber et al. 2009). If many of the firms physically surrounding a new venture are international, the likelihood of international knowledge from these firms spilling over and influencing the new firm is greater (Fernhaber et al. 2008).

Internal and External Sources of Knowledge About International Markets

As we addressed above, alliance partners, venture capital firms, and proximal firms can provide entrepreneurial ventures with international knowledge. This knowledge is not usually an element of a formal exchange of resources per se; instead, it is a secondary benefit a new venture can exploit from this relationship. While we believe these external international knowledge sources will directly influence new ventures' international activities, it is also probable that the international knowledge possessed by the TMT of an entrepreneurial firm will impact the degree to which the firm accepts and capitalizes on these knowledge sources from outside.

One may assume that new ventures that have TMTs with greater international experience are more capable at identifying the worth of their networks' international knowledge and applying that knowledge when internationalizing. However, my (Dean) colleagues and I (Fernhaber et al. 2009a, b) found that new ventures having TMTs with limited or lacking international knowledge are more likely to take advantage of external knowledge sources. More specifically, new ventures generally have a "high ratio of assumption to knowledge" (McGrath and MacMillan 1995: 4), often motivating them to find external sources to confirm they are taking the right course of action and enhance their odds of success. These external knowledge sources are valuable because they compensate for—and sometimes even replace—new ventures' limited collection of internal knowledge sources. Indeed, as Stinchcombe and March (1965) described, new ventures' dependence on social networks for survival is one of the main elements of the liability of newness. This notion implies that when new ventures have inadequate internal international knowledge, they must depend on external international knowledge sources more heavily when making strategic decisions. That is, new ventures with limited knowledge about foreign markets are more likely to be motivated to seek out and actively exploit this knowledge in the outside environment. Entrepreneurial ventures that have TMTs with more international knowledge, on the other hand, will to a limited extent rely on outside knowledge sources (even though they will still benefit from these sources) for recognizing new opportunities in international markets.

Neo-institutional theory corroborates these assertions, demonstrating that during times of uncertainty, firms are more likely to seek out and compare themselves to similar firms in their environment to understand their own situation and adjust their behavior if necessary (Haunschild and Miner 1997). In general, uncertainty can be connected to being new and/or lacking experience (Shepherd et al. 2000). For instance, studying how Japanese firms make decision about their mode of foreign entry, Lu (2002) showed that experience moderates the impact of firms' isomorphic behavior on their mode of entry decision. Firms with weaker experience in foreign entries generally draw to a greater extent on other firms' previously used entry modes. Similarly, entrepreneurial firms with weaker international experience tend to confront higher uncertainty and thus to a greater extent depend on outside firms' international knowledge for opportunity recognition.

In addition, entrepreneurial ventures' TMTs with weaker international experience tend to profit more from outside international knowledge sources since they have a larger knowledge gap that needs to be filled. Indeed, new ventures sometimes deliberately choose to exploit external knowledge when seeking international opportunities because they recognize a shortage in their own knowledge. However, this exploitation can also occur inadvertently. For instance, a new venture may enter international markets because its partners wanted to or because a particularly valuable opportunity required such entry. An absence of international experience often increases the TMT's awareness of and openness to accept knowledge from outside sources. Indeed, in my (Dean) study on new venture internationalization with colleagues (Fernhaber et al. 2009), we showed that the association between the international knowledge of an entrepreneurial firm's external knowledge sources and the firm's internationalization is more positive when there is less international knowledge within the TMT than when there is more international knowledge within the TMT.

Knowledge, Cognitive Processes, and Opportunity Identification

Previous research has shown that when firms perceive discrepancies between their prior assumptions and environmental signals, a "trigger" is activated that concentrates their attention on the interpretation of the signals and prompts the development and pursuit of a response by the organization (Dutton and Jackson 1987). However, while we know what factors influence managerial perceptions of environmental signals within organizations (Kaplan 2008; Ocasio 1997), our understanding of perceptions of opportunities is incomplete. That is, compared to perceptions of threat, we know less about the processes individuals use to identify opportunities. However, we do know, as Baron (2006: 104) argued, that opportunity identification requires pattern recognition, or the ability to "'connect the dots between changes in technology, demographics, markets, government policies and other factors." Indeed, Baron and Ensley (2006) found that experts' opportunity prototypes show higher complexity levels than prototypes of novice entrepreneurs and highlight different characteristics of both the opportunity and the business.

Although these studies are a considerable step toward understanding opportunity identification, numerous conceptual issues and empirical difficulties still hinder research in this area. Some studies, for example, investigate opportunities that were identified in the past, thus leading to limitations caused by biases due to retrospection and success (Golden 1992; Huber and Power 1985). Consequently, it continues to be challenging to uncover precisely how attention to environmental signals fosters opportunity identification (Ocasio 1997; Shepherd et al. 2007, 2017); what the perceived features of the signals are (Jackson and Dutton 1988; Julian and Ofori-Dankwa 2008); what information-processing abilities individuals have (Kuvaas 2002; Milliken 1990); what crucial resources, resource slack, or strategies firms have (Chattopadhyay et al. 2001; Thomas and McDaniel 1990); or how prior knowledge (Dimov 2007b; Shane 2000; Shepherd and DeTienne 2005) and other capabilities and resources at the individual or organizational level are utilized (Barnett 2008; Cattani and Ferriani 2008). Thus, numerous unanswered questions remain surrounding *what* factors facilitate opportunity recognition as well as *how* and *why* these factors are so crucial.

To shed light on these issues, my (Dean) colleagues and I (Grégoire et al. 2010) explored the reasoning strategies individuals utilize to identify opportunities. More specifically, the study investigated two previously unaddressed questions: *what cognitive process facilitates individuals' opportunity recognition*, and *what particular role does the individual's prior knowledge play in this process*? To this end, we created a model of opportunity identification as a cognitive process of structural alignment (Gentner 1983, 1989). Next, we carried out exercises with founders to document their think-aloud articulations during their attempts to identify new technological opportunities. An analysis of these articulations determined the degree to which entrepreneurs utilize structural-alignment processes when identifying new technological opportunities as well as the impact prior knowledge has in these processes.

These findings of structural-alignment processes have broader implications for research on organizations. Crossan et al. (1999) showed that for organizational learning, opportunity recognition is based on mechanisms at the inter-individual, team, organization, and society levels (Davidsson 2003; Dimov 2007a); however, there are also many poorly understood individual processes at the center of this multilevel phenomenon. Moreover, opportunity recognition is a prerequisite to opportunity evaluation and pursuit by both individuals and organizations (McMullen and Shepherd 2006). Thus, individual opportunity-recognition processes are crucial not only for entrepreneurial firm foundation but also for learning, adaptation, renewal, and strategy formulation more generally within organizations (Crossan and Berdrow 2003; Zott and Amit 2007).

There is a recurrent discussion among scholars about the ontological nature of opportunities. That is, do opportunities come into being as objective artifacts waiting for predisposed individuals to "discover" them, or do they come into being out of these individuals' subjective interpretations and creative behavior? This discussion has received a great deal of attention (Davidsson 2003; McMullen et al. 2007), but it is our opinion that in its current form, this debate has led to a stalemate that impedes research on one of the most relevant phenomena for organization scholars; that is, it impedes research on the processes individuals and organizations use to identify and then exploit potential opportunities (Grégoire et al. 2010; McMullen and Shepherd 2006; Shepherd et al. 2007; Shepherd 2015).

Rather than focusing on the philosophical foundations of the nature of opportunities, it may be more beneficial to examine research suggesting that opportunities stem from changes, such as changes associated with new organizational or individual knowledge, changes in the actions of important players in the economy (e.g., customers, suppliers, competitors), or widespread changes in the macro-environment (e.g., new regulations, economic cycles) (Grégoire et al. 2010; see also Shepherd et al. 2007, 2017). However, while changes like these may make existing routines and processes less optimal, they do not represent opportunities in and of themselves. As an example, take an inventor developing a new technology. While this new technology may create an objectively distinguishable environmental change, he or she does not already "have" an opportunity. Further, the new technology itself does not signify an opportunity because opportunities are associated with action targeted at reaping benefits from these changes (Grégoire et al. 2010; Grégoire and Shepherd 2012). In the entrepreneurial context, for example, new technological opportunities would stem from *applying* the technology in a specific market context (see Venkataraman and Sarasvathy 2001: 652; Eckhardt and Shane 2003).

Yet, the appropriateness of using a new technology in a specific market context is uncertain from the beginning (Knight 1921; McMullen and Shepherd 2006) due to unbalanced knowledge diffusion (Hayek 1945) and restrictions to the rationality of the person (Simon 1957), including narrow attention (Ocasio 1997; Shepherd et al. 2007, 2017); this appropriateness can only be examined in hindsight. Thus, we can conclude that the opportunity-identification process has both objective and subjective dimensions: there is the objective reality of an individual's environment and then his or her subjective interpretation of this environment and of his or her role in that environment before any objective facts become available (McMullen and Shepherd 2006).

As such, research has focused on the difference between two interdependent phases of entrepreneurial action (McMullen and Shepherd 2006; Shepherd et al. 2017). The first phase deals with the emergence of subjective individual beliefs about the existence of an opportunity for somebody who possesses the capabilities/skills necessary for exploitation (2006: 137). The second deals with individuals' assessment of the opportunity for themselves or their organization—namely, whether they have the capabilities and motivation necessary for exploitation. Thus far, the majority of work on opportunity identification has either not distinguished between the two opportunity-process phases (e.g., Baron and Ensley 2006) or has concentrated on the assessment phase (e.g., Chattopadhyay et al. 2001; Krueger and Brazeal 1994; Sarasvathy 2001; Thomas and McDaniel 1990). Yet, to advance knowledge of the underlying mechanisms that lead individuals and organizations to pursue potential opportunities, research has also focused on the first phase—the process of identifying opportunities or

> efforts to make sense of signals of change (e.g., new information about new conditions) to form beliefs regarding whether or not enacting a course of action to address this change could lead to net benefits (for instance, in terms of profits, growth, competitive jockeying and/or other forms of individual or organizational gains). (Grégoire et al. 2010: 415)

Structural Alignment Connecting the Novel to the Known

We believe that the solution to this puzzle lies partly in examining the cognitive processes people use to make sense of new information. It is well documented that individuals mentally compare new information to their prior knowledge in order to understand it. With this perspective, being able to identify opportunity-relevant patterns requires individuals to put forth cognitive effort to see "resemblances" between what happens in the world (such indications of possible environmental changes) and their mental models of circumstances that are pertinent to understanding the new information as well as to (in the case of opportunity identification) recognizing a plan to potentially benefit from these changes.

However, how does this comparison and sensemaking occur in the real world? What cognitive processes do individuals use to evaluate resemblances between new information and their prior knowledge? This issue of resemblance is the focus of cognitive research on perceptions of similarity and the utilization and outcomes of similarity considerations across a large variety of reasoning tasks (cf. Holyoak and Thagard 1996). Research in this area emphasizes that similarity perceptions regarding two or more items of interest depend on individuals' alignment of mental representations of these items (Day and Gentner 2007; Keane et al. 1994). Following on this research stream, the cognitive process of *structural alignment* (Gentner 1983, 1989) can serve as a valuable foundation to explore opportunity recognition. Structural alignment represents a cognitive "tool" individuals use to compare objects. Based on this comparison, the individual then derives implications or generates new insights. When individuals come across a new object, for example, they tend to instinctively question if anything in the new object is similar to anything they have encountered previously. Based on identified similarities, individuals then make efforts to more fully make sense of the new object. As cognitive scientists have illustrated, these considerations and the associated structural-alignment mechanism take a vital role in how individuals understand new information, learn novel ideas, and create new categories (see Holland et al. 1986). These processes include scientific innovation, the development of new product ideas, strategy development (Gavetti and Rivkin 2005, 2007), and other tasks that require creativity (Dahl and Moreau 2002; Ward 1995).

A main finding of this literature is that alignment occurs at two levels. One level centers on *superficial features*, while the other level centers on *structural relationships* (Gentner 1983, 1989). Specifically, superficial features are a mental representation's basic "parts" in addition to its characteristics and attributes (Gentner et al. 1995: 271). Structural relationships, on the other hand, are the links connecting various superficial features as part of a mental representation. Further, research has found that there are two types of *structural* relationships. The first type are first-order structural relationships, which denote one-to-one functional relationships between superficial features. These superficial features can include direct effects and action verbs. The second type are higher-order relationships, which are "relationships between relationships" and are therefore more abstract. Higher-order relationships include goal statements, causal chains, and conditional rules (Gentner et al. 1993; Holyoak 1985).

To illuminate the difference between superficial features and structural relationships, my (Dean) colleagues and I (Grégoire et al. 2010: 416) used an example of a new technology which had been developed at MIT—namely, the 3DP™ discussed in Shane (2000). We illustrated the differences between superficial features and structural relationships as follows:

> Examples of superficial features of the technology include who developed the technology (mechanical engineers at MIT), the components of the technology (mechanical arm, print head), the material it uses (ceramic powders), and what the technology produced in the lab (e.g., ceramic filters, casting molds, etc.). Examples of first-order structural relationships include how the technology operates (e.g., [mechanical arm (moves) print head]; [print head (deposits) powder]). Higher-order structural relationships include more abstract capabilities of the technology (e.g., [how the technology operates] causes [fabrication of tridimensional objects with high level of automation and precision]).

Structural-alignment processes are a significant aspect of individuals' sensemaking efforts regarding new information. When individuals are presented with a new stimulus, they evaluate how its features and relationships align with those of a pertinent "source" (Gentner 1989; Holland et al. 1986). For example, this source could be a related object, or it could be a more intangible framework including a category or theoretical model the individual holds. Yet, more frequently such a related object is a mental representation of a situation that informs the individual's understanding of the new information. This comparison of new information with a related model, object, or situation (i.e., the determination of whether a target's superficial features and structural relationships align with those of a source) enables individuals to detect patterns that convey meaning. Based on these patterns, the individuals can derive useful conclusions.

However, research on structural alignment has also shown that different sets of cognitive structures and dynamics are required to process superficial features and structural relationships (Gentner 1989; Keane et al. 1994). Consequently, these two aspects of structural alignment are likely to impact opportunity-identification efforts in different ways. On the one hand, superficial features affect how individuals search for and retrieve information from their memory (Gentner 1989; Gentner et al. 1993). Thus, a new stimulus's superficial features (e.g., the material required for operating a new technology) may trigger individuals' recollection of comparable features of an important source (e.g., a market offering the material referenced in the previous example). The source the individual recalls from memory is often shaped by his or her previous experiences or familiarity with specific features. Alternatively, it can be shaped by his or her environment or current situation (e.g., a feature may be salient for a person because of particular events in his or her life). This shaping limits the number of superficially related domains one instantly (and unconsciously) accesses (Keane et al. 1994) when scanning for pertinent references for alignment. Structural relationships, in contrast, are intertwined in a more direct manner with higher-order processes of reasoning (Keane et al. 1994). As an example, the processing and alignment associated with structural relationships affect individuals' formation of categories (Namy and Gentner 2002), solving of problems (Catrambone and Holyoak 1989, 1990), and learning (Loewenstein and Gentner 2005).

Superficial features and structural relationships can both impact people's interpretations. However, scholars have demonstrated that structural relationships are especially crucial when individuals make inferences about a stimulus that is novel and/or ambiguous (Day and Gentner 2007; Gentner 1989). As such, my (Dean) colleagues and I (Grégoire et al. 2010) theorized that people's attempts to identify opportunities are likely to stress their use and alignment of structural relationships. There are two notions underlying this stress. First, individuals are likely to draw on structural relationships when stimuli are encoded in a deep and rich way. For example, such deep and rich encoding happens when one performs a cognitively demanding or emotionally challenging task (Blanchette and Dunbar 2001; Catrambone and Holyoak 1989). The opportunity-identification task fulfills both these conditions as information required is typically ambiguous and difficult to interpret. Similarly, these tasks are usually emotionally engaging largely due to the possible outcomes they may yield for entrepreneurs and their firms (Cardon et al. 2012; Ireland et al. 2003).

Second, scholars have found that from a neuro-cognitive perspective, the brain is activated more when individuals perceive alignment of structural relationships than when they notice alignment of superficial features (Holland et al. 1986; Keane et al. 1994). Based on this partiality for the alignment of structural relationships, individuals are better able to identify and compare meaningful patterns. These patterns might include superficial similarities (but not necessarily). Indeed, researchers from several fields have documented individuals' use of structurally based "mental leaps" (Holyoak and Thagard 1996). Such mental leaps occur, for example, when individuals think creatively and/or attempt to solve scientific problems (e.g., Dahl and Moreau 2002; Dunbar 1993; Ward 1995). In the context of strategic decisions, Gavetti and Rivkin (2005) reported how Andrew Grove (the former Intel CEO) realized the risk of deserting the low-end microprocessor segment. Instead of considering the context of computer or electronic products, he related Intel's situation to what occurred in the steel sector after Nucor and mini-mills were introduced. While reinforcing bars and microprocessors do not share many comparable characteristics, Nucor's entrance and success in the steel business was very similar to Intel's entrance and success in the microprocessor sector. Thus, Grove was able to formulate a strategy that prevented Intel from experiencing a similar future because he had knowledge of the history and decline of established US steel companies. The discussion above implies that when trying to identify opportunities, individuals tend to pay more attention to the alignment of structural relationships than to the alignment of superficial features. Along these lines, my (Dean) co-authors and I revealed that the opportunity-identification process requires higher levels of cognitive effort (i.e., attention) for the alignment of structural relationships than for the alignment of superficial features (Grégoire et al. 2010).

The Role of Prior Knowledge in the Structural-Alignment Process

As mentioned earlier, scholars have shown that since knowledge is not evenly distributed throughout the population, prior knowledge provides at least a partial explanation as to why some people are able to identify specific opportunities that other people miss (e.g., Corbett 2005; Dimov

2007b; Shane 2000; Shepherd and DeTienne 2005). Overall, work in this area has argued that prior knowledge serves as a foundation for the interpretation and use of new information; however, most studies on this topic have not delineated the cognitive mechanisms by which prior knowledge affects individuals' opportunity recognition. We believe that prior knowledge likely triggers individuals' consideration of structural relationships. For instance, domain experts often find reasoning in terms of structural relationships easier because they can draw on deeper mental representations (Chi et al. 1981). Such experts are particularly good at solving problems characterized by low levels of superficial similarity but high levels of structural similarity (Keane 1988). Additionally, research has demonstrated that when people fail to solve particular problems, "failure indices" are frequently left in long-term memory. Following Seifert et al.'s (1994) "opportunistic-assimilation hypothesis," these indices remain inactive until one has an encounter with a stimulus related to addressing the problem. At that point, failure indices "serve as signposts that guide subsequent retrieval processes back to stored aspects of the problematic situation" (Seifert et al. 1994: 87). That is, prior experience with a problem can enhance an individual's attentiveness to stimuli that are relevant for finding a solution (Dimov 2004). What these perspectives demonstrate is that prior knowledge enables individuals to notice structural similarities between new information and relevant contexts although superficial connections between the two are missing.

In line with the reasoning above, my (Dean) colleagues and I (Grégoire et al. 2010) revealed that in the opportunity-recognition process, individuals' dependence on higher levels of prior knowledge requires more cognitive effort (i.e., attention) for the alignment of structural relationships than for the alignment of superficial features. The results uncovered were in line with a structural-alignment model of opportunity identification, suggesting that these cognitive processes are vital to identifying opportunities. My (Dean) colleagues and I (Grégoire et al. 2010) showed that when entrepreneurs came across information related to a novel technology, they focused on the parallels between this information and contexts in which it could be useful. Further, the structural-alignment process involves various types of similarities, each having different outcomes, and some of these similarity considerations encompass the superficial features of technologies and markets. In line with studies in cognitive psychology (e.g., Gentner 1989; Keane et al. 1994), the findings imply that these features direct individuals' early attempts to look for contexts that serve as a point of reference for assessing the significance of the stimulus (which in our example includes the identification of markets that may align with the technology). Yet, most attempts to make sense of new information and determine whether the technology and the market fit in a way that they constitute a possible opportunity primarily depend on considering and aligning structural relationships (Grégoire et al. 2010).

Most importantly, the study found that perceiving similarities between higher-order relationships seems to be a vital part of the opportunity-identification process, a notion that is supported by three additional lines of evidence. First, when participants made verbalizations highlighting similarities between the superficial features of technologies and superficial features of markets, they allocated a significantly higher amount of attention to the alignment of the structural relationships between technologies and markets, and in doing so they emphasized high-order structural relationships. Moreover, several times the entrepreneurs came up with opportunities when there were numerous structural relationships that were shared by technologies and markets but when technologies and markets had few common superficial features. Said differently, entrepreneurs' ability to notice the alignment of structural relationships enabled the transfer of technologies across domains and thus formed opportunity beliefs that were not overtly evident. Third, when the entrepreneurs placed more emphasis on a stimulus' superficial features rather than on its structural relationships, they had greater difficultly thinking of possible opportunities. Similar challenges surfaced when other matters inhibited the entrepreneurs' ability to consider structural relationships (e.g., when one participant concentrated on assessing the viability of obtaining intellectual property protection for the technology or when another participant focused on time limits). As a whole, the three lines of evidence highlight that while superficial features may direct individuals' initial thinking about new information, reasoning based on the aligning structural relationships is a vital part of opportunity recognition.

Differences in the Nature of Opportunities and the Structural-Alignment Process

The discussion above concentrated on the factors that enable some individuals or organizations to identify and act upon promising activities (cf. Gruber et al. 2010; Plambeck and Weber 2009; Short et al. 2010). Although there has been sustained interest in and theorizing about the nature and sources of opportunities (e.g., Alvarez and Barney 2010; Jackson and Dutton 1988; McMullen et al. 2007), scholars have paid less theoretical and empirical attention to the impact of differences across opportunities, particularly in regard to initial opportunity identification. However, my (Dean) colleague and I (Grégoire and Shepherd 2012) created and tested an opportunity-identification model focusing on the effects of differences across potential opportunities. Expanding the assumptions outlined above, opportunity beliefs form as a result of cognitive efforts to understand possible "matches" between new ways of supply (e.g., new services, products, technologies, or business models) and the markets in which these new means of supply can be introduced. Thus, in the context of technology transfer, the formation of opportunity beliefs hinges on the consideration entrepreneurs give to the structural alignment between new technologies and markets (as described above and specified in Grégoire et al. [2010]).

The Effects of Convergent and Divergent Variations in Alignment

When thinking about structural alignment, we need to take into consideration that superficial and structural similarities can differ independently of one another. From a modeling perspective, the question thus arises as to whether the effects of superficial and structural similarity are merely additive or whether these two forms of similarity interact with one another. To answer this question, my (Dean) colleague and I (Grégoire and Shepherd 2012) tested for a possible interaction between the two dimensions (as detailed below). However, when trying to understand the challenges associated with recognizing potential opportunities, it becomes especially important to explore the meaning and influence that differences across forms of alignment may have on the development of opportunity beliefs. This issue is particularly relevant when the superficial and structural similarities of a technology-market combination are at odds with each other.

While new technologies are often depicted as only being appropriate for specific applications (i.e., how the technology was utilized "in the lab"), entrepreneurs frequently envision other uses for technologies in entirely different markets than the inventors (or those in charge of the commercialization) originally had in mind. Indeed, Shane (2000) described how the opportunities envisioned for the technology he investigated were frequently "non-obvious" even to entrepreneurs trying to exploit other opportunities *for the same technology*. Explanations for this "non-obviousness" have generally emphasized the role of entrepreneurs' unique knowledge resources in this context. More specifically, due to their greater knowledge and understanding of particular markets and industries compared to many technology inventors, some entrepreneurs are able to recognize market applications that the inventors never could have imagined (Gruber et al. 2008, 2012; Shane 2000; Ucbasaran et al. 2009).

Over and above entrepreneurs' prior market knowledge, a complementary explanation for opportunity identification is focused attention on the distinct influence of superficial and structural similarity in the development of opportunity beliefs. In the context of our model (Grégoire and Shepherd 2012), the seeming non-obviousness of opportunities appears to be caused by divergences stemming from the low levels of superficial similarities shared between markets and technologies even though they share high levels of structural similarities.

Cognitive science researchers have found that the human mind prefers reasoning involving higher-order structural relationships when interpreting ambiguous stimuli in uncertain contexts (Gentner 1989; Holland et al. 1986). For example, when making predictions about new objects, people generally prefer predictions that proceed from a comprehensive causal system as opposed to predictions that—while equally conceivable—are not part of such a system (Clement and Gentner 1991). Similarly, studies have shown that structural matches usually lead to more brain activity compared to superficial matches because the former activate more neuronal connections (Keane et al. 1994). The implication here is that when individuals think about entrepreneurial opportunities, they are likely to be more cognitively "aroused" when they notice commonalities between a new technology's structural features and the causes of latent demand in a market than when they notice superficial similarities between the technology and the market.

Despite the mind's preference for structural similarities, recognizing and processing structural similarities without superficial parallels are especially demanding cognitive activities (cf. Catrambone and Holyoak 1989). As a result, the absence of superficial similarities characteristic of some technology-market combinations can make opportunity ideas less apparent even when a technology's capabilities correspond to the causes of latent demand in a market. In turn, individuals may feel less certain or less positive about the resulting opportunity beliefs than they would in the case of high superficial similarity. Students often experience this challenge, for example, they often have a difficult time transferring the content and solutions they learn in one domain with specific superficial elements (e.g., math problems that use particular objects or units) to other domains with logically similar problems but different superficial features (e.g., physics problems focusing on different objects and units) (cf. Bassok and Holyoak 1989; Novick and Holyoak 1991). Ultimately, the absence of superficial similarities often makes knowledge transfer more challenging.

On the other hand, a dominant focus on superficial similarities can at times result in flawed reasoning premises, such as when there are superficial similarities present without structural similarities. For example, strong similarities between a technology's superficial elements and a market could potentially offset the detrimental effects of structural discrepancies between the technology's capabilities and the causes of latent demand in the market. When this occurs, individuals' opportunity beliefs are likely to be less negative than they would have been without such strong superficial similarities.

As a whole, these observations could explain why casual observers find it difficult to identify opportunities comprising technologies that share low levels of superficial similarity but high levels of structural similarity with markets. Again, while the human brain favors making inferences based on structural relationships, identifying and processing such relationships when superficial parallels are lacking are cognitively demanding. Nevertheless, cognitive researchers have shown that low superficial/high structural reasoning is vital to making inferences that enhance knowledge in highly uncertain contexts (Holland et al. 1986) and to making creative "mental leaps" (cf. Holyoak and Thagard 1996), such as when scientists, engineers, designers, and strategists come up with imaginative solutions to complex problems (Dahl and Moreau 2002; Dunbar 1993; Gavetti and Rivkin 2005).

Based on these observations regarding superficial/structural similarities and individuals' ability to recognize non-obvious opportunities, my

(Dean) colleague and I (Grégoire and Shepherd 2012) explored the degree to which beliefs about technology-market matches with low superficial similarity levels and high structural similarity levels differ from beliefs about technology-market matches with other similarity configurations. The study found that the human mind clearly prefers reasoning involving structural relationships such that opportunity beliefs about a novel technology-market match with low superficial similarity levels but high structural similarity levels are more positive than beliefs for new technology-market matches with high superficial similarity levels but low structural similarity levels, and—rather obviously—they are also more positive than beliefs for new technology-market matches with low levels of both superficial and structural similarity. Unsurprisingly, the most positive opportunity beliefs for new technology-market matches have high levels of both superficial and structural similarities.

Thus, as we have argued, differences across possible opportunities are relevant. That is, individuals' cognitive abilities and resources are not the only factors that matter in the formation of opportunity beliefs; information differences about opportunities' underlying elements play an important role in this process as well. Consideration of the ways differences in opportunities impact structural alignment's effectiveness in generating opportunity beliefs complement studies recognizing the role these differences play in opportunity exploitation. For example, Samuelsson and Davidsson (2009) showed that the effects human and social capital have on new ventures' development activities are substantial for ventures going after *innovative opportunities* but not for ventures going after *imitative opportunities*. Further, Dahlqvist and Wiklund (2012) validated an opportunity newness measure and revealed that newness correlates with intellectual property protection and patent application. By shifting the focus away from the performance effects of exploitation-relevant differences to the inherent traits of opportunity beliefs for new supply-demand combinations, researchers can more successfully differentiate between the effects of differences across possible opportunities and the effects of individuals' motivations, resources, and capabilities.

Conclusion

In this chapter, we illustrated how individuals' prior knowledge impacts the opportunity-recognition process. While higher levels of knowledge (education) seem to facilitate opportunity recognition generally, different types of knowledge trigger the recognition of different types of opportunities (e.g., knowledge related to problems of nature can trigger the identification of environmental opportunities, and knowledge related to international markets can facilitate the identification of opportunities abroad). Knowledge related to opportunity recognition can be internal to the entrepreneur but can also be provided by external sources, such as venture capital investors. Moreover, it appears that entrepreneurs' prior knowledge plays an important role in the cognitive process of structural alignment that "connects the known with the unknown" and, in doing so, can facilitate opportunity recognition. In the next chapter, we explore how entrepreneurs' motivation, independently and conjointly with knowledge, impacts entrepreneurial cognition.

References

Alvarez, S. A., & Barney, J. B. (2010). Entrepreneurship and epistemology: The philosophical underpinnings of the study of entrepreneurial opportunities. *Academy of Management Annals, 4*(1), 557–583.

Alvarez, S. A., & Busenitz, L. W. (2001). The entrepreneurship of resource-based theory. *Journal of Management, 27*(6), 755–775.

Amabile, T. M. (1997). Entrepreneurial creativity through motivational synergy. *Journal of Creative Behavior, 31*(1), 18–26.

Anand, V., Glick, W. H., & Manz, C. C. (2002). Thriving on the knowledge of outsiders: Tapping organizational social capital. *The Academy of Management Executive, 16*(1), 87–101.

Ardichvili, A., Cardozo, R., & Ray, S. (2003). A theory of entrepreneurial opportunity identification and development. *Journal of Business Venturing, 18*(1), 105–123.

Armstrong, S., Curtis, M., Kent, R., Maxwell, D., Mousseau, F., Pearce, F., Sadler, K., Tamminga, P., & Tansey, G. (2011). In L. Knight (Ed.), *World disasters report 2011: Focus on hunger and malnutrition*. Lyons: Imprimerie Chirat, 2(1), 41–49.

Ashbolt, N. J. (2004). Microbial contamination of drinking water and disease outcomes in developing regions. *Toxicology, 198*(1), 229–238.

Audretsch, D. B., & Feldman, M. P. (1996). R&D spillovers and the geography of innovation and production. *The American Economic Review, 86*(3), 630–640.

Autio, E., Sapienza, H. J., & Almeida, J. G. (2000). Effects of age at entry, knowledge intensity, and imitability on international growth. *Academy of Management Journal, 43*(5), 909–924.

Barnett, M. L. (2008). An attention-based view of real options reasoning. *Academy of Management Review, 33*(3), 606–628.

Baron, R. A. (2006). Opportunity recognition as pattern recognition: How entrepreneurs "connect the dots" to identify new business opportunities. *Academy of Management Perspectives, 20*(1), 104–119.

Baron, R. A., & Ensley, M. D. (2006). Opportunity recognition as the detection of meaningful patterns: Evidence from comparisons of novice and experienced entrepreneurs. *Management Science, 52*(9), 1331–1344.

Bassok, M., & Holyoak, K. J. (1989). Interdomain transfer between isomorphic topics in algebra and physics. *Journal of Experimental Psychology: Learning, Memory, and Cognition, 15*(1), 153.

Baum, J. A., & Silverman, B. S. (2004). Picking winners or building them? Alliance, intellectual, and human capital as selection criteria in venture financing and performance of biotechnology startups. *Journal of Business Venturing, 19*(3), 411–436.

Baum, J. A., Calabrese, T., & Silverman, B. S. (2000). Don't go it alone: Alliance network composition and startups' performance in Canadian biotechnology. *Strategic Management Journal,* 267–294.

Blanchette, I., & Dunbar, K. (2001). Analogy use in naturalistic settings: The influence of audience, emotion, and goals. *Memory & Cognition, 29*(5), 730–735.

Bloodgood, J. M., Sapienza, H. J., & Almeida, J. G. (1996). The internationalization of new high-potential US ventures: Antecedents and outcomes. *Entrepreneurship: Theory and Practice, 20*(4), 61–77.

Boston Indicators Project. (2007). *A time like no other: Charting the time for the next revolution.* Boston: The Boston Foundation, 35(1), 137–163.

Boyd, D. P., & Gumpert, D. E. (1983). The effects of stress on early-stage entrepreneurs. *Frontiers of Entrepreneurship Research, 180,* 58–63.

Busenitz, L. W., & Barney, J. B. (1997). Differences between entrepreneurs and managers in large organizations: Biases and heuristics in strategic decision-making. *Journal of Business Venturing, 12*(1), 9–30.

Buttner, E. H. (1992). Entrepreneurial stress: Is it hazardous to your health? *Journal of Managerial Issues, 4,* 223–240.

Cardon, M. S., Foo, M. D., Shepherd, D., & Wiklund, J. (2012). Exploring the heart: Entrepreneurial emotion is a hot topic. *Entrepreneurship Theory and Practice, 36*(1), 1–10.

Carpenter, M. A., Pollock, T. G., & Leary, M. M. (2003). Testing a model of reasoned risk-taking: Governance, the experience of principals and agents, and global strategy in high-technology IPO firms. *Strategic Management Journal, 24*(9), 803–820.

Catrambone, R., & Holyoak, K. J. (1989). Overcoming contextual limitations on problem-solving transfer. *Journal of Experimental Psychology: Learning, Memory, and Cognition, 15*(6), 1147.

Catrambone, R., & Holyoak, K. J. (1990). Learning subgoals and methods for solving probability problems. *Memory & Cognition, 18*(6), 593–603.

Cattani, G., & Ferriani, S. (2008). A core/periphery perspective on individual creative performance: Social networks and cinematic achievements in the Hollywood film industry. *Organization Science*, 19(6), 824–844.

Chang, S. J. (2004). Venture capital financing, strategic alliances, and the initial public offerings of internet startups. *Journal of Business Venturing*, 19(5), 721–741.

Chatterji, A. K., Fabrizio, K. R., Mitchell, W., & Schulman, K. A. (2008). Physician-industry cooperation in the medical device industry. *Health Affairs*, 27(6), 1532–1543.

Chattopadhyay, P., Glick, W. H., & Huber, G. P. (2001). Organizational actions in response to threats and opportunities. *Academy of Management Journal*, 44(5), 937–955.

Chen, H., & Chen, T. J. (1998). Network linkages and location choice in foreign direct investment. *Journal of International Business Studies*, 29(3), 445–467.

Chi, M. T., Feltovich, P. J., & Glaser, R. (1981). Categorization and representation of physics problems by experts and novices. *Cognitive Science*, 5(2), 121–152.

Choo, F., & Trotman, K. T. (1991). The relationship between knowledge structure and judgments for experienced and inexperienced auditors. *Accounting Review*, 6(3), 464–485.

Clement, C. A., & Gentner, D. (1991). Systematicity as a selection constraint in analogical mapping. *Cognitive Science*, 15(1), 89–132.

Cohen, W. M., & Levinthal, D. A. (1990). Absorptive capacity: A new perspective on learning and innovation. *Administrative Science Quarterly*, 35, 128–152.

Cooper, A. C., Gimeno-Gascon, F. J., & Woo, C. Y. (1994). Initial human and financial capital as predictors of new venture performance. *Journal of Business Venturing*, 9(5), 371–395.

Corbett, A. C. (2005). Experiential learning within the process of opportunity identification and exploitation. *Entrepreneurship Theory and Practice*, 29(4), 473–491.

Costanza, R., D'Arge, R., de Groot, R., Farber, S., Grasso, M., & Hannon, B. (1997). The value of the world's ecosystems services and natural capital. *Nature*, 387, 253–260.

Coviello, N. E. (2006). The network dynamics of international new ventures. *Journal of International Business Studies*, 37(5), 713–731.

Coviello, N. E., & Munro, H. J. (1995). Growing the entrepreneurial firm: Networking for international market development. *European Journal of Marketing*, 29(7), 49–61.

Crossan, M. M., & Berdrow, I. (2003). Organizational learning and strategic renewal. *Strategic Management Journal*, 24(11), 1087–1105.

Crossan, M. M., Lane, H. W., & White, R. E. (1999). An organizational learning framework: From intuition to institution. *Academy of Management Review*, 24(3), 522–537.

Csikszentmihalyi, M. (1975). Play and intrinsic rewards. *Journal of Humanistic Psychology, 15*(3), 41–63.
Csikszentmihalyi, M. (2000). *Beyond boredom and anxiety.* San Francisco: Jossey-Bass.
Dahl, D. W., & Moreau, P. (2002). The influence and value of analogical thinking during new product ideation. *Journal of Marketing Research, 39*(1), 47–60.
Dahlqvist, J., & Wiklund, J. (2012). Measuring the market newness of new ventures. *Journal of Business Venturing, 27*(2), 185–196.
Daily, G. (Ed.). (1997). Nature's services: Societal dependence on natural ecosystems. *Island Press, 1*(1), 75.
Das, T. K., & Teng, B. S. (2000). A resource-based theory of strategic alliances. *Journal of Management, 26*(1), 31–61.
Davenport, T. H., & Prusak, L. (1998). *Working knowledge: How organizations manage what they know.* Cambridge, MA: Harvard Business Press.
Davidsson, P. (2003). The domain of entrepreneurship research: Some suggestions. In D. A. Shepherd & J. Katz (Eds.), *Cognitive approaches to entrepreneurship research* (pp. 315–372). Bingley: Emerald Publishing.
Davidsson, P., & Honig, B. (2003). The role of social and human capital among nascent entrepreneurs. *Journal of Business Venturing, 18*(3), 301–331.
Day, S. B., & Gentner, D. (2007). Non intentional analogical inference in text comprehension. *Memory & Cognition, 35*(1), 39–49.
Deeds, D. L., Decarolis, D., & Coombs, J. E. (1999). The impact of firm-specific capabilities on the amount of capital raised in an initial public offering: An empirical investigation of the biotechnology industry. *Strategic Management Journal, 20,* 953–968.
Dimov, D. (2004). The individuality of opportunity identification: A critical review and extension. In J. Butler (Ed.), *Opportunity identification and entrepreneurial behaviour* (pp. 135–161). Greenwich: Information Age Publishing.
Dimov, D. (2007a). Beyond the single-person, single-insight attribution in understanding entrepreneurial opportunities. *Entrepreneurship Theory and Practice, 31*(5), 713–731.
Dimov, D. (2007b). From opportunity insight to opportunity intention: The importance of person-situation learning match. *Entrepreneurship Theory and Practice, 31*(4), 561–583.
Domurath, A., & Patzelt, H. (2016). Entrepreneurs' assessments of early international entry: The role of foreign social ties, venture absorptive capacity, and generalized trust in others. *Entrepreneurship Theory and Practice, 40*(5), 1149–1177.
Dunbar, K. (1993). Concept discovery in a scientific domain. *Cognitive Science, 17*(3), 397–434.
Dunning, J. H. (2000). The eclectic paradigm as an envelope for economic and business theories of MNE activity. *International Business Review, 9*(2), 163–190.

Dutton, J. E., & Jackson, S. E. (1987). Categorizing strategic issues: Links to organizational action. *Academy of Management Review, 12*(1), 76–90.
Dutton, J. E., Worline, M. C., Frost, P. J., & Lilius, J. (2006). Explaining compassion organizing. *Administrative Science Quarterly, 51*(1), 59–96.
Dyer, J. H., & Singh, H. (1998). The relational view: Cooperative strategy and sources of interorganizational competitive advantage. *Academy of Management Review, 23*(4), 72–679.
Eckhardt, J. T., & Shane, S. A. (2003). Opportunities and entrepreneurship. *Journal of Management, 29*(3), 333–349.
Etzioni, A. (1996). The responsive community: A communitarian perspective. *American Sociological Review, 61*(1), 11.
Evans, D. S., & Leighton, L. S. (1989). Some empirical aspects of entrepreneurship. *American Economic Review, 79*(3), 519–535.
Evans, A. G., & Varaiya, N. P. (2003). Anne Evans: Assessment of a biotechnology market opportunity. *Entrepreneurship Theory and Practice, 28*(1), 87–105.
Feinberg, S. E., & Gupta, A. K. (2004). Knowledge spillovers and the assignment of R&D responsibilities to foreign subsidiaries. *Strategic Management Journal, 25*(8–9), 823–845.
Fernhaber, S. A., Gilbert, B. A., & McDougall, P. P. (2008). International entrepreneurship and geographic location: An empirical examination of new venture internationalization. *Journal of International Business Studies, 39*(2), 267–290.
Fernhaber, S. A., McDougall-Covin, P. P., & Shepherd, D. A. (2009). International entrepreneurship: Leveraging internal and external knowledge sources. *Strategic Entrepreneurship Journal, 3*(4), 297–320.
Fiske, S. T., & Taylor, S. E. (1991). *Social cognition* (2nd ed., pp. 16–15). New York: McGraw-Hill.
Florin, J., Lubatkin, M., & Schulze, W. (2003). A social capital model of high-growth ventures. *Academy of Management Journal, 46*(3), 374–384.
Frederick, D. M., & Libby, R. (1986). Expertise and auditors' judgments of conjunctive events. *Journal of Accounting Research, 28*, 270–290.
Foley, D. (2003). An examination of indigenous Australian entrepreneurs. *Journal of Developmental Entrepreneurship, 8*(2), 133.
Fried, V. H., Bruton, G. D., & Hisrich, R. D. (1998). Strategy and the board of directors in venture capital-backed firms. *Journal of Business Venturing, 13*(6), 493–503.
Gaglio, C. M., & Katz, J. A. (2001). The psychological basis of opportunity identification: Entrepreneurial alertness. *Small Business Economics, 16*(2), 95–111.
Gavetti, G., & Rivkin, J. W. (2005). How strategists really think. *Harvard Business Review, 83*(4), 54–63.
Gavetti, G., & Rivkin, J. W. (2007). On the origin of strategy: Action and cognition over time. *Organization Science, 18*(3), 420–439.
Gentner, D. (1983). Structure-mapping: A theoretical framework for analogy. *Cognitive Science, 7*(2), 155–170.

Gentner, D. (1989). The mechanisms of analogical learning. In S. Vosniadou & A. Ortony (Eds.), *Similarity and analogical reasoning* (pp. 199–233). Cambridge: Cambridge University Press.

Gentner, D., Rattermann, M. J., & Forbus, K. D. (1993). The roles of similarity in transfer: Separating retrievability from inferential soundness. *Cognitive Psychology, 25*, 524–575.

Gentner, D., Rattermann, M. J., Markman, A., & Kotovsky, L. (1995). Two forces in the development of relational similarity. In *Developing Cognitive Competence: New approaches to Process Modeling* (pp. 263–313). London: Psychology Press.

George, G., Wiklund, J., & Zahra, S. A. (2005). Ownership and the internationalization of small firms. *Journal of Management, 31*(2), 210–233.

Gimeno, J., Folta, T. B., Cooper, A. C., & Woo, C. Y. (1997). Survival of the fittest? Entrepreneurial human capital and the persistence of underperforming firms. *Administrative Science Quarterly, 42*, 750–783.

Gobbo, C., & Chi, M. (1986). How knowledge is structured and used by expert and novice children. *Cognitive Development, 1*(3), 221–237.

Golden, B. R. (1992). The past is the past—Or is it? The use of retrospective accounts as indicators of past strategy. *Academy of Management Journal, 35*(4), 848–860.

Grégoire, D. A., & Shepherd, D. A. (2012). Technology-market combinations and the identification of entrepreneurial opportunities: An investigation of the opportunity-individual nexus. *Academy of Management Journal, 55*(4), 753–785.

Grégoire, D. A., Barr, P. S., & Shepherd, D. A. (2010). Cognitive processes of opportunity recognition: The role of structural alignment. *Organization Science, 21*(2), 413–431.

Gruber, M., MacMillan, I. C., & Thompson, J. D. (2008). Look before you leap: Market opportunity identification in emerging technology firms. *Management Science, 54*(9), 1652–1665.

Gruber, M., MacMillan, I. C., & Thompson, J. D. (2012). From minds to markets: How human capital endowments shape market opportunity identification of technology start-ups. *Journal of Management, 38*(5), 1421–1449.

Gruber, M., Heinemann, F., Brettel, M., & Hungeling, S. (2010). Configurations of resources and capabilities and their performance implications: An exploratory study on technology ventures. *Strategic Management Journal, 31*(12), 1337–1356.

Haeussler, C., Patzelt, H., & Zahra, S. A. (2012). Strategic alliances and product development in high technology new firms: The moderating effect of technological capabilities. *Journal of Business Venturing, 27*(2), 217–233.

Hanks, S. H., Watson, C. J., Jansen, E., & Chandler, G. N. (1993). Tightening the life-cycle construct: A taxonomic study of growth stage configurations in high-technology organizations. *Entrepreneurship: Theory and Practice, 18*(2), 5–30.

Haunschild, P. R., & Miner, A. S. (1997). Modes of interorganizational imitation: The effects of outcome salience and uncertainty. *Administrative Science Quarterly, 42*, 472–500.

Hayek, F. A. (1945). The use of knowledge in society. *The American Economic Review, 35*, 519–530.

Hite, J. M. (2005). Evolutionary processes and paths of relationally embedded network ties in emerging entrepreneurial firms. *Entrepreneurship Theory and Practice, 29*(1), 113–144.

Hitt, M. A., Keats, B. W., & DeMarie, S. M. (1998). Navigating in the new competitive landscape: Building strategic flexibility and competitive advantage in the 21st century. *Academy of Management Executive, 12*(4), 22–42.

Holland, J. H., Holyoak, K. J., Nisbett, R. E., & Thagard, P. (1986). *Induction: Processes of inference, learning, and discovery.* Cambridge, MA: MIT Press, 42(2–3), 356–384.

Holyoak, K. J. (1985). The pragmatics of analogical transfer. *Psychology of Learning and Motivation, 19*, 59–87.

Holyoak, K. J., & Thagard, P. (1996). *Mental leaps: Analogy in creative thought.* Cambridge, MA: MIT Press.

Huber, G. P. (1991). Organizational learning: The contributing processes and the literatures. *Organization Science, 2*(1), 88–115.

Huber, G. P., & Power, D. J. (1985). Retrospective reports of strategic-level managers: Guidelines for increasing their accuracy. *Strategic Management Journal, 6*(2), 171–180.

Ireland, R. D., Hitt, M. A., & Sirmon, D. G. (2003). A model of strategic entrepreneurship: The construct and its dimensions. *Journal of Management, 29*(6), 963–989.

Jackson, S. E., & Dutton, J. E. (1988). Discerning threats and opportunities. *Administrative Science Quarterly, 33*, 370–387.

Johannisson, B. (2000). Networking and entrepreneurial growth. In D. L. Sexton & H. Landström (Eds.), *The Blackwell handbook of entrepreneurship* (pp. 368–386). Oxford: Blackwell.

Johanson, J., & Vahlne, J. E. (2003). Business relationship learning and commitment in the internationalization process. *Journal of International Entrepreneurship, 1*(1), 83–101.

Julian, S. D., & Ofori-Dankwa, J. C. (2008). Toward an integrative cartography of two strategic issue diagnosis frameworks. *Strategic Management Journal, 29*(1), 93–114.

Kaplan, S. (2008). Cognition, capabilities, and incentives: Assessing firm response to the fiber-optic revolution. *Academy of Management Journal, 51*(4), 672–695.

Keane, M. T. (1988). *Analogical problem solving.* Chichester: Ellis Horwood.

Keane, M. T., Ledgeway, S., & Duff, S. (1994). Constraints on analogical mapping: A comparison of three models. *Cognitive Science, 18*, 387–438.

Knight, F. H. (1921). *Risk, uncertainty and profit.* Washington, DC: Beard Books, 31(1), 132–152.
Knight, G. A., & Cavusgil, S. T. (2004). Innovation, organizational capabilities, and the born-global firm. *Journal of International Business Studies, 35*(2), 124–141.
Kotha, S., Rindova, V. P., & Rothaermel, F. T. (2001). Assets and actions: Firm-specific factors in the internationalization of US internet firms. *Journal of International Business Studies, 32*(4), 769–791.
Krueger, N. F., & Brazeal, D. V. (1994). Entrepreneurial potential and potential entrepreneurs. *Entrepreneurship Theory and Practice, 18,* 91–91.
Kuvaas, B. (2002). An exploration of two competing perspectives on informational contexts in top management strategic issue interpretation. *Journal of Management Studies, 39*(7), 977–1001.
Loewenstein, J., & Gentner, D. (2005). Relational language and the development of relational mapping. *Cognitive Psychology, 50*(4), 315–353.
Logan, G. D. (1990). Repetition priming and automaticity: Common underlying mechanisms? *Cognitive Psychology, 22*(1), 1–35.
Lu, J. W. (2002). Intra-and inter-organizational imitative behavior: Institutional influences on Japanese firms' entry mode choice. *Journal of International Business Studies, 33*(1), 133–137.
Lu, J. W., & Beamish, P. W. (2001). The internationalization and performance of SMEs. *Strategic Management Journal, 22*(6–7), 565–586.
McGrath, R. G., & MacMillan, I. C. (1995, July-August). Discovery-driven planning. *Harvard Business Review, 73,* 44–54.
MacMillan, I. C., Kulow, D. M., & Khoylian, R. (1989). Venture capitalists' involvement in their investments: Extent and performance. *Journal of Business Venturing, 4*(1), 27–47.
Maheswaran, D., & Sternthal, B. (1990). The effects of knowledge, motivation, and type of message on ad processing and product judgments. *Journal of Consumer Research, 17*(1), 66–73.
Margalit, A., & Halbertal, M. (2004). Liberalism and the right to culture. *Social Research, 71*(3), 529–548.
McMullen, J. S., & Shepherd, D. A. (2006). Entrepreneurial action and the role of uncertainty in the theory of the entrepreneur. *Academy of Management Review, 31*(1), 132–152.
McMullen, J. S., Plummer, L. A., & Acs, Z. J. (2007). What is an entrepreneurial opportunity? *Small Business Economics, 28*(4), 273–283.
Milliken, F. J. (1990). Perceiving and interpreting environmental change: An examination of college administrators' interpretation of changing demographics. *Academy of Management Journal, 33*(1), 42–63.
Namy, L. L., & Gentner, D. (2002). Making a silk purse out of two sow's ears: Young children's use of comparison in category learning. *Journal of Experimental Psychology: General, 131*(1), 5.

Novick, L. R., & Holyoak, K. J. (1991). Mathematical problem solving by analogy. *Journal of Experimental Psychology: Learning, Memory, and Cognition, 17*(3), 398.

Ocasio, W. (1997). Towards an attention-based view of the firm. *Strategic Management Journal, 18*, 187–206.

Oviatt, B. M., McDougall, P. P., & Loper, M. (1995). Global start-ups: Entrepreneurs on a worldwide stage. *Academy of Management Executive, 9*, 30–44.

Parris, T. M., & Kates, R. W. (2003). Characterizing and measuring sustainable development. *Annual Review of Environment and Resources, 28*, 559–586.

Patzelt, H., & Shepherd, D. A. (2011). Negative emotions of an entrepreneurial career: Self-employment and regulatory coping behaviors. *Journal of Business Venturing, 26*(2), 226–238.

Patzelt, H., Shepherd, D. A., Deeds, D., & Bradley, S. W. (2008). Financial slack and venture managers' decisions to seek a new alliance. *Journal of Business Venturing, 23*(4), 465–481.

Peredo, A. M., & Chrisman, J. J. (2006). Toward a theory of community-based enterprise. *Academy of Management Review, 31*(2), 309–328.

Plambeck, N., & Weber, K. (2009). CEO ambivalence and responses to strategic issues. *Organization Science, 20*(6), 993–1010.

Prahalad, C. K. (2007). Bottom of the pyramid. *Presentation at the Strategic Entrepreneurship Journal Launch Conference, 1*(1), 1–5.

Reuber, A. R., & Fischer, E. (1997). The influence of the management team's international experience on the internationalization behaviors of SMEs. *Journal of International Business Studies, 28*, 807–825.

Rugman, A. M. (1981). Inside the multinationals. *The economics of international markets, 34*(4), 345–355.

Ruhnka, J. C., Feldman, H. D., & Dean, T. J. (1992). The "living dead" phenomenon in venture capital investments. *Journal of Business Venturing, 7*(2), 137–155.

Samuelsson, M., & Davidsson, P. (2009). Does venture opportunity variation matter? Investigating systematic process differences between innovative and imitative new ventures. *Small Business Economics, 33*(2), 229–255.

Sapienza, H. J. (1992). When do venture capitalists add value? *Journal of Business Venturing, 7*(1), 9–27.

Sarasvathy, S. D. (2001). Causation and effectuation: Toward a theoretical shift from economic inevitability to entrepreneurial contingency. *Academy of Management Review, 26*(2), 243–263.

Saxenian, A. (1990). Regional networks and the resurgence of Silicon Valley. *California Management Review, 33*(1), 89–112.

Schneider, S. K. (1992). Governmental response to disasters: The conflict between bureaucratic procedures and emergent norms. *Public Administration Review, 52*, 135–145.

Seelos, C., & Mair, J. (2005). Social entrepreneurship: Creating new business models to serve the poor. *Business Horizons, 48,* 241–246.

Seifert, C. M., Meyer, D. E., Davidson, N., Patalano, A. L., & Yaniv, I. (1994). Demystification of cognitive insight: Opportunistic assimilation and the prepared-mind hypothesis. In R. Sternberg & J. Davidson (Eds.), *The nature of insight* (pp. 65–124). Cambridge, MA: MIT Press.

Shah, S. K., & Tripsas, M. (2007). The accidental entrepreneur: The emergent and collective process of user entrepreneurship. *Strategic Entrepreneurship Journal, 1*(1–2), 123–140.

Shane, S. (2000). Prior knowledge and the discovery of entrepreneurial opportunities. *Organization Science, 11*(4), 448–469.

Shane, S., & Venkataraman, S. (2000). The promise of entrepreneurship as a field of research. *Academy of Management Review, 25*(1), 217–226.

Shanteau, J. (1992). Competence in experts: The role of task characteristics. *Organizational Behavior and Human Decision Processes, 53*(2), 252–266.

Shepherd, D. A. (2015). Party on! A call for entrepreneurship research that is more interactive, activity based, cognitively hot, compassionate, and prosocial. *Journal of Business Venturing, 30*(4), 489–507.

Shepherd, D. A., & DeTienne, D. R. (2005). Prior knowledge, potential financial reward, and opportunity identification. *Entrepreneurship Theory and Practice, 29*(1), 91–112.

Shepherd, D. A., & Patzelt, H. (2011). The new field of sustainable entrepreneurship: Studying entrepreneurial action linking "what is to be sustained" with "what is to be developed". *Entrepreneurship Theory and Practice, 35*(1), 137–163.

Shepherd, D. A., & Patzelt, H. (2015). Harsh evaluations of entrepreneurs who fail: The role of sexual orientation, use of environmentally friendly technologies, and observers' perspective taking. *Journal of Management Studies, 52*(2), 253–284.

Shepherd, D. A., & Williams, T. A. (2014). Local venturing as compassion organizing in the aftermath of a natural disaster: The role of localness and community in reducing suffering. *Journal of Management Studies, 51*(6), 952–994.

Shepherd, D. A., Douglas, E. J., & Shanley, M. (2000). New venture survival: Ignorance, external shocks, and risk reduction strategies. *Journal of Business Venturing, 15*(5), 393–410.

Shepherd, D. A., McMullen, J. S., & Jennings, P. D. (2007). The formation of opportunity beliefs: Overcoming ignorance and reducing doubt. *Strategic Entrepreneurship Journal, 1*(1–2), 75–95.

Shepherd, D. A., Mcmullen, J. S., & Ocasio, W. (2017). Is that an opportunity? An attention model of top managers' opportunity beliefs for strategic action. *Strategic Management Journal, 38*(3), 626–644.

Short, J. C., Ketchen, D. J., Jr., Shook, C. L., & Ireland, R. D. (2010). The concept of "opportunity" in entrepreneurship research: Past accomplishments and future challenges. *Journal of Management, 36*(1), 40–65.

Simmons, J. G. (2002). Doctors and discoveries: Lives that created today's medicine. *Houghton Mifflin Harcourt, 30*(6), 825–838.

Simon, H. A. (1957). *Models of man: Social and rational; mathematical essays on rational human behavior in society setting.* New York: Wiley, *59*(7), 177.

Stinchcombe, A. L., & March, J. G. (1965). Social structure and organizations. *Handbook of Organizations, 7*, 142–193.

Sutcliffe, K. M., & Vogus, T. (2003). Organizing for resilience. In K. S. Cameron, J. E. Dutton, & R. E. Quinn (Eds.), *Positive organizational scholarship* (pp. 94–110). San Francisco: Berrett-Koehler.

Tetrick, L. E., Slack, K. J., Da Silva, N., & Sinclair, R. R. (2000). A comparison of the stress–strain process for business owners and non owners: Differences in job demands, emotional exhaustion, satisfaction, and social support. *Journal of Occupational Health Psychology, 5*(4), 464.

Thomas, J. B., & McDaniel, R. R. (1990). Interpreting strategic issues: Effects of strategy and the information-processing structure of top management teams. *Academy of Management Journal, 33*(2), 286–306.

Tilman, D., Cassman, K. G., Matson, P. A., Naylor, R., & Polasky, S. (2002). Agricultural sustainability and intensive production practices. *Nature, 418*(6898), 671–677.

Tversky, A., & Kahneman, D. (1974). Heuristics and biases: Judgement under uncertainty. *Science, 185*, 1124–1130.

Ucbasaran, D., Westhead, P., & Wright, M. (2009). The extent and nature of opportunity identification by experienced entrepreneurs. *Journal of Business Venturing, 24*(2), 99–115.

Van Wart, M., & Kapucu, N. (2011). Crisis management competencies: The case of emergency managers in the USA. *Public Management Review, 13*(4), 489–511.

Venkataraman, S. (1997). The distinctive domain of entrepreneurship research. *Advances in entrepreneurship, firm emergence and growth, 3*(1), 119–138.

Venkataraman, S., & Sarasvathy, S. D. (2001). Strategy and entrepreneurship: Outlines of an untold story, Darden Business School working paper no. 01-06.

Von Hippel, E. (1988). *The sources of innovation.* New York: Oxford University Press, 38(5), 541–552.

Ward, T. B. (1995). What's old about new ideas. In *The creative cognition approach* (pp. 157–178). Cambridge, MA: The MIT Press.

Ware, J. E., Jr., Brook, R. H., Davies, A. R., & Lohr, K. N. (1981). Choosing measures of health status for individuals in general populations. *American Journal of Public Health, 71*(6), 620–625.

Wiklund, J., & Shepherd, D. (2003). Knowledge-based resources, entrepreneurial orientation, and the performance of small and medium-sized businesses. *Strategic Management Journal, 24*(13), 1307–1314.

Williams, T. A., & Shepherd, D. A. (2016). Victim entrepreneurs doing well by doing good: Venture creation and well-being in the aftermath of a resource shock. *Journal of Business Venturing, 31*(4), 365–387.

Wright, M., Pruthi, S., & Lockett, A. (2005). International venture capital research: From cross-country comparisons to crossing borders. *International Journal of Management Reviews, 7*(3), 135–165.

Zahra, S. A., & George, G. (2002). Absorptive capacity: A review, reconceptualization, and extension. *Academy of Management Review, 27*(2), 185–203.

Zott, C., & Amit, R. (2007). Business model design and the performance of entrepreneurial firms. *Organization Science, 18*(2), 181–199.

Open Access This chapter is licensed under the terms of the Creative Commons Attribution 4.0 International License (http://creativecommons.org/licenses/by/4.0/), which permits use, sharing, adaptation, distribution and reproduction in any medium or format, as long as you give appropriate credit to the original author(s) and the source, provide a link to the Creative Commons license and indicate if changes were made.

The images or other third party material in this chapter are included in the chapter's Creative Commons license, unless indicated otherwise in a credit line to the material. If material is not included in the chapter's Creative Commons license and your intended use is not permitted by statutory regulation or exceeds the permitted use, you will need to obtain permission directly from the copyright holder.

CHAPTER 3

Motivation and Entrepreneurial Cognition

As discussed in Chap. 2, opportunity identification is one of the most essential skills of successful entrepreneurs (Ardichvili et al. 2003; Grégoire et al. 2010) and has thus gained considerable importance in the entrepreneurship literature. In addition to prior knowledge, researchers have identified motivation—the behavior-triggering force, which directs behavior and increases persistence with a course of action (Bartol and Martin 1998)—as an important antecedent of opportunity identification. How can opportunity recognition be stimulated by financial rewards? What is the motivational role of values and emotions in the entrepreneurial process? What motivations trigger entrepreneurs' identification and pursuit of opportunities related to sustaining nature and society? Finally, in what follows, we also address questions regarding the potential positive and negative outcomes of entrepreneurial motivation.

MOTIVATION AND OPPORTUNITY IDENTIFICATION

Scholars studying creativity (e.g., Amabile 1993) and a select group of scholars studying entrepreneurship (e.g., Birley and Westhead 1994; Cardon et al. 2009; Douglas and Shepherd 2002) have concluded that individuals can be driven to entrepreneurship by non-financial/intrinsic motivators. However, most work from the economics and entrepreneurship literature contends that financial reward is the primary driver behind individuals' entrepreneurial engagement (Baumol 1990; Kuratko et al. 1997;

Langan-Fox and Roth 1995). As an example, studying entrepreneurs in the Midwest, Kuratko et al. (1997: 31) discovered that "extrinsic goals concentrating on wealth" play an important role in individuals' decision to continue in entrepreneurship. Similarly, Baumol (1990: 894) argued that "how the entrepreneur acts at a given time and place depends heavily on … the reward structure in the economy … (or) the prevailing rules of the game that govern the payoff." Further, Campbell (1992) developed an economic theory of entrepreneurship, arguing that people choose to engage in entrepreneurship if the anticipated current profit value from entrepreneurial action is greater than the profit value of salaried employment. Finally, Schumpeter (1961) proposed that empire building with the goal of gaining financial reward is a significant motivator for many entrepreneurs.

To more fully understand how financial reward could initiate entrepreneurial action, we draw on motivation theorists Campbell and Pritchard (1976). These authors suggested that motivation is the choice of whether to begin putting forth effort on a particular task as well as the decision of how much effort to put forth and for how long. The first two parts of this motivational decision—namely, deciding to initiate action and determining how much effort to invest—are most important when high effort levels lead to valued end results, including high salary (Kanfer 1990; Vroom 1964).

Financial Reward

Motivation can be triggered or improved when potential financial rewards are a likely outcome. Scholars have revealed a positive association between financial income and success at particular tasks. Abbey and Dickson (1983), for example, showed that reward levels and achievement motivation are positively associated with the amount of innovations people initiate. Further, Paolillo and Brown (1978) demonstrated a positive association between innovation levels and rewards in a study of employees' ratings of the overall innovative output of their research and development (R&D) laboratory. Additionally, research on the connection between creativity and the chance to gain financial reward has suggested a positive link between the two (e.g., Woodman et al. 1993), and most creativity scholars argue that there is a strong relationship between creativity and innovativeness (Cummings and O'Connell 1978). Taken together, this research shows that the promise of financial income can increase not only people's ability to generate more opportunities but also those opportunities' level of innovativeness. Indeed, my (Dean) colleague and I (Shepherd and DeTienne 2005) demonstrated in an experiment that higher potential financial income levels lead people to identify more potential opportunities. The positive relationship found between financial reward and the amount of opportunities recognized is in line with Gilad and Levine's (1986: 46) argument that "the existence of attractive, potentially profitable business opportunities will attract and 'pull' alert individuals into entrepreneurial activities." Several researchers have explored the role the promise of financial rewards plays in *pulling* individuals into entrepreneurship (e.g., Katz 1994; Shapiro and Sokol 1982; Gilad and Levine 1986).

Shapiro and Sokol (1982) as well as other scholars (e.g., Douglas and Shepherd 2000; Schjoedt and Shaver 2007) contended that the degree to which individuals are attracted to an entrepreneurial career hinges on both pulls and pushes. In this context, "pushes" are negative characteristics of a person's present situation that encourage him or her to pursue entrepreneurship, including a fixed salary, a reward that does not correspond to the effort expended, and negative displacements. Thus, not only do potentially high financial rewards pull individuals into an entrepreneurial career, the lack of adequate financial reward in a person's present situation could push him or her into this career. In most studies about pushes, entrepreneurship represents self-employment. The motivation logic underlying this career-based argument for entry into self-employment is also likely applicable to individuals' motivation to recognize potential opportunities.

Financial Reward, Prior Knowledge, and Opportunity Identification

Even when a person is motivated to recognize opportunities, he or she is unlikely to actually identify an opportunity without having prior knowledge (see Chap. 2). Amabile (1997: 42) argued that "expertise (factual knowledge and technical proficiency) is the foundation for all creative work." Similarly, work by Fiet (2007) showed that people who use consideration sets in their opportunity-identification process uncover ideas that are more likely to result in new wealth creation. As such, my (Dean) colleagues and I (DeTienne et al. 2008) proposed that the association between financial reward, prior knowledge, and opportunity identification is more intricate than a clear-cut additive association.

Researchers have mainly explored potential prior knowledge and financial income separately; however, a concomitant consideration of the two is likely to shed additional light on opportunity identification. While the associations among prior knowledge, financial reward, and opportunity recognition have not been studied in detail, some research has shown that prior knowledge impacts the association between potential financial reward and individuals' task performance. In his work with exceptionally skilled individuals, for instance, Csikszentmihalyi (1975, 2000) found that participants with higher levels of prior knowledge gave undivided attention to a specific task at hand, which at least temporarily protected against other demands that were competing for their attention. The participants felt that they had control over the activity and that their attention was strongly task-focused. Moreover, Maheswaran and Sternthal (1990) revealed that experts (i.e., individuals with high knowledge in a particular domain) are more likely to process messages in a detailed manner in case they are provided with only content information, whereas those who are new to a task more likely process messages when provided with information related to rewards. Thus, it appears that prior knowledge can contribute some motivation in the context of a specific task regardless of whether there is financial reward associated with it.

Take, for example, George de Mestral a Swiss engineer who invented Velcro and his eight-year obsession to replicate the burr-clasping system after examining a cocklebur under a microscope. Ignoring warnings from friends and colleagues that this obsession would lead to financial devastation and personal despair, he left to work in a little mountain hut. He emerged from the hut after a long period with the underlying technology for Velcro. It took him 14 years after his initial idea to develop a commercializable product. This example clearly demonstrates how a person can be driven by the motivation to solve a problem related to one's prior knowledge instead of by financial reward. Fortunately for de Mestral, he did receive a financial reward in the end.

Applied to opportunity identification, developing a deeper understanding of potential financial reward's motivating effect on opportunity identification likely requires researchers to also consider prior knowledge. With the motivation literature as a basis, we argue that when promised financial reward, people are likely to recognize more opportunities. In addition, these opportunities are more likely to be innovative. Yet, the literature also suggests that knowledge can be a motivator and can thus lessen the positive association between financial reward and both results of opportunity recognition (i.e., number and innovativeness of potential opportunities). More specifically, prior knowledge enables individuals to "see" important linkages between ideas more quickly (Busenitz and Barney 1997; Logan 1990), thus improving their ability to recognize a larger number of opportunities.

In addition, prior knowledge provides individuals with higher creativity levels to develop opportunities that are more innovative (Cohen and Levinthal 1990; Johnson et al. 1991). Indeed, my (Dean) colleague and I (Shepherd and DeTienne 2005) showed that prior knowledge moderates the association between potential financial reward and the recognition of opportunities. Our study found that high financial reward can at least partially offset the influence of lower knowledge about customer problems on the amount of potential opportunities individuals identify and how innovative those opportunities are.

Entrepreneurial Passion

Researchers established long ago that passion is a strong motivator of action (see David Hume 1711–1778; Jean Jacques Rosseau 1712–1778) as well as of entrepreneurial decisions (Smilor 1997). We turn to self-determination theory (Deci and Ryan 2001; Gagne and Deci 2005; Ryan and Deci 2000) and its extension to passion (Vallerand et al. 2003) to gain a deeper understanding of entrepreneurial motivation. Self-determination theory proposes that individuals attempt to satisfy three basic psychological needs—need for competence, need for relatedness, and need for autonomy—and thus carefully bear these needs in mind when making decisions. When individuals are put in a decision-making situation, the intentionality of their efforts to meet these needs is either controlled or autonomous (Gagne and Deci 2005). Controlled motivation concerns a pressure to act, whereas autonomous motivation refers to individuals' voluntary participation in an activity because they find it enjoyable and interesting. This difference between autonomous and controlled intentionality is reflected in the different types of passion. As a whole, passion is a "strong inclination toward an activity that one loves and finds important, that is, self-defining and in which significant time and energy are invested" (Houlfort et al. 2015: 85). Then, depending on whether passion stems from a controlled or autonomous source, it is labeled as obsessive passion or harmonious passion (Vallerand and Houlfort 2003; Vallerand et al. 2003), respectively.

Fear Motivating Entrepreneurial (In)Action

Pursuing a potential opportunity can be highly rewarding for the individuals involved in terms of generating financial rewards (Carter 2011), positive emotions (Baron 2008; Cardon et al. 2012), and a higher status/reputation (Parker and Van Praag 2010). However, since pursuing a potential opportunity is full of uncertainty (Knight 1921; McMullen and Shepherd 2006), numerous entrepreneurial undertakings fail (Burgelman and Valikangas 2005; McGrath 1999), which can result in negative financial (Lee et al. 2007, 2011), emotional (Shepherd 2003; Shepherd et al. 2011), and social (Efrat 2005; Semadeni et al. 2008; Shepherd and Patzelt 2015) consequences for those involved (for a summary, see Ucbasaran et al. 2013). Even with the pervasiveness of failure in entrepreneurship, McGrath (1999) contended that entrepreneurs and individuals who would have otherwise become entrepreneurs generally have an anti-failure bias.

While some research has indicated that an anti-failure bias is manifest in a fear of failure and that a fear of failure usually leads to inaction (Alon and Lerner 2008; Wagner and Stenberg; for a review, see Cacciotti and Hayton 2015), some individuals appear to be able to overcome their fears and go after potential opportunities.[1] These actions are vital in creating wealth for individuals, organizations, and national economies (McGrath 1999; McMullen and Shepherd 2006; Sarasvathy 2001).

According to Conroy (Conroy 2001, 2004; Conroy et al. 2002), fear of failure can be divided into five categories: fear of feeling shame and embarrassment, fear of devaluing one's self-estimate, fear of having an uncertain future, fear of losing social influence, and fear of upsetting important others.

First, the *fear of feeling shame and embarrassment* refers to individuals' concern that a real personal flaw will be uncovered to the self and to others through a failure event (adapted from Sabini et al. 2001). Quotes from research on entrepreneurs who went through business failure illustrate this shame and embarrassment: "You kind of have ... an embarrassing grief about it that, you know, it's not a very nice feeling really. And you have a lot of regret and a lot of guilt" (Byrne and Shepherd 2015: 380). Anticipating these types of feelings over a failure can lead to fear that influences how a person assesses the financial costs of failure in the entrepreneurial decision-making process. More specifically, when entrepreneurs have greater fear of feeling shame and embarrassment, they likely weigh financial costs more when deciding whether to exploit an entrepreneurial opportunity or not. Financial losses are often noticed by stakeholders and frequently become known by others in the community. Thus, for entrepreneurs who believe it is embarrassing to fail in front of others, negative performance feedback—which is rather easy to communicate publicly—may generate feelings of embarrassment (Ashford 1986; Smith and McElwee 2011). Anticipating this shame and embarrassment may cause individuals to protect themselves from exposure to such financial risks as they believe they have simply too much at stake.

Second, *fear of devaluing one's self-estimate* refers to unease about a drop in others' appraisal of one's capabilities in relation to a group whose performance is known (adapted from Gilinsky 1949). Indeed, failure can make individuals begin to doubt their knowledge and ability to successfully undertake certain tasks (Gatewood et al. 2002; Hoang and Gimeno 2010) as well as make them question their self-worth (Jenkins et al. 2014; Laguna 2013), have lower self-esteem (Shepherd and Cardon 2009), and start to doubt the control they have over important aspects of their lives (Folkman and Moskowitz 2004; Stanton et al. 2002). In turn, entrepreneurs are likely to weigh financial costs more when they fear that failure will negatively affect their self-estimation about their own capabilities and talent. Financial performance is either the objective of pursuing an entrepreneurial opportunity or the channel for accomplishing an even greater goal (Miller et al. 2012). As such, closing a business because of financial losses is a very clear indication that the entrepreneur has failed in his or her primary aim, and it seems that the more the failure costs financially, the larger the "potential hit" to the entrepreneur's self-estimate will be—a position those who fear the devaluation of their self-estimate would not want to be in.

Third, a *fear of having an uncertain future* entails individuals' fear about not knowing where their life is heading. This fear is illustrated in work by my (Dean) colleague and me (Byrne and Shepherd 2015: 384), in which we described the situation of an entrepreneur whose business failed and his frustrations over not fully knowing what was going to unfold next: "'Suddenly you get this bit of paper from the [officials] telling you, you can't be a company director. So that, the whole vagueness and uncertainty over that bit is, ahhh.' He does not finish this sentence, he just makes an annoyed sound and shakes his head." Similar to the above, entrepreneurs who feel uneasy about such uncertainty are likely to weigh financial costs more when deciding whether to pursue an opportunity or not. A failure that costs less financially will have a lower impact on the entrepreneur's slack resources than a costlier failure. The greater the financial slack (even if it is still low), the bigger the cushion for tough times (Carroll et al. 1992; Fafchamps and Lund 2003), the greater the ability to develop future options and plans (Lentz and Tranaes 2005; Wanberg et al. 1999), and thus the more certainty about the future. Nevertheless, higher losses from a failure could make future plans unaffordable or inaccessible. That is, a substantial financially damaging failure (to the extent the entrepreneur views it as traumatic) can destroy one's central beliefs about the self, others, and life in general, making everything appear less predictable (Janoff-Bulman 1985; Haynie and Shepherd 2011). Therefore, entrepreneurs who are afraid of changing plans and uncertainty may pay a great deal of attention to potential financial costs when making decisions about opportunities.

Fourth, *fear of losing social influence* denotes people's worry that they will be less able to use their opinions and attitudes to influence others' opinions and attitudes (adapted from Martin and Hewstone 2003). The higher a failure's financial costs, the higher the probability that others will notice the failure, often resulting in stigma for the individuals involved (Cardon et al. 2011; Semadeni et al. 2008; Sutton and Callahan 1987). For instance, our research (Shepherd and Patzelt 2015) showed that individuals with substantial financial losses as a result of failure are stigmatized more than those with lower losses. Stigma is a form of social stain as the individual being stigmatized experiences defamation that harms his or her reputation (see Cardon et al. 2011; Shepherd and Patzelt 2015). Ultimately, the social influence of stigmatized individuals diminishes significantly. Sutton and Callahan (1987), for instance, reported that managers of a firm that entered Chapter 11 bankruptcy found that former associates ceased contact with them due to the failure (Sutton and Callahan 1987). Unsurprisingly, individuals who are afraid of losing social influence will likely be significantly affected by the financial costs associated with failure when making entrepreneurial decisions.

Finally, *fear of upsetting important others* refers to an individual's fear of disapproval from people critical to his or her well-being. For individuals who have this fear, large financial costs are often especially worrisome because a costly failure is likely to upset important others. For instance, the financial costs of failure not only affect the entrepreneur but can also negatively impact the firm's stakeholders and even the entrepreneur's family. Indeed, stakeholders are generally people who are important to the entrepreneur and his or her venture (Mitchell et al. 1997; Seldon and Fletcher 2015; Vandekerckhove and Dentchev 2005), friends and family often make equity investments in the business (Kotha and George 2012), and entrepreneurs frequently develop close relationships with their employees (Breugst et al. 2012). Thus, financially costly failures are likely to upset investors who could potentially lose more money (Amit et al. 1990; Mason and Harrison 2002), employees who could lose their jobs (or have to end relationships with people who are let go) (Fineman 1999; Jordan et al. 2002), and other stakeholders who could potentially lose their reputation and/or social standing (Sutton and Callahan 1987). For instance, referencing an entrepreneur whose venture failed, the *Scottish Star* newspaper (April 23, 2011) reported that "Chief executive Sam said he 'had been left with no alternative' but to pull the plug. He added: 'Making all the employees redundant is genuinely heart breaking'" (cited in Byrne and Shepherd 2015: 382). As with the other four types of fear, the more afraid an entrepreneur is of letting important stakeholders down, the more he or she is likely to emphasize the financial costs of failure when making entrepreneurial decisions.

If the Japanese proverb's argument that "fear is only as deep as the mind allows" is true, then individuals may be motivated enough to overcome their fears when making entrepreneurial decisions. Thus, a key question arises: why can some individuals overcome their fear of failure and choose to act on potential opportunities whereas others succumb to their fear and do not?

As mentioned earlier, individuals who have high obsessive passion for an activity are more likely to choose to adamantly continue their pursuit of the beloved activity (Curran et al. 2015; Houlfort et al. 2015) and to remain engaged in the activity even when presented with information suggesting the imprudence of this course of action (Stephan et al. 2009). In the context of entrepreneurship, such behavior includes disregarding (or putting minimal emphasis on) information about the high financial costs associated with failure when choosing whether to pursue potential opportunities.

Fears, Passion, and Entrepreneurial Action

One particular point of interest to theorizing about fear of failure is that obsessive passion seems to affect the way individuals make decisions under threat and can lead to maladaptive outcomes (Curran et al. 2015; Donahue et al. 2009; Hodgins and Knee 2002; Vallerand et al. 2008, 2010). Because people who "cannot help but engage in their professional activities" (Houlfort et al. 2015: 85) tend to have obsessive passion, they continue with a particular response even when they encounter signals suggesting that the response is unsuitable (i.e., they have a rigid response), which can ultimately result in negative outcomes. For example, obsessively passionate workers will continue with projects irrespective of information indicating that persisting unchanged will cause undesirable consequences (Stephan et al. 2009). They feel obligated to take on tasks for reasons besides the tasks' outcomes, so their engagement in such tasks is compulsive and rigid (Curran et al. 2015).

Additionally, obsessive passion has been linked to risky behaviors (Rip et al. 2006). Researchers have found, for instance, that obsessively passionate athletes' rigid persistence can lead to risky training, thereby increasing their vulnerability to injury (Stephan et al. 2009; Vallerand et al. 2003), and the rigid persistence of individuals who have high obsessive passion for the Internet and for soccer (Vallerand et al. 2008) is associated with poor relationship quality. Overall, obsessive passion is linked to a variety of negative outcomes at the individual level, including conflict with other life spheres (Vallerand et al. 2010), aggressive behavior (Donahue et al. 2009), and difficulties in partner relationships (Vallerand et al. 2008). For numerous other activities—such as sports, gaming, and shopping—obsessive passion often leads to unproductive outcomes, thus creating conditions that would make it difficult to continue engagement or to be successful in the long term. Thus, obsessive passion appears to overpower individuals' appraisal of threats (e.g., the threat of injury, relationship loss, etc.) associated with certain activities (i.e., activities the individual is passionate about).

People who are obsessively passionate believe they cannot live without engaging in the activity they are passionate about (Vallerand et al. 2003), and they will give that activity top priority when making decisions regarding the investment of their time and energy. As Vallerand et al. (2003: 757) fittingly remarked, obsessively passionate individuals "cannot help but to engage in the passionate activity. The passion must run its course as it controls the person." On the other hand, individuals who have low obsessive passion about a potential entrepreneurial opportunity are not as dedicated to such activity and are thus more likely to think about how investing in the focal activity will affect other aspects of their lives (Shah et al. 2002). That is, their fear of failure is associated with elements of life domains outside the focal activity. For less obsessively passionate individuals, fear of failure may motivate them to prioritize their life domains and psychological needs such that large financial opportunity costs are likely to lessen the attractiveness of acting upon potential opportunities. However, individuals who are very obsessively passionate are likely to emphasize life domains less and concentrate on the possible upsides of acting on potential opportunities. For such individuals, the entrepreneurial activity at hand is their main focus—it "commands" how they invest their time and energy. Consequently, they are less likely to become preoccupied with fears about the potential undesirable outcomes of their actions. Indeed, my (Dean) colleagues and I (Shepherd et al. 2018) showed that the negative emphasis individuals place on the financial costs of failure when making entrepreneurial decisions increases with fear of failure for those with low obsessive passion but less so for those with high obsessive passion.

Entrepreneurial Motivation for Sustaining Nature and/or Communities

Aside from knowledge (see Chap. 2), the motivation to focus attention is a key factor in opportunity recognition (Baron 2006; Kirzner 1979; McMullen and Shepherd 2006). Motivation to direct one's attention to preserving natural and communal environments likely develops when people or organizations sense that their psychological and/or physical health is at risk.

First, people are frequently motivated to take action on sustainable development opportunities that increase or preserve their personal health. For instance, damage to the natural environment from pollution jeopardizes many peoples' lives, and the overuse of natural resources decreases life support by reducing the availability of food (Sala 2006). Furthermore, research has shown that a deteriorating communal environment, including the loss of cultural identity, is associated with alcoholism (Spicer 2001) and diminished expectancy of life (McDermott et al. 1998) among members of disabled ethnic minorities. As such, individuals who face these threats are likely to be highly motivated to direct their attention to and exploit opportunities that improve practices associated with the exploitation of natural resources, diminish pollution, and eliminate oppression of ethnic groups.

In terms of psychological threats, self-determination theory attempts to explain the psychological processes underlying optimal psychological functioning and health (Ryan and Deci 2000). More specifically, the aspects of life that fulfill people's needs for competence, relatedness, and autonomy also improve psychological well-being (Ryan and Deci 2000). When something threatens these aspects of an individual's life, his or her psychological well-being is also threatened, which causes the person to dedicate more attention to the threatening part of the environment. The more attention the individual places on this threat, the more likely he or she will recognize an opportunity associated with that part of the environment.

Additionally, deteriorating natural and communal environments can jeopardize individuals' need for competence, thus motivating them to pay more attention to relevant aspects of the environment. When people begin to believe that nature is on the decline, they may start to feel that they—as part of society—are not competently managing the natural environment in a way that ensures suitable living conditions for the generations to come. For example, the negative outcomes of climate change and ozone-layer depletion will become more substantial for the next generations (Dentener et al. 2006), and the extinction of species as well as the decline of certain natural habitats including forests and oceans cannot be fully rectified in the future. In a similar vein, a deteriorating communal environment may hinder individuals from meeting their need for competence due to its impact on the next generation's well-being. As an example, family disruption harms the well-being of children and grandchildren in impacted families (Amato 2005). To the degree that individuals ascribe such negative outcomes to their own or their society's failure to preserve natural and communal environments, their need for competence will be unsatisfied and their sensitivity to opportunities that maintain the environment will increase.

Deteriorating natural and communal environments also negatively affect people's need for relatedness (i.e., their need to connect with others) (Ryan and Deci 2000). First, declining environmental conditions that will primarily harm the subsequent generation are likely to make it more challenging for individuals to develop relationships with people in that generation. For instance, children may blame their parents (or the generation of their grandparents) for leading self-centered and egoistical lives that exploited and damaged nature and for causing problems that the children and their generation will have to endure.

Second, a deteriorating natural environment generally causes unequal suffering among the earth's population; often, the individuals who suffer most did not cause the decline, thus making it challenging for both groups of people to connect. Ozone-layer depletion, global warming, and overfishing, for instance, can largely be attributed to industrial activities and use in developed regions and countries, yet the numerous and often significant costs of these activities in the form of destroyed ecosystems are forced on developing countries (Srinivasan et al. 2008). In turn, individuals from these developing countries may reproach the developed countries for their self-centeredness and irresponsibility, thus harming interpersonal relationship building across different societies.

Third, weakened communal environments can disturb salient social relationships, for example, between parents and their children when families are disrupted. With more struggles and relationship issues, people's need for relatedness is unmet. In this case, they are likely to focus on opportunities to preserve natural and communal environments to avoid harm to others in the society and the next generation.

Finally, changes to natural and communal environments could also put individuals' needs for autonomy at risk. In order to experience autonomy, individuals need to have a set of available options (Ryan and Deci 2000). However, with deteriorating environmental conditions, people's options usually decrease. For instance, global warming has killed (or is killing) coral reefs (Tourtellot 2007), and climate change has also hindered the growth of crops and other nutritious plants in many areas, thus limiting the amount and diversity of food available throughout the world. Furthermore, when social groups are disturbed, people's options for developing social ties with other individuals, especially other group members, are decreased. Thus, as these examples illustrate, the more natural and communal environmental changes lessen the options individuals have, the more their need for autonomy will remain unmet, and the more they will be inspired to focus on opportunities that preserve the environment.

People's motivation to act on sustainable opportunities seems to increase as their physical and psychological health becomes progressively threatened. That is, the more threatened people feel, the more they tend to direct their attention toward the causes of that threat, and the less attention they tend to direct toward non-threat-related information (McMullen et al. 2009). Thus, when the threat to natural and communal environments is high, individuals are highly likely to act on opportunities to preserve those environments. The threat individuals sense from declining natural and communal environments likely affects the degree to which they combine their knowledge about entrepreneurship and their environmental knowledge to identify a sustainability opportunity. Generally, after individuals perceive a threat and overcome their initial fear response, they thoughtfully search for opportunities to deal with the threat (Beck and Clark 1997). While "elaborative strategic processing of threat," people process information slowly and a "secondary appraisal process occurs in which anxious individuals evaluate the availability and effectiveness of their coping resources to deal with the perceived threat" (Beck and Clark 1997: 53). In other words, individuals whose psychological and physical health is endangered by environmental (natural or communal) deterioration will seek and assess opportunities to handle that threat and, in doing so, will be driven to utilize their prior environmental/communal knowledge as well as their entrepreneurial knowledge. As an individual undertakes assessment activities to deal with a threat, it becomes increasingly likely that he or she will uncover a complementary relationship between his or her environmental and entrepreneurial knowledge such that both forms of knowledge can be joined to help the person identify an opportunity. On the other hand, if the individual senses a lower threat from environmental decline and engages in fewer assessment activities to deal with the threat, while he or she may possess both types of knowledge (i.e., of the natural/communal environment and of entrepreneurship), he or she is unlikely to be motivated to connect the two forms of knowledge to identify an opportunity.

Entrepreneurial Motivation Toward Developing Society

Individuals and organizations vary in terms of their motivation to focus attention on generating economic and non-economic gains for disadvantaged others. We concentrate on two sources that likely explain some of this variance: the degree to which individuals feel physically and psychologically threatened by the (expected) condition of society and their altruism.

People will be more motivated to exploit opportunities to improve society when they believe that their physical well-being is at risk due to the present or expected state of society. Before 1983, for example, the institutional environment in the United States offered pharmaceutical companies few incentives to create drugs to treat rare diseases because demand for such drugs was low. As a result, many patients with rare diseases had significant difficulty obtaining much-needed medical treatment. This threat to their own health drove some of these patients to act on opportunities to change the institutional environment such that it incentivizes pharmaceutical firms to create drugs for rare diseases. Some of these patients founded the National Organization for Rare Disorders and began the Orphan Drug Act. The Orphan Drug Act is a legal framework providing marketing exclusivity for rare disease drugs to pharmaceutical companies. In turn, these actions considerably improved the medical situation not only for the patients themselves but also for others in society (Austin et al. 2006).

Furthermore, the attention individuals pay to opportunities that develop society will grow with increasing threats to their psychological needs for competence, relatedness, and autonomy (Ryan and Deci 2000). For instance, some countries' legal frameworks are incapable of dealing with corruption and violence (Paldam 2002; Karstedt 2006), so people living in these countries may believe that they (and the society they live in) are incapable of developing an institutional setting that provides them and their children peace and safety. In addition, identifying a sustainable development opportunity may enable individuals to handle a threat to their need for relatedness. For example, identifying an opportunity to prompt institutional change and improve minority rights enables individuals to develop relationships with minority groups as well as with philanthropic and volunteer supporters of the cause (Austin et al. 2006). Finally, individuals may focus their attention on entrepreneurial opportunities that develop society to meet their need for autonomy. For example, members of minority and ethnic groups often do not have equal opportunities or rights compared to the majority population in a country, which hinders their (and their children's) ability to improve their socioeconomic status and personal development. Such people are thus likely to be motivated to pursue opportunities that enhance their situation and the options available to them because these types of opportunities can help satisfy their psychological need for autonomy.

A rising threat to individuals' physical or psychological health due to the (anticipated) state of society will affect the association between their knowledge of the natural/communal environment, their entrepreneurial knowledge, and the probability that they will identify a sustainable development opportunity. As explained above, increased physical and psychological threat prompts careful consideration and the identification of opportunities to overcome that threat (Beck and Clark 1997), which in turn likely leads individuals to uncover complementarities between their environmental and entrepreneurial knowledge. For example, an individual with knowledge about both pollution-reduction technologies and auto markets may not identify opportunities to lessen air pollution by introducing new technologies into cars because he or she does not perceive air pollution caused by cars to be an issue for his or her society. However, if that same person lives in a country where many people suffer with serious health problems caused by traffic-induced air pollution, his or her need for competence may go unmet because he or she (and others) is unable to help preserve a healthy society. In turn, this psychological threat is likely to drive the individual to seek opportunities that will create a healthier society, and the individual is more likely to identify an opportunity to develop cars that put out fewer emissions based on complementarities between his or her prior knowledge of air pollution and the auto market.

Aside from threat, altruism can direct people's attention toward opportunities that develop society. This altruistic motivation to assist others generally occurs when people experience empathy and sympathy for those who are disadvantaged (Batson and Shaw 1991; Davis 1996). People who are high in empathy think and feel themselves into disadvantaged others' lives and experience emotions themselves that are similar to the others' emotions (Eisenberg 2000). Individuals who can empathize with people in very poor societies may personally experience (at least to some extent) those people's grief over providing life support for their children. It follows, then, that the more individuals empathize with the poor, the higher their motivation to pay attention to opportunities that could offset poor individuals' negative emotional experiences and distress since they are partially their own emotions. Such individuals are very likely to be motivated to act on opportunities for sustainable development that can transform poorer individuals' situation—in doing so they can also better their own emotional state. For instance, these types of individuals are likely to notice opportunities that improve poor children's health while also protecting the natural environment, such as developing inexpensive processes to convert polluted water into drinking water (Prahalad 2007).

Like empathetic individuals, sympathetic people can think and feel themselves into disadvantaged others' situations; however, unlike their empathetic counterparts, sympathetic people experience emotions that differ from these others' emotions (Eisenberg 2000). For example, those who sympathize with people who are very poor understand these people's sorrows regarding their children's health and nutrition. However, they will not personally feel this sadness, instead pitying the people for their difficult situation. Pity is an altruistic emotion that drives people to help ease the suffering of others even when giving assistance leads to significant individual costs (Dijker 2001). Overall, people who sympathize with the poor will be driven to help them and be motivated to exploit opportunities that can enhance their life.

How much empathy and sympathy motivate individuals to act on opportunities that develop people and society seems to hinge on the level of personal distress that empathy and sympathy cause them. Personal distress can stem from empathetic or sympathetic overarousal (Hoffman 1982), which occurs in highly negative emotional situations that threaten an individual's psychological well-being (Eisenberg 2000). For instance, people who empathize with those who are poor and worry about their children's nutrition personally experience that worry, which can generate personal distress.

To avoid this distress, people sometimes become less altruistic. Instead, these people concentrate more on themselves (e.g., Wood et al. 1990), thus decreasing their motivation to act on entrepreneurial opportunities that aid others. In other words, highly distressed empathetic individuals are likely to pay less attention to the poor and their suffering to avoid personally experiencing this negative emotional state. However, those who are better able to regulate their own emotions and handle their own distress will be better able to empathize and sympathize with disadvantaged others without becoming overly distressed (Eisenberg 2000). These people's psychological health is threatened less when they feel empathy and sympathy, thus making them more motivated to help others with their problems and act on potential opportunities to develop society.

Individuals' altruism, empathy, and sympathy are also likely to affect the degree to which entrepreneurial knowledge improves the positive association between prior knowledge about natural/communal environments and the likelihood of identifying sustainable development opportunities. People may have both environmental and entrepreneurial knowledge but may not be motivated to uncover complementarities between the two or combine them to identify opportunities that preserve the environment and develop society. However, altruism, empathy, and sympathy can provide such motivation.

Health and Entrepreneurial Motivation

Research has shown that people with health-related limitations often freely choose entrepreneurial careers. For instance, people who perceive barriers to advancement in more customary employment roles (e.g., individuals with disabilities) are likely to be attracted to entrepreneurial careers (Kendall et al. 2006; Callahan et al. 2002). More specifically, people with disabilities often prefer entrepreneurial careers because such careers tend to offer better accommodations for disability-related issues (Arnold and Seekins 2002; Hagner and Davies 2002). Although most organizations have made physical-access accommodations for employees in the workplace (Batavia and Schriner 2001), those with disabilities often need additional accommodations, such as flexibility to arrange their schedule around health issues and treatment. These individuals tend to highly value autonomy (Arnold and Seekins 2002; Hagner and Davies 2002). My (Dean) colleague and I (Haynie and Shepherd 2011), for example, found that soldiers and marines who were injured in Iraq and Afghanistan were driven to become entrepreneurs partially because they needed autonomy. They needed autonomy because following orders from someone else almost led to their death, and when handling their health problems, they were often forced to follow doctors' and nurses' orders. Similarly, my (Holger) colleagues and I (Wiklund et al. 2016) showed that individuals suffering from ADHD find entrepreneurship to be an attractive career path because it allows for an adjustment of the work environment to ADHD-related symptoms (e.g., varying energy levels, changing attentional foci, problems with routine activities). Indeed, statistics reveal that those who are disabled are more than twice as likely to choose self-employment than people without disabilities (US Census Bureau 2002). Thus, it appears that limitations stemming from health issues motivate such individuals to choose entrepreneurial careers. These careers offer the flexibility that enables them to take care of their health-related needs and obtain treatment.

The findings and gaps associated with this topic offer a variety of research opportunities. First, while entrepreneurial careers typically offer higher flexibility than salaried employment, the amount and type of flexibility provided across entrepreneurial careers varies. For example, venture founders who want to utilize outside capital to develop their business usually find that they must relinquish more responsibility for running the business than individuals who limit business growth to what they can finance using internal capital sources (Wasserman 2008). Along these lines, different health issues may necessitate different work-related flexibility. It is unclear what are the various flexibility needs associated with major health problems that motivate individuals to become entrepreneurs. How do these entrepreneurs take advantage of this flexibility to improve their health or lessen their health problems? Why are some entrepreneurs able to draw on flexibility more effectively to lessen their health problems than other entrepreneurs? The discussion above focused on people who are drawn to an entrepreneurial career's flexibility to deal with health problems; yet, other entrepreneurs (driven by other motives) are also likely to use the flexibility of their career to improve their health. For instance, an entrepreneurial career's flexibility could allow some to engage in recreational or sporting activities.

Second, entrepreneurial ventures are likely to differ in the autonomy they provide, and entrepreneurs are also likely to desire varying autonomy levels. Researchers can in more detail investigate the association between individuals' health problems and their desire for autonomy. For example, they can explore why some health-related problems are associated with the desire for more autonomy than other problems. How are these differences embodied in the new firms created? As detailed above, my (Dean) colleague and I (Haynie and Shepherd 2011) offered some preliminary insights about marines and soldiers who were injured in combat and their desire for autonomy; their findings imply that when a person's health-related problem is connected to loss of control (lack of control causing health-related problems or health-related problems causing lack of control), he or she is likely to strongly desire the autonomy found in an entrepreneurial career.

Third, in addition to autonomy, flexibility, and physical accommodations, what other factors do individuals with health-related problems consider when choosing the career of an entrepreneur or when choosing between different types and paths of entrepreneurial careers? As mentioned earlier, self-determination theory posits that people must also satisfy their psychological needs for competence and belonging (Ryan and Deci 2000; Deci and Ryan 1985). When poor health stops individuals from undertaking particular tasks, it appears they have an even stronger desire to decide for an entrepreneurial career through which they can develop and use new competencies (Haynie and Shepherd 2011). Thus, when becoming an entrepreneur helps individuals who have lost confidence in their competence (or the capability to display their competence) to regain that confidence, health benefits may follow (especially benefits related to psychological health).

Fourth, poor health may result in loneliness (Molloy et al. 2010). Loneliness is an emotional state that occurs when an individual feels estranged from and/or misunderstood by others and thus feels a lack of social integration (Rook 1984; Donaldson and Watson 1996). (This is different from being alone, which people sometimes seek for pleasure.) Research has shown that loneliness can worsen health-related problems (Hawkley and Cacioppo 2010; Sugisawa et al. 1994; Thurston and Kubzansky 2009). Indeed, one study showed that lonely people have a 45% higher mortality rate than people who are not lonely (Holt-Lunstad et al. 2010). How does the pursuit of an entrepreneurial career influence health-related loneliness? Entrepreneurs are frequently referred to as "lone wolfs," and "being the boss" typically separates the entrepreneur from his or her subordinates. This separation may cause feelings of isolation and loneliness (Akande 1994; Gumpert and Boyd 1984; Hannafey 2003). Yet, entrepreneurs can usually choose with whom they wish to work (Forbes et al. 2006). Additionally, some new firms are created by a founding team

(Ucbasaran et al. 2003), which enables team members to form friendships that can counteract loneliness.

Fifth, while people suffering health problems may decide to become an entrepreneur for the reasons discussed above, the costs stemming from health problems sometimes make an entrepreneurial career infeasible. Poor health can be financially costly, frequently causing many out-of-pocket expenses, lost earnings, and depleted household assets (Poterba et al. 2010). These costs can diminish one's financial resources for starting a new venture. Yet, in line with the definition of entrepreneurship as the pursuit of opportunities *beyond* the resources one presently has (Baker and Nelson 2005; Brown et al. 2001; Stevenson 1983) as well as work on effectual reasoning highlighting entrepreneurs' current resources as a starting point (Sarasvathy 2001), entrepreneurship is still viable with limited resources.

Finally, other resources aside from financial resources can be exhausted by health-related problems; poor health can also take time (Stewart et al. 2003; Weiss et al. 2000) and energy away from activities related to work (or perhaps the opposite is true in some situations—viz., an entrepreneurial venture creates energy that transforms the health issue).

ENTREPRENEURIAL MOTIVATION AND OTHERS' HEALTH

As discussed above, people who directly experience health problems are often motivated to recognize and act on opportunities to overcome their poor health. However, individuals do not need to experience health problems directly to be driven to identify and exploit opportunities to help with others' health problems. First, some individuals have prosocial motivation—namely, "the desire to expend effort based on a concern for helping or contributing to other people" (Grant and Berry 2011: 77). Prosocial motivation influences cognitive processing (Kunda 1990; Nickerson 1998). Grant and Berry (2011) found that prosocial motivation can lead to perspective taking, which enables people to generalize valuable ideas in more creative ways. Perspective taking is "a cognitive process in which individuals adopt others' viewpoints in an attempt to understand their preferences, values, and needs". This process can give individuals insight into the nature of others' health problems, which is essential for them to recognize opportunities that help solve these problems. While prosocial motivation does not necessarily eliminate self-interested actions, to at least some degree, the "rubber meets the road" with how one manages their intellectual property. For example, when reporting why he did not patent the Solar Ear (an inexpensive, durable, and solar-powered hearing aid), Howard Weinstein noted that the cost of intellectual property protection would increase the overall product price, which went against his goal of helping as many people as possible with the technology. Further, he stated, "I actually want one of the Big 5 to copy us and use their distribution power to get more low cost hearing aids and batteries to developing countries" (kopernik.info/en-us/story/howard-weinstein-solar-ear). Thus, prosocial motivation not only shapes people's cognitions to offer insight into potentially beneficial health solutions, but it also motivates them to act on these opportunities.

Second, research has shown that prosocial motivation can result in perspective taking and eventually innovations among employees (Grant and Berry 2011). Again, prosocial motivation does not necessarily exclude benefits for the actor, but prosocially motivated individuals have a desire to aid others (Grant 2007; Grant and Berry 2011). Similarly, we (Shepherd and Patzelt 2015) proposed that although health entrepreneurship may create profit for entrepreneurs, it is also highly likely to improve others' health. Researchers have the opportunity to explore phenomena that can "make a difference" (health being the dependent variable) while simultaneously furthering their careers by publishing high-quality research with a deep impact. Thus, we hope scholars are prosocially motivated when choosing their research topics.

Third, entrepreneurs are likely to vary widely in their prosocial motivation (although this remains an empirical question). What influence does such variance in prosocial motivation have on health entrepreneurship? It could be that only highly prosocially motivated people recognize and act on health-related opportunities. However, because of the high possibility of generating profit, it is more likely that "all sorts" of entrepreneurs decide to enter this industry. A more fruitful line of research could be exploring differences in exploited opportunities in relation to entrepreneurs' level of prosocial motivation. For instance, do more prosocially motivated entrepreneurs act on more radical health opportunities compared to those who are less prosocially motivated? If so, is the reason for such action because these entrepreneurs engage in more perspective taking to isolate opportunities that would be more suitable for solving health problems (consistent with Grant and Berry 2011)? Alternatively, is an entrepreneur's willingness to accept uncertainty to act on a more radical opportunity bolstered by his or her prosocial motivation? Perhaps individuals with higher prosocial motivation are more prone to exploiting opportunities that have a higher likelihood of greatly reducing others' suffering. In addition, scholars can investigate why some entrepreneurs who are prosocially motivated exploit opportunities that solve others' health problems, whereas other prosocially motivated entrepreneurs are focused on opportunities that aid others in ways unrelated to health issues.

Finally, there can be a dark side to pursuing entrepreneurial opportunities that improve others' health: (1) The process of exploiting opportunities to improve others' health may have adverse health implications for the entrepreneur, which deplete energy (and therefore motivation) from the entrepreneurial effort. (2) Potential health opportunities (as all entrepreneurial opportunities) are inherently uncertain, and their pursuit could result in failure. When failure occurs, it could come with health repercussions that negatively affect subsequent entrepreneurial motivation. Entrepreneurial grief (Shepherd 2003), for instance, is likely greater when a business failure leads to the continuation of others' suffering that was going to be improved through the venture. Further, when entrepreneurs are a key source of health benefits for others, the implications to their own health from their entrepreneurial efforts increase in importance.

Entrepreneurial Motivation and the Destruction of Nature

As detailed in Chap. 2 (and more briefly above), harm to the natural environment refers to damaging the inherent worth of the physical world (Muehlebach 2001)—namely, the earth, biodiversity, and ecosystems (Parris and Kates 2003)—and reducing a source of resources and services to support present populations and future generations (Daily 1997). There are many reasons why an opportunity's specific harm to the natural environment could adversely affect entrepreneurs' evaluations of its appeal. For instance, entrepreneurs may foresee harm to their personal and/or their venture's reputation as a result of pursuing an opportunity that damages the environment (which is in line with findings related to the relationship between illegal activity and damage to a manager's and an organization's reputation [Karpoff et al. 2008; Karpoff and Lott 1993; Wiesenfeld et al. 2008]). However, entrepreneurs are likely to judge the significance of expected losses differently because personal values are likely to influence such judgments. For example, Agle et al. (1999) showed that other-regarding values affect the importance CEOs ascribe to employees when making decisions that influence corporate performance. Values are "an enduring belief that a specific mode of conduct or end-state of existence is personally or socially preferable to an opposite or converse mode of conduct or end-state of existence" (Rokeach 1973: 5). Thus, values are guiding beliefs (Schwartz and Bilsky 1990) for decision making and ensuing action (Fishbein and Ajzen 1972; Spash 2002; Thøgersen and Olander 2002).

In terms of the natural environment, respect for nature refers to "prudence in the management of all living species and natural resources," so they can be "preserved and passed on to our descendants" as well as the realization that "current patterns of production and consumption are unsustainable and must be changed" (United Nations General Assembly 2000). Finding an opportunity that could damage the natural environment to be highly appealing is likely to be contradictory to these overall values. Thus, when provided with information about an opportunity that will negatively affect the natural environment, entrepreneurs with stronger pro-environmental values will focus more attention on that information and will emphasize it more in their opportunity evaluations than entrepreneurs with weaker pro-environmental values. Indeed, we and a colleague (Shepherd et al. 2013) revealed that when entrepreneurs assess opportunities' attractiveness, the stronger their pro-environmental values, the more they emphasize the specific harm to the natural environment resulting from the opportunities in their decision making.

However, having strong pro-environmental values does not guarantee that entrepreneurs will not try to exploit opportunities that damage the natural environment; some entrepreneurs disengage such values during the decision-making process. For instance, people who feel they lack control over their own lives but believe that events and experiences in life are controlled by fate and luck instead of their own initiative (Detert et al. 2008; Levenson 1981) tend to disengage their values more readily. These beliefs in one's capacity to exercise control include both beliefs about one's ability to effectively complete essential tasks *and* the belief that this performance influences ensuing events and outcomes.

Entrepreneurial Self-Efficacy

Self-efficacy refers to the personal belief that one can achieve whatever he or she sets out to accomplish and can thus successfully meet one's goals (Utsch et al. 1999; Zhao et al. 2005). This belief that one can achieve whatever goals he or she sets—particularly, that one can successfully start and manage a business (i.e., entrepreneurial self-efficacy [Chen et al. 1998])—may make people more likely to disengage their pro-environmental values for several reasons.

Self-regulation centers on the notion that people do things that "give them satisfaction and a sense of self-worth, and they refrain from behaving in ways that violate their moral standards because such conduct will bring self-condemnation" (White et al. 2009: 42). People's feelings of satisfaction and self-worth typically improve when they take on tasks they believe they can accomplish, and actually completing those tasks further improves their perceived competence (Ryan and Deci 2000, 2001). Consequently, "self-efficacy beliefs function as an important set of proximal determinants of human self-regulation" (Bandura 1991: 257). In terms of entrepreneurship, entrepreneurial self-efficacy denotes one's belief that he or she is able to perform the tasks involved in starting and successfully managing a venture (Chen et al. 1998). Indeed, researchers have found that entrepreneurial self-efficacy is positively related to the intention to act entrepreneurially (Zhao et al. 2005; Zhao et al. 2010) and to entrepreneurial action (Boyd and Vozikis 1994).

While one important entrepreneurial task (i.e., innovation) includes developing new ideas, products, processes, and markets, the other activities representing the subcomponents of entrepreneurial self-efficacy are associated with effective opportunity exploitation (Chen et al. 1998). Individuals are usually attracted to activities they can competently complete (Bandura and Schunk 1981; Ryan and Deci 2000), and people with high self-efficacy are frequently drawn to challenging tasks that test and develop their skills (Csikszentmihalyi 1978) as well as to experiences that offer personal fulfillment (Srivastava et al. 2010). After all, such people believe—often passionately—that they can successfully complete these challenging tasks. Thus, when presented with opportunities that could damage the natural environment, individuals with high entrepreneurial self-efficacy frequently want to seize the chance to utilize their capabilities to actively exploit them. Still, as mentioned above, individuals' moral values may ultimately limit such actions. As a result, in such situations, individuals are confronted with a conflict between actions that will enhance their satisfaction and self-worth but will concurrently breach their moral guidelines and lead to self-censure. As Bandura (2006: 171) stated, "selective moral disengagement is most likely to occur under moral predicaments in which detrimental conduct brings valued outcomes."

For individuals with low entrepreneurial self-efficacy, in contrast, there is minimal tension between satisfaction and self-worth on the one hand and moral values on the other when evaluating the appeal of opportunities that cause harm to the natural environment. Such individuals have doubts about whether the benefits of such opportunities will pan out because they are not confident in their ability to successfully exploit them. In general, people with low self-efficacy are easily deterred by obstacles (Gist 1987), which—in this context—could include their own pro-environmental values. Such individuals are also likely to feel that they have minimal control over the entrepreneurial situation and outcomes (Markman et al. 2002).

Perceived Industry Munificence

Individuals exercise agency through self-efficacy and within the bounds of system conditions (Bandura 1991). System conditions refer to "the changeability or controllability of the environment ... [and represent] the opportunity structures to exercise personal efficacy and the ease of access to those opportunity structures" (Bandura 1991: 269). A significant system condition for entrepreneurs is the industry, specifically *industry munificence*, or the "scarcity or abundance of critical resources needed by (one or more) firms operating within an environment" (Castrogiovanni 1991: 542; cf. Dess and Beard 1984).

Some industries have plentiful resources and represent a decision context in which poor and good judgments lead to similar outcomes. In other words, in such cases, high levels of industry munificence can make up for entrepreneurial and strategic weaknesses (Tsai et al. 1991). Due to their greater environmental capacity, munificent environments support growth and stability and allow businesses to develop a cushion in case of future hardship (Dess and Beard 1984). In fact, some have described these resource-rich industries as producing a tide that raises all boats (Wasserman et al. 2001). Less munificent environments (i.e., industries with less environmental capacity) (Dess and Beard 1984), on the other hand, are characterized by intense competition (Aldrich 1979), few exploitable opportunities (Covin and Slevin 1989), and hostility (Khandwalla 1976, 1977; Miller and Friesen 1983). Consequently, these resource-poor industries are more "selective," and decision makers' choices have a stronger influence on performance outcomes than in more munificent industries (Covin and Slevin 1989; Tushman 1977; Zahra and Covin 1995). Thus, there are likely to be higher personal agency beliefs in environments individuals perceive as being less munificent (in comparison to environments perceived as being more munificent) because people are more likely to feel that decisions will have a greater influence on relevant outcomes (including preventing unwanted performance outcomes).

The industry munificence individuals perceive may directly affect how much they disengage their pro-environmental values. Firms in munificent industries can grow and profit in a variety of ways (Brittain and Freeman 1980; Tushman and Anderson 1986). Thus, acting on opportunities that damage the natural environment is likely to be only one of many means to improve firm performance. Additionally, individuals may view opportunity exploitation itself as an unreasonably risky way to enhance firm performance (Covin and Slevin 1989). As a result, there is minimal conflict between the cost of passing up an opportunity and the values underlying one's assessment. Thus, under perceived conditions of munificence, individuals tend to keep their pro-environmental values fully engaged, and there is a lower likelihood that entrepreneurs will be attracted to opportunities that could cause harm to the natural environment.

In contrast, industries with less munificence are characterized by a "paucity of readily exploitable market opportunities" (Zahra and Covin 1995: 48) and very limited maneuverability. In these environments, businesses have fewer means to improve growth and profitability. This means that opportunities that could cause damage to the natural environment are part of a substantially smaller set of opportunities that could be pursued. Indeed, scholars have found that corporate entrepreneurship plays a more salient role in firm performance in resource-scarce industries than in industries with greater munificence (Covin and Slevin 1989; Miller and Friesen 1983; Zahra and Covin 1995). Therefore, when individuals perceive an industry as being less munificent, the importance of pursuing an opportunity that may harm the environment is likely to conflict with their pro-environmental values more than in more munificent contexts. In turn, this increased conflict between values and beliefs about outcomes makes decision makers more likely to disengage their values when evaluating opportunities. Such decision makers, for instance, may claim that after developing the environmentally unfriendly opportunity and/or when the industry improves, they will be better positioned to pursue only environmentally friendly opportunities in the future.

Individual Values and Entrepreneurial Motivation

Although the search for a direct association between personality traits and entrepreneurship has led to an unclear picture, the entrepreneur is clearly an essential part of the entrepreneurial process (Shook et al. 2003). During the recent revival of studies on entrepreneurs' personal characteristics, scholars have gone past looking for "trans-situational consistency in personality traits" (Shaver and Scott 2002) and have begun exploring deeper models of individual characteristics, motivation, cognition, and behavior (e.g., Baron 2004; Baum and Locke 2004; Baum et al. 2001; Busenitz and Barney 1997; Mitchell et al. 2004; Rauch and Frese 2007; Zhao et al. 2005). Take, for example, Baum et al. (2001) and Baum and Locke (2004) who showed individual characteristics such as tenacity and passion do not have a direct association with new firm growth but that these variables are associated with growth-related motivation. In addition, Rauch and Frese (2007) and Zhao and Seibert (2006) used meta-analyses to illustrate the necessity for researchers to explore more proximal moderators and mediators instead of the direct association between individual characteristics and entrepreneurial outcomes. A stronger understanding of the association between entrepreneurs and proximal outcomes, including cognition, motivation, and decision making, is likely to yield a more vivid and comprehensive view of the entrepreneurial process (Shane et al. 2003). We examine in this section how personal values motivate entrepreneurial decisions. We explore personal values since extant literature on psychology finds that one's values and his or her choices among alternatives are closely connected (Feather 1990). Therefore, a focus on personal values offers a comprehensive framework for studying decisions (Rohan 2000).

Personal values are at the core of motivated choice (Judge and Bretz 1992). Values constitute the lens through which individuals view potential actions, including how attractive these actions are. As such, personal value priorities generate valences (i.e., desirability) for prospective outcomes (Feather 1982) and "cause decisions" (Rohan 2000: 270). Thus, individuals' values influence how they define situations, evaluate alternative possibilities, and finally decide on a course of action. As entrepreneurs decide on an entrepreneurial endeavor, it is highly likely that the weight they place on the attractiveness of a successful outcome will (to some extent) depend on their personal values (Holland and Shepherd 2013).

Individuals' values stem from their cognitive representations of fundamental needs (Rokeach 1973; Schwartz 1992). Although scholars have studied values for many decades, Milton Rokeach (1973) is generally credited with starting a stream of research on values with his Rokeach Value Survey. Rokeach's work drew on the assumption that a finite number of "terminal human values" serve as individuals' internal reference points, which are the basis for judgment and motivation (Rohan 2000). Expanding Rokeach's (1973) work, Schwartz (1992) built a more comprehensive theory of values. This theory comprises an overarching structure for the value system. The theory predicts decisions and actions in numerous practical situations (Bardi et al. 2008). We call upon individual-level Schwartz values theory (1992) in this chapter. According to Schwartz (1992), there are ten basic universal value types. These value types include power, achievement, hedonism, stimulation, self-direction, universalism, benevolence, tradition, conformity, and security. Based on the differences and similarities between these values' motivational structures, Schwartz (1992) outlined four higher-order value types, specifically openness to change, self-transcendence, self-enhancement, and conservation. Higher-order values are organized in a circular manner such that adjacent values will have motivational commonalities whereas values on opposite sides of the circle will have motivations that are not compatible. While Schwartz (1992) does not expect opposing values to be negatively correlated, if an individual holds opposing values at the same time, conflicting motivations may increase internal conflict during the decision-making process (Schwartz 1992). Researchers have empirically verified that the theoretical structure of Schwartz's value types is reliable and can be generalized to various samples (Morris et al. 1998). Due to this integrated value structure, researchers can explore how related value sets impact the desirability of the financial and non-financial returns, as well as switching costs, associated with persisting with entrepreneurship (Feather 1995).

Self-Enhancement

In regard to the four higher-order values, self-enhancement comprises the values of power, achievement, and hedonism. These values center on developing one's own interests—even if it is associated with costs for others (Schwartz 1992). Thus, entrepreneurs high in self-enhancement will strive for extreme success of their ventures because they want to gain social status and recognition. These individuals are frequently prepared to dedicate substantial time and energy to display ability and success in what they are doing (Bardi and Schwartz 2003). Individual with high levels of self-enhancement generally relish in having control over resources and employees, and they recognize that creating a flourishing business can lead to a positive public image and prominent positions in society (Scheinberg and MacMillan 1988).

In the business context, achievement and power are usually associated with a firm's financial performance, often generating higher incomes and wealth. Individuals who value self-enhancement may obtain satisfaction from the opportunities for self-indulgence available to the wealthy. Looking beyond merely fulfilling their basic needs, such people are likely to seek out opportunities that satisfy wants and luxuries (Bardi et al. 2008). Indeed, many entrepreneurs maintain that the potential for high financial income and recognition are primary motivations for entering into an entrepreneurial career (Carter et al. 2003; Kuratko et al. 1997). Thus, for individuals who value power, achievement, and self-indulgence, financial returns are likely to play a more significant role in decisions regarding the attractiveness of an entrepreneurial career than for individuals who emphasize self-enhancement values to a lesser extent (Holland and Shepherd 2013).

Openness to Change

The values comprising openness to change include stimulation, hedonism, and self-direction. People who appreciate openness favor independent thought and action and derive joy from life's challenge and excitement (Schwartz 1992). These people like to try new approaches and are not scared of challenging and ultimately eliminating traditional roles or systems. In addition, individuals who are open to change find learning stimulating and enjoy using their intellectual capabilities to create innovative products (Shane et al. 1991). They also tend to have a higher promotion focus in terms of their self-regulatory system. They often seek growth and improvement toward their ideal selves (Brockner et al. 2004). Thus, people who value openness to change will emphasize the non-financial benefits of entrepreneurial action, such as self-realization and learning through experience.

People who appreciate self-enhancement and people who appreciate openness to change share the value of hedonism. Yet, they go about gratifying their desires and seeking pleasure in different ways (Schwartz 1992). Individuals who value self-enhancement receive greater satisfaction from power and achievement, whereas those who value openness to change explore new experiences and the autonomy to set their own objectives (Bardi et al. 2008). In addition, entrepreneurs drawing on openness as a principle guiding their lives will find pleasure in the freedom provided by their entrepreneurial career (Carter et al. 2003). Liberty to control one's own schedule and work life and the chance to wear many "different hats" produces psychic benefits that many entrepreneurs value as much (or more) than financial rewards. Thus, entrepreneurs who value openness to change are likely to emphasize these types of non-economic benefits from entrepreneurial action in their decision-making process more than individuals who do not value openness (Holland and Shepherd 2013).

Self-Transcendence

The values that comprise self-transcendence include universalism and benevolence. Universalism and benevolence are similar in that they both focus on others. However, universalism is typically associated with individuals outside one's close contact circle, whereas benevolence is associated with individuals inside that person's close environment (Bardi et al. 2008). These self-transcendence values inspire individuals to move beyond self-centered interests toward bettering the lives of others including personal acquaintances, their colleagues, communities in which they live, and the world overall (Schwartz 1992). People who hold these values tend to focus on being helpful, honest, and loyal to people they interact with and thrive when they have positive relationships with other individuals (Mikulincer et al. 2003). These people are inspired and motivated by enhancing their associates' lives, and they revel in the psychological benefits they receive from such benefitting others (Lyons et al. 2007).

Individuals with high self-transcendence values are likely to engage in social entrepreneurship (Hemingway 2005). These individuals may be motivated to start new ventures that encourage equal opportunities for everyone, environmental protection, better standards of living in developing nations, or other social improvements. In starting new ventures to solve such problems, self-transcendent entrepreneurs may obtain fulfillment from having an enduring positive effect on the lives of their stakeholders including employees and customers. As such, individuals with high self-transcendence values are likely to stress these forms of non-financial benefits in their entrepreneurial decisions more than those with low self-transcendence values (Holland and Shepherd 2013).

Conservation

The values associated with conservation comprise tradition, conformity, and security (Schwartz 1992). Individuals who appreciate conservation are generally committed to longstanding standards, ideals, and traditions and value societal stability, preservation of customs, and moderation in action (Schwartz 1992). For example, job applicants high in conservation value family ownership of a potential employer more than those low in conservation because family ownership is typically associated with the stability and tradition of the firm (Hauswald 2013). Thus, entrepreneurs with high conservation values will tend to prioritize stability when starting their ventures. Personal and/or family security can be another motivator behind such individuals' decision to start or persist with a venture (Kuratko et al. 1997). These people will stress self-control and caution in their actions and are likely to maintain the status quo, often keeping with conventional roles while they at the same time strive for harmonious relationships with others (Lyons et al. 2007). Additionally, individuals with high conservation values tend to attend to societal norms and generally perceive an obligation to meet responsibilities (Egri and Herman 2000). Therefore, entrepreneurs with high conservation values are also more likely to have a prevention regulatory focus, seeking to lessen discrepancies with their "ought" selves by avoiding change because they fear that change can yield negative results (Brockner et al. 2004). As such, they often focus on the potential costs of change when they decide about entrepreneurial issues.

Staw (1981) states that shared norms for consistency can result in the preference to remain dedicated to a chosen course of action even if it is failing than be seen as someone who gives up or is unable to make decisions. Staying consistent is an involuntary reaction that can enhance an individual's feeling of security in challenging situations (DeTienne et al. 2008). Because individuals with high conservation values like to maintain customs and norms, they are likely to be especially vulnerable to norms of consistency and to thus stress the costs associated with switching opportunities in their decisions to persist with their entrepreneurial endeavor (Holland and Shepherd 2013).

Motivation to Persist with Entrepreneurial Action

Researchers have studied and tested the motivation to justify previous decisions at length (Baron 1998; Keil 1995), generally referring to this topic using self-justification theory (Staw and Fox 1977). Self-justification theory is largely based on Festinger's (1957) theory of cognitive dissonance and argues that "individuals will bias their attitudes on a task in a positive direction so as to justify their previous behavior" (Staw 1981: 579). Thus, people frequently decide to continue with a course of action because they want to demonstrate to themselves (psychological self-justification) and to other people (social self-justification) their rationality and competence (Keil et al. 2000b).

Personal Sunk Costs Driving Persistence

One signal of the motivation to justify previous decisions is the top decision maker's personal sunk costs. Not only do entrepreneurs frequently invest financial resources in their ventures, but they also tend to dedicate considerable time and effort to their firms (Arkes and Blumer 1985). Their reputation may be intimately connected to their venture, thus leading to psychological or social self-justifications. While the resources an entrepreneur has already devoted to his or her firm are sunk costs and should thus be not relevant for decisions concerning the present or the future, they may actually add to a person's need for self-justification.

More specifically, sunk costs are "costs that have occurred in the past and cannot be changed by any current or future action" (Devine and O'Clock 1995) and "create a cognitive bias at a subconscious level which may be manifested in the form of emotional attachment" (Keil et al. 2000a, b). The psychological attachment associated with sunk costs may stem from individuals' need to defend previous behavior and to appear competent to others. For instance, Dean et al. (1997) showed that at the industry level, the exit rate of new ventures is negatively associated with sunk cost levels. We propose that this form of emotional attachment may also occur with entrepreneurs such that persistence in a venture will be positively associated with the level of the entrepreneurs' personal sunk costs. In this sense, sunk costs can be seen as an obstruction to exit for failing ventures and can change the exit threshold from involving only financial information to also including the need to overcome sunk costs in order to exit (Caves and Porter 1977; Rosenbaum and Lamort 1992).

Personal Self-Interest

Personal self-interest is another form of self-justification. Researchers (Graebner and Eisenhardt 2004; Jensen and Meckling 1976) have provided evidence suggesting that people tend to make decisions based on their own self-interest. Agency theory (Jensen and Meckling 1976), which deals with goal incongruency between a principal and an agent, sheds light on this notion of self-interest: "Under agency theory, goal incongruency between principal and agent can create a situation in which the agent acts to maximize his or her own utility, rather than acting in the best interests of the principal" (Keil et al. 2000a: 636). In relation to self-interest, a similar situation arises: an entrepreneur aims to maximize his or her own utility, which can result in cognitive biases regarding the firm's best interests. Such a situation frequently leads to self-justification. For instance, an entrepreneur who enjoys skiing wants to build a plant near a world-class ski region, thus deciding in line with his or her self-interest. The entrepreneur can defend this decision based on the firm's needs (e.g., it would be better to entertain important stakeholders) even when it is obvious that a less costly location would be more prudent.

Personal Opportunities

A third trigger of motivation for self-justification might result from the personal opportunities available to the entrepreneur. Cognitive psychology research (Kanfer 1990) suggests that a key aspect of motivation is being able to choose among alternative courses of action. Thus, a key motivational source for entrepreneurs could be personal opportunities they have available to them (e.g., education, other jobs, retirement), which may in turn influence the decisions they make about persistence with their venture. The literature on turnover has shown that alternative employment options play a significant role in employees leaving the organization (Jackofsky and Peters 1983; March and Simon 1958), and Graebner and Eisenhardt (2004) showed that CEOs with strong personal motivations have a higher probability of selling their firm. Similarly, McGrath (1999: 14) argued that "an entrepreneur might disband an economically profitable business if other activities appear more lucrative or interesting, if his or her interests change or if it seems that long-run growth is limited," which suggests that the motivation for persistence at least partially depends on the alternative opportunities entrepreneurs have available to them. When alternatives are available, individuals may choose the most attractive option for their own life regardless of whether that option is in their firm's best interests. On the other hand, if no alternatives outside their current firm are available or the alternatives are unattractive, entrepreneurs are more likely to persist with their current firm.

Norms for Consistency

Norms for consistency—or the notion that people continue with a course of action purely because they feel that remaining consistent is the most suitable option (Cialdini 1993; Staw and Ross 1980)—are an additional factor influencing individuals' commitment to a particular action plan (Staw 1981) and can therefore motivate entrepreneurs' persistence. As Cialdini argued (1993: 53), "Because it is a preprogrammed and mindless method of responding, automatic consistency can supply a safe hiding place from troubling realizations." Thus, entrepreneurs can search for signals within the venture indicating that persistence is the most appropriate policy and disregard information implying that adaptation is needed. Two important signals are a venture's prior success and the entrepreneur's perceptions of the venture's collective efficacy.

Prior Organizational Success

Having prior success may be another motivator of persistence when entrepreneurs believe that success is close by and that they merely need to "ride out the storm" to achieve it. Indeed, scholars have found that previous organizational success can lead to strategic persistence (Audia et al. 2000; Lant et al. 1992). Audia et al. (2000: 849), for instance, showed that "Once organizations achieve success, their natural tendency is to continue to exploit the strategies that worked in the past." Similarly, in a study on real options, McGrath (1999) highlighted three key arguments why prior success can encourage persistence. First, entrepreneurs often oversample success while simultaneously undersampling failure. In addition, prior success can lead to the underestimation of risks and overestimation of projected successes (Levinthal and March 1993: 105), thus causing them to believe that their perseverance will ultimately lead to additional successes. Second, previous success can encourage persistence because "organizations code outcomes into successes and failures and develop ideas about causes for them" (Levinthal and March 1993: 97). Stemming from their own cognitive biases, entrepreneurs often believe that their successes result from their own actions whereas failures are caused by bad luck (Staw et al. 1983). Attribution theory scholars (e.g., Shaver et al. 2001) argue that people often try to internalize success—believing that any success is the result of their own efforts—and externalize failure. Thus, entrepreneurs are likely to believe that prior success resulted from specific decisions that were made and/or from resources that were available rather than from some outside source. Therefore, the firm again will be successful in the future. Third, prior success often lessens a firm's willingness to change routines or technologies even when such changes come with added benefits (Levitt and March 1988; McGrath 1999). As such, prior success seems to make entrepreneurs more complacent and satisfied with their present situation; these entrepreneurs are less keen to make needed adaptations, thereby motivating persistence.

Perceived Collective Efficacy

Furthermore, norms for consistency may "be determined by the cultural and organizational norms surrounding individuals" (Staw 1981: 335). One organizational norm that appears to play a particularly important role in persistence decisions is collective efficacy—or a group's collective belief that it can effectively perform a specific task. According to Bandura (1986: 449), "Perceived collective efficacy will influence what people choose to do as a group, how much effort they put into it, and their staying power when group efforts fail to produce results."

While collective efficacy research is still quite new, researchers (e.g., Bandura 1986: 449) argue that "collective efficacy is rooted in self-efficacy" and therefore should function in a similar way. In a meta-analysis of research on the association between self-efficacy and persistence outcomes, Multon et al. (1991) showed that self-efficacy and persistence are positively correlated. This positive association was found across a broad range of participants, experimental designs, and measurement approaches. Furthermore, at the level of the group, scholars have shown that groups with high collective efficacy are more likely to persist than groups with low collective efficacy (e.g., Hodges and Carron 1992; Little and Madigan 1997). Entrepreneurs working in settings where collective efficacy (e.g., of the entrepreneurial team) is high are therefore likely to be more motivated to persist with their venture than those working in settings with low collective efficacy.

EXTRINSIC MOTIVATION

Economic theory researchers of firm exit assert that underperforming firms should not exist; instead, they should be exited or be eliminated from the environment. However, empirical studies provide evidence that such firms persist, sometimes with no end in sight (e.g., Gimeno et al. 1997). Earlier, we discussed potential determinants of persistence in underperforming firms, but a question still remains: why do some entrepreneurs' persistence decisions align with rational economic views whereas others do not? To explain differences among entrepreneurs' persistence decisions, we look to a core assumption of the economics-based model: extrinsic motivation.

Frequently conceptualized in research as financial income and personal wealth (Kuratko et al. 1997), extrinsic motivation refers to "a cognitive state reflecting the extent to which an individual attributes the force of his or her task behaviors to some extrinsic outcome" (Brief and Aldag 1977: 497). Researchers have long recognized the possibility of receiving a financial reward as a significant motivator for entrepreneurial behavior (Campbell 1992; Kuratko et al. 1997; Schumpeter 1961; Shepherd and DeTienne 2005). As an early example, Schumpeter (1961) proposed that empire building with the goal of gaining financial reward is a salient motivation for entrepreneurs. Further, Campbell's (1992) economic perspective on entrepreneurship suggests that a person decides to enter entrepreneurship in case the present value of profit he or she expects from entrepreneurship is greater than the expected profit from being an employee. My (Dean) colleague and I (Shepherd and DeTienne 2005) showed that potential financial rewards motivate entrepreneurs to recognize opportunities (in particular entrepreneurs with low levels of prior knowledge), and Kuratko et al. (1997: 31) revealed that "extrinsic goals concentrating on wealth" play a crucial role in sustaining entrepreneurial behavior.

Yet, there is a lack of research exploring extrinsic motivation's influence on persistence. The literatures on job satisfaction and turnover could provide useful insights to better explain this relationship. Research has repeatedly shown that there is a negative association between pay satisfaction and employee turnover (for a meta-analytic review, see Cotton and Tuttle 1986) and a positive association between job satisfaction and commitment to the organization (Johnston et al. 1990). Such research has shown that people who are happy with the financial income they receive from their job are not only less likely to leave the firm but also tend to have higher organizational commitment. The degree to which an organization meets an individual's expectations affects how committed he or she is toward the organization (Babakus et al. 1996). Thus, for the context at hand, individuals with lower extrinsic motivation are likely to be content with an underperforming firm, whereas individuals with high extrinsic motivation are likely to be less content with an underperforming firm. As with job satisfaction, people who are content in their organization are less motivated to leave.

Conclusion

In this chapter, we explored why some people are more motivated than others to engage in and persist with entrepreneurship. We found that while some motivators appear to trigger entrepreneurial action more generally (e.g., financial rewards or certain individual values), other types of motivation seem to stimulate a specific type of entrepreneurship (e.g., empathy motivating entrepreneurial action targeted toward developing societies). Interestingly, the inability to pursue a career as a salaried employee (e.g., due to injury or psychological disorder) can also stimulate entrepreneurial motivation. Finally, a key finding is that the effects of prior knowledge as described in Chap. 2 and those of motivation as described in this chapter do not seem to be independent of each other but can conjointly motivate entrepreneurial action.

NOTE

1. Fear of failure can also be associated with motivating action (Cacciotti et al. 2016).

REFERENCES

Abbey, A., & Dickson, J. W. (1983). R&D work climate and innovation in semiconductors. *Academy of Management Journal, 26*(2), 362–368.

Agle, B. R., Mitchell, R. K., & Sonnenfeld, J. A. (1999). Who matters to Ceos? An investigation of stakeholder attributes and salience, corporate performance, and CEO values. *Academy of Management Journal, 42*(5), 507–525.

Akande, A. (1994). Coping with entrepreneurial stress: Evidence from Nigeria. *Journal of Small Business Management, 32*(1), 83.

Aldrich, H. E. (1979). *Organizations and environments.* Englewood Cliffs: Prentice-Hall, 40(3), 437–453.

Alon, I., & Lerner, M. (2008). International entrepreneurship in China: Lessons from global entrepreneurship monitor. *Cell, 407*, 913–8842.

Amabile, T. M. (1993). Motivational synergy: Toward new conceptualizations of intrinsic and extrinsic motivation in the workplace. *Human Resource Management Review, 3*(3), 185–201.

Amabile, T. M. (1997). Motivating creativity in organizations: On doing what you love and loving what you do. *California Management Review, 40*(1), 39–58.

Amato, P. R. (2005). The impact of family formation change on the cognitive, social, and emotional well-being of the next generation. *The Future of Children, 15*, 75–96.

Amit, R., Glosten, L., & Muller, E. (1990). Entrepreneurial ability, venture investments, and risk sharing. *Management Science, 36*(10), 1233–1246.

Ardichvili, A., Cardozo, R., & Ray, S. (2003). A theory of entrepreneurial opportunity identification and development. *Journal of Business Venturing, 18*(1), 105–123.

Arkes, H. R., & Blumer, C. (1985). The psychology of sunk cost. *Organizational Behavior and Human Decision Processes, 35*(1), 124–140.

Arnold, N. L., & Seekins, T. (2002). Self-employment: A process for use by vocational rehabilitation agencies. *Journal of Vocational Rehabilitation, 17*(2), 107–113.

Ashford, S. J. (1986). Feedback-seeking in individual adaptation: A resource perspective. *Academy of Management Journal, 29*(3), 465–487.

Audia, P. G., Locke, E. A., & Smith, K. G. (2000). The paradox of success: An archival and a laboratory study of strategic persistence following radical environmental change. *Academy of Management Journal, 43*(5), 837–853.

Austin, J., Stevenson, H., & Wei-Skillern, J. (2006). Social and commercial entrepreneurship: Same, different, or both? *Entrepreneurship Theory and Practice, 30*, 1–22.

Babakus, E., Cravens, D. W., Johnston, M., & Moncrief, W. C. (1996). Examining the role of organizational variables in the salesperson job satisfaction model. *Journal of Personal Selling & Sales Management, 16*(3), 33–46.

Baker, T., & Nelson, R. E. (2005). Creating something from nothing: Resource construction through entrepreneurial bricolage. *Administrative Science Quarterly, 50*(3), 329–366.

Bandura, A. (1986). *Social cognitive theory.* Englewood Cliffs: Prentice-Hall, 34(2), 169–178.

Bandura, A. (1991). Social cognitive theory of self-regulation. *Organizational Behavior and Human Decision Processes, 50*(2), 248–287.

Bandura, A. (2006). Toward a psychology of human agency. *Perspectives on Psychological Science, 1*(2), 164–180.

Bandura, A., & Schunk, D. H. (1981). Cultivating competence, self-efficacy, and intrinsic interest through proximal self-motivation. *Journal of Personality and Social Psychology, 41*(3), 586.

Bardi, A., & Schwartz, S. H. (2003). Values and behavior: Strength and structure of relations. *Personality and Social Psychology Bulletin, 29*(10), 1207–1220.

Bardi, A., Calogero, R. M., & Mullen, B. (2008). A new archival approach to the study of values and value – Behavior relations: Validation of the value lexicon. *Journal of Applied Psychology, 93*(3), 483.

Baron, R. A. (1998). Cognitive mechanisms in entrepreneurship: Why and when entrepreneurs think differently than other people. *Journal of Business Venturing, 13*(4), 275–294.

Baron, R. A. (2004). The cognitive perspective: A valuable tool for answering entrepreneurship's basic "why" questions. *Journal of Business Venturing, 19*(2), 221–239.

Baron, R. A. (2006). Opportunity recognition as pattern recognition: How entrepreneurs "connect the dots" to identify new business opportunities. *Academy of Management Perspectives, 20*(1), 104–119.

Baron, R. A. (2008). The role of affect in the entrepreneurial process. *Academy of Management Review, 33*(2), 328–340.

Bartol, K. M., & Martin, D. C. (1998). Performance appraisal: Maintaining system effectiveness. *Public Personnel Management, 27*(2), 223–230.
Batavia, A. I., & Schriner, K. (2001). The Americans with disabilities act as engine of social change: Models of disability and the potential of a civil rights approach. *Policy Studies Journal, 29*(4), 690–702.
Batson, C. D., & Shaw, L. L. (1991). Evidence for altruism: Toward a pluralism of prosocial motives. *Psychological Inquiry, 2*(2), 107–122.
Baum, J. R., & Locke, E. A. (2004). The relationship of entrepreneurial traits, skill, and motivation to subsequent venture growth. *Journal of Applied Psychology, 89*(4), 587.
Baum, J. R., Locke, E. A., & Smith, K. G. (2001). A multidimensional model of venture growth. *Academy of Management Journal, 44*(2), 292–303.
Baumol, W. J. (1990). Entrepreneurship: Productive, unproductive, and destructive. *Journal of Political Economy, 98*(5, Part 1), 893–921.
Beck, A. T., & Clark, D. A. (1997). An information processing model of anxiety: Automatic and strategic processes. *Behaviour Research and Therapy, 35,* 49–58.
Birley, S., & Westhead, P. (1994). A taxonomy of business start-up reasons and their impact on firm growth and size. *Journal of Business Venturing, 9*(1), 7–31.
Boyd, N. G., & Vozikis, G. S. (1994). The influence of self-efficacy on the development of entrepreneurial intentions and actions. *Entrepreneurship Theory and Practice, 18,* 63–63.
Breugst, N., Domurath, A., Patzelt, H., & Klaukien, A. (2012). Perceptions of entrepreneurial passion and employees' commitment to entrepreneurial ventures. *Entrepreneurship Theory and Practice, 36*(1), 171–192.
Brief, A. P., & Aldag, R. J. (1977). The intrinsic-extrinsic dichotomy: Toward conceptual clarity. *Academy of Management Review, 2*(3), 496–500.
Brittain, J. W., & Freeman, J. H. (1980). Organizational proliferation and density dependent selection. In J. Kimberly & R. H. Miles (Eds.), *The organizational life cycle* (pp. 291–338). San Francisco: Jossey-Bass.
Brockner, J., Higgins, E. T., & Low, M. B. (2004). Regulatory focus theory and the entrepreneurial process. *Journal of Business Venturing, 19*(2), 203–220.
Brown, T. E., Davidsson, P., & Wiklund, J. (2001). An operationalization of Stevenson's conceptualization of entrepreneurship as opportunity-based firm behavior. *Strategic Management Journal, 22*(10), 953–968.
Burgelman, R. A., & Välikangas, L. (2005). Managing internal corporate venturing cycles. *MIT Sloan Management Review, 46*(4), 26.
Busenitz, L. W., & Barney, J. B. (1997). Differences between entrepreneurs and managers in large organizations: Biases and heuristics in strategic decision-making. *Journal of Business Venturing, 12*(1), 9–30.
Byrne, O., & Shepherd, D. A. (2015). Different strokes for different folks: Entrepreneurial narratives of emotion, cognition, and making sense of business failure. *Entrepreneurship Theory and Practice, 39*(2), 375–405.

Cacciotti, G., & Hayton, J. C. (2015). Fear and entrepreneurship: A review and research agenda. *International Journal of Management Reviews, 17*(2), 165–190.
Cacciotti, G., Hayton, J. C., Mitchell, J. R., & Giazitzoglu, A. (2016). A reconceptualization of fear of failure in entrepreneurship. *Journal of Business Venturing, 31*(3), 302–325.
Callahan, M., Shumpert, N., & Mast, M. (2002). Self-employment, choice and self-determination. *Journal of Vocational Rehabilitation, 17*(2), 75–85.
Campbell, C. A. (1992). A decision theory model for entrepreneurial acts. *Entrepreneurship: Theory and Practice, 17*(1), 21–28.
Campbell, J. P., & Pritchard, R. D. (1976). Motivation theory in industrial and organizational psychology. In M. Dunnette (Ed.), *Handbook of industrial and organizational psychology*. Chicago: Rand McNally, 12(3), 405–424.
Cardon, M. S., Wincent, J., Singh, J., & Drnovsek, M. (2009). The nature and experience of entrepreneurial passion. *Academy of Management Review, 34*(3), 511–532.
Cardon, M. S., Stevens, C. E., & Potter, D. R. (2011). Misfortunes or mistakes?: Cultural sensemaking of entrepreneurial failure. *Journal of Business Venturing, 26*(1), 79–92.
Cardon, M. S., Foo, M. D., Shepherd, D., & Wiklund, J. (2012). Exploring the heart: Entrepreneurial emotion is a hot topic. *Entrepreneurship Theory and Practice, 36*(1), 1–10.
Carroll, C. D., Hall, R. E., & Zeldes, S. P. (1992). The buffer-stock theory of saving: Some macroeconomic evidence. *Brookings Papers on Economic Activity, 1992*(2), 61–156.
Carter, S. (2011). The rewards of entrepreneurship: Exploring the incomes, wealth, and economic well-being of entrepreneurial households. *Entrepreneurship Theory and Practice, 35*(1), 39–55.
Carter, N. M., Gartner, W. B., Shaver, K. G., & Gatewood, E. J. (2003). The career reasons of nascent entrepreneurs. *Journal of Business Venturing, 18*(1), 13–39.
Castrogiovanni, G. J. (1991). Environmental munificence: A theoretical assessment. *Academy of Management Review, 16*(3), 542–565.
Caves, R. E., & Porter, M. E. (1977). From entry barriers to mobility barriers: Conjectural decisions and contrived deterrence to new competition. *Quarterly Journal of Economics, 91*, 241–261.
Chen, C. C., Greene, P. G., & Crick, A. (1998). Does entrepreneurial self-efficacy distinguish entrepreneurs from managers? *Journal of Business Venturing, 13*(4), 295–316.
Cialdini, R. (1993). *The psychology of influence*. New York: William Morrow & Co.
Cohen, W. M., & Levinthal, D. A. (1990). Absorptive capacity: A new perspective on learning and innovation. *Administrative Science Quarterly, 35*, 128–152.

Conroy, D. E. (2001). Progress in the development of a multidimensional measure of fear of failure: The performance failure appraisal inventory (PFAI). *Anxiety, Stress and Coping, 14*(4), 431–452.
Conroy, D. E. (2004). The unique psychological meanings of multidimensional fears of failing. *Journal of Sport and Exercise Psychology, 26*(3), 484–491.
Conroy, D. E., Willow, J. P., & Metzler, J. N. (2002). Multidimensional fear of failure measurement: The performance failure appraisal inventory. *Journal of Applied Sport Psychology, 14*(2), 76–90.
Cotton, J. L., & Tuttle, J. M. (1986). Employee turnover: A meta-analysis and review with implications for research. *Academy of Management Review, 11*(1), 55–70.
Covin, J. G., & Slevin, D. P. (1989). Strategic management of small firms in hostile and benign environments. *Strategic Management Journal, 10*(1), 75–87.
Csikszentmihalyi, M. (1975). Play and intrinsic rewards. *Journal of Humanistic Psychology, 15*(3), 41–63.
Csikszentmihalyi, M. (1978). Intrinsic rewards and emergent motivation. In *The hidden costs of reward: New Perspectives on the Psychology of Human Motivation* (pp. 205–216). Hillsdale: Lawrence Erlbaum Associates.
Csikszentmihalyi, M. (2000). *Beyond boredom and anxiety.* San Francisco: Jossey-Bass, 125(2), 276–302.
Cummings, L. L., & O'Connell, M. J. (1978). Organizational innovation: A model and needed research. *Journal of Business Research, 6*(1), 33–50.
Curran, T., Hill, A. P., Appleton, P. R., Vallerand, R. J., & Standage, M. (2015). The psychology of passion: A meta-analytical review of a decade of research on intrapersonal outcomes. *Motivation and Emotion, 39*(5), 631–655.
Daily, G. (1997). *Nature's services: Societal dependence on natural ecosystems.* Washington, DC: Island, 387(6630), 253–260.
Davis, M. H. (1996). *Empathy: A social psychological approach.* Boulder: Westview Press, 2, 113–126.
Dean, T. J., Turner, C. A., & Bamford, C. E. (1997). Impediments to imitation and rates of new firm failure. In *Academy of management proceedings* (pp. 103–107). Academy of Management.
Deci, E. L., & Ryan, R. M. (1985). The general causality orientations scale: Self-determination in personality. *Journal of Research in Personality, 19*(2), 109–134.
Deci, E. L., & Ryan, R. M. (2001). On happiness and human potentials: A review of research on hedonic and eudaimonic well-being. *Annual Review of Psychology, 52*(1), 141–166.
Dentener, F., Drevet, J., Lamarque, J. F., Bey, I., Eickhout, B., Fiore, A. M., et al. (2006). Nitrogen and sulfur deposition on regional and global scales: A multimodel evaluation. *Global Biogeochemical Cycles, 20*(4), 1–21.
Dess, G. G., & Beard, D. W. (1984). Dimensions of organizational task environments. *Administrative Science Quarterly,* 52–73.

Detert, J. R., Treviño, L. K., & Sweitzer, V. L. (2008). Moral disengagement in ethical decision making: A study of antecedents and outcomes. *Journal of Applied Psychology, 93*(2), 374.
DeTienne, D. R., Shepherd, D. A., & De Castro, J. O. (2008). The fallacy of "only the strong survive": The effects of extrinsic motivation on the persistence decisions for underperforming firms. *Journal of Business Venturing, 23*(5), 528–546.
Devine, K., & Clock, P. O. (1995). The effect on sunk costs and opportunity costs on a subject. *The Mid-Atlantic Journal of Business, 31*(1), 25.
Dijker, A. J. (2001). The influence of perceived suffering and vulnerability on the experience of pity. *European Journal of Social Psychology, 31*(6), 659–676.
Donahue, E. G., Rip, B., & Vallerand, R. J. (2009). When winning is everything: On passion, identity, and aggression in sport. *Psychology of Sport and Exercise, 10*(5), 526–534.
Donaldson, J. M., & Watson, R. (1996). Loneliness in elderly people: An important area for nursing research. *Journal of Advanced Nursing, 24*(5), 952–959.
Douglas, E. J., & Shepherd, D. A. (2000). Entrepreneurship as a utility maximizing response. *Journal of Business Venturing, 15*(3), 231–251.
Douglas, E. J., & Shepherd, D. A. (2002). Self-employment as a career choice: Attitudes, entrepreneurial intentions, and utility maximization. *Entrepreneurship Theory and Practice, 26*(3), 81–90.
Efrat, R. (2005). Bankruptcy stigma: Plausible causes for shifting norms. *Emory Bankruptcy Developments Journal, 22*, 481–519.
Egri, C. P., & Herman, S. (2000). Leadership in the North American environmental sector: Values, leadership styles, and contexts of environmental leaders and their organizations. *Academy of Management Journal, 43*(4), 571–604.
Eisenberg, N. (2000). Emotion, regulation, and moral development. *Annual Review of Psychology, 51*(1), 665–697.
Fafchamps, M., & Lund, S. (2003). Risk-sharing networks in rural Philippines. *Journal of Development Economics, 71*(2), 261–287.
Feather, N. T. (1982). Human values and the prediction of action: An expectancy-valence analysis. In N. T. Feather (Ed.), *Expectations and actions: Expectancy-value models in psychology* (pp. 263–292). Hillsdale: LEA.
Feather, N. T. (1990). Bridging the gap between values and actions: Recent applications of the expectancy-value model. In E. T. Higgins & R. M. Sorrentino (Eds.), *Handbook of motivation and cognition: Foundations of social behavior* (Vol. 2, pp. 151–192). New York: Guilford Press.
Feather, N. T. (1995). Values, valences, and choice: The influences of values on the perceived attractiveness and choice of alternatives. *Journal of Personality and Social Psychology, 68*(6), 1135.
Festinger, L. (1957). *A theory of cognitive dissonance*. Stanford: Stanford University Press.
Fiet, J. O. (2007). A prescriptive analysis of search and discovery. *Journal of Management Studies, 44*(4), 592–611.

Fineman, S. (1999). Emotion and organizing. In S. R. Clegg & C. Hardy (Eds.), *Studying organization: Theory and method* (pp. 289–310). London: Sage.
Fishbein, M., & Ajzen, I. (1972). Attitudes and opinions. *Annual Review of Psychology, 23*(1), 487–544.
Folkman, S., & Moskowitz, J. T. (2004). Coping: Pitfalls and promise. *Annual Review of Psychology, 55,* 745–774.
Forbes, D. P., Borchert, P. S., Zellmer-Bruhn, M. E., & Sapienza, H. J. (2006). Entrepreneurial team formation: An exploration of new member addition. *Entrepreneurship Theory and Practice, 30,* 225–248.
Gagné, M., & Deci, E. L. (2005). Self-determination theory and work motivation. *Journal of Organizational Behavior, 26*(4), 331–362.
Gatewood, E. J., Shaver, K. G., Powers, J. B., & Gartner, W. B. (2002). Entrepreneurial expectancy, task effort, and performance. *Entrepreneurship Theory and Practice, 27*(2), 187–206.
Gilad, B., & Levine, P. (1986). A behavioral model of entrepreneurial supply. *Journal of Small Business Management, 24,* 45.
Gilinsky, A. S. (1949). Relative self-estimate and the level of aspiration. *Journal of Experimental Psychology, 39*(2), 256.
Gimeno, J., Folta, T. B., Cooper, A. C., & Woo, C. Y. (1997). Survival of the fittest? Entrepreneurial human capital and the persistence of underperforming firms. *Administrative Science Quarterly, 42,* 750–783.
Gist, M. E. (1987). Self-efficacy: Implications for organizational behavior and human resource management. *Academy of Management Review, 12*(3), 472–485.
Graebner, M. E., & Eisenhardt, K. M. (2004). The seller's side of the story: Acquisition as courtship and governance as syndicate in entrepreneurial firms. *Administrative Science Quarterly, 49*(3), 366–403.
Grant, A. M. (2007). Relational job design and the motivation to make a prosocial difference. *Academy of Management Review, 32*(2), 393–417.
Grant, A. M., & Berry, J. W. (2011). The necessity of others is the mother of invention: Intrinsic and prosocial motivations, perspective taking, and creativity. *Academy of Management Journal, 54*(1), 73–96.
Grégoire, D. A., Barr, P. S., & Shepherd, D. A. (2010). Cognitive processes of opportunity recognition: The role of structural alignment. *Organization Science, 21*(2), 413–431.
Gumpert, D. E., & Boyd, D. P. (1984). The loneliness of the small-business owner. *Harvard Business Review, 62*(6), 18.
Hagner, D., & Davies, T. (2002). "Doing my own thing": Supported self-employment for individuals with cognitive disabilities. *Journal of Vocational Rehabilitation, 17*(2), 65–74.
Hannafey, F. T. (2003). Entrepreneurship and ethics: A literature review. *Journal of Business Ethics, 46*(2), 99–110.

Hauswald, H. (2013). Family businesses' ability to attract new talent: Who is attracted and under what conditions? In *Stakeholder trust in family businesses, Familienunternehmen und KMU*. Wiesbaden: Springer Gabler.

Hawkley, L. C., & Cacioppo, J. T. (2010). Loneliness matters: A theoretical and empirical review of consequences and mechanisms. *Annals of Behavioral Medicine, 40*(2), 218–227.

Haynie, J. M., & Shepherd, D. (2011). Toward a theory of discontinuous career transition: Investigating career transitions necessitated by traumatic life events. *Journal of Applied Psychology, 96*(3), 501.

Hemingway, C. A. (2005). Personal values as a catalyst for corporate social entrepreneurship. *Journal of Business Ethics, 60*(3), 233–249.

Hoang, H., & Gimeno, J. (2010). Becoming a founder: How founder role identity affects entrepreneurial transitions and persistence in founding. *Journal of Business Venturing, 25*(1), 41–53.

Hodges, L., & Carron, A. V. (1992). Collective efficacy and group performance. *International Journal of Sport Psychology, 23*(1), 48–59.

Hodgins, H. S., & Knee, C. R. (2002). The integrating self and conscious experience. In E. L. Deci & R. M. Ryan (Eds.), *Handbook of selfdetermination research* (pp. 87–100). Rochester: University of Rochester Press.

Hoffman, M. L. (1982). Development of prosocial motivation: Empathy and guilt. In *The development of prosocial behavior* (pp. 281–313). New York: Academic.

Holland, D. V., & Shepherd, D. A. (2013). Deciding to persist: Adversity, values, and entrepreneurs' decision policies. *Entrepreneurship Theory and Practice, 37*(2), 331–358.

Holt-Lunstad, J., Smith, T. B., & Layton, J. B. (2010). Social relationships and mortality risk: A meta-analytic review. *PLoS Medicine, 7*(7), e1000316.

Houlfort, N., Fernet, C., Vallerand, R. J., Laframboise, A., Guay, F., & Koestner, R. (2015). The role of passion for work and need satisfaction in psychological adjustment to retirement. *Journal of Vocational Behavior, 88*, 84–94.

Jackofsky, E. F., & Peters, L. H. (1983). Job turnover versus company turnover: Reassessment of the March and Simon participation hypothesis. *Journal of Applied Psychology, 68*(3), 490.

Janoff-Bulman, R. (1985). The aftermath of victimization: Rebuilding shattered assumptions. *Trauma and its Wake, 1*, 15–35.

Jenkins, A. S., Wiklund, J., & Brundin, E. (2014). Individual responses to firm failure: Appraisals, grief, and the influence of prior failure experience. *Journal of Business Venturing, 29*(1), 17–33.

Jensen, M. C., & Meckling, W. H. (1976). Theory of the firm: Managerial behavior, agency costs and ownership structure. *Journal of Financial Economics, 3*(4), 305–360.

Johnson, P. E., Jamal, K., & Berryman, R. G. (1991). Effects of framing on auditor decisions. *Organizational Behavior and Human Decision Processes, 50*(1), 75–105.

Johnston, M. W., Parasuraman, A., Futrell, C. M., & Black, W. C. (1990). A longitudinal assessment of the impact of selected organizational influences on salespeople's organizational commitment during early employment. *Journal of Marketing Research*, 333–344.

Jordan, P. J., Ashkanasy, N. M., & Hartel, C. E. (2002). Emotional intelligence as a moderator of emotional and behavioral reactions to job insecurity. *Academy of Management Review*, 27(3), 361–372.

Judge, T. A., & Bretz, R. D. (1992). Effects of work values on job choice decisions. *Journal of Applied Psychology*, 77(3), 261.

Kanfer, R. (1990). Motivation theory and industrial and organizational psychology. In M. D. Dunnette (Ed.), *Handbook of industrial and organizational psychology* (Vol. 1, 2nd ed., pp. 75–130). Palo Alto: Consulting Psychologists Press.

Karpoff, J. M., & Lott, J. R., Jr. (1993). The reputational penalty firms bear from committing criminal fraud. *The Journal of Law and Economics*, 36(2), 757–802.

Karpoff, J. M., Lee, D. S., & Martin, G. S. (2008). The consequences to managers for financial misrepresentation. *Journal of Financial Economics*, 88(2), 193–215.

Karstedt, S. (2006). Democracy, values, and violence: Paradoxes, tensions, and comparative advantages of liberal inclusion. *The Annals of the American Academy of Political and Social Science*, 605(1), 50–81.

Katz, J. A. (1994). Modelling entrepreneurial career progressions: Concepts and considerations. *Entrepreneurship: Theory and Practice*, 19(2), 23–40.

Keil, M. (1995). Escalation of commitment in information systems development: A comparison of three theories. *Academy of Management Journal*, 8, 348–353.

Keil, M., Mann, J., & Rai, A. (2000a). Why software projects escalate: An empirical analysis and test of four theoretical models. *Management Information Systems Quarterly*, 24, 631–664.

Keil, M., Tan, B. C., Wei, K. K., Saarinen, T., Tuunainen, V., & Wassenaar, A. (2000b). A cross-cultural study on escalation of commitment behavior in software projects. *Management Information Systems Quarterly*, 24, 299–325.

Kendall, E., Buys, N., Charker, J., & MacMillan, S. (2006). Self-employment: An under-utilised vocational rehabilitation strategy. *Journal of Vocational Rehabilitation*, 25(3), 197–205.

Khandwalla, P. N. (1976). The design of effective top management style. *Vikalpa*, 1(2), 41–58.

Khandwalla, P. N. (1977). *The design of organizations*. New York: Houghton Mifflin Harcourt P, 29(7), 770–791.

Kirzner, I. M. (1979). *Perception, opportunity, and profit*. Chicago: University of Chicago Press, 2(3), 1–16.

Knight, F. H. (1921). *Risk, uncertainty and profit*. Washington, DC: Beard Books, 31(1), 132–152. kopernik.info/en-us/story/howard-weinstein-solar-ear

Kotha, R., & George, G. (2012). Friends, family, or fools: Entrepreneur experience and its implications for equity distribution and resource mobilization. *Journal of Business Venturing*, 27(5), 525–543.

Kunda, Z. (1990). The case for motivated reasoning. *Psychological Bulletin, 108*, 480.
Kuratko, D. F., Hornsby, J. S., & Naffziger, D. W. (1997). An examination of owner's goals in sustaining entrepreneurship. *Journal of Small Business Management, 35*(1), 24.
Laguna, M. (2013). Self-efficacy, self-esteem, and entrepreneurship among the unemployed. *Journal of Applied Social Psychology, 43*(2), 253–262.
Langan-Fox, J., & Roth, S. (1995). Achievement motivation and female entrepreneurs. *Journal of Occupational and Organizational Psychology, 68*(3), 209–218.
Lant, T. K., Milliken, F. J., & Batra, B. (1992). The role of managerial learning and interpretation in strategic persistence and reorientation: An empirical exploration. *Strategic Management Journal, 13*(8), 585–608.
Lee, S. H., Peng, M. W., & Barney, J. B. (2007). Bankruptcy law and entrepreneurship development: A real options perspective. *Academy of Management Review, 32*(1), 257–272.
Lee, S. H., Yamakawa, Y., Peng, M. W., & Barney, J. B. (2011). How do bankruptcy laws affect entrepreneurship development around the world? *Journal of Business Venturing, 26*(5), 505–520.
Lentz, R., & Tranaes, T. (2005). Job search and savings: Wealth effects and duration dependence. *Journal of Labor Economics, 23*(3), 467–489.
Levenson, H. (1981). Differentiating among internality, powerful others, and chance, 1–15.
Levinthal, D. A., & March, J. G. (1993). The myopia of learning. *Strategic Management Journal, 14*(S2), 95–112.
Levitt, B., & March, J. G. (1988). Organizational learning. *Annual Review of Sociology, 14*(1), 319–338.
Little, B. L., & Madigan, R. M. (1997). The relationship between collective efficacy and performance in manufacturing work teams. *Small Group Research, 28*(4), 517–534.
Logan, G. D. (1990). Repetition priming and automaticity: Common underlying mechanisms? *Cognitive Psychology, 22*(1), 1–35.
Lyons, S. T., Duxbury, L., & Higgins, C. (2007). An empirical assessment of generational differences in basic human values. *Psychological Reports, 101*(2), 339–352.
Maheswaran, D., & Sternthal, B. (1990). The effects of knowledge, motivation, and type of message on ad processing and product judgments. *Journal of Consumer Research, 17*(1), 66–73.
March, J. G., & Simon, H. A. (1958). *Organizations, 57*(9), 705–717.
Markman, G. D., Balkin, D. B., & Baron, R. A. (2002). Inventors and new venture formation: The effects of general self-efficacy and regretful thinking. *Entrepreneurship Theory and Practice, 27*(2), 149–165.
Martin, R., & Hewstone, M. (2003). Majority versus minority influence: When, not whether, source status instigates heuristic or systematic processing. *European Journal of Social Psychology, 33*(3), 313–330.

Mason, C. M., & Harrison, R. T. (2002). Is it worth it? The rates of return from informal venture capital investments. *Journal of Business Venturing, 17*(3), 211–236.

McDermott, R., O'Dea, K., Rowley, K., Knight, S., & Burgess, P. (1998). Beneficial impact of the homelands movement on health outcomes in central Australian aborigines. *Australian and New Zealand Journal of Public Health, 22*(6), 653–658.

McGrath, R. G. (1999). Falling forward: Real options reasoning and entrepreneurial failure. *Academy of Management Review, 24*(1), 13–30.

McMullen, J. S., & Shepherd, D. A. (2006). Encouraging consensus-challenging research in universities. *Journal of Management Studies, 43*(8), 1643–1669.

McMullen, J. S., Shepherd, D. A., & Patzelt, H. (2009). Managerial (in) attention to competitive threats. *Journal of Management Studies, 46*(2), 157–181.

Mikulincer, M., Gillath, O., Sapir-Lavid, Y., Yaakobi, E., Arias, K., Tal-Aloni, L., & Bor, G. (2003). Attachment theory and concern for others' welfare: Evidence that activation of the sense of secure base promotes endorsement of self-transcendence values. *Basic and Applied Social Psychology, 25*(4), 299–312.

Miller, D., & Friesen, P. H. (1983). Strategy-making and environment: The third link. *Strategic Management Journal, 4*(3), 221–235.

Miller, T. L., Grimes, M. G., McMullen, J. S., & Vogus, T. J. (2012). Venturing for others with heart and head: How compassion encourages social entrepreneurship. *Academy of Management Review, 37*(4), 616–640.

Mitchell, R. K., Agle, B. R., & Wood, D. J. (1997). Toward a theory of stakeholder identification and salience: Defining the principle of who and what really counts. *Academy of Management Review, 22*(4), 853–886.

Mitchell, R. K., Busenitz, L., Lant, T., McDougall, P. P., Morse, E. A., & Smith, J. B. (2004). The distinctive and inclusive domain of entrepreneurial cognition research. *Entrepreneurship Theory and Practice, 28*(6), 505–518.

Molloy, G. J., McGee, H. M., O'neill, D., & Conroy, R. M. (2010). Loneliness and emergency and planned hospitalizations in a community sample of older adults. *Journal of the American Geriatrics Society, 58*(8), 1538–1541.

Morris, M. W., Williams, K. Y., Leung, K., Larrick, R., Mendoza, M. T., Bhatnagar, D., et al. (1998). Conflict management style: Accounting for cross-national differences. *Journal of International Business Studies, 29*(4), 729–747.

Muehlebach, A. (2001). "Making place" at the United Nations: Indigenous cultural politics at the UN working group on indigenous populations. *Cultural Anthropology, 16*(3), 415–448.

Multon, K. D., Brown, S. D., & Lent, R. W. (1991). Relation of self-efficacy beliefs to academic outcomes. *A meta-analytic investigation, 38*(1), 30–38.

Nickerson, R. S. (1998). Confirmation bias: A ubiquitous phenomenon in many guises. *Review of General Psychology, 2*, 175.

Paldam, M. (2002). The cross-country pattern of corruption: Economics, culture and the seesaw dynamics. *European Journal of Political Economy, 18*(2), 215–240.
Paolillo, J. G., & Brown, W. B. (1978). How organizational factors affect R&D innovation. *Research Management, 21*(2), 12–15.
Parker, S. C., & Van Praag, M. (2010). Group status and entrepreneurship. *Journal of Economics and Management Strategy, 19*(4), 919–945.
Parris, T. M., & Kates, R. W. (2003). Characterizing and measuring sustainable development. *Annual Review of Environment and Resources, 28*, 559–586.
Poterba, J. M., Venti, S. F., & Wise, D. A. (2010). *The Asset Cost of Poor Health* (No. w16389). Cambridge, MA: National Bureau of Economic Research.
Prahalad, C.K. (2007). Bottom of the pyramid. *Presentation at the Strategic Entrepreneurship Journal Launch Conference,* 1(1), 1.
Rauch, A., & Frese, M. (2007). Let's put the person back into entrepreneurship research: A meta-analysis on the relationship between business owners' personality traits, business creation, and success. *European Journal of Work and Organizational Psychology, 16*(4), 353–385.
Rip, B., Fortin, S., & Vallerand, R. J. (2006). The relationship between passion and injury in dance students. *Journal of Dance Medicine & Science, 10*(1–1), 14–20.
Rohan, M. J. (2000). A rose by any name? The values construct. *Personality and Social Psychology Review, 4*(3), 255–277.
Rokeach, M. (1973). *The nature of human values.* New York: Free press.
Rook, K. S. (1984). The negative side of social interaction: Impact on psychological well-being. *Journal of Personality and Social Psychology, 46*(5), 1097.
Rosenbaum, D. I., & Lamort, F. (1992). Entry, barriers, exit, and sunk costs: An analysis. *Applied Economics, 24*(3), 297–304.
Ryan, R. M., & Deci, E. L. (2000). Self-determination theory and the facilitation of intrinsic motivation, social development, and well-being. *American Psychologist, 55*(1), 68.
Ryan, R. M., & Deci, E. L. (2001). On happiness and human potentials: A review of research on hedonic and eudaimonic well-being. *Annual Review of Psychology, 52*(1), 141–166.
Sabini, J., Garvey, B., & Hall, A. L. (2001). Shame and embarrassment revisited. *Personality and Social Psychology Bulletin, 27*(1), 104–117.
Sala, E. (2006). Top predators provide insurance against climate change. *Trends in Ecology & Evolution, 21*(9), 479–480.
Sarasvathy, S. D. (2001). Causation and effectuation: Toward a theoretical shift from economic inevitability to entrepreneurial contingency. *Academy of Management Review, 26*(2), 243–263.
Scheinberg, S., & MacMillan, I. (1988). *An eleven-country study of the motivation to start a business.* Wellesley: Frontiers of Entrepreneurship Research, Babson College.

Schjoedt, L., & Shaver, K. G. (2007). Deciding on an entrepreneurial career: A test of the pull and push hypotheses using the panel study of entrepreneurial dynamics data. *Entrepreneurship Theory and Practice, 31*(5), 733–752.
Schumpeter, J. A. (1961). *The theory of economic development: An inquiry into profits, capital, credit, interest, and the business cycle* (trans: R. Opie, p. 244). Cambridge, MA: Harvard University Press.
Schwartz, S. H. (1992). Universals in the content and structure of values: Theoretical advances and empirical tests in 20 countries. *Advances in Experimental Social Psychology, 25*, 1–65.
Schwartz, S. H., & Bilsky, W. (1990). Toward a theory of the universal content and structure of values: Extensions and cross-cultural replications. *Journal of Personality and Social Psychology, 58*(5), 878–891.
Selden, P. D., & Fletcher, D. E. (2015). The entrepreneurial journey as an emergent hierarchical system of artifact-creating processes. *Journal of Business Venturing, 30*(4), 603–615.
Semadeni, M., Cannella, A. A., Jr., Fraser, D. R., & Lee, D. S. (2008). Fight or flight: Managing stigma in executive careers. *Strategic Management Journal, 29*(5), 557–567.
Shah, J. Y., Friedman, R., & Kruglanski, A. W. (2002). Forgetting all else: On the antecedents and consequences of goal shielding. *Journal of Personality and Social Psychology, 83*(6), 1261–1281.
Shane, S., Kolvereid, L., & Westhead, P. (1991). An exploratory examination of the reasons leading to new firm formation across country and gender. *Journal of Business Venturing, 6*(6), 431–446.
Shane, S., Locke, E. A., & Collins, C. J. (2003). Entrepreneurial motivation. *Human Resource Management Review, 13*(2), 257–279.
Shapiro, A., & Sokol, L. (1982). The social dimensions of entrepreneurship. In A. C. Kent, L. D. Sextopn, & H. K. Vesper (Eds.), *Encyclopedia of entrepreneurship* (pp. 72–90).
Shaver, K. G., & Scott, L. R. (2002). Person, process, choice. *Entrepreneurship: Critical Perspectives on Business and Management, 2*(2), 334.
Shaver, K. G., Gartner, W. B., Crosby, E., Bakalarova, K., & Gatewood, E. J. (2001). Attributions about entrepreneurship: A framework and process for analyzing reasons for starting a business. *Entrepreneurship: Theory and Practice, 26*(2), 5–33.
Shepherd, D. A. (2003). Learning from business failure: Propositions of grief recovery for the self-employed. *Academy of Management Review, 28*(2), 318–328.
Shepherd, D. A., & Cardon, M. S. (2009). Negative emotional reactions to project failure and the self-compassion to learn from the experience. *Journal of Management Studies, 46*(6), 923–949.
Shepherd, D. A., & DeTienne, D. R. (2005). Prior knowledge, potential financial reward, and opportunity identification. *Entrepreneurship Theory and Practice, 29*(1), 91–112.

Shepherd, D. A., & Patzelt, H. (2015). Harsh evaluations of entrepreneurs who fail: The role of sexual orientation, use of environmentally friendly technologies, and observers' perspective taking. *Journal of Management Studies, 52*(2), 253–284.

Shepherd, D. A., Patzelt, H., & Wolfe, M. (2011). Moving forward from project failure: Negative emotions, affective commitment, and learning from the experience. *Academy of Management Journal, 54*(6), 1229–1259.

Shepherd, D. A., Patzelt, H., & Baron, R. A. (2013). "I care about nature, but...": Disengaging values in assessing opportunities that cause harm. *Academy of Management Journal, 56*(5), 1251–1273.

Shepherd, D. A., Thorgren, S., & Wincent, J. (2018). *Fear of failure promoting opportunity pursuit: Potential payoffs, fear of failure, and obsessive passion* (Working paper). Lulea, Sweden.

Shook, C. L., Priem, R. L., & McGee, J. E. (2003). Venture creation and the enterprising individual: A review and synthesis. *Journal of Management, 29*(3), 379–399.

Smilor, R. W. (1997). Entrepreneurship: Reflections on a subversive activity. *Journal of Business Venturing, 12*(5), 341–346.

Smith, R., & McElwee, G. (2011). After the fall: Developing a conceptual script-based model of shame in narratives of entrepreneurs in crisis! *International Journal of Sociology and Social Policy, 31*(1/2), 91–109.

Spash, C. L. (2002). *Greenhouse economics: Values and ethics*. London: Taylor and Francis.

Spicer, P. (2001). Culture and the restoration of self among former American Indian drinkers. *Social Science & Medicine, 53*(2), 227–240.

Srinivasan, T. U., Carey, S. P., Hallstein, E., Higgins, P. A. T., Kerr, A. C., Koteen, L. E., et al. (2008). The debt of nations and the distribution of ecological impacts from human activities. *Proceedings of the National Academy of Sciences of the United States of America, 105*, 1768–1773.

Srivastava, A., Locke, E. A., Judge, T. A., & Adams, J. W. (2010). Core self-evaluations as causes of satisfaction: The mediating role of seeking task complexity. *Journal of Vocational Behavior, 77*(2), 255–265.

Stanton, A. L., Danoff-burg, S., & Huggins, M. E. (2002). The first year after breast cancer diagnosis: Hope and coping strategies as predictors of adjustment. *Psycho-Oncology, 11*(2), 93–102.

Staw, B. M. (1981). The escalation of commitment to a course of action. *Academy of Management Review, 6*(4), 577–587.

Staw, B. M., & Fox, F. V. (1977). Escalation: The determinants of commitment to a chosen course of action. *Human Relations, 30*(5), 431–450.

Staw, B. M., & Ross, J. (1980). Commitment in an experimenting society: A study of the attribution of leadership from administrative scenarios. *Journal of Applied Psychology, 65*(3), 249.

Staw, B. M., McKechnie, P. I., & Puffer, S. M. (1983). The justification of organizational performance. *Administrative Science Quarterly, 28,* 582–600.
Stephan, Y., Deroche, T., Brewer, B. W., Caudroit, J., & Le Scanff, C. (2009). Predictors of perceived susceptibility to sport-related injury among competitive runners: The role of previous experience, neuroticism, and passion for running. *Applied Psychology, 58*(4), 672–687.
Stevenson, H. H. (1983). *A perspective on entrepreneurship.* Boston: Harvard Business School, 30(1), 1–22.
Stewart, W. F., Ricci, J. A., Chee, E., Morganstein, D., & Lipton, R. (2003). Lost productive time and cost due to common pain conditions in the US workforce. *JAMA, 290*(18), 2443–2454.
Sugisawa, H., Liang, J., & Liu, X. (1994). Social networks, social support, and mortality among older people in Japan. *Journal of Gerontology, 49*(1), S3–S13.
Sutton, R. I., & Callahan, A. L. (1987). The stigma of bankruptcy: Spoiled organizational image and its management. *Academy of Management Journal, 30*(3), 405–436.
Thøgersen, J., & Ölander, F. (2002). Human values and the emergence of a sustainable consumption pattern: A panel study. *Journal of Economic Psychology, 23*(5), 605–630.
Thurston, R. C., & Kubzansky, L. D. (2009). Women, loneliness, and incident coronary heart disease. *Psychosomatic Medicine, 71*(8), 836.
Tourtellot, J. B. (2007). 111 islands. *National Geographic Traveler, 24*(8), 108–127.
Tsai, W. M. H., MacMillan, I. C., & Low, M. B. (1991). Effects of strategy and environment on corporate venture success in industrial markets. *Journal of Business Venturing, 6*(1), 9–28.
Tushman, M. L. (1977). Special boundary roles in the innovation process. *Administrative Science Quarterly, 22,* 587–605.
Tushman, M. L., & Anderson, P. (1986). Technological discontinuities and organizational environments. *Administrative Science Quarterly, 31,* 439–465.
Ucbasaran, D., Lockett, A., Wright, M., & Westhead, P. (2003). Entrepreneurial founder teams: Factors associated with member entry and exit. *Entrepreneurship Theory and Practice, 28*(2), 107–128.
Ucbasaran, D., Shepherd, D. A., Lockett, A., & Lyon, S. J. (2013). Life after business failure: The process and consequences of business failure for entrepreneurs. *Journal of Management, 39*(1), 163–202.
United Nations millennium declaration. (2000). *United Nations General Assembly, 35*(4), 347–359.
U.S. Census Bureau. (2002). *Census 2000 summary file.* Retrieved http://factfinder.census.gov
Utsch, A., Rauch, A., Rothfufs, R., & Frese, M. (1999). Who becomes a small scale entrepreneur in a post-socialist environment: On the differences between entre-

preneurs and managers in East Germany. *Journal of Small Business Management,* *37*(3), 31.
Vallerand, R. J., & Houlfort, N. (2003). Passion at work. *Emerging Perspectives on Values in Organizations,* 175–204.
Vallerand, R. J., Blanchard, C., Mageau, G. A., Koestner, R., Ratelle, C., Léonard, M., et al. (2003). Les passions de l'ame: on obsessive and harmonious passion. *Journal of Personality and Social Psychology, 85*(4), 756.
Vallerand, R. J., Ntoumanis, N., Philippe, F. L., Lavigne, G. L., Carbonneau, N., Bonneville, A., et al. (2008). On passion and sports fans: A look at football. *Journal of Sports Sciences, 26*(12), 1279–1293.
Vallerand, R. J., Paquet, Y., Philippe, F. L., & Charest, J. (2010). On the role of passion for work in burnout: A process model. *Journal of Personality, 78*(1), 289–312.
Vandekerckhove, W., & Dentchev, N. A. (2005). A network perspective on stakeholder management: Facilitating entrepreneurs in the discovery of opportunities. *Journal of Business Ethics, 60*(3), 221–232.
Vroom, V. H. (1964). *Work and motivation.* New York: Willey.
Wanberg, C. R., Kanfer, R., & Rotundo, M. (1999). Unemployed individuals: Motives, job-search competencies, and job-search constraints as predictors of job seeking and reemployment. *Journal of Applied Psychology, 84*(6), 897.
Wasserman, N. (2008). The founder's dilemma. *Harvard Business Review, 86,* 102–109.
Wasserman, N., Nohria, N., & Anand, B. N. (2001). When does leadership matter? *The contingent opportunities view of CEO leadership,* 2–4.
Weiss, K. B., Sullivan, S. D., & Lyttle, C. S. (2000). Trends in the cost of illness for asthma in the United States, 1985–1994. *Journal of Allergy and Clinical Immunology, 106*(3), 493–499.
White, J., Bandura, A., & Bero, L. A. (2009). Moral disengagement in the corporate world. *Accountability in Research, 16*(1), 41–74.
Wiesenfeld, B. M., Wurthmann, K. A., & Hambrick, D. C. (2008). The stigmatization and devaluation of elites associated with corporate failures: A process model. *Academy of Management Review, 33*(1), 231–251.
Wiklund, J., Patzelt, H., & Dimov, D. (2016). Entrepreneurship and psychological disorders: How ADHD can be productively harnessed. *Journal of Business Venturing Insights, 6,* 14–20.
Wood, J. V., Saltzberg, J. A., Neale, J. M., Stone, A. A., & Rachmiel, T. B. (1990). Self-focused attention, coping responses, and distressed mood in everyday life. *Journal of Personality and Social Psychology, 58*(6), 1027.
Woodman, R. W., Sawyer, J. E., & Griffin, R. W. (1993). Toward a theory of organizational creativity. *Academy of Management Review, 18*(2), 293–321.

Zahra, S. A., & Covin, J. G. (1995). Contextual influences on the corporate entrepreneurship-performance relationship: A longitudinal analysis. *Journal of Business Venturing, 10*(1), 43–58.

Zhao, H., & Seibert, S. E. (2006). The big five personality dimensions and entrepreneurial status: a meta-analytical review. *Journal of Applied Psychology, 91*, (2), 259–271.

Zhao, H., Seibert, S. E., & Hills, G. E. (2005). The mediating role of self-efficacy in the development of entrepreneurial intentions. *Journal of Applied Psychology, 90*(6), 1265.

Zhao, H., Seibert, S. E., & Lumpkin, G. T. (2010). The relationship of personality to entrepreneurial intentions and performance: A meta-analytic review. *Journal of Management, 36*(2), 381–404.

Open Access This chapter is licensed under the terms of the Creative Commons Attribution 4.0 International License (http://creativecommons.org/licenses/by/4.0/), which permits use, sharing, adaptation, distribution and reproduction in any medium or format, as long as you give appropriate credit to the original author(s) and the source, provide a link to the Creative Commons license and indicate if changes were made.

The images or other third party material in this chapter are included in the chapter's Creative Commons license, unless indicated otherwise in a credit line to the material. If material is not included in the chapter's Creative Commons license and your intended use is not permitted by statutory regulation or exceeds the permitted use, you will need to obtain permission directly from the copyright holder.

CHAPTER 4

Attention and Entrepreneurial Cognition

While there are numerous possible reasons explaining why managers of incumbent firms have trouble recognizing and responding to strategically important discontinuous change (e.g., economic incentives (Christensen 1997), rigid routines (Levinthal and March 1993), and/or poor competitive analysis systems (Zahra and Chaples 1993; McMullen et al. 2009)), scholars have recently begun focusing on the role managerial attention plays in this context (Eggers and Kaplan 2009; Kaplan 2008; Maula et al. 2013). Attention refers to a non-specific and limited cognitive resource that is required for mental activities and differs across individuals and tasks (Kahneman 1973). What environmental stimuli direct individuals' attention toward or away from entrepreneurial tasks? How are knowledge and attention related? How do entrepreneurial individuals allocate attention across different entrepreneurial tasks, such as opportunity exploitation or poorly performing entrepreneurial projects, and how do cognitive processes impact entrepreneurs' attention allocation? This chapter tries to answer these questions.

TRANSIENT ATTENTION AND OPPORTUNITY IDENTIFICATION

How managers allocate attention guides their engagement with the firm's external context to identify changes that represent entrepreneurial opportunities. These processes can be more top down or more bottom up. Thus far, the majority of research has utilized top-down processes to explore the association between the allocation of attention (Cho and Hambrick 2006; Ocasio 1997) and the ability to recognize and make sense of new opportunities (Eisenhardt and Schoonhoven 1990; Tripsas and Gavetti 2000). Researchers have given these top-down processes different names, but each of these different conceptualizations generally outlines a set of knowledge structures that managers draw on to engage with their environment to recognize, make sense of, and respond to signals from the environment (Bogner and Barr 2000)—namely, signals that indicate potential opportunities. A knowledge structure is "a kind of mental template that individuals impose on an information environment to give it form and meaning" (Walsh 1995: 281). Top managers utilize knowledge structures as a foundation from which they can build subjective representations of the environment that can be used to shape decisions (Dutton and Jackson 1987; Starbuck and Milliken 1988).

Knowledge structures focus managerial attention on potentially relevant features of their organization's environment (Kaplan and Tripsas 2008). Researchers have shown that such focused attention can trigger strategic persistence and improved performance when industries are changing at a slow pace (Nadkarni and Narayanan 2007). For example, consistent with these top-down explanations, Polaroid's failure to profit from the commitment it made early to digital imaging technology stems from its top managers' inability to utilize the most appropriate structure of knowledge for changes that had occurred in the organizational environment. Consequently, Polaroid ultimately ended up with "quite limited technical strength in this emerging market" (Tripsas and Gavetti 2000: 1157).

More recent work investigating bottom-up attention-allocation processes—where prominent features of the environment grab people's attention whether or not they are anticipated (Ocasio 2011)—provides an alternative or possibly complementary mode to top-down processes. Rindova et al. (2010) showed that sequences of action with the gestalt characteristics of grouping, simplicity, and motif were connected to better evaluations received from potential investors for ventures trying to adjust to a radical change. They contended that rather than knowledge structures concentration attention on situational features that are projected to be important, managers use gestalt properties to look for and understand patterns within situations characterized by discontinuous change (Whitson and Galinsky 2008). These managers make sense of events as they occur (Ariely and Carmon 2000; Ariely and Zauberman 2000). In a similar vein, my (Dean) colleagues and I (Shepherd et al. 2007) investigated how a big-picture depiction of the environment (a gist) activates a bottom-up process. In this process striking environmental changes that would have gone unnoticed in top-down processing capture top managers' attention. Research like this provides an alternative explanation to top-down processes for clarifying how managers discern the unanticipated while questing the comparative performance of top-down versus bottom-up processes in how individuals notice, make sense of, and use information to form opportunity beliefs.

High Levels of Top-Down Attention Allocation and Recognizing Environmental Change

Individuals learn core concepts from their prior experiences, which then become part of their knowledge structures (Nadkarni and Narayanan 2007; Walsh 1995). Core concepts generate particular environmental expectations that then guide how managers allocate attention in a top-down manner. Top-down attention allocation allows managers to attain predictability, efficiency, and reliability by focusing attention on environmental features that they believe to yield possible opportunities. In addition, these managers do attend less to features that are not believed to be important (Nadkarni and Barr 2008). *Incremental environmental changes* refer to changes in consumer preferences, design elements, competitive dynamics, and institutions that are in line with the firm's present trajectory and require few modifications in how product components are combined and connected into a "big picture" (Henderson and Clark 1990). Since incremental environmental changes generally take place where and when they are anticipated to do so (Sirmon et al. 2007), individuals are likely to notice such changes when they allocate transient attention to them by top-down processing. For these managers, the complexity of their knowledge structures additionally improves their ability to detect incremental change as they draw on knowledge of their firm's current situation to allocate attention to environmental features they expect to be important.

While high top-down attention allocation enables managers to detect incremental change, it also prevents them from noticing discontinuous change (cf., Rosenkopf and Nerkar 2001; Tripsas and Gavetti 2000). *Discontinuous environmental changes* entail new formations of consumer preferences, design components, and/or competitive dynamics that do not match the firm's present trajectory and could thus potentially disturb the present situation and initiate a new course of action (compare Gatignon et al. 2002).

Work on perception in the psychology literature has shown that when individuals put great emphasis on their knowledge structures when they allocate their attention, they are less likely to detect unanticipated stimuli. This is true even when stimuli are very striking. In numerous experiments, for instance, scholars have shown that individuals assigned a particular task often do not perceive information not relevant to that specific task regardless of how conspicuous the information is (e.g., Neisser 1976). Yet, when individuals are told that the task at hand is only slightly important, they will attend to the prominent stimulus, while individuals who are told the task is highly important are less likely to do so. Apparently, when individuals believe a task is only slightly important, they are more likely to ease up on top-down processing and engage in more bottom-up processing, which frees their transient attention to capture signals of unanticipated environmental change. On the other hand, when individuals believe a task is highly important, they are more likely to direct their attention to where change is anticipated, thereby tying up transient attention such that they do not perceive signals of unanticipated environmental change.

Strategy researchers have dedicated a great deal of energy toward investigating how top-down processing decreases managers' ability to detect discontinuous change. For instance, the top managers of Liz Claiborne effectively used top-down attention-allocation processes to respond to changes that matched their prevalent knowledge structures (i.e., incremental changes). However, these processes also blinded him to discontinuous changes:

> Environmental changes had decreased the value of a part of Liz Claiborne's set of choices (in particular, those concerning production and distribution). Small, incremental changes—exploring the local neighborhood of the current position—no longer sufficed. At the same time, larger, systematic changes lay outside the mental maps of existing management. Different mental maps of the changed performance landscape were required to move Liz Claiborne to a new performance peak. (Siggelkow 2001: 853)

Low Levels of Top-Down Attention Allocation (More Bottom-Up Processing) and Recognizing Environmental Change

When top managers engage in bottom-up processing, they enable the environment to capture their attention. Specifically, attention capture refers to how aspects inherent in a particular situation draw attention to themselves in case people do not search for them actively (Pashler et al. 2001). In their study on the Challenger disaster, Starbuck and Milliken (1988) highlighted how individuals are more likely to pay attention to novel information than information that is less novel. Similarly, Rindova et al. (2010) showed that the most prominent elements of a situation are also the elements that will most likely capture managers' attention seemingly due to the particularly distinct nature of the signals. Thus, by allowing environmental changes to grab their attention, decision makers are more open to possible surprises (Wyble et al. 2013). Since the most prominent features of a situation (either alone or in relation to other environmental features) are those most likely to capture managers' attention (Shepherd et al. 2007), bottom-up processing can help managers pay more attention to unexpected indicators of changes in their environment.

On the other hand, bottom-up processing can also cause prominent environmental features to arouse and attract managers' attention even when those features are only marginally related to the firm's technologies, products, and markets (see Franconeri et al. 2005; Franconeri and Simons 2003). Researchers have shown that prominent environmental changes sometimes take people down the wrong path (Kruglanski and Boyatzi 2012) and can disrupt cognitive processing (Frey and Eagly 1993). In addition, bottom-up processing lessens people's use of trial-and-error knowledge from their previous experiences. In this case, they might "reinvent the wheel" and repeat past mistakes, leading them to allocate attention to environmental features that have already been established as not being strategically crucial or not matching the organization's range of actions (Katila and Ahuja 2002; Levinthal and Rerup 2006).

Thus, compared to bottom-up attention allocation, a high top-down process enables managers to detect incremental changes. At the same time, it obstructs the detection of discontinuous changes. This idea is in line with Eggers and Kaplan's (2009) discovery that firms grow slower in a market that is radically new when managers focus on current technologies (high top-down attention allocation) as compared to focusing on emerging technologies (bottom-up attention allocation). Similarly, my (Dean) colleagues and I (Shepherd et al. 2017) recently proposed that top managers' likelihood of detecting incremental change is greater when their attentional processing is more top down compared to when it is more bottom up. However, their probability of detecting discontinuous change is greater for attentional processing that is more bottom up compared to attentional processing that is more top down.

Managers' Task Demands and Top-Down Attention Allocation

The necessity to reach a specific level of performance is called *task demands*. Task demands grow as individuals take on greater *task challenges* (Hambrick et al. 2005: 476), which frequently arise from inside the firm. For instance, "large firms with technologically interdependent units that are geographically far-flung, with complex matrix structures, require significant co-ordination and integration" (Hambrick et al. 2005: 476), which in turn generates numerous challenges requiring top managers' attention. The external environment can also contribute task challenges for an organization. Hostile external environments, for example, can cause a variety of managerial challenges that necessitate attention. These challenges include ensuring resource conservation, understanding threat characteristics, and developing successful strategies in a competitive marketplace (Miller and Friesen 1983). Additionally, more complex environments can also pose challenges as managers must take into account many fluctuating parameters and potential contingencies (Aldrich 1979; Eisenhardt 1989), including competitors' actions and responses (Hambrick et al. 1996; McMullen et al. 2009). The task challenges arising from both of these environments constitute conflicting demands for managers' information processing.

There is also heterogeneity in the performance demands that owners and stakeholders from different organizations place on top managers. For instance, an attentive board of directors is likely to implement high managerial task demands. More specifically, a board of directors monitors the performance of top management. With increasing attention of the board's members, there is an increasing need for top managers to defend strategic decisions and moves through proposals to the board (Castaner and Kavadis 2013). Indeed, the vigilance of a board tends to increase when there is a higher percentage of external directors (Lim 2015), the CEO does not chair the board (Finkelstein and D'Aveni 1994; Kesner and Johnson 1990), the CEO does not appoint board members (Zajac and Westphal 1994), and ownership is very concentrated (Castaner and Kavadis 2013). In addition, top decision makers' task demands tend to increase when they are facing activist shareholders (Walls et al. 2012).

Because top managers' attentional capability has its limits (Ocasio 1997; Simon 2013), high levels of demands for one task make it necessary that they dedicate more attention to detecting environmental signals central to that task (e.g., collecting information regarding the efficiency of the firm). These types of tasks may compete for attention with the task of detecting signals of change in the external environment. In the face of competing multiple tasks and limited attention, managers will utilize their experience to determine how they should allocate their attention (Hambrick and Mason 1984). This experience may stem from their education (Carpenter 2002; Wiersema and Bantel 1992), functional backgrounds (Finkelstein and Hambrick 1990), and/or prior jobs (Beyer et al. 1997). As the demands that are competing between tasks—including the observation of the environment—increase, managers' attention is more likely to be divided (e.g., Han and Humphreys 2002; Rodriguez et al. 2002). They are likely to direct available transient attention toward central concepts of the task-related knowledge structure and away from concepts that are only peripheral. In turn, these peripheral concepts do not receive managers' transient attention, making it difficult for top managers to recognize changes in the environment that are novel or unfamiliar.

On the other hand, top managers with fewer task demands are less likely to depend on top-down attention-allocation processes. Such managers still focus on concepts that are at the core of their knowledge structures. However, these managers have higher levels of transient attention they can allocate to peripheral concepts and thus have a higher chance of noticing unanticipated environmental changes that signal opportunities. Based on this reasoning, my (Dean) colleagues and I (Shepherd et al. 2017) contended that higher levels of competing task demands cause decision makers to draw more heavily on top-down processing of attention to recognize changes in their environment.

Knowledge Structure Complexity and Recognizing Environmental Change

Unlike technology and market changes that are incremental and discontinuous (and thus consistent and inconsistent with a firm's current trajectory, respectively), architectural changes represent opportunities because they alter how product or service components are combined and connected to form a coherent whole (Henderson and Clark 1990). In the case of architectural changes, design features that are at the core and thus the primary components of the product are unaltered (Henderson and Clark 1990). People frequently have more difficulties recognizing architectural changes than they have difficulties recognizing incremental changes because the former are concealed in the interactions and connections between components, thus leading to minimal observable surface change. To recognize architectural changes, individuals must have a complex knowledge structure (which entails connections that are rich and deep) that serves as the foundation for understanding the nature of such changes and how components are integrated and connected, although the components themselves are not modified. For instance, in the 1970s, Xerox—the plain-paper copiers pioneer—began seeing other firms pop up selling new copiers that were smaller in size and were more dependable than the existing products Xerox offered. Even though the new copiers did not incorporate significantly novel engineering or scientific knowledge, and although Xerox had come up with the core underlying technologies and had vast industry experience, the firm made mistakes and false starts for almost eight years before they had a viable product ready for entry (Henderson and Clark 1990).

Architectural modifications are frequently harder to detect since they are concealed in the exchanges and interconnections between components. Thus, managers need rich and deep knowledge structures. Nadkarni and Narayanan (2007) stressed that knowledge structures differ in *complexity*—namely, the scope and diversity of the concepts embedded in individuals' cognitive structures—*and* in the number, richness, and depth of these concepts' interconnections (Kiss and Barr 2015; Nadkarni and Narayanan 2007).[1] The complexity of knowledge structures may increase flexibility in strategic decision making (Nadkarni and Narayanan 2007) because it enhances managers' ability to detect more signals in their environment (Sutcliffe 1994; Walsh 1995). Therefore, managers who possess knowledge structures with greater complexity tend to be better at detecting incremental changes in the environment and then utilizing the knowledge they gain to make strategic decisions (Kiss and Barr 2015). Managers with knowledge structures that are more simple, on the other hand, not only have a smaller number of core concepts but also less rich and more shallow linkages between the concepts they possess, thus making them less able to detect architectural environmental changes. As such, my (Dean) colleagues and I (Shepherd et al. 2017) argued that managers' likelihood of detecting architectural change increases with the complexity of their knowledge structures.

Attention Toward Early-Stage Exploration and Opportunity Evaluation Speed

Decision speed is frequently conceived of as "how quickly organizations execute all aspects of the decision making process" (Forbes 2005: 355). High decision speed has been linked to exceptional performance (Bourgeois and Eisenhardt 1988; Bingham and Eisenhardt 2011; Eisenhardt 1989; for an exception, see Perlow et al. 2002). Managers who make quick decisions enable their firms to act on opportunities before they vanish (Baum and Wally 2003; Stevenson and Gumpert 1985). In addition, quick decisions associated with opportunity exploitation demonstrate to stakeholders that the firm is flexible and proactive (Langley 1995). Further, quick decision making improves organizational learning because it enables the firm to make more decisions in a limited period of time and therefore provides more experiences and a higher number of interactions that expose information that is salient for learning (Baum and Wally 2003; Eisenhardt 1989; Forbes 2005). Quick strategic decisions can also lead to a first-mover advantage (Lieberman and Montgomery 1988) or a set of transient advantages (McGrath 2013). Researchers have also shown that decision speed is particularly important as a response to environmental dynamism (Baum and Wally 2003; Eisenhardt and Martin 2000; Judge and Miller 1991). However, quick decisions in dynamic environments are rather difficult to make because dynamism makes it more difficult for firms to understand the market and then inform how to make decisions (Priem et al. 1995).[2] As such, a "central debate in the strategy, organization, and entrepreneurship literature surrounds how leaders effectively manage their organization and strategies in dynamic environments" (Eisenhardt et al. 2010: 1263).

Individuals may improve the speed of their decisions by using information that is real-time, developing and considering a greater number of alternatives, relying on intuition that is based on their experiences, and using techniques that actively resolve potential conflicts (Eisenhardt 1989). Moreover, the speed of making decisions increases when decision makers are younger (Forbes 2005), employ heuristics for opportunity recognition (Bingham and Eisenhardt 2011), utilize routines to guide their decision making (Helfat and Peteraf 2003), trust in their own intuition (Miller and Ireland 2005; Wally and Baum 1994), and rely on past experiences (Forbes 2005).

Extant studies thus shed light on how important it is to make decisions quickly to recognize transient opportunities and to achieve high firm performance. These studies have also explored the antecedents to organizations' decision speed. Yet, research in this area has generally considered the speed of a firm's decision making to be rather universal as opposed to being heterogeneous within a firm depending on the decisions at hand (e.g., Baum and Wally 2003; Eisenhardt 1989; Forbes 2005; Judge and Miller 1991). Therefore, this research stream does not yet provide a deep understanding of decision-making speed for different assessment decisions in the different stages of the opportunity progression process.

To begin to overcome this lack of understanding, my (Dean) colleague and I (Bakker and Shepherd 2017) explored the vital role of *attention* in this context (Ocasio 1997). As discussed earlier, when faced with large and complex option sets, individuals are unable to dedicate full attention to all matters simultaneously; rather, they are likely to focus their attention on a restricted set of issues (Lavie et al. 2010; Ocasio 2011). However, firms can develop methods to enhance their decision-making speed in areas of particular interest. My (Dean) colleague and I (Bakker and Shepherd 2017) built on Cho and Hambrick's (2006) notion of attentional orientation (which in turn drew on Ocasio's work on attention (1997, 2011)) to theorize on a firm's attention level toward specific opportunity-advancement stages. Attention ranged from higher attention levels focused on earlier-stage exploration activities and related assessment decisions to higher attention levels focused on later-stage exploitation activities and related assessment decisions. The study found that firms that focus their attention on earlier-stage exploration activities tend to confront different issues than firms that pay more attention to the exploitation of potential opportunities. Exploration focuses the attention of individuals on seeking something novel by constantly scanning the environment for indications of wealth-generating opportunities (Brown and Eisenhardt 1997; McGrath 1999). In contrast, exploitation focuses the attention of individuals on current opportunities and on the capabilities required to take advantage of them (Rothaermel and Deeds 2004). The degree of attention a manager focuses on specific opportunity-advancement stages affects the relative speed of decision making for a particular potential opportunity based on three characteristics: *experience* (Levitt and March 1988; Ocasio 1997), *standard operating procedures* (Cyert and March 1963; Gavetti et al. 2007; Ocasio 1997), and *confidence* (Levitt and March 1988; March and Shapira 1987).

Experience and Managers' Attention

Firms gain experience and learn by repeatedly executing certain tasks and activating routines (Levitt and March 1988). Because of differences in important activities, firms that focus more attention on earlier-stage exploration tend to have different experiences than those that focus their attention on later-stage development or exploitation. Early-stage exploration entails search, discovery, and experimentation; in contrast, exploitation entails refinement, implementation, and execution (March 1991). These domain-specific activities and the resulting experience are likely to affect decision-making speed. More specifically, managers with domain-specific experience will allocate less time collecting information; these managers already possess a strong knowledge base to draw from (Forbes 2005). Moreover, such managers are also likely to analyze information more quickly since they possess an organizing framework that "facilitates the storage, recall, and interpretation of data" (Forbes 2005: 358).

Standard Operating Procedures and Managers' Attention

Firms generally develop standard operating programs, practices, and routines over time (Cyert and March 1963; Gavetti et al. 2007), which can be viewed as a set of behavioral rules learned as the firm tries to adjust to operating conditions (Cyert and March 1963). Not only do we contend that different attentional orientations guide individuals toward diverse experiences, but we also argue these different orientations result in the development of different kinds of operating procedures. For example, practices and routines associated with prospecting deal with how to allot slack resources to explore possible opportunities (George 2005), how to normalize and learn from minor failures (Sitkin 1992), and how to effectively redistribute resources from one firm to another (Brown and Eisenhardt 1997). Routines and practices related to exploitation, on the other hand, entail the management of risk and preservation of strategic congruence (Greve 2007; March 1991), the refinement of current technologies and attainment of efficiency (Csaszar 2013; March 1991), and the ramping up of operations to reach economies of scale and scope (Lavie et al. 2010). As these examples illustrate, standard operating procedures influence and direct the decisions firms make (Cyert and March 1963) as well as affect their speed. These practices also enable the transmission of past learning, which can then be applied again in new situations

(Cyert and March 1963), and they can set rules for collecting, filtering, and processing information (Cyert and March 1963).

Confidence and Manager's Attention

Focusing attention on particular tasks not only helps individuals build domain-specific experience and create operating procedures that are standardized, it also improves managers' confidence—or the "the strength of belief in the goodness, accuracy, and appropriateness of one's judgments" (Budescu and Yu 2007: 154)—in that particular domain (Levitt and March 1988; March and Shapira 1987). When managers focus on earlier-stage exploration activities, they are more likely to engage in collecting, analyzing, and assessing information about prospecting ventures. In this context, knowledge that is specific to a domain and the arrangement of this knowledge will improve individuals' confidence as they make decisions in their knowledge domain (cf. Einhorn and Hogarth 1985). In turn, confidence helps managers overcome the anxiety that frequently arises in uncertain situations (Eisenhardt 1989; Eisenhardt and Martin 2000) and helps them "act quickly and decisively" (Judge and Miller 1991: 450; Baum and Wally 2003).

A particularly important exploration-related activity is *terminating unpromising projects and ventures at an early stage* (McGrath 1999). Due to the higher unpredictability of potential results, exploration in ventures at an early stage is intrinsically more uncertain and more likely to end in failure than exploration of ventures that are at a later stage (Gupta et al. 2006; McGrath 1999). Consequently, firms that focus their attention on earlier-stage exploration activities often have to decide whether to terminate a venture at an early stage. In turn, these firms generally gain experience handling these types of ventures and thus develop more standard operating procedures to detect faults and terminate ventures early on (McGrath 1999) compared to firms that focus their attention on later-stage exploration or exploitation. Moreover, firms focusing on earlier-stage exploration are likely to collect and process domain-specific information more quickly (Forbes 2005) and more confidently use that information (Judge and Miller 1991) to make decisions on a focal venture's ultimate fate. Thus, these traits and behaviors enhance the speed with which managers terminate ventures during the prospecting stage.

Venture progression during the prospecting stage necessitates heterogeneous experiences, standard operating procedures, and confidence.

Venture progression is dissimilar to venture termination in numerous ways. First, the decision to advance a venture centers less on constraining downside risk, but more on the realization of upside potential (Bowman and Hurry 1993; McGrath 1999). Advancing a venture from prospecting to developing requires one to invest in a previously recognized opportunity—an early decision to pursue one venture over others. Advancing a venture therefore represents a move toward opportunity exploitation (Choi et al. 2008; Choi and Shepherd 2004). In contrast to firms that allocate attention toward later-stage development and exploitation, firms that focus more attention on earlier-stage exploration activities tend to heed information indicating the venture's upside potential or have the experience, operating procedures, or confidence needed to quickly advance a venture. My (Dean) colleague and I (Bakker and Shepherd 2017) showed that in the prospecting stage (i.e., the earliest venture-development stage), a greater orientation toward earlier-stage exploration activities enhances the speed by which managers decide about termination, but it diminishes the speed by which they make decisions about venture progression. Thus, having an attentional orientation toward earlier opportunity-advancement stages enables firms to make certain, but not necessarily all, decisions more rapidly.

Attention to Poorly Performing Entrepreneurial Projects

Research has also explored how managers and team members of entrepreneurial projects attend to the poor performance of these projects and how this attention influences project termination.

Team Members' Attention and Project Termination

Along with our co-authors, we (Shepherd et al. 2014) shed light on the connection between the timing of project termination and learning from failure from the standpoint of individuals working on the project. These insights in turn have implications for the management of entrepreneurial firms. First, team members are able to decrease negative emotions after the failure of their project by adopting an engineering mindset. An engineering mindset directs more of the individuals' attention toward the criticality of a firm's overall engineering challenge than toward any specific project.

With an engineering mindset directing people's attention, the failure of their project results in minimal negative emotion. In addition, there are fewer barriers to rapidly redeploying (human and other) resources to a subsequent project. Yet, in case project team members perceive the transition to a new project to be delayed, they tend to develop negative emotions. Interestingly, those with an engineering mindset also tend to develop more negative emotions when a project (especially one that performs poorly) is *not* terminated than when it is terminated. An engineering mindset represents a cognitive script for creative problem-solving; this mindset stresses the importance of the engineering process in terms of undertaking challenging tasks that are critical to the organization over and above remaining committed to a particular project the organization no more deems important.

Second, delayed termination gives team members time to contemplate personal errors (i.e., slipups in a specific process, wrong calculations, etc.), issues related to the organization as a whole (i.e., management choices that resulted in failure, problems with coordination between departments, etc.), technical issues (i.e., engineering-related problems), and issues related to industry or markets (i.e., influence of institutions or the government on product development, the inclusion of customers, etc.). These types of reflections often serve as a foundation for lessons learned that can be verbalized and documented when there is enough time left—two steps required for the organization to learn from its experiences (see Zollo and Winter 2002). On the other hand, team members involved in quick termination of projects have minimal time to learn from their project failure experiences. This minimal time for learning is especially troubling in an organizational environment that rapidly redeploys resources because after a project is terminated, there is no time for team members' reflection, verbalization, or documentation of the lessons they learned from the experience. Additionally, even if team members can engage in reflection, they are unlikely to find time to exchange their thoughts with others, which will hinder learning at the level of the team, nor are they likely to document the lessons they have learned, which hinders learning of the organization overall. Thus, in organizations that rapidly redeploy resources after project termination, team members, teams, and even the organizations themselves typically do not learn from the failures they experience after it has occurred but rather before the event.

Finally, members of teams often harness the negative emotions they feel from their project's "creeping death" to initiate learning from failure.

When negative emotions are used in this way, they can be very supportive for learning because such emotions indicate to the team members that something is not right, that the organization does not find the project worthwhile anymore, and that individuals' reassignment to a more salient engineering challenge is being delayed. As they wait for redeployment, team members can direct the negative emotions arising from their unfilled need for a prominent engineering challenge toward a new challenge—specifically capturing the learnings from failure. By refocusing attention away from the delay, team members can learn from the failure experience. Thus, the negative emotions arising from creeping death enable rather than impede learning from failure.

Overall, the team members' perspective emphasizes people's reactions to project-termination timing and the effects of these reactions on learning from the failure of a project. Namely, when it comes to creeping death, the project team members are able to (1) lessen negative emotions arising from failure by stressing the key role of the engineering challenge instead of a particular project; (2) have time to contemplate, verbalize, and document the lessons they have learned (in the case of rapid deployment, this time is available before the actual termination event); and (3) redirect negative emotions stemming from creeping death to learning from the failure.

Managers' Attention and Project Termination

My (Holger) colleague and I (Behrens and Patzelt 2016) built on the attention-based view of the firm (Ocasio 1997) to study how managers terminate corporate entrepreneurship projects considering the properties of the portfolio, their attentional focus (reflected by managers' past project failure experience), situated attention (reflected by the firm's growth rate), and attention's structural distribution within the organization (reflected by managers' hierarchical positions). The study yielded several insights. First, managers differ in their allocation of attention to different aspects of the project portfolio, more specifically in the attention they allocate to a project's fit with the firm's portfolio strategy and the portfolio's balance of incremental versus radical projects. Therefore, the study highlights that understanding managerial attention allocation in project terminations requires consideration of interactions between portfolio characteristics and effects at the level of the firm, the individual, and the organization.

Second, managers' prior failure experience influences how they allocate attention in future decisions about project terminations—an impact that goes beyond their emotions and learning from failure (McGrath 1999; Shepherd et al. 2009, 2011, 2013, 2014). Specifically, more prior failure experiences accelerate how an entrepreneurial project's low strategic fit enhances the probability that a project is terminated. Therefore, prior failure experience has far-reaching consequences on a firm's future composition of the project portfolio and therefore strategic entrepreneurship. Moreover, the study highlights that prior failure experiences are cumulative in nature (Shepherd et al. 2013) such that more prior failures have a stronger impact on attention allocation than fewer prior failures.

Finally, the negative impact of a project's contribution to portfolio balance on the propensity of termination is stronger for top managers than for middle managers, illustrating the divergent thinking among managers at different organizational levels (Floyd and Wooldridge 1997; Hornsby et al. 2009; Kuratko et al. 2005). The finding also shows that managers' attention allocation is different for project start and termination. While middle managers allocate more attention to the project's strategic context for project start decisions compared to top managers (Behrens et al. 2014), for termination decision, middle managers attend less to strategic aspects (e.g., a project's strategic fit and portfolio balance) than top managers. Top managers seem to be more prone to resource investments in the start of new projects that are exploratory than in these projects' continuation.

METACOGNITION TO FOCUS ENTREPRENEURS' ATTENTION

Researchers have argued that "successful future strategists will exploit an entrepreneurial mindset . . . [namely,] the ability to rapidly sense, act, and mobilize, even under uncertain conditions" (Ireland et al. 2003: 963–989). Such a notion implies that the ability to both notice and adapt to uncertainty is a key skill of successful managers (McGrath and McMillan 2000; Ireland et al. 2003). When conceptualizing the notion of an *entrepreneurial mindset*, Ireland et al. (2003) described cognitive tasks, such as interpreting opportunities as goal change, continually reflecting on and challenging one's "dominant logic" in changing environments, and reconsidering "deceptively simple questions" about what one believes to be true in regard to markets and the firm. The cognitive tasks associated with an entrepreneurial mindset embody what we more generally call *cognitive adaptability*. Cognitive adaptability refers to the degree to which people are dynamic, flexible, self-regulating (Jost et al. 1998), and *engaged* in developing numerous decision frameworks aimed at sensing and processing environmental changes and then choosing from those various alternatives to successfully understand, plan, and implement an array of personal, social, and organizational objectives in a shifting world. Here, decision frameworks refer to organized prior knowledge about individuals and situations that are formed to actively build a meaningful reality (Fiske and Taylor 1991).

Metacognition can be a process that engages these decision frameworks. According to Schraw and Dennison (1994: 460), metacognition is "the ability to reflect upon, understand, and control one's learning." More specifically, metacognition is a higher-order cognitive process that helps organize people's knowledge and what they recognize about themselves, situations, tasks, and environments to enable effective and *adaptable* cognitive functioning when faced with input from environments that are dynamic and complex (Brown and Eisenhardt 1997). Metacognition is often seen as a conscious process (also known as metacognitive awareness (Flavell 1979)) that occurs in social contexts (Jost et al. 1998). Allen and Armour-Thomas (1993: 204) argued that it is "meaningless to ask a question about any type of thinking without asking concomitant questions about contextual forces in which such thinking is situated" (Allen and Armour-Thomas 1993: 204).

Using metacognition research as a foundation and integrating it with relevant social cognition work (selectively reviewed below), my (Dean) colleague and I (Haynie and Shepherd 2009) proposed the notion of cognitive adaptability, which occurs when individuals perceive and then ascribe meaning to environmental features in relation to their own goal orientation and then utilize their metacognitive knowledge and experiences to develop several alternative decision frameworks aimed at interpreting, planning, and implementing objectives to "manage" an environment that is mutable. Individuals then choose and employ a particular framework from the multiple alternatives and end up with some result (i.e., cognitive [understanding and comprehension] and/or behavioral [action]). Individuals then evaluate these outcomes in relation to their goal orientation, which in turn informs ensuing decision-framework generation and selection (Haynie and Shepherd 2009; Haynie et al. 2012).

Goal Orientation

Motives affect how individuals perceive and interpret context (Griffin and Ross 1991), and context can also define individuals' motives (Wyer and Srull 1989). As such, we propose that this relationship is the foundation for the development and use of metacognitive strategies. For instance, in entrepreneurship, these motivations could be to increase one's share in a specific market, improve manufacturing productivity, or achieve higher sales. In other words, the goals managers pursue are often seen as a function—or as a result—of the environment those goals originated in. Therefore, we argue that the *origins* of cognitive adaptability stem from the combined effects of (1) the setting the individual functions within and (2) his or her motivations whereby the person interprets context. To capture this relationship between context and motivation, my (Dean) colleague and I (Haynie and Shepherd 2009) proposed the term goal orientation, which specifically refers to *the degree to which a person interprets environmental changes in relation to a broad array of personal, social, and organizational goals.* Goal orientation engages metacognitive knowledge and metacognitive experience as metacognitive resources.

Metacognitive Knowledge

Metacognitive knowledge is one's conscious understanding of cognitive processing in relation to (1) people, (2) tasks, and (3) strategy (Flavell 1979). First, metacognitive knowledge of *people* has both an external and internal focus. Externally focused metacognitive knowledge refers to understanding what other individuals, such as potential customers, competitors, and investors, think about their firms and environments. Internally focused metacognitive knowledge refers to understanding and acknowledging one's own biases, values, and intellectual strengths and weaknesses. For instance, a manager may know that he or she is better at sensing external stakeholders' needs than those of employees or other mid-level managers. Second, metacognitive knowledge of *tasks* relates to understanding the nature of a particular challenge as well as having knowledge of solutions to similar tasks that could be implemented for the task at hand. Lastly, metacognitive knowledge of *strategy* entails the procedures one uses to ensure that a particular decision framework is suitable in light of one's goal orientation and metacognitive knowledge of people and tasks. More specifically, metacognitive knowledge of strategy is the process of referencing previously learned strategies for functionally similar tasks and altering those strategies for the task at hand. Thus, my (Dean) colleague and I (Haynie and Shepherd 2009) established an overall definition for metacognitive knowledge as the *degree to which an individual depends on what he or she already knows about people, tasks, and strategy when generating multiple decision frameworks aimed at interpreting, planning, and implementing goals to "manage" a changing environment.*

Metacognitive Experience

Metacognitive experience refers to experiences that are affective, are based on cognitive activity, and serve as a channel through which prior *experiences, memories, intuitions, and emotions* may be used as resources in the process of making sense of a specific task, problem, or situation (Flavell 1979). For instance, an individual has a metacognitive experience if he or she feels that a specific task is challenging to undertake or understand. In the next step, he or she draws on that prior experience to yield the creation of a new decision framework for a new but similar task. Like past experiences, emotions and intuitions related to prior situations can shape the generation of decision frameworks for novel tasks. As an example, emotions like fear, anger, joy, or grief or that are connected to an event in the past may serve to influence—at a metacognitive level—the development of future decision frameworks aimed at novel events, tasks, or situations similar to those from which the experienced emotions stemmed. Intuitions serve a similar function in the metacognitive creation of decision frameworks: if the individual tends to draw on intuitions resulting from prior experiences, those intuitions will likely influence the development of future decision frameworks aimed at new tasks, events, or situations. A manager, for instance, may draw a decision based on a "hunch," which reflects his or her reliance on intuition (Miller and Ireland 2005). In simple terms, metacognitive experiences enable people to make sense of their social world more easily (Earley and Ang 2003) and thus, together with metacognitive knowledge, help individuals choose a decision framework. Therefore, my (Dean) colleague and I (Haynie and Shepherd 2009: 697) referred to metacognitive knowledge as the *degree to which the individual depends on idiosyncratic experiences, emotions, and intuitions when generating multiple decision frameworks aimed at interpreting, planning, and implementing goals to "manage" a changing environment.*

Metacognitive Choice

Thus, individuals select and use a particular decision framework (chosen among the set of available alternatives) in the context of their goal orientation to plan and implement objectives to "manage" dynamic environments. This selection among numerous decision frameworks is similar to a golfer choosing a particular club based on his or her goals for a specific shot. Each club in the golfer's bag can be seen as an alternative path to action and goal realization—getting the ball to the green and into the hole. Yet, depending on the nature of the specific shot at hand (e.g., in a sand trap versus on the fairway), there is a "most suitable" club for that shot—namely, the club that will help the golfer realize his or her goal. An individual who is cognitively adaptable and draws on his or her metacognitive knowledge and experience generates various alternative decision frameworks as possibilities (different clubs) to interpret an altered reality and then chooses the most suitable option from that set of possibilities in light of his or her goals to most effectively reach that goal. Thus, my (Dean) colleague and I (Haynie and Shepherd 2009: 700) defined metacognitive choice as the *degree to which the individual engages in the active process of choosing the most suitable option among multiple decision frameworks that helps him or her best interpret, plan, and implement a response in order to "manage" a changing environment.*

Monitoring

Implementing the chosen decision framework will result in action that generates feedback to additional adaptive cognitions (Flavell 1979). According to Flavell (1979), the purpose of a metacognitive strategy is to feel confident that the goal has been accomplished. In line with Flavell's proposition, metacognition has mechanisms to evaluate the result of implementing a specific decision framework in relation to one's goal orientation, metacognitive knowledge, and metacognitive experience (Flavell 1979). Monitoring a person's own cognitions happens both during and after the process of interpreting, planning, and implementing a response to an altered reality. Depending on the particular characteristics of the association between current performance and a person's goal orientation, monitoring this relationship may prompt him or her to reassess their motivation (Locke et al. 1984; Locke and Latham 1990; Nelson and Narens 1994) and/or his or her metacognitive knowledge, metacognitive experience, and/or the particular decision framework chosen based on the setting at hand (i.e., metacognitive choice). As such, monitoring refers to *looking for and utilizing feedback to reassess one's goal orientation, metacognitive knowledge, metacognitive experience, and metacognitive choice in order to "manage" a changing environment* (Haynie and Shepherd 2009: 700).

Learning to Think Metacognitively

Over the past decade, researchers have explored various instructional approaches that harness metacognition to improve reasoning (Kramarski et al. 2001). Mevarech and Kramarski (1997) created an instructional method to help students enhance their mathematical reasoning by developing their metacognitive skills through four types of questions based on (1) comprehension, (2) connection, (3) strategy, and (4) reflection (Mevarech and Kramarski 2003: 469). We refer to these questions as "metacognitive questions" as they are used to stimulate learners' metacognition.

First, *comprehension questions* are intended to encourage one to think about whether he or she really understands the nature of a particular problem before starting to address it. This understanding forms from carefully considering the situation such that one identifies a problem, its nature, and its implications. The following are examples of questions encouraging students to think about comprehension: What is the core of the problem? What is the key question asked? What meanings do the key concepts convey?

Second, *connection questions* are intended to encourage students to think about a particular problem in terms of its similarities and differences with problems he or she has faced and solved before. These questions urge students to draw on existing knowledge and experiences without generalizing from them too much. Questions like the following prompt learners to think about these connections: How can I relate this problem to problems I addressed previously? In what ways does this problem differ from those I worked on in the past, and how does it differ?

Third, *strategic questions* are intended to encourage students to think about which strategies are most suitable for solving a problem and why. These questions urge learners to contemplate the what, why, and how underlying their approach to a problem. The following are examples of strategic questions: What is the strategy/tactic/principle best suited for me to address this problem? Why is this strategy/tactic/principle so particularly appropriate? How can I put together information I need for solving the problem? How can I realize the plan?

Fourth, *reflection questions* are intended to encourage students to think about their understanding and feelings as they progress through the problem-solving process. These tasks help students generate their own feedback (i.e., develop a feedback loop in their solution process) to provide the chance to change. Examples of reflection questions include the following: What am I doing? It there any sense in what I am doing? Are there particular challenges I have to address? How do I feel about it? In what way can I verify the proposed solution to the problem? Is it possible to draw on a different approach to tackle this task?

Metacognitive training helps decision makers (1) develop and answer a set of self-addressed questions that are in line with those described above (Kramarski et al. 2002); (2) clarify why it is important to ask and answer these types of questions (Kramarski and Zeichner 2001); and (3) utilize these questions when contemplating or reflecting on new ideas (Kramarski et al. 2002), such as potential opportunities. A significant number of empirical studies have found that metacognitive skills (as represented by asking and answering the questions outlined above) enable learning (e.g., Kramarski and Zeichner 2001; Mevarech and Kramarski 2003). Overall, these questions prompt people to think about their learning, which can positively affect their subsequent task performance. For instance, metacognitive training improves individuals' (1) adaptability to new situations (i.e., it provides a foundation on which an individual's prior knowledge and experience influence his or her learning or problem-solving in a novel situation (Mayer and Wittrock 1996: 48)), (2) creativity (i.e., it can result in unique and flexible solutions, ideas, or perceptions (Runco and Chand 1995)), and (3) communication of the thinking underlying a specific response (Mevarech and Kramarski 2003). Each of these skills is very valuable for entrepreneurs.

Conclusion

Managers' attention is a limited resource, and where they allocate attention influences several aspects of the entrepreneurial process, including environmental changes and the recognition, evaluation, and exploitation of opportunities. Research has uncovered several factors at the individual, organizational, and environmental level that explain how entrepreneurs allocate attention. In this chapter, we illustrated that cognitive processes, particularly metacognition, impact individuals' attention allocation and thereby entrepreneurial outcomes. We now turn to the topic of entrepreneurial identity, which has attracted considerable scholarly interest over the last several years.

NOTES

1. The different knowledge structure forms (e.g., categories, schemas, mental models, and logics) differ in complexity. For greater analytical and conceptual simplicity, we decided not to distinguish among the various knowledge structure forms but to instead characterize them based on complexity.
2. While environmental dynamism and velocity are different constructs, they are "closely related in practice" (Baum and Wally 2003: 1110).

REFERENCES

Aldrich, H. E. (1979). *Organizations and environments*. Englewood Cliffs: Prentice-Hall, 16(2), 183–214.

Allen, B. A., & Armour-Thomas, E. (1993). Construct validation of metacognition. *The Journal of Psychology, 127*(2), 203–211.

Ariely, D., & Carmon, Z. (2000). Gestalt characteristics of experiences: The defining features of summarized events. *Journal of Behavioral Decision Making, 13*(2), 191–201.

Ariely, D., & Zauberman, G. (2000). On the making of an experience: The effects of breaking and combining experiences on their overall evaluation. *Journal of Behavioral Decision Making, 13*(2), 219.

Bakker, R. M., & Shepherd, D. A. (2017). Pull the plug or take the plunge: Multiple opportunities and the speed of venturing decisions in the Australian mining industry. *Academy of Management Journal, 60*(1), 130–155.

Baum, J., & Wally, S. (2003). Strategic decision speed and firm performance. *Strategic Management Journal, 24*(11), 1107–1129.

Behrens, J., & Patzelt, H. (2016). Corporate entrepreneurship managers' project terminations: Integrating portfolio-level, individual-level, and firm-level effects. *Entrepreneurship Theory and Practice, 40*(4), 815–842.

Behrens, J., Ernst, H., & Shepherd, D. A. (2014). The decision to exploit an R&D project: Divergent thinking across middle and senior managers. *Journal of Product Innovation Management, 31*(1), 144–158.

Beyer, J. M., Chattopadhyay, P., George, E., Glick, W. H., & Pugliese, D. (1997). The selective perception of managers revisited. *Academy of Management Journal, 40*(3), 716–737.

Bingham, C. B., & Eisenhardt, K. M. (2011). Rational heuristics: The 'simple rules' that strategists learn from process experience. *Strategic Management Journal, 32*(13), 1437–1464.

Bogner, W. C., & Barr, P. S. (2000). Making sense in hypercompetitive environments: A cognitive explanation for the persistence of high velocity competition. *Organization Science, 11*(2), 212–226.

Bourgeois, L. J., III, & Eisenhardt, K. M. (1988). Strategic decision processes in high velocity environments: Four cases in the microcomputer industry. *Management Science, 34*(7), 816–835.

Bowman, E. H., & Hurry, D. (1993). Strategy through the option lens: An integrated view of resource investments and the incremental-choice process. *Academy of Management Review, 18*(4), 760–782.
Brown, S. L., & Eisenhardt, K. M. (1997). The art of continuous change: Linking complexity theory and time-paced evolution in relentlessly shifting organizations. *Administrative Science Quarterly, 42*(1), 1–34.
Budescu, D. V., & Yu, H.-T. (2007). Aggregation of opinions based on correlated cues and advisors. *Journal of Behavioral Decision Making, 20*(2), 153–177.
Carpenter, M. A. (2002). The implications of strategy and social context for the relationship between top management team heterogeneity and firm performance. *Strategic Management Journal, 23*(3), 275–284.
Castañer, X., & Kavadis, N. (2013). Does good governance prevent bad strategy? A study of corporate governance, financial diversification, and value creation by French corporations, 2000–2006. *Strategic Management Journal, 34*(7), 863–876.
Cho, T. S., & Hambrick, D. C. (2006). Attention as the mediator between top management team characteristics and strategic change: The case of airline deregulation. *Organization Science, 17*(4), 453–469.
Choi, Y. R., & Shepherd, D. A. (2004). Entrepreneurs' decisions to exploit opportunities. *Journal of Management, 30*(3), 377–395.
Choi, Y. R., Lévesque, M., & Shepherd, D. A. (2008). When should entrepreneurs expedite or delay opportunity exploitation? *Journal of Business Venturing, 23*(3), 333–355.
Christensen, C. M. (1997). *The innovator's dilemma*. Cambridge: Harvard Business School.
Csaszar, F. A. (2013). An efficient frontier in organization design: Organizational structure as a determinant of exploration and exploitation. *Organization Science, 24*(4), 1083–1101.
Cyert, R. M., & March, J. G. (1963). *A behavioral theory of the firm*. Englewood Cliffs: Prentice-Hall, 2, 15(3), 457–460.
Dutton, J. E., & Jackson, S. E. (1987). Categorizing strategic issues: Links to organizational action. *Academy of Management Review, 12*(1), 76–90.
Earley, P. C., & Ang, S. (2003). *Cultural intelligence: Individual interactions across cultures*. Stanford: Stanford University Press.
Eggers, J. P., & Kaplan, S. (2009). Cognition and renewal: Comparing CEO and organizational effects on incumbent adaptation to technical change. *Organization Science, 20*(2), 461–477.
Einhorn, H. J., & Hogarth, R. M. (1985). Ambiguity and uncertainty in probabilistic inference. *Psychological Review, 92*(4), 433.
Eisenhardt, K. M. (1989). Making fast strategic decisions in high-velocity environments. *Academy of Management Journal, 32*(3), 543–576.
Eisenhardt, K. M., & Martin, J. A. (2000). Dynamic capabilities: What are they? *Strategic Management Journal, 21*(10), 1105–1121.

Eisenhardt, K. M., & Schoonhoven, C. B. (1990). Organizational growth: Linking founding team, strategy, environment, and growth among US semiconductor ventures, 1978–1988. *Administrative Science Quarterly, 35*(3), 504–529.
Eisenhardt, K. M., Furr, N. R., & Bingham, C. B. (2010). Microfoundations of performance: Balancing efficiency and flexibility in dynamic environments. *Organization Science, 21*(6), 1263–1273.
Finkelstein, S., & D'aveni, R. A. (1994). CEO duality as a double-edged sword: How boards of directors balance entrenchment avoidance and unity of command. *Academy of Management Journal, 37*(5), 1079–1108.
Finkelstein, S., & Hambrick, D. C. (1990). Top-management-team tenure and organizational outcomes: The moderating role of managerial discretion. *Administrative Science Quarterly, 35*(3), 484–503.
Fiske, S. T., & Taylor, S. E. (1991). McGraw-Hill series in social psychology. In *Social cognition*. New York: Mcgraw-Hill Book Company, 102(2), 246–268.
Flavell, J. H. (1979). Metacognition and cognitive monitoring: A new area of cognitive–developmental inquiry. *American Psychologist, 34*(10), 906.
Floyd, S. W., & Wooldridge, B. (1997). Middle management's strategic influence and organizational performance. *Journal of Management Studies, 34*(3), 465–485.
Forbes, D. P. (2005). Are some entrepreneurs more overconfident than others? *Journal of Business Venturing, 20*(5), 623–640.
Franconeri, S. L., & Simons, D. J. (2003). Moving and looming stimuli capture attention. *Attention, Perception, & Psychophysics, 65*(7), 999–1010.
Franconeri, S. L., Hollingworth, A., & Simons, D. J. (2005). Do new objects capture attention? *Psychological science, 16*(4), 275–281.
Frey, K. P., & Eagly, A. H. (1993). Vividness can undermine the persuasiveness of messages. *Journal of Personality and Social Psychology, 65*(1), 32.
Gatignon, H., Tushman, M. L., Smith, W., & Anderson, P. (2002). A structural approach to assessing innovation: Construct development of innovation locus, type, and characteristics. *Management Science, 48*(9), 1103–1122.
Gavetti, G., Levinthal, D., & Ocasio, W. (2007). Neo-Carnegie: The Carnegie school's past, present, and reconstructing for the future. *Organization Science, 18*(3), 523–536.
George, G. (2005). Slack resources and the performance of privately held firms. *Academy of Management Journal, 48*(4), 661–676.
Greve, H. R. (2007). Exploration and exploitation in product innovation. *Industrial and Corporate Change, 16*(5), 945–975.
Griffin, D. W., & Ross, L. (1991). Subjective construal, social inference, and human misunderstanding. *Advances in Experimental Social Psychology, 24*, 319–359.
Gupta, A. K., Smith, K. G., & Shalley, C. E. (2006). The interplay between exploration and exploitation. *Academy of Management Journal, 49*(4), 693–706.
Hambrick, D. C., & Mason, P. A. (1984). Upper echelons: The organization as a reflection of its top managers. *Academy of Management Review, 9*(2), 193–206.

Hambrick, D. C., Cho, T. S., & Chen, M. J. (1996). The influence of top management team heterogeneity on firms' competitive moves. *Administrative Science Quarterly*, 659–684.

Hambrick, D. C., Finkelstein, S., & Mooney, A. C. (2005). Executive job demands: New insights for explaining strategic decisions and leader behaviors. *Academy of Management Review*, 30(3), 472–491.

Han, S., & Humphreys, G. W. (2002). Segmentation and selection contribute to local processing in hierarchical analysis. *The Quarterly Journal of Experimental Psychology: Section A*, 55(1), 5–21.

Haynie, M., & Shepherd, D. A. (2009). A measure of adaptive cognition for entrepreneurship research. *Entrepreneurship Theory and Practice*, 33(3), 695–714.

Haynie, J. M., Shepherd, D. A., & Patzelt, H. (2012). Cognitive adaptability and an entrepreneurial task: The role of metacognitive ability and feedback. *Entrepreneurship Theory and Practice*, 36(2), 237–265.

Helfat, C. E., & Peteraf, M. A. (2003). The dynamic resource-based view: Capability lifecycles. *Strategic Management Journal*, 24(10), 997–1010.

Henderson, R. M., & Clark, K. B. (1990). Architectural innovation: The reconfiguration of existing product technologies and the failure of established firms. *Administrative Science Quarterly*, 35, 9–30.

Hornsby, J., Kuratko, D., Shepherd, D., & Bott, J. (2009). Managers' corporate entrepreneurial actions: Examining perception and position. *Journal of Business Venturing*, 24(3), 236–247.

Ireland, R. D., Hitt, M. A., & Sirmon, D. G. (2003). A model of strategic entrepreneurship: The construct and its dimensions. *Journal of Management*, 29(6), 963–989.

Jost, J. T., Kruglanski, A. W., & Nelson, T. O. (1998). Social metacognition: An expansionist review. *Personality and Social Psychology Review*, 2(2), 137–154.

Judge, W. Q., & Miller, A. (1991). Antecedents and outcomes of decision speed in different environmental context. *Academy of Management Journal*, 34(2), 449–463.

Kahneman, D. (1973). *Attention and effort*. Englewood Cliffs: Prentice-Hall, 57(9), 705–717.

Kaplan, S. (2008). Cognition, capabilities, and incentives: Assessing firm response to the fiber-optic revolution. *Academy of Management Journal*, 51(4), 672–695.

Kaplan, S., & Tripsas, M. (2008). Thinking about technology: Applying a cognitive lens to technical change. *Research Policy*, 37(5), 790–805.

Katila, R., & Ahuja, G. (2002). Something old, something new: A longitudinal study of search behavior and new product introduction. *Academy of Management Journal*, 45(6), 1183–1194.

Kesner, I. F., & Johnson, R. B. (1990). An investigation of the relationship between board composition and stockholder suits. *Strategic Management Journal*, 11(4), 327–336.

Kiss, A. N., & Barr, P. S. (2015). New venture strategic adaptation: The interplay of belief structures and industry context. *Strategic Management Journal, 36*(8), 1245–1263.
Kramarski, B., & Zeichner, O. (2001). Using technology to enhance mathematical reasoning: Effects of feedback and self-regulation learning. *Educational Media International, 38*(2–3), 77–82.
Kramarski, B., Mevarech, Z. R., & Arami, M. (2002). The effects of metacognitive instruction on solving mathematical authentic tasks. *Educational Studies in Mathematics, 49*(2), 225–250.
Kramarski, B., Mevarech, Z. R., & Lieberman, A. (2001). Effects of multilevel versus unilevel metacognitive training on mathematical reasoning. *The Journal of Educational Research, 94*(5), 292–300.
Kruglanski, A. W., & Boyatzi, L. M. (2012). The psychology of closed and open mindedness, rationality, and democracy. *Critical Review, 24*(2), 217–232.
Kuratko, D. F., Ireland, R. D., Covin, J. G., & Hornsby, J. S. (2005). A model of middle-level managers' entrepreneurial behavior. *Entrepreneurship Theory and Practice, 29*(6), 699–716.
Langley, A. (1995). Between "paralysis by analysis" and "extinction by instinct". *Sloan Management Review, 36*(3), 63.
Lavie, D., Stettner, U., & Tushman, M. L. (2010). Exploration and exploitation within and across organizations. *Academy of Management Annals, 4*(1), 109–155.
Levinthal, D. A., & March, J. G. (1993). The myopia of learning. *Strategic Management Journal, 14*(S2), 95–112.
Levinthal, D., & Rerup, C. (2006). Crossing an apparent chasm: Bridging mindful and less-mindful perspectives on organizational learning. *Organization Science, 17*(4), 502–513.
Levitt, B., & March, J. G. (1988). Organizational learning. *Annual Review of Sociology, 14*(1), 319–338.
Lieberman, M. B., & Montgomery, D. B. (1988). First-mover advantages. *Strategic Management Journal, 9*(S1), 41–58.
Lim, E. N. (2015). The role of reference point in CEO restricted stock and its impact on R&D intensity in high-technology firms. *Strategic Management Journal, 36*(6), 872–889.
Locke, E. A., & Latham, G. P. (1990). Work motivation and satisfaction: Light at the end of the tunnel. *Psychological Science, 1*(4), 240–246.
Locke, E. A., Frederick, E., Lee, C., & Bobko, P. (1984). Effect of self-efficacy, goals, and task strategies on task performance. *Journal of Applied Psychology, 69*(2), 241.
March, J. G. (1991). Exploration and exploitation in organizational learning. *Organization Science, 2*(1), 71–87.
March, J. G., & Shapira, Z. (1987). Managerial perspectives on risk and risk taking. *Management Science, 33*(11), 1404–1418.

Maula, M. V., Keil, T., & Zahra, S. A. (2013). Top management's attention to discontinuous technological change: Corporate venture capital as an alert mechanism. *Organization Science, 24*(3), 926–947.

Mayer, R. E., & Wittrock, M. C. (1996). Problem-solving transfer. In D. C. Berliner & R. C. Calfee (Eds.), *Handbook of educational psychology* (pp. 47–62). New York: Routledge.

McGrath, R. G. (1999). Falling forward: Real options reasoning and entrepreneurial failure. *Academy of Management Review, 24*(1), 13–30.

McGrath, R. G. (2013). *The end of competitive advantage: How to keep your strategy moving as fast as your business*. Boston: Harvard Business Review Press, 56(5), 64.

McGrath, R. G., & MacMillan, I. C. (2000). *The entrepreneurial mindset: Strategies for continuously creating opportunity in an age of uncertainty* (Vol. 284). Boston: Harvard Business Press, 27(2), 185–203.

McMullen, J. S., Shepherd, D. A., & Patzelt, H. (2009). Managerial (in)attention to competitive threats. *Journal of Management Studies, 46*(2), 157–181.

Mevarech, Z. R., & Kramarski, B. (1997). IMPROVE: A multidimensional method for teaching mathematics in heterogeneous classrooms. *American Educational Research Journal, 34*(2), 365–394.

Mevarech, Z. R., & Kramarski, B. (2003). The effects of metacognitive training versus worked-out examples on students' mathematical reasoning. *British Journal of Educational Psychology, 73*(4), 449–471.

Miller, D., & Friesen, P. H. (1983). Strategy-making and environment: The third link. *Strategic Management Journal, 4*(3), 221–235.

Miller, C. C., & Ireland, R. D. (2005). Intuition in strategic decision making: Friend or foe in the fast-paced 21st century? *The Academy of Management Executive, 19*(1), 19–30.

Nadkarni, S., & Barr, P. S. (2008). Environmental context, managerial cognition, and strategic action: An integrated view. *Strategic Management Journal, 29*(13), 1395–1427.

Nadkarni, S., & Narayanan, V. K. (2007). Strategic schemas, strategic flexibility, and firm performance: The moderating role of industry clockspeed. *Strategic Management Journal, 28*(3), 243–270.

Neisser, U. (1976). *Cognition and reality: Principles and implications of cognitive psychology*. New York: WH Freeman/Times Books/Henry Holt & Co.

Nelson, T. O., Kruglanski, A. W., & Jost, J. T. (1998). Knowing thyself and others: Progress in metacognitive social psychology. In V. Y. Yzerbyt, G. Lories, & B. Dardenne (Eds.), *Metacognition: Cognitive and social dimensions* (pp. 69–89). Thousand Oaks: Sage.

Ocasio, W. (1997). Towards an attention-based view of the firm. *Strategic Management Journal, 18*, 187–206.

Ocasio, W. (2011). Attention to attention. *Organization Science, 22*(5), 1286–1296.

Pashler, H., Johnston, J. C., & Ruthruff, E. (2001). Attention and performance. *Annual Review of Psychology, 52*(1), 629–651.

Perlow, L. A., Okhuysen, G. A., & Repenning, N. P. (2002). The speed trap: Exploring the relationship between decision making and temporal context. *Academy of Management Journal, 45*(5), 931–955.

Priem, R. L., Rasheed, A. M., & Kotulic, A. G. (1995). Rationality in strategic decision processes, environmental dynamism and firm performance. *Journal of Management, 21*(5), 913–929.

Rindova, V., Ferrier, W. J., & Wiltbank, R. (2010). Value from gestalt: How sequences of competitive actions create advantage for firms in nascent markets. *Strategic Management Journal, 31*(13), 1474–1497.

Rodriguez, V., Valdes-Sosa, M., & Freiwald, W. (2002). Dividing attention between form and motion during transparent surface perception. *Cognitive Brain Research, 13*(2), 187–193.

Rosenkopf, L., & Nerkar, A. (2001). Beyond local search: Boundary-spanning, exploration, and impact in the optical disk industry. *Strategic Management Journal, 22*(4), 287–306.

Rothaermel, F. T., & Deeds, D. L. (2004). Exploration and exploitation alliances in biotechnology: A system of new product development. *Strategic Management Journal, 25*(3), 201–221.

Runco, M. A., & Chand, I. (1995). Cognition and creativity. *Educational Psychology Review, 7*(3), 243–267.

Schraw, G., & Dennison, R. S. (1994). Assessing metacognitive awareness. *Contemporary Educational Psychology, 19*(4), 460–475.

Shepherd, D. A., Covin, J. G., & Kuratko, D. F. (2009). Project failure from corporate entrepreneurship: Managing the grief process. *Journal of Business Venturing, 24*(6), 588–600.

Shepherd, D. A., Haynie, J. M., & Patzelt, H. (2013). Project failures arising from corporate entrepreneurship: Impact of multiple project failures on employee's' accumulated emotions, learning, and motivation. *Journal of Product Innovation Management, 30*(5), 880–895.

Shepherd, D. A., McMullen, J. S., & Jennings, P. D. (2007). The formation of opportunity beliefs: Overcoming ignorance and reducing doubt. *Strategic Entrepreneurship Journal, 1*(1–2), 75–95.

Shepherd, D. A., McMullen, J. S., & Ocasio, W. (2017). Is that an opportunity? An attention model of top managers' opportunity beliefs for strategic action. *Strategic Management Journal, 38*(3), 626–644.

Shepherd, D. A., Patzelt, H., & Wolfe, M. (2011). Moving forward from project failure: Negative emotions, affective commitment, and learning from the experience. *Academy of Management Journal, 54*(6), 1229–1259.

Shepherd, D. A., Patzelt, H., Williams, T. A., & Warnecke, D. (2014). How does project termination impact project team members? Rapid termination, 'creeping death', and learning from failure. *Journal of Management Studies, 51*(4), 513–546.

Siggelkow, N. (2001). Change in the presence of fit: The rise, the fall, and the renaissance of Liz Claiborne. *Academy of Management Journal, 44*(4), 838–857.

Simon, H. A. (2013). *Administrative behavior.* New York: Simon and Schuster.

Sirmon, D. G., Hitt, M. A., & Ireland, R. D. (2007). Managing firm resources in dynamic environments to create value: Looking inside the black box. *Academy of Management Review, 32*(1), 273–292.

Sitkin, S. B. (1992). Learning through failure: The strategy of small losses. *Research in Organizational Behavior, 14,* 231–266.

Starbuck, W. H., & Milliken, F. J. (1988). Challenger: Fine-tuning the odds until something breaks. *Journal of Management Studies, 25*(4), 319–340.

Stevenson, H., & Gumpert, D. (1985). The heart of entrepreneurship. *Harvard Business Review, 63*(2), 85–94.

Sutcliffe, K. M. (1994). What executives notice: Accurate perceptions in top management teams. *Academy of Management Journal, 37*(5), 1360–1378.

Tripsas, M., & Gavetti, G. (2000). Capabilities, cognition, and inertia: Evidence from digital imaging. *Strategic Management Journal, 21*(10), 1147–1161.

Walls, J. L., Berrone, P., & Phan, P. H. (2012). Corporate governance and environmental performance: Is there really a link? *Strategic Management Journal, 33*(8), 885–913.

Wally, S., & Baum, J. R. (1994). Personal and structural determinants of the pace of strategic decision making. *Academy of Management Journal, 37*(4), 932–956.

Walsh, J. P. (1995). Managerial and organizational cognition: Notes from a trip down memory lane. *Organization Science, 6*(3), 280–321.

Whitson, J. A., & Galinsky, A. D. (2008). Lacking control increases illusory pattern perception. *Science, 322*(5898), 115–117.

Wiersema, M. F., & Bantel, K. A. (1992). Top management team demography and corporate strategic change. *Academy of Management Journal, 35*(1), 91–121.

Wyble, B., Folk, C., & Potter, M. C. (2013). Contingent attentional capture by conceptually relevant images. *Journal of Experimental Psychology: Human Perception and Performance, 39*(3), 861.

Wyer, R. S., & Srull, T. K. (Eds.). (1989). *Social intelligence and cognitive assessments of personality* (Vol. 2). London: Lawrence Earlbaum.

Zahra, S. A., & Chaples, S. S. (1993). Blind spots in competitive analysis. *Academy of Management Executive, 7*(2), 7–28.

Zajac, E. J., & Westphal, J. D. (1994). The costs and benefits of managerial incentives and monitoring in large US corporations: When is more not better? *Strategic Management Journal, 15*(S1), 121–142.

Zollo, M., & Winter, S. G. (2002). Deliberate learning and the evolution of dynamic capabilities. *Organization Science, 13*(3), 339–351.

Open Access This chapter is licensed under the terms of the Creative Commons Attribution 4.0 International License (http://creativecommons.org/licenses/by/4.0/), which permits use, sharing, adaptation, distribution and reproduction in any medium or format, as long as you give appropriate credit to the original author(s) and the source, provide a link to the Creative Commons license and indicate if changes were made.

The images or other third party material in this chapter are included in the chapter's Creative Commons license, unless indicated otherwise in a credit line to the material. If material is not included in the chapter's Creative Commons license and your intended use is not permitted by statutory regulation or exceeds the permitted use, you will need to obtain permission directly from the copyright holder.

CHAPTER 5

Entrepreneurial Identity

Identity refers to the meanings that individuals attach to themselves (Gecas 1982) and is often understood as the answer to the question "Who am I?" (Stryker and Burke 2000). Answering this question allows people to fulfill a basic need to be distinct from others, which is important for psychological (Fromkin and Snyder 1980) and physical (Markus and Kitayama 1991) health. Nevertheless, although the notion that entrepreneurs are different and distinct is a key topic in entrepreneurship studies (e.g., Baker and Nelson 2005; Yli-Renko et al. 2001) and founding and growing a venture may fulfill the psychological need to be unique (Teal and Carroll 1999) and therefore to develop a unique self-identity, doing so may thwart the need to feel belonging (Ashforth and Mael 1989; Tajfel 2010). An unmet need for belonging can lead to feeling isolated (Brewer 1991); this feeling can negatively influence the individual's physical and psychological well-being (Leonardelli and Brewer 2001). In this chapter, we develop a framework for entrepreneurs' dealing with multiple *micro-identities* (Ashforth et al. 2000; Pratt and Forman 2000) and specify entrepreneurs' strategies to achieve an "ideal" balance between belongingness and distinctiveness (Shepherd and Haynie 2009a). We also explore how individuals can lose their work identities and the role of entrepreneurship in identity recovery and reconstruction.

Distinctiveness

As just mentioned, individuals have a psychological need to feel unique and different from others (Brewer and Pickett 1999; Hornsey and Jetten 2004; Cantor et al. 2002). This feeling of uniqueness is the basis for developing a sense of distinction from others that plays a key role in the development and sustenance of identity (Brewer 1991; Fromkin and Snyder 1980).[1] Empirical studies have found that distinguishing oneself from others serves as the foundation for the construction of a unique identity (Teal and Carroll 1999). Moreover, a perceived *lack* of distinctiveness appears to prompt people to behave in ways that differentiate themselves from referent groups (Tajfel and Turner 1979a, b). This differentiation in turn helps them more clearly define their identities (Turner 1987). As an example, Vignoles et al. (2000) emphasized studies illustrating the prominence of distinctiveness at the identity level, arguing that (1) individuals can memorize information more effectively if it helps them to illustrate how they are different from others (Leyens et al. 1997), (2) groups are seen as being more diverse if the evaluator belongs to the group (Brewer 1993; Park and Rothbart 1982), (3) feelings of intense similarity to other individuals are linked to negative emotions (Fromkin and Snyder 1980), (4) individuals feel a greater sense of identification with groups that are distinct (Brewer and Pickett 1999), and (5) individuals tend to view themselves as less like others than others are to themselves (Codol 1984, 1987).

While the search for distinctiveness has been linked to the motivation to enhance one's self-esteem (Abrams and Hogg 1988), theoretical work (Brewer 1991) and empirical studies (Brewer et al. 1993; Vignoles et al. 2000) have shown that the need for distinctiveness is a "universal human motive" (Brewer and Pickett 1999) enabling self-definition or comparative appraisal of people's identity (Brewer 1991: 478) and that it is separate from self-esteem (Brewer 1991). Thus, we suggest that distinctiveness plays a central role in developing a meaningful sense of an entrepreneurial identity and therefore a notion of who one is as an individual (Vignoles et al. 2000).

Belonging

While people pursue distinctiveness, theory has suggested that doing so could come at the expense of fulfilling the need to belong (Baumeister and Leary 1995; Brewer 1991). According to Baumeister and Leary, the need to belong is a "powerful, fundamental, and extremely pervasive motivation" (1995: 1). The majority of work on social identity has centered on the advantages of inclusiveness—namely, to be a member of a relevant in-group. Being a member of a group meets the need to belong and is embodied in a desire to develop and preserve long-lasting attachments to other people (Baumeister and Leary 1995). While a number of perspectives have described the benefits of inclusion within a group, the most prominent perspectives have been social identity theory (Tajfel and Turner 1979a, b, 1986) and self-categorization theory (Oakes et al. 1994).

Social identity theory (Tajfel and Turner 1979a, b, 1986) proposes that people are motivated to interpret groups they are a member of favorably as a way to improve their own feelings of self-worth. In addition, work has shown that with more identification with an out-group (i.e., a group that is distinct from the mainstream), his or her perceptions of the mainstream group become more negative (Gramzow and Gaertner 2005). A great deal of work has shown that people often go to extremes to employ group membership in such a manner. Many psychologists, for instance, see the 1999 tragedy at Columbine High School—where two marginalized, outcast students fired on others in their class—as a powerful (even though rare) example of the potential mental consequences stemming from feelings of isolation, rejection, and not belonging. In line with social identity theory, self-categorization theory argues that the pervasiveness of an individual's social identity depends on his or her comparison with others. Indeed, research on self-categorization theory has shown that the importance of a person's social identity emerges from the specific comparisons with others in a social environment (Oakes et al. 1994).

Ultimately, there is substantial evidence showing that people have a strong need to belong and that they behave in a way that this need becomes satisfied. The feeling of belonging appears to be a strong human driver (Baumeister and Leary 1995). Said differently, individuals generate positive emotions from enhanced belongingness (McAdams and Bryant 1987; McAdams 1985) and negative emotions from reduced belongingness (Leary 1990). These negative emotions have been associated with loneliness and anxiety (Tice and Baumeister 1990)—negative emotions that can diminish one's physical and psychological health.

The studies discussed above stress a potential tradeoff in fulfilling psychological needs related to individuals' self-identity. Scholars argue that maintaining distinctiveness is essential for individuals to develop self-identity, yet feeling a sense of belonging and identifying with social groups are basic human motivations. Thus, for entrepreneurs distinctiveness appears to reduce belongingness and vice versa (Brewer 1991: 478). We will challenge this notion later.

OPTIMAL DISTINCTIVENESS THEORY

Optimal distinctiveness theory argues that people want to be affiliated with groups that enable them to optimally balance their belongingness need and the distinctiveness need (Brewer 1991, 1993). Studies have proposed an inverted U-shaped association between distinctiveness and its advantages (Brewer and Pickett 1999; Brewer and Weber 1994). These studies have argued that this association is caused by the conflict between the need for "differentiation of the self from others" and a need for "inclusion of the self into larger social collectives," which counteract each other (Brewer 1993: 3; Vignoles et al. 2000: 339). Optimal distinctiveness theory is in line with Fromkin and Snyder's (1980) theories of uniqueness. Fromkin and Snyder suggested that a moderate level of distinctiveness is the most acceptable and that both very high and very low levels of distinctiveness are the worst for the individual. Optimal distinctiveness theory, created by Brewer (1991), has been "restricted to the discussion of distinctiveness at the level of the group membership." Extending this notion, Brewer and Gardner (1996) applied the same logic to self-representation at the individual and interpersonal levels. This application proposes that the conflicting assimilation and differentiation needs become manifest at the level of the individual in terms of similarity and uniqueness (Vignoles et al. 2000: 340).

THE IDENTITY DISTINCTIVENESS OF ENTREPRENEURIAL INDIVIDUALS

An entrepreneurial role generally enables people to meet their distinctiveness need in ways that are in line with the theoretical and empirical findings discussed above. This role provides people with autonomy (e.g. Akande 1994; Boyd and Gumpert 1983; Kuratko and Hodgetts 1995) that enables them to have more influence in their venture's development and, more generally, more control over their lives (Kolvereid 1996; Longenecker et al. 1988). Entrepreneurs can situate their ventures in relation to other ventures (and maybe even other entrepreneurs) in a way that maximizes distinctiveness (Guth and Ginsberg 1991; Lumpkin and

Dess 1996; Naman and Slevin 1993), and they can build hurdles to imitation that help uphold their own and their venture's distinctiveness (Yip 1982). Although a conventional strategy view would see such behavior as competitive maneuvering and the attempt to enhance one's position in the market, social identity theory suggests that these behaviors also differentiate entrepreneurs from a potential "out-group." This differentiation increases entrepreneurs' notion of the self as being something that is different and unique (Teal and Carroll 1999).

Moreover, compared to more traditional careers, the "freedom" associated with an entrepreneurial role provides a great deal of control over and feedback for the advancement of one's self-identity. In other words, the distinctiveness characteristic of the entrepreneurial process, together with the array of actions and behaviors individuals undertake to meet entrepreneurial ends (e.g., creating a new venture, exploiting a new opportunity), offers these people a range of possibilities to distinguish themselves from other people. Narratives of new venture founders illustrated that some people see "the enterprise in terms of personal growth or fulfillment." Such people believe that "life would not have been complete without proving one had the ability to successfully start a business" (Bruno et al. 1992: 297). In addition, Cova and Svanfeldt (1993) contended that some business founders "create a product that flows from their own internal desires and needs. They create primarily to express subjective conceptions of beauty, emotion, or some aesthetic ideal" (297). Overall, entrepreneurs appear to have substantial opportunities to undertake differentiation activities that align well with their desire to fulfill their need for a unique notion of self.

Scholars have been particularly interested in what makes entrepreneurs distinct from other individuals. Teachers of entrepreneurship classes tend to center their instruction on teaching students to "think outside the box" or to "color outside the lines" since most believe these actions will lead to success in the entrepreneurial context. Researchers explore how entrepreneurs are different from others in terms of their knowledge (Shane 2000), personality (Korunka et al. 2003), motivation (Naffziger et al. 1994), and cognition (Busenitz and Barney 1997). Given our interest in difference as being essential to entrepreneurial behavior and action (and constituting the basis for entrepreneurs' fulfillment of their distinctiveness needs), it is crucial to concurrently think about existing studies suggesting that when individuals distinguish themselves as entrepreneurs, they may not be fulfilling their belongingness needs. In turn, these unmet feelings for belongingness can ultimately diminish individuals' psychological health.

For instance, some evidence has suggested that founders often put relationships within their personal environment including their family at risk (Ufuk and Ozgen 2001) and tend to feel isolated (Hannafey 2003), lonely (Akande 1994; Gumpert and Boyd 1984) and chronically stressed (Akande 1994). Research has shown that these types of feelings result in increased problems for one's physical well-being (Buttner 1992; Ufuk and Ozgen 2001), psychological well-being (Jamal and Badawi 1995; Naughton 1987; Eden 1975), and satisfaction at work (Buttner 1992; c.f. Naughton 1987). Gumpert and Boyd (1984), for instance, reported that a little more than half of 210 small business owner-managers explained that they "frequently feel a sense of loneliness" and experienced higher stress. The authors attributed the feelings of being lonely to the specific role of entrepreneurs. For instance, many of these individuals responded that they did not have a confidant with whom they could share their major worries, that the intense time requirements associated with business foundation and management isolated them from other people, and that "there's this distance you have to maintain as [owner] manager" (Gumpert and Boyd 1984: 20).

These empirical findings and anecdotes illustrate the possible dark side of entrepreneurship. Yet, founders may vary in the extent to which they experience the dark side. For example, many new ventures are started by an entrepreneurial team (Ucbasaran et al. 2003; Breugst et al. 2015; Breugst and Shepherd 2017; Klotz et al. 2014). Members of this founding team unite to make shared decisions to reach collective venture goals (West 2007) and form team spirit (Lechler 2001). Thus, team members may help fulfill entrepreneurs' belongingness needs and reduce the dark side of entrepreneurship.

Even within entrepreneurial teams, however, one individual typically emerges as the "lead entrepreneur" (Ensley et al. 2000). This structure is often necessary because without some kind of formalizing responsibilities and roles as well as putting someone in charge, the success of a venture is likely to decline (Sine et al. 2006; Stinchcombe 1965). Increased formalization structurally differentiates the lead entrepreneur from other founding team members, which can sometimes lead to conflict and negative interactions between the team's members (Stinchcombe 1965). For instance, Boyd and Gumpert (1983) showed that more than two-thirds of founders who started a venture with partners eventually dissolved their founder teams. Regardless of the distinct role of the lead entrepreneur and potential conflict among team members, founding team members likely satisfy part of the individual entrepreneur's need to belong.

We argue that while an entrepreneurial role may fulfill people's need for distinctiveness, the need for belonging is often left unmet, thus ultimately diminishing psychological health. Thus, entrepreneurs who cannot find the right "balance" between distinctiveness and belonging may experience the dark side of entrepreneurship and the negative effects that result from it (see Kets de Vries 1985). Consider the following as an example:

> When Daniel C. chose to abandon his 20-year career as a corporate executive and acquire a small structural steel company, he assumed that his prime concerns would be financing the venture and marketing his wares. Certainly these have been challenges, but they paled beside the unexpected demon that surfaced in his new life and for which he was totally unprepared. Its name, for a want of a better, is loneliness. Daniel reflects: "I'd never thought about loneliness before because I'd never met it. In corporate life, there was always someone to share ideas with—my boss or another colleague. They knew what I was saying because they had been there. . . . Now it seems I have no one. Sure, there is an association of structural steel people, but they are my competition. I learned early on that pricing talk is resolutely avoided at association meetings, but even if we don't talk about prices, there are tensions between us simply because we're competitors." . . . To his surprise, Daniel realized that his new role aggravated the headaches and the ulcer that were his usual signs of stress. Daniel's feelings and experience are common among small-company owners [Based on a survey of 450 small business CEOs]. (Gumpert and Boyd 1984: 18)

The next section introduces our framework to clarify the association between belonging and distinctiveness when entrepreneurs (try to) manage the borders separating their micro-identities (see Shepherd and Haynie 2009a).

ENTREPRENEURS' OPTIMAL DISTINCTIVENESS AND PSYCHOLOGICAL HEALTH

Research usually view people as psychologically healthy when their life is "congruent or meshing with deeply held values that are holistically or fully engaged" (Ryan and Deci 2001: 146). Specifically, optimal distinctiveness theory proposes that medium levels of distinctiveness lead to psychological health. The association is illustrated in Fig. 5.1, where the Y-axis represents

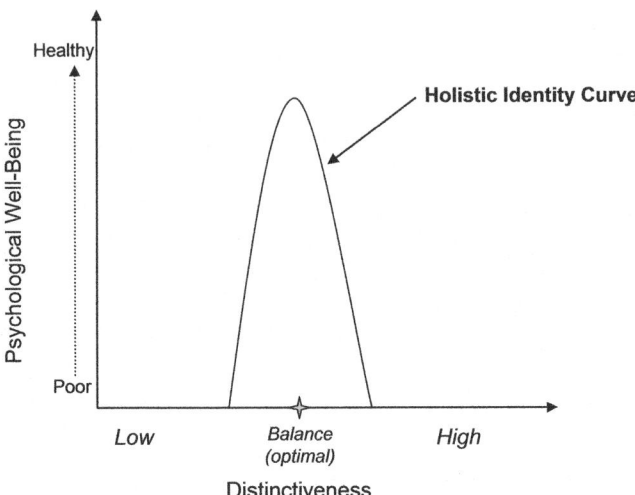

Fig. 5.1 Optimal distinctiveness for an entrepreneuring individual's identity

psychological well-being, the X-axis represents the distinctiveness level, and the curve represents the individual's psychological well-being at different distinctiveness levels. As the figure shows, at low distinctiveness levels (far left), a specific identity offers minimal distinctiveness, so the person shows low psychological well-being. His or her psychological well-being improves with growing distinctiveness until an optimum is reached. After that point, further growing distinctiveness (going right on the X-axis) leads to decreased well-being (due to lower belongingness levels). The upper point of the inverted-U curve signifies this optimum for a particular person and represents the point at which belonging and distinctiveness are well-balanced and there are maximum levels of psychological well-being and health.

For entrepreneurs, the question then becomes whether they can "reshape" their psychological well-being curve to lessen the tradeoff between belonging and distinctiveness. By lessening this tradeoff, entrepreneurs may be able to counteract the implications stemming from the dark side of their entrepreneurial career. To begin to address this issue, my (Dean) colleague and I (Shepherd and Haynie 2009a) integrated the notion of "balance" from optimal distinctiveness theory with studies proposing that people can manage several micro-identities (Ashforth et al. 2000; Pratt and Foreman 2000). Based on this integration, we created a framework to

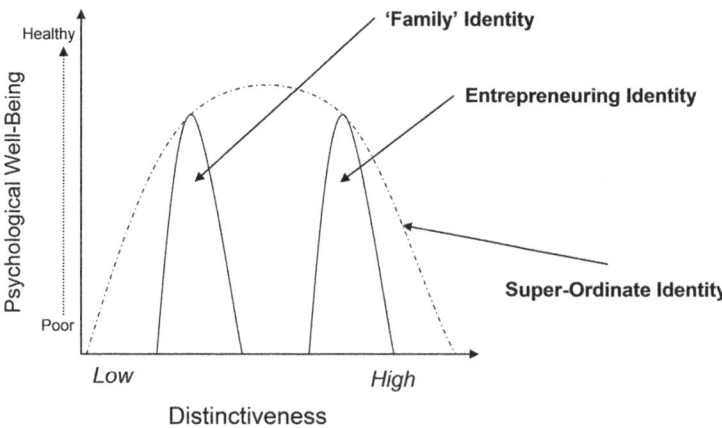

Fig. 5.2 Micro-identities and the 'super-ordinate' identity

understand how entrepreneurs can optimally balance belonging and being distinct and at the same time pursue the highly distinctive role identity associated with being a founder. We argued that through the maintenance and management of various micro-identities, entrepreneurs can develop a *super-ordinate identity* curve. This super-ordinate identity is a holistic representation of a founder's various micro-identities. Some micro-identities may be associated with belonging and others with distinctiveness, which can help mitigate the tradeoff between the two (Shepherd and Haynie 2009a). This relationship is shown in Fig. 5.2.

Entrepreneurs' micro-identities can be defined by the degree to which they maintain multiple *role* identities (Greenhaus and Powell 2006). Overall, the number of micro-identities a particular person maintains depends on the number of role identities that he or she incorporates when constructing an overall self-identity (the super-ordinate identity curve). While an entrepreneurial identity is itself likely formed from various micro-identities, this added complexity is unnecessary for model development.

Individuals define their identities by the peripheral and central traits characteristic of a specific role (Ashforth et al. 2000: 475). A person may define his or her "entrepreneurial identity" as encompassing a set of central (e.g., strategic orientation, commitment to opportunity, control of resources [Brown et al. 2001]) and peripheral attributes, which together form this person's entrepreneurial identity.[2] This same person may also see his or her "parent" role identity as encompassing a set of central (e.g., role model, protector) and peripheral (e.g., repair person, kids' taxi, etc.) traits, which in sum form the parenthood role identity. All micro-identities have their own curve describing the distinctiveness- well-being relationship, with the maximum of the inverted-U curve representing the best balancing of distinctiveness and belonging with respect to the particular micro-identity. The optimal distinctiveness when an individual enacts an entrepreneurial identity differs from the optimal distinctiveness level when that same person enacts other micro-identities. This optimum is also different from an entrepreneur's super-ordinate identity curve (if he or she has more than one micro-identity) as we will outline in more detail below. As an example, the distinctiveness need is more likely to be fulfilled by a person's entrepreneurial identity than by his or her parent identity.

There are boundaries between each of these micro-identities, also known as identity boundaries, or the "physical, temporal, emotional, cognitive, and/or relational limits that define entities [identities] as separate from one another" (Ashforth et al. 2000: 474). An identity boundary may, for example, be defined by a building: once the person enters his or her workplace, that person takes on the identity associated with his or her vocation. Yet, identity boundaries can also be less tangible (e.g., than a building) and more cognitive in nature. Consider a founder who gets a phone call from a business partner while driving. Even though he or she may be heading to the mountains for a weekend getaway, the business call requires an identity transition defined by the person's entrepreneur micro-identity boundary. Although we detail the characteristics that define identity boundaries later, it is important to note here that entrepreneurs who maintain only one identity aligning to their ventures are likely less psychologically healthy than entrepreneurs who additionally maintain micro-identities related to belongingness.

Entrepreneurs likely differ in the number of micro-identities they have, and these micro-identities are fairly invariant over time. There is also likely to be variance in the weight entrepreneurs assign to their distinct micro-identities (as they are a part of one's holistic self-identity) in terms of meeting their personal distinctiveness and belongingness needs. For example, a founder may have various micro-identities that indicate belongingness—such as being a family member, sports team member, or church goer—but may only try to fulfill the need for belonging through one (or a few) of those micro-identities (Oswald and Suter 2004; Stewart 2003).

Entrepreneurs' choice of strategies for managing identities will influence the degree to which various micro-identities channel both distinctiveness and belongingness (and therefore improved psychological health). An identity-management strategy's effectiveness hinges on how one's various micro-identities are separated and interact. However, the challenges associated with managing identity (so as to maximize psychological well-being) lie in effectively transitioning between micro-identities—namely, switching from one identity to another so one can "psychologically (and where relevant, physically) exit one role and enter another" (Ashforth et al. 2000: 477). The idea of transitioning between identity boundaries is often viewed as a psychological transaction cost (see Ortona and Scacciati 1992). High psychological costs of leaving one identity and entering another lead to higher costs to one's psychological well-being. Two micro-identity-management strategies—compartmentalization and integration—have implications for a person's psychological well-being via an individual's distinct entrepreneurial identity.

COMPARTMENTALIZATION AND INTEGRATION AS STRATEGIES FOR MICRO-IDENTITY MANAGEMENT

Compartmentalization is a strategy used to maintain an identity that indicates distinctiveness (i.e., their entrepreneurial identity) and one that indicates belonging, choosing between the micro-identities at various times and in multiple situations (Shepherd and Haynie 2009a). Entrepreneurs using a compartmentalization strategy rarely switch between micro-identities in order to manage boundaries, specifically to reduce the boundary transition costs. For instance, a founder may also be a father or mother, thus having a parenting identity that addresses his or her need for belonging (Oswald and Suter 2004). Using a strategy of compartmentalization to manage his or her micro-identities, this entrepreneur *separates* his or her entrepreneurial role from non-work roles by taking on one identity after the other through intermittent transitions. With this approach, the individual is able to internalize his or her micro-identity as an entrepreneur while at work and then switch to other identities (e.g., father/mother, friend, athlete, etc.) when outside work.

A compartmentalization strategy does not alter the shape of the curve of the entrepreneurial identity; rather, it adds an additional curve representing the entrepreneur's non-work micro-identity. In the example, we use two

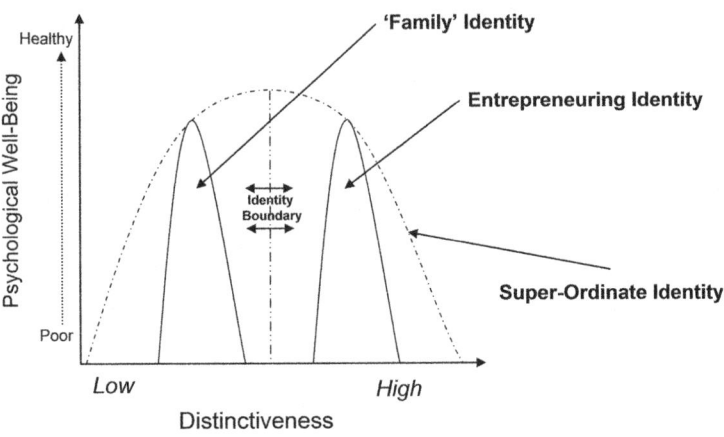

Fig. 5.3 Compartmentalization of micro-identities

curves representing two identities (refer to Fig. 5.3 (Shepherd and Haynie 2009a)). On the far right is the entrepreneurial identity curve, which confers distinctiveness while the person participates in founding activities. On the left is the non-work curve, which confers belonging while he or she participates in activities not associated with work. Compartmentalizing various micro-identities allows one to develop a super-ordinate identity that maximizes his or her psychological well-being by fulfilling his or her distinctiveness needs (through the entrepreneurial identity) and his or her belongingness needs (e.g., through the identity as a father or mother, sports team member, etc.).

Yet, managing identity with the goal of reducing identity conflict through compartmentalization may be challenging for many entrepreneurs. A large research stream has focused on exploring identity conflict, particularly work-family conflict (Lobel 1991). This work has argued that efforts to maintain separate identities using compartmentalization may not work (Lobel 1991). Greenhaus and Beutell (1985), for instance, uncovered three theoretical types of conflict between work roles and family roles: (1) time-based conflict, which occurs when the amount of time needed for the identity as an entrepreneur and the identity as a father or mother is extreme or conflicting (e.g., the individual is required to be in two places at the same time); (2) strain-based conflict, which occurs when the strain (e.g., fatigue or illnesses) caused by the stresses of one role makes it harder to adequately execute the other role; and (3) behavior-based conflict, which occurs when the behavior required is different between identities. For instance, the strain associated with the uncertainty of founding activities may make it challenging for an individual to successfully immerse him- or herself in the father/mother identity.

While compartmentalization is at one end of the identity-management strategies continuum, *integration* is at the other end. Integration is a strategy entrepreneurs use to manage multiple micro-identities and in doing so lessen the tradeoff between addressing the needs to be distinct and to belong by *uniting* the identity-conferring distinctiveness and an identity-conferring belonging. With this strategy, both identities can be enacted (almost) *simultaneously* through transitioning frequently. Integration is an effort to combine identities into "a single, all-purpose mentality, one way of being, one amorphous self" (Nippert-Eng 1996: 568). A straightforward example of an integrated identity can be found in a family firm. In a family business, the roles characterized by one's micro-identities—which are very prominent in the strategy of compartmentalization—are in essence merged together when one utilizes an integration strategy. The goal of integration is to overcome the conflicting demands associated with multiple micro-identities by enacting various identities at the same time or by quickly switching between them. In Fig. 5.4, my (Dean) colleague and I (Shepherd and Haynie 2009a) illustrate this strategy, with two different identities being replaced by one identity.

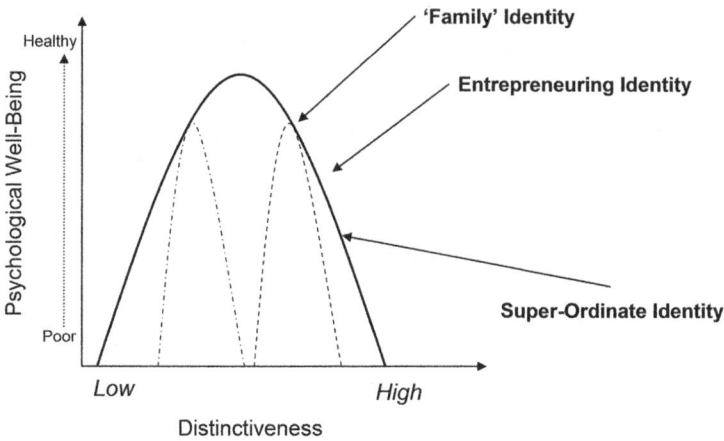

Fig. 5.4 Integration of micro-identities

Similar to compartmentalization, entrepreneurs may have a hard time employing integration strategies to manage several identities. Attempts to lessen separation between micro-identities may lead to unforeseen interruptions of one micro-identity because of another. Such interactions can be a way to minimize the tradeoff between being distinct and belonging; however, they may also be a source of distraction. Further, these distractions may occur without warning (Hall 2002), leading to an interruption of the individual's immersion in a particular identity. For instance, a friend's phone call can interrupt one's immersion in his or her entrepreneurial micro-identity, and a call from a coworker can interrupt one's immersion in an interaction with friends. In each of these instances, the entrepreneur may have decreased psychological well-being due to feelings that neither the need for distinction nor the need for belonging is being adequately fulfilled as well as bewilderment and worry about which identity is the one that is most important (Ashforth et al. 2000). With compartmentalization strategies, where individuals maintain their separate identities, these types of interruptions are unlikely.

With the above descriptions of compartmentalization and integration strategies, it is critical to note that we are not suggesting that the extreme form of such a strategy is usual or suitable. We just propose that these strategies are endpoints on a continuum on which people allocate themselves as either following more compartmentalization or more integration when managing multiple micro-identities. Moreover, because of the different benefits and costs for compartmentalization and integration, it is likely that entrepreneurs differ in their evaluations for strategies to manage identities based on fulfilling their personal distinctiveness and belongingness needs. Indeed, individuals may have power over the degree to which they pursue strategies for being distinctive and/or to belong. Researchers usually assert that enacting an entrepreneur identity will more likely meet one's need for distinctiveness, whereas enacting other "collective" micro-identities will more likely meet one's belonging need. Some individuals will favor more compartmentalization (i.e., they prefer the benefits of compartmentalization more than those of integration or may be better positioned to handle the challenges associated with compartmentalization), whereas some individuals may favor higher integration for similar reasons. My (Dean) colleague and I (Shepherd and Haynie 2009a) argued that despite entrepreneurs' preference for either compartmentalization or integration, they all usually want to (1) fulfill their needs for being distinct and to belong, (2) reduce issues in identity transition related to "the effort required to become psychologically and physically disengaged from one identity and re-engaged in another identity" (adapted from Ashforth et al. 2000: 473), and (3) lessen the occurrence and scale of identity conflict.

To apply this idea of compartmentalization and integration to entrepreneurs as they attempt to balance distinctiveness and belonging, we now explore how boundaries and synergies between identities influence the degree to which compartmentalization and integration are suitable strategies for balancing entrepreneurs' needs to be distinct and to belong. We form our theorizing based on the idea that boundaries and potential synergies between micro-identities constitute strategic constraints, which is in line with the socially constructed nature of identities (Ashforth et al. 2000). Following this line of arguments, identity is not exclusively controlled by a person; rather, the individual "takes" the role characteristics that other people "offer" (Katz and Kahn 1978). Yet, our arguments do not depend on this assumption but instead imply that, for instance, entrepreneurs can strengthen or weaken identity boundaries. In other words, identities can be the outcome of negotiation (Swann 1987) wherein social reality not only shapes people (Turner 1987) but individuals also influence social reality (McNulty and Swann 1994). For instance, people utilize things like impression management and partner choice to bring others to view them as they view themselves (Swann 2005).

IDENTITY BOUNDARIES, IDENTITY SYNERGIES, AND MANAGEMENT STRATEGY

Above, we outlined a continuum of strategies for managing identities by explaining the anchors of that continuum—compartmentalization and integration. The key question becomes why would (or should) an individual choose any strategy (more compartmentalized vs. more integrated) as the more suitable way to balance distinctiveness and belonging. We suggest that the success of an entrepreneur's chosen strategy in terms of maximizing well-being is dependent on the dual consideration of potential synergies between micro-identities that are in conflict (possible benefits from identity transitions). Moreover, this success also depends on the characteristic of the identities' boundaries (costs associated with identity transitions). Figure 5.5 develops and illustrates this model (Shepherd and Haynie 2009a).

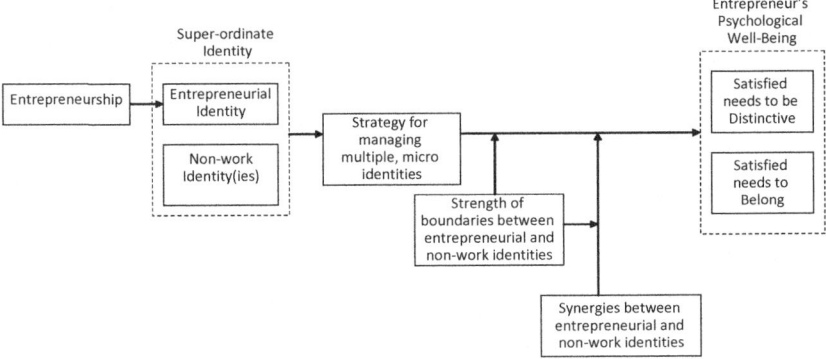

Fig. 5.5 Managing entrepreneurs' multiple micro-identities to maximize PWB

Specifically, identity synergy denotes the degree of relatedness among identities, with higher levels of convergence between identities resulting in a higher likelihood that each identity will improve the success of the other. As an example, Pratt and Foreman (2000) described a person with strong religious beliefs (a strong micro-identity related to one's role in the church) deciding to work for a religious organization, thereby serving to "align one's religious and work-related identities" (Pratt and Foreman 2000: 23). Another example could be a family firm in which one's "family" micro-identity (a key element of which is being a "provider") aligns with managing the firm to feed the family. Identity synergy occurs in the case that one identity improves the outcomes of a different identity—for instance, the family identity increases the founder identity's ability to fulfill the distinctiveness need and/or the founder identity increases the family identity's ability to meet the belongingness need. For instance, identity synergy outside the family firm context is the case of Phil Knight, the founder of Nike. His identity as a University of Oregon track team member in the early 1960s combined with the desire to uphold his identity as a running community member after graduation motivated him to develop a groundbreaking running shoe. Not only did Knight's founder identity confer and fulfill his need for distinctiveness, it also furthered his identification with the running community, thus enabling him to maintain an identity that fulfilled his belongingness needs, with each identity ultimately improving the other identity's performance.

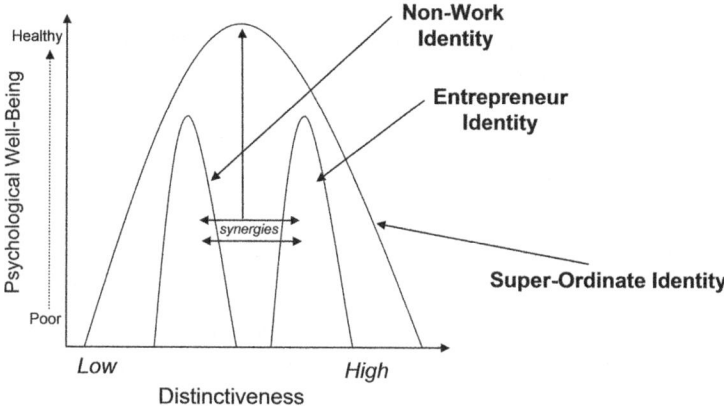

Fig. 5.6 Optimal distinctiveness and psychological well-being

The way my colleague and I (Shepherd and Haynie 2009a) conceptualized synergies' role regarding conflicting micro-identities is equivalent to how organization scholars describe the relationship between people, groups, and performance. This stream of research has shown that when synergies exist between members of a specific group, the group's overall performance will exceed the sum of each group member's individual performances (Watson et al. 1991). Along these same lines, we propose that at the micro-identity level, synergies between identities *both* "broaden" and "raise" the super-ordinate identity curve. That is, when there are synergies between an individual's micro-identities, the benefits for the founder's holistic identity are greater than the sum of each identity's benefits. The benefits in this case are improved psychological well-being due to fulfilling both the distinctiveness and belongingness needs. We illustrate this idea in Fig. 5.6.

Next, we characterize the boundaries defining entrepreneurs' micro-identities as being either strong or weak. When boundaries are strong they are impermeable and inflexible whereas weak boundaries are permeable and flexible. This boundary flexibility denotes the degree to which one's identities are associated with distinct contexts or situations. Boundary permeability describes how vulnerable a boundary is being interrupted and distracted, which makes it necessary that the individual transitions between identities. Impermeable boundaries permit only few intrusions into a specific identity from a different identity's roles and activities, whereas permeable boundaries are more vulnerable to intrusions. Inflexible boundaries that are rigid serve for the definition of a particular micro-identity in terms of its identity-specific features, such as working hours, places, interactions, and even personality traits. For instance, an entrepreneurial identity tied to having to be in the office from 7:00 a.m. to 6:00 p.m. is an inflexible boundary. Boundaries that are flexible, on the other hand, are characterized by transitions between competing micro-identities that are not well-defined and nuanced. With flexible boundaries, conflicting micro-identities are indistinct.

Integrating these notions of synergy and boundary into strategies for compartmentalizing and integrating identities helps form a framework of specific conditions that we can use to explore a particular strategy for entrepreneurs attempting to balance their needs for identity distinctiveness and belonging. My (Dean) colleague (Shepherd and Haynie 2009a) and I dichotomize the continuous variables of this model in Fig. 5.7 for illustrative purposes.

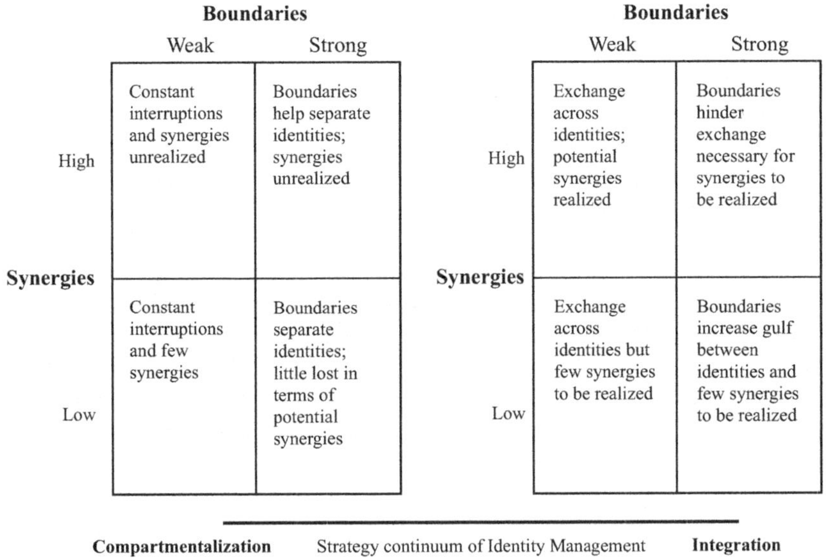

	Boundaries			Boundaries	
Synergies	Weak	Strong	Synergies	Weak	Strong
High	Constant interruptions and synergies unrealized	Boundaries help separate identities; synergies unrealized	High	Exchange across identities; potential synergies realized	Boundaries hinder exchange necessary for synergies to be realized
Low	Constant interruptions and few synergies	Boundaries separate identities; little lost in terms of potential synergies	Low	Exchange across identities but few synergies to be realized	Boundaries increase gulf between identities and few synergies to be realized

Compartmentalization   Strategy continuum of Identity Management   Integration

Fig. 5.7 Managing multiple identities

Compartmentalization of Micro-Identities

The most effective compartmentalization strategies have strong boundaries. Strong boundaries help entrepreneurs keep their identities as entrepreneurs and identities that are not related to work distinct. In other words, interruptions from one identity to another are minimal. These rare transitions between identities enable the individual to balance his or her distinctiveness and belonging needs. For instance, moving from a family identity to a founder identity at the beginning of a day fulfills a founder's need for distinctiveness, and the transition from a founder identity to that of an athlete at the end of the day fulfills his or her need to belong. Yet, trying to maintain separate identities with deliberately infrequent transitions using a compartmentalization strategy makes it challenging to establish synergies. That is, two identities need to integrate for the effective realization of synergies (Allred et al. 2005; Schweiger and Goulet 2005), so realizing potential synergies hinges on the degree to which identities interact and are coordinated (Larsson and Finkelstein 1999). Therefore, entrepreneurs who utilize compartmentalization to manage multiple micro-identities have increased psychological well-being in the case of strong boundaries between identities but have decreased psychological well-being when there are weak boundaries (Shepherd and Haynie 2009a).

Integrating Micro-Identities

Entrepreneurs use integration strategies to mitigate the tradeoff between distinctiveness and belonging by uniting their entrepreneur identity related to being distinct with their identity related to belonging such that they can enact both identities at the same time (or almost at the same time) through frequent transitions. As mentioned earlier, the benefit of this type of strategy is realizing potential identity synergies. However, for one to benefit from potential synergies using an integration strategy, there have to be weak identity boundaries. For instance, there is often a blurred line between "market" and "home" in many family firms because the family and the firm are intimately entwined (Hamilton 2006). Weak boundaries lessen the challenges and psychological efforts of moving between identities, which is a prerequisite to capitalize on synergies. With growing boundary strength, however, the gulf between one's identities is wider, thus necessitating more effort for bridging the gulf. This increased effort enhances the psychological costs that come with frequent identity transitions. As such, with increasing boundary strength, possible synergistic benefits will become weaker or less likely to materialize. We therefore argue that when boundaries are inflexible and impermeable, it becomes more challenging—if not entirely impossible—for an individual drawing on a strategy of integration to capture the advantages of possible synergies between a distinct identity and other identities and fulfill their need to belong. However, even when boundaries are flexible and permeable and synergies do not develop, the entrepreneur must deal with the costs associated with weak boundaries. These costs can include identity conflict resulting from blurred identity boundaries such that one identity's (e.g., the entrepreneurial identity's) roles and responsibilities spill over into another identity and vice versa (Williams and Alliger 1994) without the synergistic benefits.

Consider, for example, the integration of one's founder and parental identities at a single table that at the same time represents (or frequently transitions between being) a kitchen table (parental identity) and a boardroom table (founder identity). The weakness of the boundaries improves the integration strategy's effectiveness at managing these founder and family-related identities to balance distinctiveness and belonging. Despite Friedman's (1991) argument that family firm interests are in most cases not in full alignment (1991), some founders' non-entrepreneurial identities can improve their role as entrepreneur. For instance, Stewart (2003: 387) highlighted the crucial role of family kinship in improving entrepreneurial activities: "relatives provide a diffuse, long term source of social support that underwrites the capacity of entrepreneurs to take short term risks (Mattessich and Hill 1976)." It could be that the feeling of belonging resulting from a family identity could enhance one's entrepreneurial role by increasing the distinctiveness of the identity. Research has also highlighted some examples of synergies in which the role of entrepreneur bolsters individuals' feelings of belonging. For instance, work in a family firm could help strengthen one's marriage (Wicker and Burley 1991).

Thus, synergies can raise the psychological well-being curve more than would occur if the effects of the two micro-identities were simply added together. However, for this to happen, there has to be potential for realizing synergies due to a boundary between two micro-identities that is characterized by permeability and flexibility and a strategy to achieve integration. Configurations that involve psychological integration will not be able to yield the same fit and thus will not result in similar psychological well-being advantages. While compartmentalization can lead to a suitable "fit" in the case of boundaries with little permeability and the lack of synergies, this "best" configuration of compartmentalization improves well-being to a lesser extent than the "best" configuration of integration as the latter can harness potential synergies. Therefore, with high identity synergy potential, individuals who use integration to manage multiple micro-identities likely have higher psychological well-being when identity boundaries are weaker than when they are stronger (Shepherd and Haynie 2009a). Moreover, in case there are higher levels of synergies and weaker boundaries, entrepreneurs with greater identity integration have higher well-being than would result from any other blend of strategy, boundary strength, and synergy level (Shepherd and Haynie 2009a).

Work Roles, Organizational Identification, and Disjunctive Transitions

As discussed previously, one's vocation is central to his or her identity. In other words, individuals' answer to the question "Who Am I?" often centers on a work role: I am a teacher, a doctor, an architect, a marine, and so on. Scholars have tended to investigate the relationship between identity and career in terms of occupational socialization (Nicholson 1984), role transitions (Nicholson 1984), and the processes underlying the identity conflict and change that stems from such transitions (Ashforth 2001; Ashforth et al. 2000; Ashforth and Mael 1989). This stream of research has two common cases: a relatively stable identity conflicting with changing role expectations (Swann 1987, 2005) and an evolving notion of the self conflicting with fixed role expectations (Snyder and Swann 1978; Stryker 1987). Both cases begin an incremental identity-change process that unfolds over time and is usually presumed to be path dependent—that is, future work roles are generally presumed to be explicitly "related" to one's prior career roles (Rosenbaum 1979). Additionally, although we know that vocational identity change is a path-dependent process, there is a dearth of research on identity change in response to events that almost immediately "strip" a person of his or her closely held and valued vocational identity, thus breaking his or her career path (e.g., entrepreneurial failure). Vocational identity can be defined in terms of both work role—"a set of expectations about behavior, attitudes, and values associated with a specified position (Schlenker and Gutek 1987: 287; Stryker 1968; Cantor and Mischel 1979)—and organizational identification, "a psychological state wherein the individual perceives himself or herself to be part of a larger whole" (Rousseau 1998: 217; Dutton et al. 1994).

One such career path-breaking event is a trauma. A trauma is a situation in which an individual is "confronted with an event or events that involved actual or threatened death or serious injury, or a threat to the physical integrity of self or others" and "the person's response involved intense fear, helplessness, or horror" (APA 1994). Traumatic events can destroy individuals' fundamental beliefs that life is benevolent and meaningful and that the self is worthy (Janoff-Bulman 1989). We have a strong understanding of how individuals cope with such events (Benight et al. 1999; Bonanno 2004), but we are only beginning to discover trauma's effects on people's vocational and entrepreneurial identities.

Unfortunately, trauma is a relatively common experience in today's increasingly global organizational environment, which is affected by war, terrorism, and discontinuous organizational change. Investigating the mechanisms underlying the transition to new roles and organizations for people who go through disjunctive transitions like those often necessitated by trauma will enable scholars to more fully understand the degree to which such individuals are able to contribute to their community's and nation's economy (Audretsch 2007).

For instance, my colleague and I (Haynie and Shepherd 2011) explored the nature of vocational identity change initiated by trauma in a sample of US soldiers and marines who were disabled while serving in Iraq and Afghanistan. This was an ideal context for investigation because the connection between identity and vocation is pervasive and purposefully developed by organizations to improve members' organizational identification. Indeed, the sociology and psychology literatures are full of studies describing how the routines, symbols, and artifacts comprising military culture have a powerful and continued influence on military personnel's identity (Budd 2007; Hale 2008; Lande 2007). However, the military essentially "forces" most individuals who are disabled from wartime injuries into career transitions, deeming them unsuitable for continued organizational membership. Individuals in the study reported that their conceptions of the self became detached from their work role and the organization they had initially identified so strongly with in a single point in time—after the gunshot or bomb blast that left them injured. One soldier described this idea: "I know that Sergeant Joshua Smith is not who I am anymore and not who my family or society needs me to be. But I'm not sure who I am now."

The study's sample included ten soldiers and marines who were disabled during combat. After being discharged from the military due to their disability, each enrolled in a vocational retraining program focused on entrepreneurship. The theory developed sheds light on the thoughts, emotions, and behaviors characterizing individuals who have adjusted well after a trauma—namely, those who have relatively high subjective well-being and have made progress toward achieving new vocational milestones. The study compared these individuals with others who adjusted less well after trauma. Based on the similarities and differences among our cases, there emerged a model explaining how vocational identity change occurs after a traumatic experience.

The First Step: Identity Foundation

Scholars have centered on investigating why—as a response to an identity threat—some people are better at creating and subsequently internalizing a new conception of the self compared to others who find completing this task difficult and/or are slow in doing so. Evidence has shown that these differences are directly related to the process of negotiating and overcoming identity conflict (e.g., Burke 1991, 2003; Ibarra 1999). As discussed earlier, because individuals generally have multiple identities (Ashforth et al. 2000; Pratt and Foreman 2000), identity conflict can occur when one identity's (e.g., parent) behavioral expectations go against another identity's (e.g., business owner) behavioral expectations. Researchers have explored instances when a stable identity conflicts with changing role expectations, for example, career change (Swann 1987, 2005), marriage (Burke 2006), and divorce (Rahav and Baum 2002). Results from these studies point to an incremental identity-change process whereby new behavioral expectations are developed in response to an evolving conception of self. According to Ibarra (1999: 764), "people adapt to new roles by experimenting with provisional selves that serve as trials" for a future identity. Overall, this research stream proposes people who experience identity conflict can alter their focused attention, beliefs, and behaviors to trigger the identity-change process (Snyder and Swann 1978; Stryker 1987) or can alter others' expectations to overcome identity conflict (Swann 1987, 2005). For both approaches, the underlying assumption is that identity conflict automatically and immediately initiates identity negotiation (Burke 1991, 2003). That is, because identity is so important to psychological well-being, resolving identity conflict or ambiguity receives an individual's immediate attention (Burke 1991, 2003; Brewer 1991; Tajfel and Turner 1979a, b).

When identity change is necessitated by trauma, however, the study mentioned above (Haynie and Shepherd 2011) provides some counterevidence to the above assumptions. More specifically, the study found that although some participants in the sample eventually employed identity-building activities to create a new vocational identity during the entrepreneurship training program, the process for doing so was neither automatic nor instantaneous. Individuals who go through traumatic experiences are confronted with challenges that are more urgent than identity conflict as trauma introduces threats that are more detrimental to human existence than threats to identity. Along these lines, the study found that there are generally two stages in the trauma-recovery process. In Stage 1, individuals concentrate on reconstructing their fundamental assumptions about the world and humanity. In Stage 2, they focus on rebuilding a new conception of self based on a socially situated vocational identity standard.

One of the study participants, Aaron, is a good example of this process. Aaron was a marine, and his identity was strongly tied to his work role and organization. Aaron almost died in combat when an explosive went off and pinned him under a vehicle for several hours before he was rescued. Remembering his thoughts not long after his injury, Aaron recounted the following:

> I was a 23 year old cocky Marine. I was fit, tops in the Marine Corps, and then it happened. I was completely helpless, hopeless. I couldn't do anything for myself. As soon as my first injury happened my confidence was gone, and I was shattered, I doubted myself. I didn't care about life anymore. I saw the evil side of humanity, and I didn't need it—I didn't want to live anymore. It was a night and day difference. It's like I was fed up with everything and honestly came to the point where I was suicidal. I came to the point in my life where I didn't care if I lived or died.

In line with the results of trauma, Aaron's experience destroyed his basic assumptions that life is benevolent and meaningful and that he is a worthy person (Janoff-Bulman 1989). After his trauma, Aaron had to reorient himself psychologically by rebuilding those destroyed assumptions before he could engage in any form of identity negotiation or change. For theory building, we refer to this orientation as *identity foundation*: a set of internalized and closely held beliefs and assumptions about the world and humanity that serve as the basis for future actions that will enable the self to realize meaning and purpose. Before constructing this identity foundation, Aaron was unable to develop, form, or negotiate a new vocational identity. Aaron used several coping mechanisms to create a new identity foundation, some of which were problem focused—centered on overcoming the issue causing distress—and some of which were emotion focused, centered on alleviating the negative emotions stemming from the issue (for a distinction, see Folkman and Moskowitz 2004). For instance, he reported how he often overused alcohol and others drugs, and how he slept through large parts of the day. Aaron reported that his alcohol and drug use were a way to "numb myself. I didn't care. I was very reckless. There was a point in my life when I came back, and after I got get out of the hospital, I was just very reckless in my life. It was foolish and stupid—I'd say it was very wrong, but that's just what happened." He also took minor useful steps toward building his new identity foundation. For instance, he began recognizing obstacles hindering him from creating a new basis for meaning and purpose in his life. In one example of such behavior, he described how he realized his friends enabled his dysfunctional behaviors: "Well, they held me back for sure. Just going out and drinking and hanging out and just cutting loose. But with that shit I wasn't going anywhere in life. Just the same stupid stuff." In addition, he started going to professional counseling. Performing these simple coping activities helped Aaron reach a foundational level of psychological subsistence, thus positioning him to begin taking steps toward negotiating a new identity. He had in no way accepted his traumatic experience, but he had adequately oriented himself to begin forming a new identity, which can be seen in the following statement:

> It was a very slow transition. It wasn't like I just woke up one day, and you know I'm going to put all that stuff aside, and I'm going to turn the page and end a chapter in my life. I was unhappy with life, I was unhappy with where I was at, and I knew I was going to do the stuff that I needed to get to where I wanted to go, so I started making changes. . . . I think as humans we all need to have hope. I think that's a purpose for living. I think without a purpose to live, that's self-explanatory. You've got to have a purpose to live.

Studies on trauma (Janoff-Buhlman 1992; Magwaza 1999; Solomon et al. 1997) have argued that recovering from traumatic events involves reconstructing shattered *assumptions of the world* and *of the self* to reestablish psychological balance (Janoff-Buhlman 1992). While my (Dean) colleague and I (Haynie and Shepherd 2011) supported this idea, the findings also showed that the onset of this reconstruction process for each assumption is sequential. More specifically, the analysis across cases showed that the process of rebuilding shattered assumptions of the world to establish an identity foundation starts before rebuilding shattered assumptions of self, thus making this process a *necessary condition* for vocational identity change to occur in a meaningful and positive way.

Trauma, Identity Change, and Entrepreneurial Career Motivations

Expanding on the career literature, past studies have concentrated on entrepreneurship as a career option for particular groups (e.g., individuals with disabilities, women, ethnic minorities, immigrants) that are "shut out" of or face barriers to advancement in "traditional" occupational roles (Kendall et al. 2006). For instance, self-employment often guarantees that individuals with disabilities have the job accommodations they need (Wiklund et al. 2016) as well as more flexibility for other elements of their lives (Arnold and Seekins 2002; Hagner and Davies 2002). Those who are disabled frequently show interest in entrepreneurial careers (Callahan et al. 2002) with higher self-employment rates among people with disabilities than among individuals without disabilities (Arnold and Seekins 2002; U.S. Census 2002). An entrepreneurial career may also help stigmatized inmates who face considerable problems finding salaried employment to earn their living after release from prison (Patzelt et al. 2014).

Therefore, exploring motivations for entrepreneurship among people who have lost their vocational identity due to a trauma will shed light on what factors are important in forming a new vocational identity. Overall, there are two motivations in this context: an entrepreneurial career due to perceived or real barriers to other vocations (push motivation) and an entrepreneurial career due to a desire to fulfill some psychological need (pull motivation).

Sometimes, one is pushed toward entrepreneurship due to physical limitations that he or she believes "shut the door" to certain careers. More interestingly, my (Dean) colleague and I (Haynie and Shepherd 2011) uncovered a second push motivation that manifests itself as a perceived limit to employment based on experiencing trauma, coping with trauma, and undergoing ongoing identity change. The need for autonomy is important in the process of vocational identity change following trauma.

Aaron reported that he felt "helpless and hopeless" after being injured, and he had to depend entirely on others—doctors, nurses, friends, and family—during his physical recovery. Think about how this prolonged period of reliance on others and lack of control likely affected Aaron (and other individual in similar posttrauma situations) psychologically. Aaron and those in a similar position went from being healthy with a strong well-being to being entirely dependent on others for their survival. Another veteran hurt during combat summarized this push motivation toward entrepreneurship as a career option best: "After all this, I've been so dependent on everybody else for everything. I need to feel like I have a say." The career and entrepreneurship literatures have not fully explored this type of push motivation; however, it is likely to help explain why—despite substantial accessibility and accommodation improvements for individuals with disabilities in the workplace over the past decade (Batavia and Schriner 2001)—those who are disabled are more than two times as likely to be self-employed than individuals in the general public (U.S. Census 2002). The desire for autonomy and control after prolonged periods of reliance on others limits these individuals' future vocation options, shutting the door on certain vocational opportunities just like physical limitations do.

In addition to this push motivation, my (Dean) colleague and I (Haynie and Shepherd 2011) uncovered psychological needs that attract these individuals to entrepreneurship as a career. People are often pulled to entrepreneurial careers due to a fundamental need for competence as well as the need to be seen as competent by others. Our participants discussed the appeal of being seen as a person who can make something great from nothing and can provide for employees, and some talked about entrepreneurship as an opportunity to show that they have the capabilities needed to be successful.

More pertinent to trauma-induced identity change are the two pull motivations that seem to differentiate between individuals who are well adjusted (i.e., coping well with their new life outside their previous career) and those who are less well adjusted. These pull motivations include the desire for security and espoused excitement/passion over the emerging vocational identity. Security is a fundamental human need, and for individuals who have not developed an identity foundation, it appears that an entrepreneurial career can fulfill this need (Haynie and Shepherd 2011). Interestingly, while some individuals mentioned they were pulled toward entrepreneurship because of the security it offers, this pull motivation was practically absent among individuals who were well adjusted (Haynie and Shepherd 2011).

Another pull motivation identified was an espoused passion for entrepreneurship and its related aspects. Similar to security, this pull motivation distinguishes between individuals based on how well adjusted they are. Each of the participants who had adjusted well after their traumatic experience noted passion as being a key pull toward entrepreneurship. For well-adjusted individuals, espoused passion for entrepreneurship directs their attention away from the past (i.e., their trauma) *and* away from the present (i.e., barriers created by their disability) such that a future orientation has formed. Instead of having a detailed plan for their life, these individuals' pull motivation enables their new identity to develop; it has not yet been fully determined. This outcome contrasts to the outcomes of less well-adjusted individuals. Individuals who have adjusted less well to their trauma are focused more on the present, and the need for security—namely, their need to find a path that will lead them to tomorrow—is greater than the more abstract idea of an imagined future along a new path. Having no identity foundation, these individuals believe that their futures are more or less pre-determined by the outside factors, that they have no control over it. As a result, individuals who are less well adjusted often continue to feel some hopelessness, believing they are on the same path with insurmountable barriers ahead.

Competence Transference

An additional consideration in this context of trauma and entrepreneurship is the connection between the far and more recent past and the future as it relates to transference of competences—namely, taking the knowledge and competencies one learns in one context and successfully applying them in another context (e.g., entrepreneurship). The career literature frequently talks about cognitions to transfer vocational competences (e.g., knowledge, skills, and abilities) from the past to the present/future (Carless 2005; Edwards 1991; O'Reilly et al. 1991). My (Dean) colleague and I (Haynie and Shepherd 2011) uncovered two types of competence transference in our study. These types differentiated those who adjusted successfully from those who failed to adjust: (1) *career* competence transference, which includes applying the competencies one acquired from a previous to a burgeoning new career, and (2) *coping* competence transference, which includes applying the knowledge, skills, and abilities one developed from coping with a traumatic experience to a burgeoning new career.

For well-adjusted individuals, the data revealed the connections between the past, present, and future related to applying acquired competences to their new emerging career were readily obvious. Aaron, for instance, discussed how he learned to be disciplined in the military, and how this competence was beneficial in entrepreneurship: "And ultimately I think probably the biggest factor is discipline, because I think you have to have discipline to be able to follow through with any of it. Beyond the discipline, if you don't have discipline it's not going to happen. I would just guess that if you look at some of the most successful people, it comes down to discipline." Likewise, other well-adjusted participants had a strong tendency to link the prior skills and knowledge they learned about themselves and others when coping with their trauma to their burgeoning entrepreneurial identity and venture. For example, Aaron said that having to cope with trauma helped him realize his personal strengths: "You know what? All that shit that happened to me I would never take it back; I would never trade it. Not that I could to go through it again, but I am what I am today because of the things that happened before." In addition, my (Dean) colleague and I (Haynie and Shepherd 2011) found that rather than submissively assuming transference, well-adjusted individuals concentrated on the competences they had developed in the past and ways they could utilize those competences in the future. In order to accomplish this transfer, they thought about their prior competences in a more abstract way—namely, more structurally, more generalizably, and more portably.

In contrast, individuals who were less well adjusted (1) felt that they had learned few skills in the military that could help in their new career, suggesting instead that they had a "competence disadvantage" because of their past career experiences; (2) noted fewer skills stemming from coping with their trauma; and (3) concentrated on the surface-level mismatch between their past (in this case, being in the military and coping with trauma) and their future career.

Entrepreneurship as a Means of Identity Play

As discussed above, while people usually value their career and the associated identity, events occasionally result in the termination of that identity altogether (Ebaugh 1988; Latack and Dozier 1986; Latack et al. 1995), thus requiring such people to re-create that part of the self. Recent identity research has investigated identity play as a means to transition to new identities (Ibarra and Petriglieri 2010; Mainemelis and Ronson 2006; Savin-Baden 2010; Schrage 1999; Winnicott 1975) as such play liberates individuals from the constraints of behavioral consistency to explore different notions of a future self (Ibarra and Petriglieri 2010; Mainemelis and Ronson 2006).

Early research on identity play (Ibarra and Petriglieri 2010) has argued that individuals must have access to a quite safe place to experiment with potential identities (Ibarra 2004; Kets de Vries and Korotov 2007). However, an "involuntary career transition, sparked by an unexpected job loss, may not provide sufficient psychological safety to allow for identity play" (Ibarra and Petriglieri 2010: 20). More specifically, individuals who experience work-related losses (e.g., failed entrepreneurs; Shepherd 2003) frequently feel grief—the negative emotional reaction in response to losing something important—and then go through a time of liminality (Ashforth 2001) during which they "struggle to establish a 'new normal' around the changed sense of self" (Conroy and O'Leary-Kelly 2014). Such loss often threatens individuals' sense of self because they generally feel a disconnect between their current and future work identities and then have to "take stock, re-evaluate, revise, re-see, and re-judge" their work identity (Strauss 1997: 102). Although important, transitioning from one work identity to another is usually challenging because one must not only give up an old identity but also create a new one.

Hitting Rock Bottom and Realizing a Lost Identity

Losing a business can make some entrepreneurs believe that their current situation in life is quite negative. This belief often makes the entrepreneur feel that he or she has *hit rock bottom*. Hitting rock bottom refers to a crystallization of discontent based on the development of "associative links among a multitude of unpleasant, unsatisfactory, and otherwise negative features of one's current life situation" (Baumeister 1991: 281–282). The effect of hitting rock bottom is significant, indicating that a threshold was reached that generated "a large mass of negative features" strong enough to "undermine a person's commitment to a role, relationship, or involvement" and that unrelated reservations or negative feelings were insufficient in undermining that commitment (Baumeister 1994: 282).[3] For instance, an entrepreneur may view certain negative events (e.g., missed sales forecasts, supply chain problems) as isolated events that are standard barriers to ultimately reaching success. After the crystallization of discontent, however, the entrepreneur may see these same events as part of a broad failure pattern that comes with his or her entrepreneurial role.

Regardless of efforts to safeguard themselves from the negative feedback associated with their life situations, entrepreneurs may begin to see "bad days turning into bad years," causing them to believe that their future will probably "contain much of the same" (Bauer et al. 2005: 1182). Hitting rock bottom in this way—because one has formed associative connections between the negative features and outcomes of their lives—triggers a number of problems (Baumeister 1994) that ultimately bring negativity to a *climax* such that the individual's commitment to his or her role is changed in a fundamental way. For instance, many people have recounted hitting rock bottom over dissatisfaction with religious groups (Jacobs 1984; Wright 1984), marriage (Vaughan 1990), and criminal behavior (Paternoster and Bushway 2009).

Hitting rock bottom generates an emotional crisis, or an extremely negative state that people want to escape from (Jacobs 1984; Paternoster and Bushway 2009; Vaughan 1990; Wright 1984). When this occurs, the individual will likely see his or her life in a substantially different light, radically changing his or her perspectives on roles, commitments, and relationships that make up his or her life (Baumeister 1994; Maitlis 2009). A failed entrepreneur, for instance, may need to change relationships with certain friend groups (e.g., restrict or eliminate costly activities), alter financial commitments (e.g., sell expensive homes, more to a lower-cost neighborhood), and drop certain community memberships (e.g., country club, etc.), which can dramatically affect his or her everyday life (Newman 1988). On the other hand, individuals are unlikely to hit rock bottom when they lose a job that is not highly valued or can be easily regained/replaced and when losing that job is not seen as highly threatening. In such cases, my (Dean) colleague and I (Shepherd and Williams 2018) theorized that there is no crystallization of discontent that individuals need to escape.

Cognitive Deconstruction and Escaping Identity Loss

Some people face the crystallization of discontent from hitting rock bottom and overcome it through *cognitive deconstruction* (Twenge et al. 2003). More specifically, people may try to get away from the disconnect between their present and future work identities by decreasing their self-awareness and meaningful thought—that is, they can put themselves in a numb state (Dixon and Baumeister 1991). Similarly, cognitive deconstruction after hitting rock bottom is a state with no emotions (Pennebaker 1989; Twenge et al. 2003) because people actively evade their emotions (Baumeister 1990; Stillman et al. 2009), and it removes meaning from awareness as well as "blots out threatening implications . . . it is a refusal of insight and a denial of implications or contexts" (Baumeister 1990: 92). A cognitive deconstructive state is different from the emotions one feels from work-related loss before hitting rock bottom. More specifically, people who are in a deconstructed state are mainly cognizant of the self and their particular situation in terms of a constricted time perspective that narrowly focuses on the present (instead of the past or future), concrete actions and sensations at a superficial level (instead of more abstract, wide-ranging ideas at a higher level), and proximal goals (instead of distal goals from the past or about the future) (Baumeister 1990; Twenge et al. 2003). Through cognitive deconstruction, people can avoid thoughts related to the loss of their work identity and thus avoid the negative emotions that come with that loss (see Pennebaker 1989, 1993).

While deconstructed cognition eases the difficulties associated with identity loss, maintaining this cognitive state for a prolonged period of time is challenging due to the dysfunctional behaviors that come along with this state of mind, such as disinhibition (Baumeister and Vohs 2002), passivity (i.e., avoiding responsibility or self-assessment) (Ringel 1976), lack of emotion (Williams and Broadbent 1986), and irrational (rather than meaningful) thoughts (Neuringer 1972). Therefore, periods of an emotionless state are generally disrupted by periods of high negative emotions (Baumeister 1990; Wegner et al. 1986). Such spikes in negative emotions are particularly detrimental as people are unable to accurately evaluate the consequences of extreme actions, such as self-violence (Baumeister 1988) and even suicide (Baumeister 1990). Moreover, people have limited self-regulatory resources (Muraven and Baumeister 2000), so before long, the effort required to continue a deconstructed state becomes too exhausting (Kashdan and Breen 2007; Vohs et al. 2005). In turn, this exhaustion leads to higher levels of lethargy and passivity (Baumeister 1990; Twenge et al. 2003), perceptions that time is dragging (Twenge et al. 2003), and less genuine social interactions with others (John and Gross 2004; Kashdan and Breen 2007). When one reaches this state, his or her recovery process has been suspended (or not even really started), and the person begins to experience chronic dysfunction (Baumeister 1994; McIntosh and McKeganey 2000).

Recovering from Identity Loss Through Identity Play

Although identity loss can result in negative outcomes, a potential upside of such loss is the rare opportunity for people to *reboot* not only their careers (Zikic and Klehe 2006) but also their central work identity via identity play. The idea of "play" is somewhat similar to deconstructed cognition in that it offers an escape (although a very different kind of escape) from one's current reality (Csikszentmihalyi 1997). Play enables the individual to withdraw "from the reigning order and the necessities of the present and offers spaces for imagination, for creation, and for everyday creativity" (Hjorth 2005: 392; Kark 2011). Although similar to cognitive destruction in terms of enabling an escape, play provides a healthier route forward by triggering processes that will ultimately generate a new work identity that is positive (Shepherd and Williams 2018).

When people undertake *identity play*, they generate and engage provisional identities to determine whether they could serve as future identities (Ibarra and Petriglieri 2010). In this context, *provisional identities* are temporary conceptualizations of the self that must be "refined with experience" to become lasting (Ibarra 1999: 767; see also Ibarra 2004). Importantly, identity play is *not directed at a goal*; rather, it centers on discovery, enjoyment, and "rehearsing future possibilities" (Ibarra and Petriglieri 2010: 12; see also Csikszentmihalyi 1990; Miller 1973; Sutton-Smith 2009). The identities that result from such play are "trials for possible, but not yet fully elaborated" work identities (Ibarra 2005: 3). Identity play is the best context in which to create and explore temporary conceptualizations of the self as it is contextually positioned at the threshold of one's current reality and future possibilities (Ibarra and Petriglieri 2010: 11; Petriglieri and Petriglieri 2010). At this threshold, through identity play, individuals can explore alternatives without completely committing to them in the present; instead, these alternatives signify opportunities for the future (Winnicott 1975, 2001, 2005; Schrage 1999). People are likely to be very creative when thinking about various features of a prior identity that could be applied to a new identity or when forming entirely new possible concepts of the self. For instance, a failed entrepreneur may consider how the skills and knowledge he or she gained when founding a business could be utilized in a corporate setting, take exams to apply to law school, or undertake other low-risk exploration activities. When this occurs, hitting rock bottom frees the entrepreneur to actively investigate future possibilities (Shepherd and Williams 2018).

While identity play has a lot of potential updates, it needs to happen in a space that encourages exploring, discovering, and testing untried behaviors (Schrage 1999; Winnicott 1975, 2001, 2005). This space is not necessarily a physical place but a mindset, a mindset that is ready and willing to suspend or violate traditional rules without worrying about outcomes, such as penalties or exclusion (Glynn 1994; Van Maanen and Schein 1979), or about "strings being attached" to actions (Ibarra and Petriglieri 2010). Identity play also helps individuals move away from focusing on the past and present, thus liberating their identity from the weight and restrictions of validation in a social setting (Ibarra and Petriglieri 2010; Winnicott 1975, 2005). Unlike cognitive deconstruction, however, during identity play, the individual does not omit meaning making but instead investigates an array of potential *future* selves (Holzman 2009), thus facilitating identity creation and recovery (Shepherd and Williams 2018).

First, after they have hit rock bottom, people divert their focus away from the negative outcomes of identity loss in an effort to get away from the present (Jacobs 1984; Paternoster and Bushway 2009; Vaughan 1990; Wright 1984), which can help lessen negative affect (Baumeister 1994). By reducing negative emotions (Fredrickson 1998), play helps the individual escape without the constraint of a limited focus on well-rehearsed actions (e.g., identity protection or restructuring). As an escape oriented toward the future, identity play focuses on positive outcomes after hitting rock bottom that are manageable and help in creating a positive new work identity. Consider, for example, a founder whose venture has failed: he or she may escape the negative emotions caused by thinking about the failure through playing with alternative career options, concentrating on several positive future results (e.g., obtaining a secure corporate job with substantial benefits, considering jobs in non-profit organizations, etc.). This positive attention directed toward the future could be further strengthened as the entrepreneur thinks "I would have never considered and pursued these opportunities had my venture been successful."

Second, to avoid the emotional consequences of hitting rock bottom, people can move their focus away from particular aims and results to overall processes. An injured military veteran, for example, may stop concentrating on reaching a higher military rank and thinking about "what might have been" and instead begin focusing on alternative career options, such as running a small organization, engaging in a new venture with other veterans, volunteering to speak to other people facing similar setbacks, and so on. Such an escape offers a process-oriented enabling space for identity play (Glynn 1994; Miller 1973) centered on means instead of ends such that one's actions are circuitous and probing instead of linear and directed (Miller 1973). Due to this process focus, activities associated with identity play are not controlled by unyielding rationality or a strong desire for efficiency. Instead, these activities promote finding enjoyment in the journey and the decision process, "including intuition, emotion, and taking a leap of faith" (Ibarra and Petriglieri 2010: 13), all of which encourage creative thinking and action (Isen et al. 1987). Further, while pleasure is an important motivation for play (Ibarra and Petriglieri 2010), being present in the activity at hand may in and of itself lead to positive emotional experiences (Csikszentmihalyi 1997; Mainemelis and Ronson 2006), including enjoyment. Generating positive emotions can counteract lingering negative emotions (Fredrickson et al. 2000) and further expand one's focus and cognitive processes (Fredrickson 2001; Fredrickson and Branigan 2005), thus encouraging the imaginative formation of alternative identities from identity play (Shepherd and Williams 2018).

Third, to avoid the emotional crisis and "meaning vacuum" associated with hitting rock bottom, people can concentrate less on distal goals (or on past unreached goals, for that matter, such as those stemming from identity loss) and focus more on proximal activities (i.e., what opportunities they can envision or play with in the proximal future). As mentioned earlier, identity play includes proximal activities and actions related to testing temporary identities as possible identities, which in turn leads individuals to uncover principles and skills "that are relevant in reality beyond play" (Senge 1990: 314) (see also Miller 1973; Sutton-Smith 2009). Such play involves activities related to investigating low-risk explorative notions of future identities (Brown and Starkey 2000), an enduring process until the individual at hand finds a positive identity (that is likely provisional in nature) (Dutton et al. 2010) or an identity that at least could be positive (Maitlis 2009). For instance, after an entrepreneur loses his or her business, he or she may try numerous diverse identities, including entrepreneurship consultant or teacher, business angel, venture capital investor, employee in an entrepreneurial company, running a government agency promoting entrepreneurship, and so on, by visiting different locations and experimenting with these identities. Thus, getting away from the emotional weight triggered by the crystallization of discontent allows people like this to "play" by offering time and freedom from distal goals (e.g., for the last example, meeting conductor demands, performing at live events) to explore new identity possibilities. While the emphasis is on immediate trials, individuals test new notions of the self (created through play) by projecting them into the relatively near future. Without the constraints of distal goals, the failed entrepreneur can freely generate and strive for near goals, such as creating and trying on provisional identities developed through identity play.

Finally, while fantasy in a cognitively deconstructed state may be detrimental (Baumeister 1990), as part of identity play it may be very useful. Identity play "generally unfolds at the threshold between fantasy and reality, or the boundary between dreams (i.e., the possible selves in our heads) and reality (i.e., concrete possibilities available in the given world at any given time)" (Ibarra and Petriglieri 2010: 15). Thus, fantasy is insufficient for identity play as it requires flirtations across the boundary between dream and reality. Fantasy in a cognitively deconstructed state is problematic because it is free of any reality, thus making it rather ineffective in generating identity alternatives. However, when individuals play out identity fantasies, they are able to creatively explore (Brown and Starkey 2000) or flirt with ideas of a provisional future self that actually have meaning in reality, which can improve the chance of forming an identity that is positive (Shepherd and Williams 2018). For instance, the failed entrepreneur may play out his or her fantasy of working in a non-profit organization as an alternative new identity by working with a local non-profit for two weeks.

DISCIPLINE FOLLOWING OPEN IDENTITY PLAY

The association between play and the formation of a new positive work identity is likely shaped by the degree to which the cognitive process includes disciplined imagination. *Disciplined imagination* denotes an evaluation and selection process in which individuals introduce discipline through the "consistent application of selection criteria to trial-and-error thinking" and in which they trigger imagination through the "deliberate diversity introduced into the problem statements, thought trials, and selection criteria that comprise that thinking" (Weick 1989: 516; see also Shepherd and Williams 2018). The construction of these aspects of disciplined imagination—namely, the problem descriptions, thought experiments, and criteria applied for evaluation and selection—likely influences a person's ability to form conceivable outcomes. The outcome is a plausible new identity that is worth additional identity refinement and validation. Without forming a suitably plausible new identity, the individual is unlikely to engage in identity refinement or socially validate his or her new identity and will continue to play, thus delaying recovery.

Although identity play can generate possible new work identities, before a new identity can be enacted fully, the individual will likely have to engage in finer-grained identity refinement and social validation. Individuals seem to undertake a deeper analysis of a possible identity conjecture beyond the testing involved in thought trials by assessing their new identity using internal standards of self-beliefs (Ibarra 1999; Rafaeli and Sutton 1989) and external feedback based on other people's responses to their potential implementation of the new role (Ibarra and Petriglieri 2010; Meister et al. 2014). These internal and external forms of feedback provide information about the match between the alternative identity and the role it corresponds to (Bandura 1977; Weick 1979). A gap between the new possible work identity and the individual's role when performing this work requires *refinement* to "close the gap." In other words, the individual has to tailor the new identity to fit the new work role (Deaux 1991; Erez and Earley 1993). Pratt et al. (2006: 248) conducted a study on physician residents and showed that identity refinement includes three forms of identity customization. Physician residents used either splinting or patching to close a large gap between identifying a new work identity and performing its corresponding role. In this context, splinting refers to "a temporary identity to use until the identity develop[s] and [becomes] stronger (and then [can] be cast aside)," and patching refers to using one identity to mask holes or deficiencies in the new identity's correlation with the new work tasks (Pratt et al. 2006). For smaller gaps (which may result from effectively employing splinting or patching), the physicians appeared to use enriching to further refine their new identity. That is, although the new identity's basic features remain identical, through enriching, one obtains a more profound, richer, and more detailed understanding of the identity (Pratt et al. 2006). Overall, these refinement mechanisms enable identity adaptation (Ibarra 1999).

In addition to the three identity customization practices just listed, gaps can also be closed, and fit can be reached by altering characteristics of the work role to align it more closely with the new identity. Wrzesniewski and Dutton (2001), for instance, revealed that people take part in job crafting to redefine and re-imagine their work roles and then more closely align those work roles with work they feel is more meaningful (at least vis-à-vis their identity). Returning to our previous example, a failed entrepreneur could attempt to refine his or her new identity in pedagogy by first limiting its scope. For instance, the entrepreneur could choose to limit him- or herself to only teaching high-potential or adult students with ambitious performance-related goals instead of taking on beginner students. Similarly, he or she could develop corporate training for executives in entrepreneurial organizations or new industries. These sorts of refining activities are likely to help individuals align their budding new identity with their desired work identity.

Further, a new identity must also be *socially validated*. Research has shown that identity construction involves interaction in social contexts (Ibarra 1999; Meister et al. 2014; Sveningsson and Alvesson 2003). Said differently, people can try an alternative identity and thus make identity claims in social contexts. The claims an individual makes about a new identity trigger a reaction from others—namely, this alternative identity is accepted, rejected, or renegotiated by these "others" (Conroy and O'Leary-Kelley 2014; Ibarra 1999). It is important to note that this validation stage follows periods of less-directed, more fluid exploration of possible identities that did not involve any (or only very minimal) social validation. For example, the failed entrepreneur from our example before may decide to explore working in various government organizations, such as the Small Business Administration. In the early stages of exploration, he or she may not share this idea with anyone. However, after realizing the idea is plausible compared to other identity options pursued during play, the entrepreneur may begin seeking social validation. The ensuring social interaction is likely to provide information about any lingering deficiencies, asymmetries, or holes in the budding new work identity and about the need for additional refinements (McNulty and Swann 1994; Meister et al. 2014).

Social interaction not only helps validate a new work identity, but it can also help an individual further refine the identity. By sharing a new identity with others, the individual not only gets feedback, but those others can also aid in coproducing a more conceivable version of the identity by supporting particular features, adding new information, and facilitating the establishment of middle ground (Boje 1991; Conroy and O'Leary-Kelly 2014; Ibarra and Barbulescu 2010; Polletta and Lee 2006). Role models are a particularly important source of social validation for an alternative work identity (Ashforth 2001; Ibarra 1999; Pratt et al. 2006). Role models display the skills, styles, and behaviors that are appropriate in a social setting, and individuals can adopt and develop these skills, styles, and behaviors as a basis for their new work identity (Ibarra 1999). For example, the failed entrepreneur who decided to work for the Small Business Administration may observe an employee who is a highly regarded mentor for new businesses. Observing this individual may provide the entrepreneur with an illustration of good mentoring skills and behaviors in talking to and promoting mentees, which the entrepreneur may adopt and use as a basis to build up his or her new work identity as a successful startup mentor.

When a new identity is socially validated, the individual can adopt it as a positive identity; however, when there is no social validation, the individual can either abandon it or further refine and test the identity through another validation round. For instance, the failed entrepreneur might turn to his or her instructors or role models for validation and guidance, enabling the entrepreneur to coproduce this new identity in mentoring while obtaining validation and legitimacy at the same time. Such social validation is likely to facilitate individuals' transition to a new identity and serve as a continuing source of identity reinforcement and support.

Individuals can facilitate the refinement and validation of a new identity by occasionally drawing on identity play. For example, identity play can aid in splinting to overcome a major "boundary crossing" (Pratt et al. 2006; Van Maanen and Schein 1979) between a new identity and its associated work roles. Because splinting entails using a temporary identity until the new identity becomes more robust (Pratt et al. 2006), the challenge is "finding" a temporary identity that can serve as the splint while the primary identity develops. Just as identity play can aid in generating possible new identities, it can also likely help individuals generate possible "splints" when refining a new identity. Similarly, when one undertakes refinement through patching, he or she must generate an additional identity to make up for deficiencies with the new identity (Pratt et al. 2006). Identity play can be helpful in generating this "patch." For instance, a failed entrepreneur pursuing a conventional identity as a corporate employee may experience deficiencies from a lacking entrepreneurial role. To patch these deficiencies, the entrepreneur may ask to take on project-style work in the new employee role and to lead/"own" the project. Thus, he or she would be able to choose a team and work with more autonomy within the larger corporate structure. While perhaps not ideal, these patches likely help the entrepreneur transition to the new corporate employee identity.

Identity play can even help failed entrepreneurs enrich a new identity. More specifically, through identity play, an individual can explore a new identity in perhaps more extreme contexts, which can provide more profound, richer, and more nuanced information about the new identity. An individual could play with taking on different role models, combining different role features, and/or combining and recombining various roles.

An injured veteran, for example, may combine a more stable role of running a small business, which would have few connections to his or her former work identity, with a riskier work identity as a motivational speaker for other injured veterans or for people who have gone through hardship. By playing with the motivational speaker identity, the injured veteran will likely be exposed to others who have struggled, thus gaining a greater and deeper understanding about both the lost identity and the nuance and (possible) importance of the new identity.

Identity play can also be beneficial in helping entrepreneurs engage their social context to refine a new identity and receive social validation. For instance, other people can be involved in identity play, and through this more social form of play, rules and limits are formed and adjusted (Barrett 1998; Nachmanovitch 1990) in an interpersonal negotiation process. By "playing with others," individuals can coproduce an outcome to help refine the new identity and ultimately obtain social validation. For instance, the failed entrepreneur may engage family members (Newman 1988) and other people he or she encountered during identity play in generating new versions of a budding identity. The end result of this coproduction process could be a more nuanced version of the identity as well as higher acceptance of the new identity among new professional and/or social circles. If the audience rejects the new provisional identity (generated through identity play), the entrepreneur can re-engage in identity play to develop a new potential identity that can then be refined and socially validated.

So far, we have mainly discussed *what* paths entrepreneurs may take after the loss of a work identity. Now, we turn to *why* entrepreneurs choose one path over another and why there are likely varying levels of success among people attempting to create a new positive work identity. My (Dean) colleague and I (Shepherd and Williams 2018) argued that *individuals with a stronger promotion focus are more likely to undertake identity play to escape the negative emotions stemming from identity loss—from rock bottom—than individuals with a weaker promotion focus.*

Identity Conflict in Family Firms and an Expedited Entrepreneurial Process

Many businesses are run and owned by family members (Heck and Trent 1999; Rogoff and Heck 2003; Wortman 1994), which can lead to tension within both the family and the firm (Daily and Dollinger 1992; Harvey and Evans 1994; Kellermanns and Eddleston 2004). Family conflict can be the outcome of business issues, such as different goals related to financial targets or product/service offerings. Family conflict can also arise from seemingly routine issues such as hours of operation. In addition, business conflict may stem from family issues, including the amount of time family members are not at home, conflicts between spouses, or inattentiveness to crucial family matters. In these cases, conflicts are often directly caused by the direct and frequent interaction between family members, the family, and the firm.

Exploring the behavioral expectations that come with both the family member identity and the entrepreneurial identity is key to understanding the implications of role conflict in entrepreneurial context settings.[4] In the entrepreneurial context (e.g., family businesses), the boundaries between conflicting identities are often blurred and ill defined (Danes and Olson 2003). When the roles are considered independently (e.g., family member and business owner), the behavioral expectations for each role are developed based on input from the social environment. In other words, the social environment establishes "identity standards" related to what behaviors are acceptable for particular identities (Burke 2003). Although individuals may not universally share these socially ascribed standards (and they are certainly likely to vary across cultures (Choi et al. 1997)), individuals can compare their actions and behaviors to these social categories to determine if they are acceptable for a given identity. When an individual internalizes a particular identity and then acts counter to expectations for that role, identity conflict can result.

However, a common cause of identity conflict in the context of entrepreneurship begins at the *intersection* of the family identity and firm identity. Thus, family business identity conflict *occurs when the individual activates both his or her family identity and business identity, but acting in a way consistent with one identity concurrently necessitates behaviors that are incompatible with the other identity.*

Building on identity control and social identity theory, my (Dean) colleague and I (Shepherd and Haynie 2009b) concluded that the family and business identities are combined within a meta-identity—what we termed the *family business meta-identity*. This family business meta-identity is a higher-level identity that delineates "who we are as family" and "who we are as a business" such that it captures these occasionally competing identities. Thus, through this meta-identity, individuals can resolve conflict where family and firm overlap. Focusing on opportunity evaluation as an activity that likely generates conflict between one's family identity and his or her business identity, we illustrate how the meta-identity can resolve identity conflict by employing prior solutions from other conflicts that have been similar in nature, or by changing the meta-identity (by negotiation) to mitigate new conflicts.

While we recognize that the heterogeneity of viewpoints, knowledge, and experience that lead to conflict can improve decision comprehensiveness (Bantel 1993), we also theorize on the "dark side" of conflict for family firms—namely, the notion that time periods of prolonged identity conflict can result in negative outcomes for family members' psychological health (e.g., Frone et al. 1992), family disfunction (e.g., Kinnunen and Mauno 1998), and deterioration of firm performance (e.g., Beckhard and Dyer 1983). Thus, "lingering" identity conflict can be a barrier to efficient decision making in the entrepreneurial context.

Identity, Identity Conflict, and the Entrepreneurial Firm

We must consider the larger context in which people work and pursue all types of human interaction in order to fully understand how they conceptualize their own identities (Burke 2003; Fiske and Taylor 1991). Theories of social identity have typically centered on the premise of social categories (Tajfel and Turner 1979a, b, 1986). Social categories are based on similarity within the group in terms of the behaviors and attributes that are ideal for the particular social group (Cantor and Mischel 1977; Fiske and Taylor 1991). For instance, when someone is described as a "business owner," it calls to mind a specific meaning and specific characteristics that describe and limit the social category of "firm owners," such as the ways those individuals behave, dress, and talk; with whom they associate; their educational level; and so on. People who share more characteristics with other members in a category will be viewed as a member of the group more quickly, consensually, and consistently (Fiske and Taylor 1991). This social categorization is crucial for groups for two main reasons: (1) social categories provide "order" in the social context, and (2) social categories situate groups within that context (Ashforth and Mael 1989; Turner 1987). In other words, social categorization enables individuals to develop an identity that is based on a social comparator (Burke 2003). However, groups generally maintain multiple identities, thus making the idea of a socially situated identity more complex than it may initially seem (Ashforth et al. 2000).

The various identities that can represent membership in a given group when taken together tend to be associated with specific expected behaviors. These expectations are largely defined by the standards and traditions dictated by the overall social environment (Stryker and Burke 2000; Stryker and Statham 1985). Compared to non-family business, in family businesses, individuals often have to balance competing expectations regarding their behaviors for at least the family role and the entrepreneurial role. Because one's identity is characterized by expectations of behaviors for a socially attributed role (Stryker and Burke 2000), we define the family identity as *the set of behavioral expectations associated with the family role* (Shepherd and Haynie 2009b). Psychologists and sociologists in general contend that the family role embodies expectations about behaviors related to nurturing (Giordano 2003), protection (Goldberg et al. 1999), care giving (Lechner 1993), loyalty and commitment to the family (Knoester et al. 2007), and perceptions of collective gain/loss (Berger and Janoff-Bulman 2006). Families may outline their specific behavioral expectations in various forms, such as in a family creed or culture, which is manifest in traditions, stories, and artifacts.

In a similar way, we define the business owner identity *as the set of behavioral expectations associated with the business owner role* (Shepherd and Haynie 2009b). Both psychological and business perspectives generally state that the role as a business owner is associated with expectations about behaviors that yield extrinsic returns (e.g., growth, financial earnings, public recognition) (Kuratko et al. 1997), commitment to the firm and its members (Muse et al. 2005), legitimacy in a social context (Malach-Pines et al. 2005), and security and prosperity for the family (Kuratko et al. 1997). Businesses may convey their specific behavioral expectations in their mission statement and/or the firm's culture (Anderson et al. 2008).

The family and business roles in an entrepreneurial firm can mutually reinforce each other but also lead to role expectations that are conflicting. The expectations and demands from work and family often lead to such conflict, which has led many scholars to explore mechanisms to mitigate conflict between conventional work and family roles via compartmentalization (Bird et al. 1983). Unlike for traditional employment, for family business entrepreneurs, compartmentalization strategies are likely an insufficient and unsuitable mechanism to deal with or prevent conflict stemming from competing expectations related to identities of being a family member and a business owner. First, for most entrepreneurial ventures, the physical and temporal boundaries underlying effective compartmentalization are generally not appropriate or practical. Discussion of business matters pops up at dinner, work times have to be coordinated with kids' baseball schedules, and plans for a weekend spent with the family likely overlap with moving stock at the family firm, for example. In these types of situations, the self-regulation needed to compartmentalize these closely linked identities is likely to cause mental stress (Baumeister et al. 2000), thus resulting "in poor performance on subsequent tasks requiring self-control" (Seeley and Gardner 2003: 104).

Second, compartmentalization prevents the entrepreneur or the family firm from taking advantage of synergies between the family and business identities. These synergies could positively contribute to the performance of the family firm (Kellermanns and Eddleston 2004) and to the entrepreneur's and family members' psychological well-being (Shepherd and Haynie 2009b). Research has suggested, for instance, that systemic family influences can enhance firm success (Habbershon et al. 2003; Kellermanns and Eddleston 2004). Characteristics that are generated and strengthened through family relationships, such as trust, loyalty, and commitment, often serve the business aims as well. Additionally, the families' unique knowledge about members' specific skills, limitations, and belief systems may help family businesses more effectively implement their strategies compared to businesses that do not have such strong family involvement.

Importantly, in terms of identity conflict in entrepreneurial businesses, identity at a higher level represents the identities of family and business as well as their intersection. We take this focus because for many entrepreneurial businesses, this intersection is likely to represent a distinct case defined by the *shared meaning* between the family and business owner identities. The intersection of these two identities is activated and shared at the same time and regularly. We now return to identity control theory and the notion of a meta-identity to manage the family and business identities as well as the intersection between the two.

A Meta-Identity Perspective on the Family Business Role Identity

Drawing on social identity theory, identity control theory (ICT) (Burke 2003) focuses on how one's identity influences *behaviors*. That is, the roles individuals take on connect themselves to the social environment and others within that environment, thus creating a socially situated identity "standard." In other words, how individuals view their identity and how they act are relative to a socially derived standard. The focus of ICT is on how individuals' identity and behavior connect. For instance, the teacher role is connected to students, the father role is connected to children, and interactions between these groups are assessed as being either consistent or inconsistent with a social standard. ICT diverges from other social identity theories, however, because it stresses identity change.

According to Burke (2003, see also Deaux 1992, 1993), when identities share meanings, intersect, and are activated together, there will be a hierarchy of meaning, in which identities higher in the hierarchy "control the meanings of identities lower in the hierarchy." For many entrepreneurial businesses, the family business meta-identity is a higher-level identity that not only conveys to family members "who we are as a family" and "who we are as a business" but also details the intersection of the these identities. A defined family business meta-identity can help ease identity conflicts between the (lower-level) family and business identities when the conflicts are similar to those experienced in the past. In addition, this meta-identity changes as individuals engage in "negotiating, modifying, developing, and shaping expectations through interaction" (Burke 2003). The process of role transformation unfolds when people confront environmental situations that initiate identity conflict between the competing roles of family member and business owner that are unlike past identity conflicts. Because of the negative outcomes associated with prolonged and intense periods of identity conflict, it is particularly important to delineate changes of the family business meta-identity.

Family, Business, Opportunities, and Identity Conflict

While many actions and tasks entrepreneurs undertake could lead to conflict between the family and business identities, identity conflict is particularly likely to arise from the important task of opportunity evaluation. Opportunity evaluation can instigate identity conflict in entrepreneurial ventures for two main reasons: (1) the task is prolonged and is a chance to pursue novel paths, thus suggesting a highly uncertain environment (Knight 1921; McMullen and Shepherd 2006), and (2) opportunity evaluation makes the entrepreneur imagine the future activities and behaviors that may be necessary to effectively take advantage of that opportunity, thus making those activities and behaviors explicit. Explicit future activities and behaviors can be compared to the current expected behaviors related to the family firm identity.

Decisions about taking action on a particular opportunity and when to do so are vital for a growing venture's ultimate survival (Bourgeois and Eisenhardt 1988). In the end, entrepreneurship is about acting "upon the possibility that one has identified an opportunity worth pursuing" (McMullen and Shepherd 2006). Action results from the development of a belief that an opportunity for someone is actually an opportunity that the family firm can, and wants to, exploit. Thus, one must believe that pursing the potential opportunity is both desirable and feasible for the family business. When evaluating a novel opportunity, the family firm must answer questions with a joint understanding of and belief in "who we are" as a family firm. For instance, evaluating an opportunity requires the family business to determine whether "this [is] an opportunity for us," which likely often includes other questions: "Is this opportunity desirable for the family and for the firm?" "Can we successfully exploit this opportunity given our current knowledge, resources, and capabilities?"

Regarding identity conflict between the family and business identities, the opportunity-evaluation process is likely to result in either (1) an opportunity that does not generate identity conflict, or (2) an opportunity that generates identity conflict that shows similarity to prior identity conflicts, or (3) an opportunity that generates conflict without similarity to prior identity conflicts.

Opportunities That Do Not Cause Identity Conflict

Sometimes, opportunity evaluation is not associated with identity conflict because the family firm believes the opportunity aligns with both the family identity *and* the business identity. For instance, pursing an opportunity to develop and market a new high-quality toy for education purposes may align with the expectations associated with the role of a business owner and the role of a family member. In this case, no identity conflict develops as the expected behavior of the family member role does not hinder the entrepreneur from meeting the expectations of the firm owner role. In a similar vein, a potential opportunity could be at odds with the role expectation of both identities. An example could be the opportunity to introduce a toy that has no market (i.e., children do not want to use it) and in addition is produced cheaply and coated in toxic paint. In this case as well no identity conflict exists since opportunity exploitation would be incompatible with the expectations of the business owner role as it represents a detrimental business decision and would also be inconsistent with expectations of the family role associated with the child safety and care.

Indeed, both decisions are likely to be quick because in the first hypothetical case, the family business can easily decide to exploit the opportunity, while in the second hypothetical case, the family business can easily choose to forego the potential opportunity.

On the other hand, when the family business perceives a potential opportunity to be consistent with one identity but inconsistent with the other, identity conflict arises. When this occurs, the conflict consumes individuals' capacity to process information, thus making the decision process slower (Weick 1990; Staw et al. 1981). Moreover, there may well be procrastination—namely, postponing a behavior that one feels is emotionally unattractive although it is cognitively important because it can lead to desirable future results (Van Eerde 2000). In case the individual experiences a new form of identity conflict, that conflict is likely to continue (i.e., not be resolved immediately). This persistent identity conflict stemming from opportunity evaluation will likely affect the family business in a negative way by causing the entrepreneur to delay the decision to abandon the opportunity search and either exploit or reject the opportunity.

Opportunities That Cause Identity Conflict Similar to the Past

The degree to which identity conflict postpones the emergence of opportunity beliefs hinges on how similar the conflict is to prior conflicts. Identity conflict triggers reference to his or her family business meta-identity, which attempts to align identities lower in the hierarchy (family and business identities) as well as reconcile their individual meanings. This meta-identity embodies the shared meaning between the family and business identities as well as their intersection. The meta-identity also captures known practices to overcome conflict based on prior incidences that caused conflict between family and business identities. Thus, the meta-identity enacts routines to compare the present conflict with prior conflicts to evaluate whether and how the conflict is similar or different from those that have been resolved in the past. When the current identity conflict is *consistent* with one encountered in the past, the identity conflict is considered "similar." Similar means that no matter what the source of conflict is, it is "located" at the same intersection point of the family identity and the business identity as the prior conflict to which it was compared. For instance, say a family firm assessed an opportunity that requires higher family commitment to the business in the form of more work time and weekends at the firm. This new commitment level also affects the family, requiring the children to quit their weekend sports programs, for instance. In this case, the intersection of the family and business identities is embodied in the conflict's nature—namely, the most suitable (for this specific family) balance of commitment to both family and business activities. If the entrepreneur faces a future opportunity that causes identity conflict over a similar matter, he or she can resolve the conflict by referencing a past solution. These past solutions to identity conflict exist as an element of the larger family business meta-identity (i.e., as content).

Opportunities That Cause Conflict Dissimilar to the Past

Individuals will not always have past experience that can be applied to mitigating identity conflict caused by a new opportunity. Every opportunity is different and carries its own uncertainty that can be a new point of intersection between the family and business identities. When a new intersection forms, the family firm's meta-identity repertoire will not include a routine that can help resolve the identity conflict. (Many new family businesses likely encounter this situation often.) To overcome this new identity conflict, the family has to alter its current family business meta-identity by changing its underlying belief of "who we are as a family business." Modifying the family business meta-identity entails role transformation, or the process of "negotiating, modifying, developing, and shaping expectations through interaction" (Burke 2003). This role transformation has to occur within existing structures of the family and through interactions between family members.

The dynamic role-transformation process takes place in a social setting and includes behaviors that align perceptions of the types of behaviors which are (or are not) suitable given the existing identity standard. The identity standard for the family firm is shaped by a shared understanding of the expected behaviors for both the family and business roles as well as for the interaction of the two. Thus, to change (i.e., modify or extend) that standard, the family must craft a new collective understanding of "who we are." Consider the earlier example when the family evaluated an opportunity that was inconsistent with their shared understanding of balancing activities related to work and family, respectively. To exploit the opportunity, the family would need to undertake role renegotiation to transform their collective understanding of the family firm identity.

The literature has validated this idea of a negotiated identity (Burke 1991, 2003). When the conflict cannot be resolved by a meta-identity's current routines (i.e., the conflict is different from prior conflicts), the meta-identity needs adaptation to include a new conception of the family business intersection. This adaptation leads to a change in "who we are" that then alters "who we are as a family" and "who we are as a business." An outcome of the conflict-resolution process, this transformation adds to the family business's repertoire of solutions that can be used to overcome future identity conflict. How quickly identity conflict can be resolved (and thus how quickly opportunity beliefs can be formed) depends on the overall effectiveness and efficiency of renegotiation.

Conclusion

We have argued in this chapter that an entrepreneurial career provides multiple opportunities for individuals to develop a meaningful and unique self-identity. To overcome the cognitive and psychological challenges associated with balancing the fulfillment of the basic need to be distinct with the basic need to belong, entrepreneurs can apply integration or compartmentalization strategies to manage their work-related and non-work-related microidentities. We have also illustrated how traumatic events can disrupt one's occupational identity, and that entrepreneurship as an alternative career may help reconstruct it and in doing so help individuals recover emotionally and psychologically. Finally, we have focused on the specific case of family firm owner-managers and argued how these managers can resolve potential identity conflict from their roles as family members and business owners. The next chapter will explore the role of emotions in entrepreneurship and how they are related to entrepreneurial cognition.

Notes

1. We concentrate on the individual level in this chapter.
2. We do not provide one definition for "entrepreneurial identity" because although people are likely to share common characteristics, we also expect variation, and it is a person's idea of his or her own entrepreneurial identity that influences psychological well-being.
3. People likely have different negative features in their lives, create different associative connections between these features, and, thus, have different experiences with and timing of hitting rock bottom. Future studies can investigate individual variation in the development, nature, and timing of hitting rock bottom, especially in relation to identity loss.
4. In line with the social psychology literature, we use "identity" and "role identity" interchangeably (e.g., Burke 1991; Burke and Tully 1977; Stryker 1968; Stryker and Burke 2000).

References

Abrams, D., & Hogg, M. A. (1988). Comments on the motivational status of self-esteem in social identity and intergroup discrimination. *European Journal of Social Psychology, 18*(4), 317–334.

Akande, A. (1994). Coping with entrepreneurial stress: Evidence from Nigeria. *Journal of Small Business Management, 32*(1), 83–87.

Allred, B. B., Boal, K. B., & Holstein, W. K. (2005). Corporations as stepfamilies: A new metaphor for explaining the fate of merged and acquired companies. *Academy of Management Executive, 19*(3), 23–37.

American Psychiatric Association, APA. (1994). *Diagnostic and statistical manual of mental disorders, fourth edition: DSM-IV.* Washington, DC: APA.

Anderson, C., Spataro, S. E., & Flynn, F. J. (2008). Personality and organizational culture as determinants of influence. *Journal of Applied Psychology, 93*(3), 702–710.

Arnold, N. L., & Seekins, T. (2002). Self-employment: A process for use by vocational rehabilitation agencies. *Journal of Vocational Rehabilitation, 17*(2), 107–113.

Ashforth, B. (2001). *Role transitions in everyday life: An identity-based perspective.* Mahwah: Lawrence Erlbaum.

Ashforth, B. E., & Mael, F. (1989). Social identity theory and the organization. *Academy of Management Review, 14*(1), 20–39.

Ashforth, B. E., Kreiner, G. E., & Fugate, M. (2000). All in a day's work: Boundaries and micro role transitions. *Academy of Management Review, 25*(3), 472–491.

Audretsch, D. B. (2007). *The entrepreneurial society.* Oxford: Oxford University Press.

Baker, T., & Nelson, R. E. (2005). Creating something from nothing: Resource construction through entrepreneurial bricolage. *Administrative Science Quarterly, 50*(3), 329–366.

Bandura, A. (1977). Self-efficacy: Toward a unifying theory of behavioral change. *Psychological Review, 84*(2), 191–215.

Bantel, K. A. (1993). Comprehensiveness of strategic planning: The importance of heterogeneity of a top team. *Psychological Reports, 73*(1), 35–49.

Barrett, F. J. (1998). Managing and improvising: Lessons from jazz. *Career Development International, 3*(7), 283–286.

Batavia, A. I., & Schriner, K. (2001). The Americans with disabilities act as engine of social change: Models of disability and the potential of a civil rights approach. *Policy Studies Journal, 29*(4), 690–702.

Bauer, J. J., McAdams, D. P., & Sakaeda, A. R. (2005). Crystallization of desire and crystallization of discontent in narratives of life-changing decisions. *Journal of Personality, 73*(5), 1181–1214.

Baumeister, R. F. (1988). Masochism as escape from self. *Journal of Sex Research, 25*(1), 28–59.

Baumeister, R. F. (1990). Suicide as escape from self. *Psychological Review, 97*(1), 90.
Baumeister, R. F. (1991). *Meanings of life.* New York: Guilford Press.
Baumeister, R. F. (1994). The crystallization of discontent in the process of major life change. In T. F. Heatherton & J. L. Weinberger (Eds.), *Can personality change?* (pp. 281–297). American Psychology Association: Washington, DC.
Baumeister, R. F., & Leary, M. R. (1995). The need to belong: Desire for interpersonal attachments as a fundamental human motivation. *Psychological Bulletin, 117*(3), 497.
Baumeister, R. F., & Vohs, K. D. (2002). The pursuit of meaningfulness in life. In C. R. Snyder & S. J. Lopez (Eds.), *Handbook of positive psychology* (pp. 608–618). New York: Oxford University Press.
Baumeister, R. F., Dale, K. L., & Muraven, M. (2000). Volition and belongingness: Social movements, volition, self-esteem, and the need to belong. *Self, Identity, and Social Movements, 13,* 230–242.
Beckhard, R., & Dyer, W. G. (1983). Managing change in the family firm-issues and strategies. *Sloan Management Review, 24*(3), 59–65.
Benight, C. C., Swift, E., Sanger, J., Smith, A., & Zeppelin, D. (1999). Coping self-efficacy as a mediator of distress following a natural disaster. *Journal of Applied Social Psychology, 29*(12), 2443–2464.
Berger, A. R., & Janoff-Buhlman, R. (2006). Costs and satisfaction in close relationships: The role of loss–gain framing. *Personal Relationships, 13*(1), 53–68.
Bird, G. A., Bird, G. W., & Scruggs, M. (1983). Role-management used by husbands and wives in two-earner families. *Family and Consumer Sciences Research Journal, 12*(1), 63–70.
Boje, D. M. (1991). The storytelling organization: A study of story performance in an office-supply firm. *Administrative Science Quarterly, 36,* 106–126.
Bonanno, G. A. (2004). Loss, trauma, and human resilience: Have we underestimated the human capacity to thrive after extremely aversive events? *American Psychologist, 59*(1), 20–28.
Bourgeois, L. J., III, & Eisenhardt, K. M. (1988). Strategic decision processes in high velocity environments: Four cases in the microcomputer industry. *Management Science, 34*(7), 816–835.
Boyd, D. P., & Gumpert, D. E. (1983). The effects of stress on early-stage entrepreneurs. In *Frontiers of entrepreneurship research* (pp. 180–190). Wellesley: Babson College.
Breugst, N., & Shepherd, D. A. (2017). If you fight with me, I'll get mad! A social model of entrepreneurial affect. *Entrepreneurship Theory and Practice, 41*(3), 379–418.
Breugst, N., Patzelt, H., & Rathgeber, P. (2015). How should we divide the pie? Equity distribution and its impact on entrepreneurial teams. *Journal of Business Venturing, 30*(1), 66–94.
Brewer, M. B. (1991). The social self: On being the same and different at the same time. *Personality and Social Psychology Bulletin, 17*(5), 475–482.

Brewer, M. B. (1993). Social identity, distinctiveness, and in-group homogeneity. *Social Cognition, 11*(1), 150–164.
Brewer, M. B., & Gardner, W. (1996). Who is this "We"? Levels of collective identity and self representations. *Journal of Personality and Social Psychology, 71*(1), 83–93.
Brewer, M. B., & Pickett, C. L. (1999). Distinctiveness motives as a source of the social self. *Psychology of the Social Self, 14,* 71–87.
Brewer, M. B., & Weber, J. G. (1994). Self-evaluation effects of interpersonal versus intergroup social comparison. *Journal of Personality and Social Psychology, 66*(2), 268–275.
Brewer, M. B., Manzi, J. M., & Shaw, J. S. (1993). Ingroup identification as a function of depersonalization, distinctiveness, and status. *Psychological Science, 4*(2), 88–92.
Brown, A. D., & Starkey, K. (2000). Organizational identity and learning: A psychodynamic perspective. *Academy of Management Review, 25*(1), 102–120.
Brown, T. E., Davidsson, P., & Wiklund, J. (2001). An operationalization of Stevenson's conceptualization of entrepreneurship as opportunity-based firm behavior. *Strategic Management Journal, 22*(10), 953–968.
Bruno, A. V., McQuarrie, E. F., & Torgrimson, C. G. (1992). The evolution of new technology ventures over 20 years: Patterns of failure, merger, and survival. *Journal of Business Venturing, 7*(4), 291–302.
Budd, F. (2007). US air force wingman culture: A springboard for organizational development. *Organization Development Journal, 25*(3), 17–22.
Burke, P. J. (1991). Identity processes and social stress. *American Sociological Review, 56,* 836–849.
Burke, P. J. (2003). Relationships among multiple identities. *Advances in Identity Theory and Research,* 195–214.
Burke, P. J. (2006). Identity change. *Social Psychology Quarterly, 69*(1), 81–96.
Burke, P. J., & Tully, J. C. (1977). The measurement of role identity. *Social Forces, 55*(4), 881–897.
Busenitz, L. W., & Barney, J. B. (1997). Differences between entrepreneurs and managers in large organizations: Biases and heuristics in strategic decision-making. *Journal of Business Venturing, 12*(1), 9–30.
Buttner, E. H. (1992). Entrepreneurial stress: Is it hazardous to your health? *Journal of Managerial Issues, 4*(2), 223–240.
Callahan, M., Shumpert, N., & Mast, M. (2002). Self-employment, choice and self-determination. *Journal of Vocational Rehabilitation, 17*(2), 75–85.
Cantor, N., & Mischel, W. (1977). Traits as prototypes: Effects on recognition memory. *Journal of Personality and Social Psychology, 35*(1), 38–48.
Cantor, N., & Mischel, W. (1979). Prototypes in person perception. *Advances in Experimental Social Psychology, 12,* 3–52.
Cantor, N., Kemmelmeier, M., Basten, J., & Prentice, D. A. (2002). Life task pursuit in social groups: Balancing self-exploration and social integration. *Self and Identity, 1*(2), 177–184.

Carless, S. A. (2005). Person–job fit versus person–organization fit as predictors of organizational attraction and job acceptance intentions: A longitudinal study. *Journal of Occupational and Organizational Psychology, 78*(3), 411–429.

Choi, I., Nisbett, R. E., & Smith, E. E. (1997). Culture, category salience, and inductive reasoning. *Cognition, 65*(1), 15–32.

Codol, J. P. (1984). Social differentiation and undifferentiation. In H. Tajfel (Ed.), *The social dimension: Volume 1: European developments in social psychology* (pp. 314–337). Cambridge: Cambridge University Press.

Codol, J. P. (1987). Comparability and incomparability between oneself and others: Means of differentiation and comparison reference points. *Cahiers de Psychologie Cognitive/Current Psychology of Cognition, 7*(1), 87–105.

Conroy, S. A., & O'Leary-Kelly, A. M. (2014). Letting go and moving on: Work-related identity loss and recovery. *Academy of Management Review, 39*(1), 67–87.

Cova, B., & Svanfeldt, C. (1993). Societal innovations and the postmodern aestheticization of everyday life. *International Journal of Research in Marketing, 10*(3), 297–310.

Csikszentmihalyi, M. (1990). *Flow. The psychology of optimal experience.* New York: Harper Perennial.

Csikszentmihalyi, M. (1997). *Finding flow: The psychology of engagement with everyday life.* New York: Basic Books.

Daily, C. M., & Dollinger, M. J. (1992). An empirical examination of ownership structure in family and professionally managed firms. *Family Business Review, 5*(2), 117–136.

Danes, S. M., & Olson, P. D. (2003). Women's role involvement in family businesses, business tensions, and business success. *Family Business Review, 16*(1), 53–68.

De Vries, M. F. K., & Korotov, K. (2007). Creating transformational executive education programs. *Academy of Management Learning & Education, 6*(3), 375–387.

Deaux, K. (1991). Social identities: Thoughts on structure and change. In R. C. Curtis (Ed.), *The relational self: Theoretical convergences in psychoanalysis and social psychology* (pp. 77–93). New York: Guilford.

Deaux, K. (1992). Personalizing identity and socializing self. In G. Breakwell (Ed.), *Social psychology of identity and the self-concept* (pp. 9–33). London: Academic.

Deaux, K. (1993). Reconstructing social identity. *Personality and Social Psychology Bulletin, 19*(1), 4–12.

Dixon, T. M., & Baumeister, R. F. (1991). Escaping the self: The moderating effect of self-complexity. *Personality and Social Psychology Bulletin, 17*(4), 363–368.

Dutton, J. E., Dukerich, J. M., & Harquail, C. V. (1994). Organizational images and member identification. *Administrative Science Quarterly, 39*(2), 239–263.

Dutton, J. E., Roberts, L. M., & Bednar, J. (2010). Pathways for positive identity construction at work: Four types of positive identity and the building of social resources. *Academy of Management Review, 35*(2), 265–293.

Ebaugh, H. R. F. (1988). *Becoming an ex: The process of role exit*. Chicago: University of Chicago Press.
Eden, D. (1975). Organizational membership vs self-employment: Another blow to the American dream. *Organizational Behavior and Human Performance, 13*(1), 79–94.
Edwards, J. R. (1991). Person-job fit: A conceptual integration, literature review, and methodological critique. *International Review of Industrial/Organizational Psychology, 6*, 283–357. London: Wiley.
Ensley, M. D., Carland, J. W., & Carland, J. C. (2000). Investigating the existence of the lead entrepreneur. *Journal of Small Business Management, 38*(4), 59–77.
Erez & Earley. (1993). *Culture, self-identity, and work*. New York: Oxford University Press.
Fiske, S. T., & Taylor, S. E. (1991). *Social cognition, McGraw-Hill series in social psychology*. New York: Mcgraw-Hill Book Company.
Folkman, S., & Moskowitz, J. T. (2004). Coping: Pitfalls and promise. *Annual Review of Psychology, 55*, 745–774.
Fredrickson, B. L. (1998). What good are positive emotions? *Review of General Psychology, 2*(3), 300.
Fredrickson, B. L. (2001). The role of positive emotions in positive psychology. *American Psychologist, 56*(3), 218–226.
Fredrickson, B. L., & Branigan, C. (2005). Positive emotions broaden the scope of attention and thought-action repertoires. *Cognition & Emotion, 19*(3), 313–332.
Fredrickson, B. L., Mancuso, R. A., Branigan, C., & Tugade, M. M. (2000). The undoing effect of positive emotions. *Motivation and Emotion, 24*(4), 237–258.
Friedman, S. D. (1991). Sibling relationships and intergenerational succession in family firms. *Family Business Review, 4*(1), 3–20.
Fromkin, H. L., & Snyder, C. R. (1980). The search for uniqueness and valuation of scarcity. In K. Gergen, M. Greenberg, & R. Willis (Eds.), *Social exchange: Advances in theory and research* (pp. 57–75). New York: Plenum.
Frone, M. R., Russell, M., & Cooper, M. L. (1992). Antecedents and outcomes of work-family conflict: Testing a model of the work-family interface. *Journal of Applied Psychology, 77*(1), 65.
Gecas, V. (1982). The self-concept. *Annual Review of Sociology, 8*(1), 1–33.
Giordano, P. C. (2003). Relationships in adolescence. *Annual Review of Sociology, 29*(1), 257–281.
Glynn, M. A. (1994). Effects of work task cues and play task cues on information processing, judgment, and motivation. *Journal of Applied Psychology, 79*(1), 34–45.
Goldberg, S., Grusec, J. E., & Jenkins, J. M. (1999). Confidence in protection: Arguments for a narrow definition of attachment. *Journal of Family Psychology, 13*(4), 475–483.
Gramzow, R. H., & Gaertner, L. (2005). Self-esteem and favoritism toward novel in-groups: The self as an evaluative base. *Journal of Personality and Social Psychology, 88*(5), 801–815.

Greenhaus, J. H., & Beutell, N. J. (1985). Sources of conflict between work and family roles. *Academy of Management Review, 10*(1), 76–88.
Greenhaus, J. H., & Powell, G. N. (2006). When work and family are allies: A theory of work-family enrichment. *Academy of Management Review, 31*(1), 72–92.
Gumpert, D. E., & Boyd, D. P. (1984). The loneliness of the small-business owner. *Harvard Business Review, 62*(6), 18.
Guth, W. D., & Ginsberg, A. (1991). Guest editor's introduction: Corporate entrepreneurship. *Strategic Management Journal, 7*(1), 5–15.
Habbershon, T. G., Williams, M., & MacMillan, I. C. (2003). A unified systems perspective of family firm performance. *Journal of Business Venturing, 18*(4), 451–465.
Hagner, D., & Davies, T. (2002). "Doing my own thing": Supported self-employment for individuals with cognitive disabilities. *Journal of Vocational Rehabilitation, 17*(2), 65–74.
Hale, H. C. (2008). The development of British military masculinities through symbolic resources. *Culture & Psychology, 14*(3), 305–332.
Hall, D. T. (2002). *Careers in and out of organizations*. Thousand Oaks: Sage.
Hamilton, E. (2006). Whose story is it anyway? Narrative accounts of the role of women in founding and establishing family businesses. *International Small Business Journal, 24*(3), 253–271.
Hannafey, F. T. (2003). Entrepreneurship and ethics: A literature review. *Journal of Business Ethics, 46*(2), 99–110.
Harvey, M., & Evans, R. E. (1994). Family business and multiple levels of conflict. *Family Business Review, 7*(4), 331–348.
Haynie, J. M., & Shepherd, D. (2011). Toward a theory of discontinuous career transition: Investigating career transitions necessitated by traumatic life events. *Journal of Applied Psychology, 96*(3), 501–524.
Heck, R. K., & Trent, E. S. (1999). The prevalence of family business from a household sample. *Family Business Review, 12*(3), 209–219.
Hjorth, D. (2005). Organizational entrepreneurship: With de Certeau on creating heterotopias (or spaces for play). *Journal of Management Inquiry, 14*(4), 386–398.
Holzman, L. (2009). *Vygotsky at work and play*. London: Routledge.
Hornsey, M. J., & Jetten, J. (2004). The individual within the group: Balancing the need to belong with the need to be different. *Personality and Social Psychology Review, 8*(3), 248–264.
Ibarra, H. (1999). Provisional selves: Experimenting with image and identity in professional adaptation. *Administrative Science Quarterly, 44*(4), 764–791.
Ibarra, H. (2004). Working identity: Unconventional strategies for reinventing your career. *Harvard Business Press, 34*(3), 325–374.
Ibarra, H. (2005). *Identity transitions: Possible selves, liminality and the dynamics of career change* (Working paper no. 31/OB). INSEAD.

Ibarra, H., & Barbulescu, R. (2010). Identity as narrative: Prevalence, effectiveness, and consequences of narrative identity work in macro work role transitions. *Academy of Management Review, 35*(1), 135–154.
Ibarra, H., & Petriglieri, J. L. (2010). Identity work and play. *Journal of Organizational Change Management, 23*(1), 10–25.
Isen, A. M., Daubman, K. A., & Nowicki, G. P. (1987). Positive affect facilitates creative problem solving. *Journal of Personality and Social Psychology, 52*(6), 1122–1131.
Jacobs, J. (1984). The economy of love in religious commitment: The deconversion of women from nontraditional religious movements. *Journal for the Scientific Study of Religion, 23*(2), 155–171.
Jamal, M., & Badawi, J. A. (1995). Job stress, type-a behavior and employees' well-being among Muslim immigrants in North America: A study of work force diversity. *International Journal of Commerce and Management, 5*(4), 6–23.
Janoff-Bulman, R. (1989). Assumptive worlds and the stress of traumatic events: Applications of the schema construct. *Social Cognition, 7*(2), 113–136.
Janoff-Bulman, R. (1992). *Shattered assumptions: Towards a new psychology of trauma.* New York: Free Press.
John, O. P., & Gross, J. J. (2004). Healthy and unhealthy emotion regulation: Personality processes, individual differences, and lifespan development. *Journal of Personality, 72*(6), 1301–1334.
Kark, R. (2011). Games managers play: Play as a form of leadership development. *Academy of Management Learning & Education, 10*(3), 507–527.
Kashdan, T. B., & Breen, W. E. (2007). Materialism and diminished well–being: Experiential avoidance as a mediating mechanism. *Journal of Social and Clinical Psychology, 26*(5), 521–539.
Katz, D., & Kahn, R. L. (1978). *The social psychology of organizations* (Vol. 2). New York: Wiley.
Kellermanns, F. W., & Eddleston, K. A. (2004). Feuding families: When conflict does a family firm good. *Entrepreneurship Theory and Practice, 28*(3), 209–228.
Kendall, E., Buys, N., Charker, J., & MacMillan, S. (2006). Self-employment: An under-utilised vocational rehabilitation strategy. *Journal of Vocational Rehabilitation, 25*(3), 197–205.
Kets de Vries, M. F. (1985). The dark side of entrepreneurship. *Harvard Business Review, 85*(6), 160–167.
Kinnunen, U., & Mauno, S. (1998). Antecedents and outcomes of work-family conflict among employed women and men in Finland. *Human Relations, 51*(2), 157–177.
Klotz, A. C., Hmieleski, K. M., Bradley, B. H., & Busenitz, L. W. (2014). New venture teams: A review of the literature and roadmap for future research. *Journal of Management, 40*(1), 226–255.
Knight, F. H. (1921). *Risk, uncertainty and profit.* Washington, DC: Beard Books.

Knoester, C., Petts, R. J., & Eggebeen, D. J. (2007). Commitments to fathering and the well-being and social participation of new, disadvantaged fathers. *Journal of Marriage and Family, 69*(4), 991–1004.

Kolvereid, L. (1996). Prediction of employment status choice intentions. *Entrepreneurship: Theory and Practice, 21*(1), 47–58.

Korunka, C., Frank, H., Lueger, M., & Mugler, J. (2003). The entrepreneurial personality in the context of resources, environment, and the startup process: A configurational approach. *Entrepreneurship Theory and Practice, 28*(1), 23–42.

Kuratko, D. F., & Hodgetts, R. M. (1995). *Entrepreneurship: A contemporary approach.* Fort Worth: Dryden Press.

Kuratko, D. F., Hornsby, J. S., & Naffziger, D. W. (1997). An examination of owner's goals in sustaining entrepreneurship. *Journal of Small Business Management, 35*(1), 24–33.

Lande, B. (2007). Breathing like a soldier: Culture incarnate. *The Sociological Review, 55*(s1), 95–108.

Larsson, R., & Finkelstein, S. (1999). Integrating strategic, organizational, and human resource perspectives on mergers and acquisitions: A case survey of synergy realization. *Organization Science, 10*(1), 1–26.

Latack, J. C., & Dozier, J. B. (1986). After the ax falls: Job loss as a career transition. *Academy of Management Review, 11*(2), 375–392.

Latack, J. C., Kinicki, A. J., & Prussia, G. E. (1995). An integrative process model of coping with job loss. *Academy of Management Review, 20*(2), 311–342.

Leary, M. R. (1990). Responses to social exclusion: Social anxiety, jealousy, loneliness, depression, and low self-esteem. *Journal of Social and Clinical Psychology, 9*(2), 221–229.

Lechler, T. (2001). Social interaction: A determinant of entrepreneurial team venture success. *Small Business Economics, 16*(4), 263–278.

Lechner, V. M. (1993). Support systems and stress reduction among workers caring for dependent parents. *Social Work, 38*(4), 461–469.

Leonardelli, G. J., & Brewer, M. B. (2001). Minority and majority discrimination: When and why. *Journal of Experimental Social Psychology, 37*(6), 468–485.

Leyens, J. P., Yzerbyt, V. Y., & Rogier, A. (1997). Personality traits that distinguish you and me are better memorized. *European Journal of Social Psychology, 27*(5), 511–522.

Lobel, S. A. (1991). Allocation of investment in work and family roles: Alternative theories and implications for research. *Academy of Management Review, 16*(3), 507–521.

Longenecker, J. G., McKinney, J. A., & Moore, C. W. (1988). Egoism and independence: Entrepreneurial ethics. *Organizational Dynamics, 16*(3), 64–72.

Lumpkin, G. T., & Dess, G. G. (1996). Clarifying the entrepreneurial orientation construct and linking it to performance. *Academy of Management Review, 21*(1), 135–172.

Magwaza, A. S. (1999). Assumptive world of traumatized South African adults. *Journal of Social Psychology, 139*(5), 622–630.

Mainemelis, C., & Ronson, S. (2006). Ideas are born in fields of play: Towards a theory of play and creativity in organizational settings. *Research in Organizational Behavior, 27,* 81–131.

Maitlis, S. (2009). Who am I now? Sensemaking and identity in posttraumatic growth. In L. Morgan Roberts & J. E. Dutton (Eds.), *Exploring positive identities and organizations: Building a theoretical and research foundation* (pp. 47–76). New York: Psychology Press.

Malach-Pines, A., Levy, H., Utasi, A., & Hill, T. L. (2005). Entrepreneurs as cultural heroes: A cross-cultural, interdisciplinary perspective. *Journal of Managerial Psychology, 20*(6), 541–555.

Markus, H. R., & Kitayama, S. (1991). Culture and the self: Implications for cognition, emotion, and motivation. *Psychological Review, 98*(2), 224–253.

Mattessich, P., & Hill, R. (1976). Family enterprise and societal development: A theoretical assessment. *Journal of Comparative Family Studies, 7*(2), 147–158.

McAdams, D. P. (1985). *Power, intimacy, and the life story.* Homewood: Dow-Jones-Irwin.

McAdams, D. P., & Bryant, F. B. (1987). Intimacy motivation and subjective mental health in a nationwide sample. *Journal of Personality, 55*(3), 395–413.

McIntosh, J., & McKeganey, N. (2000). Addicts' narratives of recovery from drug use: Constructing a non-addict identity. *Social Science & Medicine, 50*(10), 1501–1510.

McMullen, J. S., & Shepherd, D. A. (2006). Encouraging consensus-challenging research in universities. *Journal of Management Studies, 43*(8), 1643–1669.

McNulty, S. E., & Swann, W. B., Jr. (1994). Identity negotiation in roommate relationships: The self as architect and consequence of social reality. *Journal of Personality and Social Psychology, 67*(6), 1012–1023.

Meister, A., Jehn, K. A., & Thatcher, S. M. (2014). Feeling misidentified: The consequences of internal identity asymmetries for individuals at work. *Academy of Management Review, 39*(4), 488–512.

Miller, S. (1973). Ends, means, and galumphing: Some leitmotifs of play. *American Anthropologist, 75*(1), 87–98.

Muraven, M., & Baumeister, R. F. (2000). Self-regulation and depletion of limited resources: Does self-control resemble a muscle? *Psychological Bulletin, 126*(2), 247–259.

Muse, L. A., Rutherford, M. W., Oswald, S. L., & Raymond, J. E. (2005). Commitment to employees: Does it help or hinder small business performance? *Small Business Economics, 24*(2), 97–111.

Nachmanovitch, S. (1990). *Free play: Improvisation in life and art.* New York: Putnam.

Naffziger, D. W., Hornsby, J. S., & Kuratko, D. F. (1994). A proposed research model of entrepreneurial motivation. *Entrepreneurship: Theory and Practice, 18*(3), 29–43.

Naman, J. L., & Slevin, D. P. (1993). Entrepreneurship and the concept of fit: A model and empirical tests. *Strategic Management Journal, 14*(2), 137–153.

Naughton, T. J. (1987). A conceptual view of workaholism and implications for career counseling and research. *Career Development Quarterly, 35*(3), 180–187.

Neuringer, C. (1972). Suicide attempt and social isolation on the MAPS test. *Suicide and Life-threatening Behavior, 2*(3), 139–144.

Newman, K. S. (1988). Falling from grace: The experience of downward mobility in the American middle class. *Free Press, 115*(2), 243–267.

Nicholson, N. (1984). A theory of work role transitions. *Administrative Science Quarterly*, 172–191.

Nippert-Eng, C. (1996). Calendars and keys: The classification of "home" and "work". *Sociological Forum, 11*(3), 563–582.

Oakes, P. J., Haslam, S. A., & Turner, J. C. (1994). *Stereotypes and social reality.* Oxford: Basil Blackwell.

O'Reilly, C. A., Chatman, J., & Caldwell, D. F. (1991). People and organizational culture: A profile comparison approach to assessing person-organization fit. *Academy of Management Journal, 34*(3), 487–516.

Ortona, G., & Scacciati, F. (1992). New experiments on the endowment effect. *Journal of Economic Psychology, 13*(2), 277–296.

Oswald, R. F., & Suter, E. A. (2004). Heterosexist inclusion and exclusion during ritual: A "straight versus gay" comparison. *Journal of Family Issues, 25*(7), 881–889.

Park, B., & Rothbart, M. (1982). Perception of outgroup homogeneity and levels of social categorization: Memory for the subordinate attributes of ingroup and outgroup members. *Journal of Personality and Social Psychology, 42*(6), 1051–1068.

Paternoster, R., & Bushway, S. (2009). Desistance and the "feared self": Toward an identity theory of criminal desistance. *Journal of Criminal Law and Criminology, 99*, 1103–1156.

Patzelt, H., Williams, T. A., & Shepherd, D. A. (2014). Overcoming the walls that constrain us: The role of entrepreneurship education programs in prison *Academy of Management Learning & Education, 13*(4), 587–620.

Pennebaker, J. W. (1989). Confession, inhibition, and disease. *Advances in Experimental Social Psychology, 22*, 211–244.

Pennebaker, J. W. (1993). Putting stress into words: Health, linguistic, and therapeutic implications. *Behaviour Research and Therapy, 31*(6), 539–548.

Petriglieri, G., & Petriglieri, J. L. (2010). Identity workspaces: The case of business schools. *Academy of Management Learning & Education, 9*(1), 44–60.

Polletta, F., & Lee, J. (2006). Is telling stories good for democracy? Rhetoric in public deliberation after 9/11. *American Sociological Review, 71*(5), 699–721.

Pratt, M. G., & Foreman, P. O. (2000). Classifying managerial responses to multiple organizational identities. *Academy of Management Review, 25*(1), 18–42.

Pratt, M. G., Rockmann, K. W., & Kaufmann, J. B. (2006). Constructing professional identity: The role of work and identity learning cycles in the customization of identity among medical residents. *Academy of Management Journal, 49*(2), 235–262.

Rafaeli, A., & Sutton, R. I. (1989). The expression of emotion in organizational life. *Research in Organizational Behavior, 11*(1), 1–42.

Rahav, G., & Baum, N. (2002). Divorced women: Factors contributing to self-identity change. *Journal of Divorce & Remarriage, 37*(3–4), 41–59.

Ringel, E. (1976). The pre suicidal syndrome. *Suicide and Life-threatening Behavior, 6*(3), 131–149.

Rogoff, E. G., & Heck, R. K. Z. (2003). Evolving research in entrepreneurship and family business: Recognizing family as the oxygen that feeds the fire of entrepreneurship. *Journal of Business Venturing, 18*(5), 559–566.

Rosenbaum, J. E. (1979). Tournament mobility: Career patterns in a corporation. *Administrative Science Quarterly, 24*(2), 220–241.

Rousseau, D. M. (1998). Why workers still identify with organizations. *Journal of Organizational Behavior, 19*(3), 217–233.

Ryan, R. M., & Deci, E. L. (2001). On happiness and human potentials: A review of research on hedonic and eudaimonic well-being. *Annual Review of Psychology, 52*(1), 141–166.

Savin-Baden, M. (2010). Changelings and shape shifters? Identity play and pedagogical positioning of staff in immersive virtual worlds. *London Review of Education, 8*(1), 25–38.

Schlenker, J. A., & Gutek, B. A. (1987). Effects of role loss on work-related attitudes. *Journal of Applied Psychology, 72*(2), 287–293.

Schrage, M. (1999). Serious play: How the world's best companies simulate to innovate. *Harvard Business Press, 18*(4), 247–257.

Schweiger, D. M., & Goulet, P. K. (2005). Facilitating acquisition integration through deep-level cultural learning interventions: A longitudinal field experiment. *Organization Studies, 26*(10), 1477–1499.

Seeley, E. A., & Gardner, W. L. (2003). The "selfless" and self-regulation: The role of chronic other-orientation in averting self-regulatory depletion. *Self and Identity, 2*(2), 103–117.

Senge, P. M. (1990). *The fifth discipline: The art and practice of the learning organization.* New York: Doubleday.

Shane, S. (2000). Prior knowledge and the discovery of entrepreneurial opportunities. *Organization Science, 11*(4), 448–469.

Shepherd, D. A. (2003). Learning from business failure: Propositions of grief recovery for the self-employed. *Academy of Management Review, 28*(2), 318–328.

Shepherd, D., & Haynie, J. M. (2009a). Birds of a feather don't always flock together: Identity management in entrepreneurship. *Journal of Business Venturing*, 24(4), 316–337.

Shepherd, D., & Haynie, J. M. (2009b). Family business, identity conflict, and an expedited entrepreneurial process: A process of resolving identity conflict. *Entrepreneurship Theory and Practice*, 33(6), 1245–1264.

Shepherd, D., & Williams, T. (2018). Hitting rock bottom after job loss: Bouncing back to create a new positive work identity. *Academy of Management Review*, 43(1).

Sine, W. D., Mitsuhashi, H., & Kirsch, D. A. (2006). Revisiting burns and stalker: Formal structure and new venture performance in emerging economic sectors. *Academy of Management Journal*, 49(1), 121–132.

Snyder, M., & Swann, W. B. (1978). Hypothesis-testing processes in social interaction. *Journal of Personality and Social Psychology*, 36(11), 1202–1212.

Solomon, Z., Iancu, I., & Tyano, S. (1997). World assumptions following disaster. *Journal of Applied Social Psychology*, 27(20), 1785–1798.

Staw, B. M., Sandelands, L. E., & Dutton, J. E. (1981). Threat rigidity effects in organizational behavior: A multilevel analysis. *Administrative Science Quarterly*, 26(4), 501–524.

Stewart, A. (2003). Help one another, use one another: Toward an anthropology of family business. *Entrepreneurship Theory and Practice*, 27(4), 383–396.

Stillman, T. F., Baumeister, R. F., Lambert, N. M., Crescioni, A. W., DeWall, C. N., & Fincham, F. D. (2009). Alone and without purpose: Life loses meaning following social exclusion. *Journal of Experimental Social Psychology*, 45(4), 686–694.

Stinchcombe, A. L. (1965). Organizations and social structure. *Handbook of Organizations*, 44(2), 142–193.

Strauss, A. L. (1997). *Mirrors and masks: The search for identity*. Glencoe: Transaction Publishers.

Stryker, S. (1968). Identity salience and role performance: The relevance of symbolic interaction theory for family research. *Journal of Marriage and the Family*, 30, 558–564.

Stryker, S. (1987). Identity theory: Developments and extensions. In K. Yardley & T. Honess (Eds.), *Self and identity: Psychosocial perspectives* (pp. 89–103). Oxford: Wiley.

Stryker, S., & Burke, P. J. (2000). The past, present, and future of an identity theory. *Social Psychology Quarterly*, 63(4), 284–297.

Stryker, S., & Statham, A. (1985). Symbolic interaction and role theory. In G. Lindzey & E. Aronson (Eds.), *Handbook of social psychology* (pp. 311–378). New York: Random House.

Sutton-Smith, B. (2009). *The ambiguity of play*. Cambridge, MA: Harvard University Press.

Sveningsson, S., & Alvesson, M. (2003). Managing managerial identities: Organizational fragmentation, discourse and identity struggle. *Human Relations,* 56(10), 1163–1193.
Swann, W. B. (1987). Identity negotiation: Where two roads meet. *Journal of Personality and Social Psychology,* 53(6), 1038–1051.
Swann Jr, W. B. (2005). The self and identity negotiation. *Interaction Studies,* 6(1), 69–83.
Tajfel, H. (2010). *Social identity and intergroup relations.* Cambridge: Cambridge University Press.
Tajfel, H., & Turner, J. C. (1979a). An integrative theory of intergroup conflict. *The Social Psychology of Intergroup Relations, 33,* 33–47.
Tajfel, H., & Turner, J. C. (1979b). An integrative theory of intergroup conflict. In *The social psychology of intergroup relations.* Monterey: Brooks Cole.
Tajfel, H., & Turner, J. C. (1986). The social identity theory of intergroup behavior. In S. Worchel, & W. G. Austin (Eds.), *Psychology of intergroup relations.* Chicago: Nelson, 34(3), 325–374.
Teal, E. J., & Carroll, A. B. (1999). Moral reasoning skills: Are entrepreneurs different? *Journal of Business Ethics,* 19(3), 229–240.
Tice, D. M., & Baumeister, R. F. (1990). Self-esteem, self-handicapping, and self-presentation: The strategy of inadequate practice. *Journal of Personality,* 58(2), 443–464.
Turner, J. H. (1987). Toward a sociological theory of motivation. *American Sociological Review,* 52(1), 234–227.
Twenge, J. M., Catanese, K. R., & Baumeister, R. F. (2003). Social exclusion and the deconstructed state: Time perception, meaninglessness, lethargy, lack of emotion, and self-awareness. *Journal of Personality and Social Psychology,* 85(3), 409.
U.S. Census Bureau. (2002). *Census 2000 summary file.* Retrieved http://factfinder.census.gov
Ucbasaran, D., Lockett, A., Wright, M., & Westhead, P. (2003). Entrepreneurial founder teams: Factors associated with member entry and exit. *Entrepreneurship Theory and Practice,* 28(2), 107–128.
Ufuk, H., & Özgen, Ö. (2001). Interaction between the business and family lives of women entrepreneurs in Turkey. *Journal of Business Ethics,* 31(2), 95–106.
Van Eerde, W. (2000). Procrastination: Self-regulation in initiating aversive goals. *Applied Psychology,* 49(3), 372–389.
Van Maanen, J. E., & Schein, E. H. (1979). Toward a theory of organizational socialization. *Research in Organizational Behavior, 1,* 209–264.
Vaughan, D. (1990). Autonomy, interdependence, and social control: NASA and the space shuttle challenger. *Administrative Science Quarterly,* 35(2), 225–257.
Vignoles, V. L., Chryssochoou, X., & Breakwell, G. M. (2000). The distinctiveness principle: Identity, meaning, and the bounds of cultural relativity. *Personality and Social Psychology Review,* 4(4), 337–354.

Vohs, K. D., Baumeister, R. F., & Ciarocco, N. J. (2005). Self-regulation and self-presentation: Regulatory resource depletion impairs impression management and effortful self-presentation depletes regulatory resources. *Journal of Personality and Social Psychology, 88*(4), 632–657.
Watson, W. E., Michaelsen, L. K., & Sharp, W. (1991). Member competence, group interaction, and group decision making: A longitudinal study. *Journal of Applied Psychology, 76*(6), 803–809.
Wegner, D. M., Vallacher, R. R., Kiersted, G. W., & Dizadji, D. (1986). Action identification in the emergence of social behavior. *Social Cognition, 4*(1), 18–38.
Weick, K. (1979). *The social psychology of organizing*. Reading: Addison-Wesley.
Weick, K. E. (1989). Theory construction as disciplined imagination. *Academy of Management Review, 14*(4), 516–531.
Weick, K. E. (1990). The vulnerable system: An analysis of the Tenerife air disaster. *Journal of Management, 16*(3), 571–593.
West, G. P. (2007). Collective cognition: When entrepreneurial teams, not individuals, make decisions. *Entrepreneurship Theory and Practice, 31*(1), 77–102.
Wicker, A. W., & Burley, K. A. (1991). Close coupling in work-family relationships: Making and implementing decisions in a new family business and at home. *Human Relations, 44*(1), 77–92.
Wiklund, J., Patzelt, H., & Dimov, D. (2016). Entrepreneurship and psychological disorders: How ADHD can be productively harnessed. *Journal of Business Venturing Insights, 6*, 14–20.
Williams, K. J., & Alliger, G. M. (1994). Role stressors, mood spillover, and perceptions of work-family conflict in employed parents. *Academy of Management Journal, 37*(4), 837–868.
Williams, J. M., & Broadbent, K. (1986). Autobiographical memory in suicide attempters. *Journal of Abnormal Psychology, 95*(2), 144.
Winnicott, D. W. (1975). Transitional objects and transitional phenomena. In D. Winnicott (Ed.), *Through pediatrics to psychoanalysis* (pp. 229–242). London: Karnac.
Winnicott, D. W. (2001). *Playing and reality*. New York: Basic Books.
Winnicott, D. W. (2005). The potential space. In *Playing and reality*. London: Routledge.
Wortman, M. S. (1994). Theoretical foundations for family-owned business: A conceptual and research-based paradigm. *Family Business Review, 7*(1), 3–27.
Wright, S. A. (1984). Post-involvement attitudes of voluntary defectors from controversial new religious movements. *Journal for the Scientific Study of Religion, 23*, 172–182.
Wrzesniewski, A., & Dutton, J. E. (2001). Crafting a job: Revisioning employees as active crafters of their work. *Academy of Management Review, 26*(2), 179–201.

Yip, G. S. (1982). *Barriers to entry: A corporate-strategy perspective*. Lexington: Lexington Books/Health and Company.

Yli-Renko, H., Autio, E., & Sapienza, H. J. (2001). Social capital, knowledge acquisition, and knowledge exploitation in young technology-based firms. *Strategic Management Journal, 22*(6–7), 587–613.

Zikic, J., & Klehe, U. C. (2006). Job loss as a blessing in disguise: The role of career exploration and career planning in predicting reemployment quality. *Journal of Vocational Behavior, 69*(3), 391–409.

Open Access This chapter is licensed under the terms of the Creative Commons Attribution 4.0 International License (http://creativecommons.org/licenses/by/4.0/), which permits use, sharing, adaptation, distribution and reproduction in any medium or format, as long as you give appropriate credit to the original author(s) and the source, provide a link to the Creative Commons license and indicate if changes were made.

The images or other third party material in this chapter are included in the chapter's Creative Commons license, unless indicated otherwise in a credit line to the material. If material is not included in the chapter's Creative Commons license and your intended use is not permitted by statutory regulation or exceeds the permitted use, you will need to obtain permission directly from the copyright holder.

CHAPTER 6

Emotion and Entrepreneurial Cognition

Entrepreneurship is a highly emotional endeavor; it has often been portrayed as an "emotional rollercoaster" with multiple ups and downs that impact entrepreneurs' emotional experiences. For example, entrepreneurs may experience passion, joy, satisfaction, flow, enthusiasm, and excitement from work, but also bitter disappointment, distress, worry, anger, and grief (Shepherd et al. 2011; Baron 2008; Cardon et al. 2009; Patzelt and Shepherd 2011; Foo et al. 2009; Boyd and Gumpert 1984; Schindehutte et al. 2006). The psychology literature has long acknowledged that emotions can impact how people think and decide. For example, Affect-as-Information Theory (Frijda 1986; Schwarz and Clore 1983) states that individuals ask themselves (implicitly) how they feel about a particular situation and, based on this information component, make decisions. The Broaden-and-Build Theory (Fredrickson 1998) assumes that positive emotions influence cognition by broadening individuals' thought-action repertoires. On the other hand, it is also well documented that people can use their cognitive resources to influence emotional experiences (Folkman and Moskowitz 2004; Lazarus and Folkman 1984a, b). We will now explore the association between emotions and cognition in entrepreneurship.

POSITIVE EMOTIONS AND ENTREPRENEURIAL COGNITION

Individuals develop passion for their work when they value their work highly, like performing work-related activities, and do so regularly (Vallerand et al. 2003), thus leading them to incorporate work into their personal identity. For instance, Bill Gates and Steve Jobs were not merely the founders and former CEOs of Microsoft and Apple. Rather, the businesses they founded also partially defined who they were as people, and their work activities became significant parts of their identities. However, managers vary in terms of how much they incorporate work activities into their identity (Cardon et al. 2009; Shepherd and Haynie 2009), which results in either harmonious passion or obsessive passion. While harmonious and obsessive passion are correlated to a degree, both are not the opposite ends of a continuum (Vallerand et al. 2003).

Harmonious Passion and Entrepreneurs' Opportunity Exploitation

Harmonious passion *is an autonomous internalization of an activity in one's identity that causes the individual to decide to pursue that activity* (Vallerand et al. 2003). As a result, people experiencing harmonious work-related passion readily and autonomously undertake work-related activities. For instance, when these entrepreneurs brainstorm new ideas with innovation team members, obtain the resources needed to turn the resulting ideas into products, and create product-development budgets, they engage in these activities with no (or only minimal) obligations attached. In other words, such entrepreneurs' motivation does not stem from their firm's goal to reach specific outputs, from social pressure at work, or from the need to feed the family. In addition, while work plays an important role in the development of these individuals' identity as an entrepreneurial manager, this does not mean that work necessarily dominates other parts of their lives. Rather, these entrepreneurs can balance different elements in their lives when creating their identity. For instance, a harmoniously passionate entrepreneur may incorporate roles as a family member, golfer, and guitar player into his or her overall identity.

By autonomously internalizing work into their identities, harmoniously passionate entrepreneurs are able to flexibly perform work activities and believe that they have control over their entrepreneurial endeavors. These feelings of flexibility and control make such entrepreneurs experience positive emotions. They are absorbed by their work and experience flow (Vallerand et al. 2003). For example, some corporate entrepreneurs have reported putting their entire heart into their work (Shepherd et al. 2011). When entrepreneurs have positive affective experiences, they are more likely to pursue new opportunities they identify.

Moreover, harmoniously passionate entrepreneurs tend to use heuristics less but engage more in analytic strategies because positive emotional experiences enhance cognitive flexibility by enabling entrepreneurs to build on or connect cognitive frameworks in a novel manner (Baron 2004; Ward 2004). For instance, a positive affective state indicates that the decision maker can use mental resources to broaden his or her thought-action repertoire (Fredrickson 1998). Thus, harmoniously passionate entrepreneurs experiencing positive emotions will more likely discover non-obvious alternatives to sidestep challenges associated with exploiting new opportunities (cf. Baron 2008), therefore demonstrating firsthand the creativity underlying successful innovation processes (Bharadwaj and Menon 2000).

Additionally, because of their positive emotional state at work, harmoniously passionate entrepreneurs are more likely to believe there are fewer risks associated with exploiting a new opportunity. When individuals experience positive affect, they are more likely to believe they have control over environmental influences (Alloy and Abramson 1979), thus influencing the level of risk and outcome uncertainty these individuals perceive, both of which can be significant barriers to new opportunity exploitation (McMullen and Shepherd 2006; Mullins and Forlani 2005). Entrepreneurs who perceive they are in control over the uncertainties associated with opportunity exploitation will be more likely to act on a novel opportunity (Mullins and Forlani 2005). This association holds although the entrepreneur might possess incomplete information about the context they operate in (Choi and Shepherd 2004). Overall, harmoniously passionate entrepreneurs will also spend less energy gathering and analyzing information, and they are more likely to act on opportunities than less passionate entrepreneurs who feel they have limited control over their context.

Obsessive Passion and Entrepreneurs' Opportunity Exploitation

Obsessive passion "results from a controlled internalization of the activity into one's identity" (Vallerand et al. 2003: 757). Controlled internalization stems from the perception of a duty to undertake an activity due to intrapersonal or interpersonal obligations related to it. For instance, an entrepreneur could be part of an entrepreneurship club that requires members to create a particular amount of new products/services every year in order to be accepted. Alternatively, entrepreneurs' self-esteem can be connected to the performance of their development projects, causing them to put forth substantial energy into these projects. This intensive dedication to projects is likely to make work an important part of such entrepreneurs' identities. Entrepreneurs experiencing obsessive passion are generally not able to balance their work, family, and additional roles during identity formation well. This is because entrepreneurial activities take up an overly large part of their overall identity, which can lead to conflict with other roles and activities they pursue in their lives (see Vallerand et al. 2003).

Unlike harmonious passion, obsessive passion does not drive people to act based on positive affective experiences; rather, obsessively passionate individuals have an "internal compulsion" to pursue activities (Vallerand et al. 2003: 757). This felt obligation to work can also lead entrepreneurs to go after new additional opportunities. For instance, entrepreneurs who do not experience obsessive passion about their work may feel that exploiting a certain opportunity would take too much of the venture's resources or would be too risky, thus making them decide not to pursue the opportunity further. However, entrepreneurs high in obsessive passion will think less about resources and risk. Instead, they will consider whether exploiting the opportunity would lead to acceptance within the venture, among stakeholders (e.g., financiers), and/or in the entrepreneurial community. Furthermore, acting on new opportunities may also enable the obsessively passionate entrepreneur to uphold his or her self-image as "being so entrepreneurial that not opportunity is missed," which in turn will help maintain self-esteem. Studies have supported these arguments by demonstrating that in environments in which difficult and distant goals (such as developing a new product opportunity to market) are the norm, people often have trouble resisting the urge to concentrate on a proximal reward (e.g., acceptance in the entrepreneurial community) at the expense of ignoring goals that are more distal (Metcalfe and Mischel 1999).

Obsessively passionate entrepreneurs often experience negative emotions outside work (Vallerand et al. 2003). Because of the obligations related to their business and the necessity they perceive to perform business-related activities, it is frequently challenging or even impossible for these individuals to concentrate on activities outside work (cf. Vallerand et al. 2003). For instance, when spending time with friends and family, entrepreneurs who feel obsessive passion are likely to continually think of and discuss business issues and try to identify novel innovation opportunities. Such entrepreneurs may even pick up hobbies associated with the generation of novel ideas. Entrepreneurs in the information technology (IT) sector, for instance, may visit meetings of computer hobbyists in their free time in computer clubs and may form close social relationships within these clubs. Talking with these friends about recent happenings in the IT sector can help the entrepreneurs develop new product ideas or validate work ideas outside their normal work-related context. The larger the number of ideas entrepreneurs who feel obsessive passion generate from exchanges with their close personal environment and the better the validation of current ideas within this environment, the greater will be their tendency to act on new opportunities.

Obsessively passionate entrepreneurs' problems to find balance between their roles related to business and outside the business context (e.g., family) could lead them to allocate greater amounts of time to business issues. Indeed, role theorists argue that engaging multiple roles at the same time can cause role conflict that consumes people's coping resources (Allen 2001). As a means to lessen this role conflict, obsessively passionate entrepreneurs often focus their energy on their role in business, neglecting their family life and other non-work-related activities. In addition, these entrepreneurs generally utilize the available work time and energy to focus attention on exploiting new opportunities. As such, the *more obsessively passionate an entrepreneur is, the more likely he or she will choose to exploit an opportunity.*

The Moderating Effect of Non-work-Related Excitement

Although passion for work alters entrepreneurs' emotional state when they undertake work activities, entrepreneurs can also experience emotions stemming from sources external to the work context. Specifically, entrepreneurs may experience affective changes that are—unlike passion for work— triggered subconsciously or unconsciously by happenings outside the business context (Cardon et al. 2009). These emotions can then also be experienced in the entrepreneur's business context (Isen and Geva 1987).

In one study of innovative owner-managers' decisions, we and our colleague (Klaukien et al. 2013) explored non-work-related excitement. Excitement is a strong and positive emotional experience that is likely to influence entrepreneurs' judgment and decisions (Baron 2008; Russel 1980). For instance, excitement outside the work environment may stem from anticipating seeing a new movie or doing another pleasurable activity after work, winning a sports game, looking forward to an upcoming party, or celebrating children's graduation.[1] If this non-work-related excitement spills over to the entrepreneurs' business context, it could affect their evaluations of new opportunities. As mentioned briefly above, entrepreneurs may also experience excitement due to their passion for work (Cardon et al. 2009). However, as the above examples show, many additional sources of excitement exist. We untangle these sources and, for this section, focus on excitement originating outside entrepreneurs' work context.

Excitement will likely lessen the influence harmonious passion for work has on the decision to act on recognized opportunities. As discussed earlier, harmonious passion encourages entrepreneurs to pursue new opportunities since it causes positive emotions at work. In turn, the positive experiences make entrepreneurs feel that they have more control over possible resource limitations and the competitive environment, both of which could jeopardize new product/service (Mullins and Forlani 2005). In addition, positive affective experiences improve entrepreneurs' creativity as a prerequisite to effectively developing new products (Bharadwaj and Menon 2000). However, experiencing positive affect has an upper limit, after which further stimuli are unlikely to yield additional positive emotional experiences (Westermann et al. 1996). Because excitement is a positive affective experience with a high activation level (Russel 1980), it takes a significant amount of entrepreneurs' emotional capacity, providing less space for positive emotions stemming from harmonious work-related passion. In other words, when entrepreneurs with high harmonious passion experience high excitement levels from outside the business context, they generate lower positive emotions from work-related activities since their overall levels of positive emotions are mainly a result of excitement from non-work-related activities.

For instance, an entrepreneur who won the lottery may have a very high excitement level when he or she enters the business the next day. Since the entrepreneur already has high positive emotions, performing business-related tasks is unlikely to add to his or her overall positive emotional experience (cf. Westermann et al. 1996). In such cases, entrepreneurs' work-related passion is unlikely to affect their risk perceptions and perceptions of control over resources and competition as well as their creativity, all of which would enable new product/service development (Bharadwaj and Menon 2000; Mullins and Forlani 2005). On the other hand, entrepreneurs with lower excitement levels may experience considerable positive emotions from their work-related passion since they have "room" for more positive emotions. As such, harmonious passion has a stronger influence on these entrepreneurs' perceptions of risk, control, and creativity and is more likely to trigger the decision to pursue new opportunities.

Unlike non-work-related excitement playing a negative moderating (i.e., substituting) role in the association between harmonious passion and the decision to exploit new opportunities, excitement likely magnifies the strength of the association between obsessive passion and opportunity exploitation. Obsessive passion motivates entrepreneurs to exploit opportunities due to perceived work-related obligations (e.g., social norms within the entrepreneurial community) which is likely to lessen their self-regulation capabilities that are needed to avoid exploitation when the situation at hand is unsuitable for exploitation. Non-work-related excitement can further reduce obsessively passionate entrepreneurs' ability to resist exploiting opportunities. The ability to resist opportunity exploitation and self-regulate is based on entrepreneurs' handling future-oriented (i.e., distant in time) goals and on their in-depth assessment of whether pursuing a potential opportunity aligns with those goals (e.g., whether opportunity exploitation would contribute to venture success or comply with the R&D team's resources). When entrepreneurs encounter a stimulus that focuses their attention on an alternative goal (Simon 1957), these goal-directed actions may be interrupted, and the new goal may become the one pursued (Carver and Scheier 2001).

Excitement can be a strong emotional stimulus (Russel 1980) distracting entrepreneurs' attention from their ventures' distant goals. Rather, excitement often motivates people to take action immediately (Russel 1980). Thus, compared to entrepreneurs with low excitement levels, highly excited entrepreneurs are more vulnerable to immediate work-related obligations and will show a stronger tendency to behave in accordance with those obligations to the detriment of goals that are more distant. For instance, if obsessively passionate entrepreneurs' social context expects them to roll out a significant number of new products/services and not overlook important new opportunities, entrepreneurs high in excitement will focus less on assessing whether a new product/service will benefit their firm in the long run. Instead, they are likely to pay more attention to the social pressures urging immediate exploitation. Entrepreneurs with lower excitement levels, however, are likely to be less focused on action and will put forth more effort in assessing whether exploiting the new opportunity aligns with their firm's distant goals. Thus, the obligations obsessively passionate entrepreneurs attach to their work activities will have a stronger influence on their opportunity exploitation when they are highly excited than when they have low excitement levels.

Managers' Emotional Displays and Employees' Willingness to Act Entrepreneurially

Managers are often seen as economic individuals making rational choices and are unaffected by their emotions (e.g., Chandler 1961). Although researchers have long recognized that managers' rationality is bounded (e.g., Simon 1957), research has only recently started to explore the role of managers' emotions in their decision-making processes (e.g., Fineman 2003; Huy 1999). Yet, emotions and their displays among others are frequently a part of social interactions between people and substantially affect others' cognition and actions (e.g., Hochschild 2012). Therefore, the emotions managers display while interacting with employees impact those employees' behavior (Rafaeli and Sutton 1987). Here, we define emotional displays as noticeable reactions in a person's voice, face, and behavior that appear to indicate his or her currently experienced emotions (Lewis 1998).

Because a primary task of being a manager entails motivating employees to act in the organization's interest (Yukl 2006), it is necessary for managers to display emotions based on the behavior they would like to elicit from employees. Newcombe and Ashkanasy (2002) showed that an individual's facial expressions can more powerfully affect an observer's rating of that person's leadership than the objective information that was delivered, thus highlighting the considerable influence managers' emotional displays can have on employees. Scholars have also revealed that emotional displays change the receiver's interpretation of a verbal message (e.g., Archer and Akert 1977) and that the signaled emotions of an individual can alter the receiver's emotional state (Pugh 2001) and thus influence his or her decisions and actions.

The emotions a sender displays might not mirror his or her "felt" emotions (Ekman and Oster 1979; Hochschild 2012). Take, for example, a server who flashes a welcoming smile to a guest to obtain a larger tip even though he or she is annoyed (Rafaeli and Sutton 1987). Indeed, the distinction between managers' displayed emotions and those they feel gives them the chance to outwardly display only emotions that make employees align their performance with the goals of the organization regardless of the managers' current inner emotions (Dasborough and Ashkanasy 2002). However, managers must be able to control their displayed emotions and show only those emotions that suit their objectives. This ability ultimately reflects managers' *emotional intelligence* (Mayer and Salovey 1997).

The influence of this emotional display on the receiver rests on his or her expectations about the sender's role. For instance, while service personnel generally intend to smile in a friendly manner toward customers, funeral directors are expected to express sadness to a relative of the deceased (Rafaeli and Sutton 1987). Role expectations and emotional displays even change at the individual level. People expect surgical nurses, for instance, to show few emotions in the operating room. On the other hand, during their work with patients and their relatives, the emotions they display should be warm and sociable (Denison and Sutton 1990). We will now concentrate on the manager's role as one who encourages entrepreneurial behavior among employees and, specifically, investigate how these managers' emotional displays improve or reduce employees' willingness to act entrepreneurially.

It is important for firms to increase the willingness to act entrepreneurially for employees for several reasons. First, entrepreneurial behavior is crucial for all organizations to generate knowledge and convert it into novel products (Shane and Venkataraman 2000), an activity that is especially critical given the competitiveness of current business environments. Further, firms need to pursue corporate entrepreneurship projects to respond to environmental hostility and dynamism (Ireland and Hitt 1999). Furthermore, when employees have an entrepreneurial mindset, they are more likely to identify novel business opportunities with high growth potential that the firm could miss if it does not have entrepreneurial employees (McGrath and MacMillan 2000).

Entrepreneurial motivation studies present several factors that influence individuals' willingness to act in an entrepreneurial way. For example, Shane et al. (2003) highlighted people's risk-taking propensity, goal setting, and drive as primary motivators of entrepreneurs. We suggest that the emotions a manager displays about an entrepreneurial project relay signals to employees that shape their perceptions about risk/uncertainty as well as influence project goals and the energy employees are willing to put forth. Finally, emotions can be contagious. Namely, the emotions managers display can spill over to employees, impacting their emotional experiences and motivation for entrepreneurial action. Our specific focus in this section is on the emotions of satisfaction, frustration, worry, bewilderment, and strain. Yet, we also capture confidence, which some authors describe as an emotion (e.g., Barbalet 1996). However, confidence seems to be more based on cognition than the other emotions. As such, confidence may affect the extent to which the other emotions influence employees.

Displays of Confidence

Confidence is an "emotion of assured expectation" (Barbalet 1996: 76) that encourages action (Barbalet 1996)—a feeling that one is able to successfully handle situations given the resources one has at hand (Collins Cobuild 1987). Confidence displays visually indicate that the manager believes in employees' ability to successfully accomplish tasks necessary for innovation, which in turn can inspire employees to act entrepreneurially.

Entrepreneurial projects are highly uncertain for those involved in terms of their financial welfare, psychic well-being, and career security (Liles 1976). An individual will act entrepreneurially if a project's perceived uncertainty is below his or her personal threshold of acceptable risk for that project. Because the confidence managers display signals to employees that specific projects can be managed in a way that leads to success, employees' perceptions regarding the uncertainty of such projects will be lessened. Although confidence indicates that project outcomes are within the team's control, managers and employees may still encounter substantial challenges. In fact, these challenges may lead to emotional experiences and displays. Because employees generally view managers as experts on their projects, managers' confidence displays can be especially a strong inspiration for behavior (Carson et al. 1993). Thus, the confidence managers display shows employees that projects are realistic and the likelihood of success is high.

Positive Emotional Displays

While scholars dispute the definition of emotion, they generally agree that "an emotion is a valenced affective reaction to perceptions of situations" (Richins 1997: 127). Further emotions are signals of individuals' overall well-being (Rafaeli and Sutton 1987). The range of emotions people experience is vast (Averill 1975), and researchers have developed numerous categorizations to try to organize our understanding of these nuanced reactions. Some scholars suggest that there are few "basic emotions" and that all other emotions are derived from these basic emotions (compare Ekman 1992; Frijda 1986). In this section, we investigate managers' displays of five common emotions that are in line with these basic emotions (Ekman 1992; Frijda 1986). Indeed, research has found that they are prominent during processes of organizational change (Brundin 2002) such as corporate entrepreneurship (Guth and Ginsberg 1990).

According to Rafaeli and Sutton (1987) and others (cf. Russel 1980), emotions are either positive or negative. A positive emotion "reflects the extent to which a person feels enthusiastic, active, and alert" and "is a state of high energy, full concentration, and pleasurable engagement" (Watson et al. 1988: 1063). One positive emotion is satisfaction, which is based on a belief that one's performance is higher than normal or expected (Fisher 2003). Research has investigated numerous forms of satisfaction (e.g., job satisfaction (Fisher 2003) and customer satisfaction (Rafaeli and Sutton 1987; Pugh 2001)), generally finding that individuals feel satisfaction when they have previously received positive feedback.

Managers who outwardly display their satisfaction provide a visual indicator to employees that their project performs above expectations. In turn, this outward display of satisfaction will likely heighten employees' entrepreneurial motivation for three reasons. First, people often assume that past success applies to the future as well, thus believing that returns will be higher and risk lower than objectively the case (Levinthal and March 1993). As such, when managers display satisfaction with a project, employees will feel that the project is likely to succeed. Thus, employees' perceived uncertainty will fall below employees' acceptable threshold. Second, when managers signal high satisfaction and a high likelihood of project success, employees are more likely to meet high personal goals related to the project; high personal goals can be a strong motivation to act entrepreneurially (Baum et al. 2001). Finally, setting challenging goals for themselves can improve employees' drive, or their "willingness to put forth effort" (Shane et al. 2003: 268), which is a requirement for entrepreneurial behavior.

Negative Emotional Displays

A negative emotion refers to "a general dimension of subjective distress and unpleasurable engagement that subsumes a variety of aversive mood states, including anger, contempt, disgust, guilt, fear, and nervousness" (Watson et al. 1988: 1063). Negative emotions appear to have a harmful impact on the relationship between managers and employees by weakening trust between the two parties and thus significantly upsetting their relationship (Liden and Graen 1980). When investigating emotional displays during radical organizational change, Brundin (2002) discovered that frustration, worry, bewilderment, and strain are commonly experienced negative emotions that are obstacles to implementing the intended change.

Frustration happens when "an instigated goal-response (or predicted behavioral sequence) is interrupted or interdicted" (Fox and Spector 1999: 916). Stemming from the basic emotion of anger (Ekman 1992), frustration frequently causes counter-productive behaviors (Fox and Spector 1999) and poor performance (McColl-Kennedy and Andersson 2002). As a result, managers need to neutralize employee frustration as soon as they notice it (Humphrey 2002). When managers themselves indicate their frustration, they signal that the group is not meeting performance standards for the current project stage. Thus, employees are likely to feel that the project is more uncertain, so only individuals with an exceedingly high propensity for risk taking will see the project as feasible and become involved. Furthermore, if the team does not meet previously set goals for the project stage at hand, these goals may be diminished, which offsets the motivational influence of high goals that trigger entrepreneurial action (Baum et al. 2001). In addition, reducing goals also lessens employees' willingness to put effort into the project (Shane et al. 2003).

Further, *worry* is a negative emotion-laden and uncontrollable chain of thoughts and images (Borkovec et al. 1983). It is a common characteristic of anxiety disorder (Langlois et al. 2000) and often causes feelings of insecurity and intolerance of uncertainty (Francis and Dugas 2004). Worry emerges when people try to resolve problems with uncertain outcomes that could ultimately be negative (Borkovec et al. 1983). Managers displaying worry signal to employees that they feel project development is uncertain and could result in failure. With more worry displayed by managers, the uncertainty employees attach to the project and their negative expectations of the project's future will increase. High uncertainty has a detrimental effect on entrepreneurial motivation (similar to frustration, as discussed above). Moreover, the imagined uncertainty employees feel about the entrepreneurial project's progress will likely cause them to set lower performance goals for the entire project, ultimately reducing their motivation to act entrepreneurially (Baum et al. 2001).

Stemming from insufficient understanding, *bewilderment* is an ambiguity experience that is considered unacceptable by others (Meyerson 1990). Meyerson (1990) showed that bewilderment is a frequent emotional experience among hospital social workers that is regularly kept secret because it is seen as an indication of being weak. Yet, settings that are less formal and more relaxed can constitute "safe havens," where people are free to show their bewilderment openly (Meyerson 1990). Displays of bewilderment indicate that managers are having trouble understanding a project's current challenges due to its complexity. Since employees frequently view managers as experts, in such cases, they are likely to feel that they too will have trouble understanding their own task within the project. Therefore, employees will perceive the tasks and outcomes associated with the project as ambiguous, so only employees with a high tolerance for uncertainty will become involved (similar to frustration, as discussed earlier).

Strain is another important negative emotion in the managerial context. People experience strain as tiredness, exhaustion, and sometimes even depression with results from overly high job demands (Karasek 1979; Fineman 2003). Researchers have found that continuous strain may result in dangerous physical symptoms including high blood pressure and as a consequence various cardiovascular diseases (Schnall et al. 1994). Displays of strain indicate that managers perceive the current project stage places overly high demands on him or her. Thus, employees are likely to believe the project demands very high effort. These employees are only likely to continue their commitment and motivation in the project when they have high drive (Shane et al. 2003) and tolerance for uncertainty.

The Moderating Role of Managers' Emotional Displays

Brundin et al. (2008) argued that, from employees' viewpoint as receivers of managers' signals, displayed positive and negative emotions interact with displayed confidence in explaining employees' entrepreneurial motivation. Consider, for instance, a manager who signals to employees a particular confidence level regarding a specific project. This signal shows employees that the project's outcome is under their collective control (Barbalet 1996). If the manager additionally signals a positive emotion, he or she indicates that the project is currently performing well. Because people tend to extrapolate past success into the future (Levinthal and March 1993), employees are likely to believe that the project's future is less uncertain. Thus, since the effect of the level of confidence a manager displays on employees' willingness to act entrepreneurially is influenced by the project uncertainty perceived, the additional display of satisfaction strengthens this signal because it lessens the uncertainty employees perceive regarding managerial displays of confidence.

In contrast, managers' displays of negative emotions are likely to have a negative impact on the effect of signaled confidence on employees' entrepreneurial motivations. For instance, bewilderment displays suggest that the manager is having trouble understanding the actual project stage's complexity (Meyerson 1990). When a manager shows bewilderment, his or her employees may think the manager is unable to effectively explain the goals and tasks for this project stage and will thus perceive the project as more uncertain. Along the same lines, when a manager shows strain, thus signaling that his or her current job duties are at the high end of his or her tolerance (Parker and Sprigg 1999), employees are likely to assume that the project requires more personal effort on their part and will be unsure whether those efforts will be enough for project success. As a result, employees will likely feel there is more uncertainty regarding the actual level of signaled confidence than when there is no display of negative emotions.

Interestingly, and opposite our expectations, we and our colleagues (Brundin et al. 2008) found that managers' displays of frustration boost the positive association between managers' confidence displays and employees' entrepreneurial motivation. In other words, managers' displays of control over outcomes are more positively related to employees' motivation to act entrepreneurially when the managers also signal that present goals are not being met and that the team is underachieving. Therefore, when employees perceive (from managerial signals) below-expectation performance of the project, it is even more important for managers to indicate that they are confident and that the project is likely to succeed in the future. Seeing this confidence despite current underperformance potentially motivates employees to even enhance their efforts in order to turn the project around and realize successful project outcomes. A study of radical organizational change supports this conjecture, showing that perception of frustration among leaders propel change activities when the leaders seem to truly believe the project will succeed (Brundin 2002). It appears that confidence is important in this context not only because it positively affects employees' willingness but also because when it is displayed outwardly, it influences the effect of outward display of other positive and negative emotions. These results add to prior findings reported by Shea (1999) which revealed that highly confident supervisors have a stronger impact on team members than those with less confidence. However, Shea (1999) did not consider contingencies between confidence displays and displays of positive and negative emotions, which, as we and a colleague (Brundin et al. 2008) showed, can have a substantial influence on subordinates' motivation.

Above, we introduced the role negative emotions play in the entrepreneurial context—namely, managers' displays of negative emotions and the impact thereof on employees' entrepreneurial motivation (Brundin et al. 2008). However, negative emotions can also have a more straightforward and impactful influence on entrepreneurial cognition, which we discuss next.

Negative Emotions, Affective Commitment, and Learning from Experience

There has been a significant theoretical movement toward developing a better understanding of organizational knowledge. In this literature, organizational knowledge is viewed as the assumptions and expectations organizational members hold about the cause-and-effect relationship in the domains in which the firm operates (Huber 1991; Walsh and Ungson 1991). While there has been increased research on knowledge at the level of the organization, this stream of work has mainly concentrated on transfer and acquisition of knowledge from sources outside the firm (Ahuja 2000; Hansen 1999). In contrast, scholars have focused less on the ways new knowledge is generated (McFadyen and Cannella 2004). One significant exception is work on how an individual's interpersonal relationships can contribute to knowledge creation (e.g., McFadyen and Cannella 2004; Yli-Renko et al. 2001). Despite these recent studies, however, we know little about how members of an organization create new knowledge that is actionable based on their own experiences. Actionable knowledge in organizations is generated when a member of the organization learns from his or her experience (Huy 1999; Kim 1993) and is then dedicated to act to aid his or her organization based on the newly acquired knowledge (Kanter 1968; Leonard-Barton 1995).

Researchers believe that failure is an experience that can trigger individuals' learning. Project failure is an especially common event, in particular for individuals in innovation (Burgelman and Valikangas 2005; Shepherd and Cardon 2009; Sminia 2003) and research-based firms and organizations (DiMasi et al. 2003). Moreover, project failures are common for people in organizations facing contexts that are quickly changing (Deeds et al. 2000; McGrath et al. 2006) and complex (Gassmann and Reepmeyer 2005; Iacovou and Dexter 2005). Here, project failure is *the termination of an endeavor that was aimed to generate value for the organization but did not meet its intended goals* (Shepherd et al. 2009a). For example, in interviews we conducted and reported in Shepherd et al. (2011), research scientists referred to project failure as the project being "over" (a research scientist in chemistry), "buried" (a research scientist in theoretical physics), and having reached a "dead end" (research scientist in biochemistry). They also reported that the termination of projects is an implicit part of their jobs. Since failure "upsets the status quo" (Chuang and Baum 2003) and causes individuals to seek potential solutions (McGrath 2001; Petrovski 1985), often people within organizations, including scientific researchers (Popper 1959), engineers (Petrovski 1985), and organizational leaders (Sitkin 1992), learn more from failing than from succeeding. Thus, we refer to *learning from failure* as "the sense that one is acquiring, and can apply, knowledge and skills" (Spreitzer et al. 2005: 538) and in doing so stress people's subjective learning perception (Huy 1999; Kim 1993; Weick 1979), which is in line with sensemaking studies. However, opportunities to learn from failure may not always end in knowledge the organization can act on because the individuals may have trouble effectively processing information revealed by the failure (Weick 1990; Weick and Sutcliffe 2007). In addition, the failure may cause negative emotions that lessen individuals' dedication to acting for the organization's benefit. Indeed, we and our colleague (Shepherd et al. 2011) built on psychology research on coping with loss (Archer and Freeman 1999; Stroebe and Schut 2001; Shepherd 2003) to explore how individuals learn from failure and maintain their affective organizational commitment as a prerequisite to move past project failure. The study used psychological theories of loss (Archer and Freeman 1999; Stroebe and Schut 2001) to theorize a model explaining how individuals within organizations move on after project failure.

Moving on after project failure requires individuals to view projects as a means to explore held assumptions, approach project failure as feedback to test these assumptions, and make decisions on following projects based on that feedback (McGrath 1999). These actions require individuals to learn from the failure of their previous project and be willing to adapt their beliefs to reach organizational goals. Specifically, we explore how individuals process project failure as feedback—influenced by the time passed since the project has failed, individuals' coping orientation, and their beliefs regarding the extent to which the organization normalizes failure—to facilitate learning from the failed project. We also investigate how negative emotions stemming from project failure can influence individuals' affective commitment to reaching organizational goals, how time passed since the failure and perceptions regarding the extent to which the organizational environment normalizes failure directly impact negative emotions, and how individuals' coping orientations—namely, loss, restoration, and oscillation orientations—impact the association between time since project failure and the resulting negative emotions about the failure event.

Entrepreneurial Project Failure and Negative Emotions

Employees in organizations tend to form feelings of psychological ownership (Pierce et al. 2001) for projects such that they believe they have control over and deep knowledge of the project based on heavy investments of effort, time, and energy. As a result of these feelings of psychological ownership, individuals' self-identities often become interwoven with that of the project and/or project team. When resources are reallocated after a project failure, the team is likely split up and allocated to other projects, thus leading to the loss of close relationships. In such situations, part of an individual's self-identity can be lost; this loss can result in dysfunctional effects for the individual (Pierce et al. 2001).

There are a number of examples of employees who describe project failure to yield substantial negative emotions; these individuals see project failures as the low point of their career (Eggen and Witte 2006), experience bitter disappointment (Cunningham 2004), and feel emotionally devastated (Dillion 1998). Further, research team members have reported feeling a variety of emotions after project failure, including denial, anger, personal pain, sadness, dismay, worry, anxiety, annoyance, frustration, and depression (Dillon 1998; Murray and Cox 1989). In our study with a colleague (Shepherd et al. 2011), interviews with research scientists also revealed several negative emotions caused by project failure. For example, when asked about their feelings after their most recent project failure, the scientists interviewed reported the following: "To see that you and the team were not able to lead it [a project] to a successful completion was altogether disappointing" (economics); "There was this huge effort put into the project, and to accept that is was for nothing was really difficult" (economics); "I was completely frustrated" (chemistry); "It was really painful. ... I think we were all equally depressed" (biochemistry); "When the project does not work out, you start thinking whether your work makes any sense or not. ... You start doubting [the work] more and more" (mechanical engineering); "It was really frustrating, I was quite furious. ... For example, to reduce the anger whenever I got an email [from a project team member], I read it only the next day. I had to sleep on it to deal with all the frustration" (theoretical physics).

However, does every project failure lead to overly negative emotions? Is there variation in the level of negative emotions generated by project failures? With these questions in mind, we employ self-determination theory (SDT) to theorize on how people generate negative emotions from project failure because SDT (1) centers on individuals' psychological well-being, which has been associated with emotions; (2) focuses on criteria of importance based on the person's context; and (3) has been explored at length in organizational settings. In this context, **psychological well-being** *is the degree to which a person experiences self-acceptance, positive relationships with other people, mastery, autonomy, personal growth, and purpose in life* (Ryff 1989).

The goal of SDT is to explain the psychological processes that enable optimum psychological functioning and well-being (Ryan and Deci 2000; Deci and Ryan 2000: 262). A person's environment provides nutriments that satisfy three needs associated with psychological well-being: competence, relatedness, and autonomy. When these needs are not met, psychological well-being decreases. Meeting these needs varies between project team members and within the individual team members across projects (Sheldon et al. 1996). Overall, people are driven to achieve high performance on projects that will help them satisfy their psychological needs. The motivation behind these performance desires mirrors intrinsic motivation since it entails active involvement in tasks that the person considers as interesting and that enable personal growth (Deci and Ryan 2000).

While projects that help individuals meet their basic needs will lead to higher intrinsic motivation compared to projects that fulfill these needs less, they are also likely to lead to more substantial negative emotions if they fail. This idea of project salience based on how much it fulfills these psychological needs is in line with previous scholarly work on commitment via people's psychological ownership and personal work engagement. Specifically, psychological ownership occurs when a person believes that a specific project belongs to him or her in a way that identity bonding between the person and his or her project has emerged and meaning and emotions related to possessiveness and ownership have formed despite the fact that the person has no legal right to the project (Pierce et al. 2001). Moreover, personal work engagement describes how much of their personal selves people bring to their work roles (Kahn 1990) and the degree to which there is "the simultaneous employment and expression of a person's preferred self in task behaviors that promote connections to work and to others, personal presence, and active, full role performances" (Kahn 1990: 700). Main elements of psychological ownership include autonomy and relatedness, and main elements of personal engagement include relatedness and competence. Kahn (1990) denotes these latter elements as meaningfulness, which occurs when individuals feel useful, worthwhile, and valuable when participating in some type of activity. When projects satisfy people's needs for autonomy, relatedness, and competence, those people will start to feel psychological ownership for those projects and will be to a great extent personally engaged in the projects. Thus, higher psychological ownership and personal engagement for a project will cause stronger negative emotional reactions in the case of failure.

Project Failure, Need for Competence, and Negative Emotions

A project importance to a person partially depends on the degree to which the project contributes to fulfilling his or her need for competence. Once the project is stopped, this need is unmet (i.e., thwarted). The psychological need for **competence** *is met when a person received feedback indicating that he or she is performing well at a task*, and this need is thwarted when feedback indicates poor performance (Deci and Ryan 2000). The motivation literature provides a large body of evidence linking tasks that fulfill needs for competence and individuals' motivation to complete those tasks (Vallerand and Reid 1984).

Projects help meet employees' need for competence. To start with, projects often allow for the improvement of individuals' learning (Dweck 1986) and generate mastery over feelings (Butler 1992). In turn, these feelings demonstrate the generation of competence (Rawsthorne and Elliot 1999). Further, the culture of a particular project team may contribute to fulfilling competence needs as a productive competitive environment within or across project teams can confirm employees' competence (Tjosvold et al. 2003). In addition, group membership can address competence needs. Namely, a group can itself form confidence in its competence (Gist 1987; Lindsley et al. 1995). Group members will not only value this competence but it can also contribute to their self-identity (Tajfel and Turner 1979, 1986).

Thus, employees' psychological well-being is likely to decrease when they (1) lose a project which they believe is an important source of learning for valued skills and/or for which they perceive to possess high levels of task-related competence, (2) lose a culture within the team that sustains productive competition but is substituted by a culture of caustic competitiveness with individuals who do not support their endeavors and behaviors, or (3) lose the membership in a competent group and are allocated to a group that is less capable. In addition, individuals often view group membership turnovers as losing a central aspect of their identity, thus decreasing his or her feelings of competence and self-worth (Steele 1988). Losing these important elements through the failure of a project and are not completely substituted by, for example, the next project thwarts the individual's competence need, causing negative emotions. Because projects are likely to differ in the degree they fulfill people's need for competence, they are also likely to differ in the degree to which this need is thwarted in the case of failure.

Project Failure, Need for Autonomy, and Negative Emotions

A project's importance is also affected by how much the project fulfills a person's psychological need for autonomy. **Autonomy** at work *is a form of personal control that offers employees the opportunity to choose when, where, and how they do their work* (Thompson and Prottas 2006). As with the need for competence, projects differ in how much autonomy they offer to those involved. Generally, people tend to value situations they have personal control over more than situations controlled by external forces. Leaders can provide employees autonomy through empowerment (Logan and Ganster 2007; Lok et al. 2005), structures with low levels of formality (O'driscoll et al. 2006), participation in important decisions, and opportunities for extensive self-management (Liden and Tewksbury 1995). Autonomy can also be supported through organizational processes and structures that encourage the sharing of information, independent activities, and decision making within a team setting (Blanchard et al. 1995). Researchers have shown that environments that offer people more autonomy improve well-being (Deci et al. 1989), increase one's satisfaction with the job (Purasuraman and Alutto 1984), and diminish the levels of stress people experience (Purasuraman and Alutto 1984; Thompson and Prottas 2006). However, autonomy can be undercut by incentives and evaluations, which have been shown to reduce creative outcomes (Amabile 1997), finding solutions for problems that are complex in nature (McGraw and McCullers 1979), and processing of information deeply and conceptually (Deci and Ryan 2000).

The processes, structures, and management systems that help fulfill project team members' autonomy needs can become different in the case of project failure. For instance, when management terminates a project, employees may see that project termination as a threat to their sense of control (Dirks et al. 1996). This threat perception is particularly problematic when individuals have felt psychological ownership over or have identified themselves with the project at hand (Pierce et al. 2001); the individuals may feel a sense of loss, frustration, and stress (Pierce et al. 2001). Thus, project failure can thwart the fulfillment of autonomy needs, thereby causing negative emotional reactions among project members. Because projects differ in the degree to which they fulfill the need for autonomy, there will also be differences in the degree to which this need is thwarted after project failure.

Project Failure, Need for Relatedness, and Negative Emotions

A project's importance is also likely to be affected by how much the project fulfills the psychological need for relatedness. **Relatedness** *entails feeling connected to and understood by others* (Patrick et al. 2007). For instance, there is evidence that people's motivation increases when their environment shows a sense of secure relatedness (Ryan and La Guardia 2000; Ryan et al. 1994). Indeed, studies have also found that people have a need to feel related to other people and behave in ways to fulfill that need. Further, people tend to experience positive emotions from increased relatedness to other members of their group (McAdams and Bryant 1987; McAdams 1985) and more negative emotions with decreasing relatedness (Leary 1990). These negative emotions can include anxiety (Tice and Baumeister 1990; Craighead et al. 1979) and loneliness (Russell et al. 1984). Low feelings of relatedness within one's group can also have negative consequences for their physical and psychological health (De Longis et al. 1988).

Entrepreneurial projects often offer organizational members the chance to fulfill their need for relatedness. This need can be satisfied, for instance, through supervisor and/or coworker support (Caverley et al. 2007; Thompson and Prottas 2006), identification with an organizational group (Richter et al. 2006), and/or identification with the organization itself (Ashforth 2001; Barker and Tompkins 1994). As with the other needs, the need for relatedness can be thwarted by project failure since, for example, it can be associated with losing a specific valued coworker relationship (cf Vince and Broussine 1996). Indeed, this loss and other changes stemming from project failure can harm employees' attachment to other people, which in the past provided the employees a foundation for experiencing relatedness at work (Vince and Broussine 1996) and thus boosted their psychological well-being. Consistently, employees with less-supportive team members and managers have been found to typically have lower psychological well-being (Gilbreath and Benson 2004).

Psychological well-being can also be decreased when an individual's identity is jeopardized by an entrepreneurial project failure that breaks apart the team, leading to the redeployment of prior teammates within the firm.

This identity threat is especially extensive for employees who perceive that their team is an extension of the self (Belk 1988). After project failure, the threat to the individual's social identity thwarts his or her relatedness need and causes a negative emotional reaction (Aquino and Douglas 2003; De Longis et al. 1988). Like the other needs, projects likely differ in how much they fulfill the need for relatedness and thus differ in how much they thwart this need if they fail.

Negative Emotions and Learning from Project Failure

Research has found that negative emotions hinder people's information processing (Mogg et al. 1990; Wells and Matthews 1994), which is required for learning. We acknowledge that negative emotions can benefit learning. Negative emotions, for instance, indicate that something important is at risk or has been lost (Luce et al. 1997). As a result, people may direct their attention to the cause of the loss (Clore 1992; Pieters and Raaij 1987). This attention allocation is a prerequisite for learning based on enhanced scanning and information processing related to the cause of the loss (Cacioppo et al. 1999; Weick 1979) and for the motivation to initiate change (Lazarus 1993). Yet, in other situations, negative emotions can also limit individuals' information scanning (Gladstein and Reilly 1985; Staw et al. 1981; Sutton and D'Aunno 1989) and disrupt their processing of information that is obtained (Mathews et al. 1990), thus diminishing learning. Furthermore, negative emotions can also redirect individuals' scarce information-processing capacity from the event itself to the emotional reactions to the event (Nolen-Hoeksema and Morrow 1991). Overall, any learning advantages that come from negative emotions are usually overshadowed by its disadvantages, and, in particular, for tasks that are highly complex (Huber 1985).

Effective learning from entrepreneurial project failure starts to materialize when the employee compares the project's actual performance with the initial plan for particular project tasks to improve his or her understanding of the performance gap and failure cause (McGrath 1999: 23). Learning frequently entails the repetition of strategies, routines, and/or practices that previously have been used successfully in one's own or other organizations (e.g., vicarious learning (Kim and Miner 2007)). However, learning can also occur from the study of failures because failures drive people to seek out new models, activities, and/or routines (Kim and Miner 2007). When individuals are able to effectively learn after an entrepreneurial project failure, it gives the organization information about its assumptions (e.g., about product favorability, strategic direction, etc.) that can improve its decision making going forward (McGrath 1999). Therefore, learning from project failure entails understanding the reasons for the failure, evaluating the core assumptions that drove the failed project to determine whether they are worth keeping, and creating capabilities to alter the strategies, processes, and procedures that resulted in the failure. While entrepreneurial project failure can create useful opportunities for organizational learning (Corbett et al. 2007; McGrath 1999; Sitkin 1992), when such failures are associated with emotional challenges, organizational members are unlikely to discuss them, thus compromising learning (McGrath 1999; Shepherd 2003; Shepherd et al. 2009a, b; Shepherd et al. 2013).

Just like we anticipate heterogeneity in the negative emotions a person experiences across project failures and heterogeneity in emotion levels across team members for a specific project failure, we also expect individuals' responses to negative emotional experiences to vary. The question that arises is why some individuals are better than others at overcoming the negative emotional interference to learning that can occur after a failure experience. We argue that self-regulation (specifically self-compassion) moderates the association between the negative emotions in response to a project failure and the learning benefits for the individual. Based on the social psychology and failure literatures, we explore how different aspects of self-compassion can help employees learn from the failure of their project.

Negative emotions can weaken people's recalling of information about the past and can cause perceptions of disconnection from and avoidance of close relationships with other people in the social environments inside and outside work (Hogan et al. 2001). In particular, negative emotions stemming from entrepreneurial project failure will impact individuals' affective organizational commitment. Affective commitment, or *a person's identification with and involvement in an organization* (O'Reilly and Chatman 1986), represents their motivation to "give energy and loyalty to the organization" (Kanter 1968: 499). Research has shown that employees' affective commitment can lead to better performance at the level of the individual (Sinclair et al. 2005; Vandenberghe et al. 2004) and the organization (Gong et al. 2009). Thus, employees often see project failure as a type of negative feedback regarding their work efforts. The experience of such negative emotions is a mediator in the association between the negative feedback individuals receive and how they regulate their personal goals (Ilies and Judge 2005), indicating that after project failure, goals congruence between the level of the individual and the organization diminishes as compared to their congruence before the failure event. However, after time, an individual's emotional attachment to a failed project gradually breaks, and his or her thinking about the project or events associated with the failure event cause fewer negative emotions. New projects and social relationships become more central and start to fulfill the individual's previously thwarted psychological needs, thus helping regain his or her affective commitment to the organization.

Intelligent-Failure Management Through Normalization

In environments where failure consequences are especially detrimental, dividing complex tasks into smaller subtasks enables individuals to generate a series of small wins; these small wins in turn drive constructive behavior (Weick 1984). Such wins are likely to generate task-related self-efficacy and thus positively impact task performance for ensuing forms of the task that are more difficult (Bandura 1991). A potential drawback of "small wins" is that due to their "smallness," people may not pay as much attention to the task at hand, leading them to search for less information (Sitkin 1992). As a different strategy, "intelligent failure" recognizes the advantages of failure if "(1) they [the projects undertaken] result from thoughtfully planned actions, (2) have uncertain outcomes, (3) are of modest scale, (4) are executed and responded to with alacrity, and (5) take place in domains that are familiar enough to permit effective learning" (Sitkin 1992: 243). For *alacrity* to arise, individuals must fail without the experience of negative emotions, which can occur when the organizational environment normalizes failure for employees.

Normalization denotes institutionalized processes whereby the extraordinary (in our case, failure) is made more commonplace. More specifically, stimuli that are threatening, uncommon, consequential, or have personal meaning may stimulate deep emotions. A normalization process makes these stimuli less important and less arousing, thus making them more ordinary (Ashforth and Kreiner 2002: 217). Generally, normalization stems from habituation or desensitization processes. Habituation—which can be triggered by interactions with others and is a social process (Ashforth and Kreiner 2002)—involves recurring exposure to the same stimulus that ultimately leads to increasingly weaker responses. Desensitization involves exposure to stimuli of growing unpleasantness. Through desensitization, the discrepancy between anticipated and actually experienced stimuli is diminished, thus decreasing the emotions experienced (St-Onge 1995). For instance, in several entrepreneurial failures of escalating significance, the discrepancy between anticipated and experienced failures becomes smaller, so the most recent failure causes fewer negative emotions as compared to failures without predecessors.

Normalization can also improve a person's persistence with what he or she initially perceives as a task that is aversive. For instance, when recounting how he learned to deal with disgust at handling corpses to continue the task, a hospital orderly stated, "After a while, I got used to it. Each time it got a little easier. It's just not that big a deal anymore" (Reed 1989: 48). When the failure of projects is normalized, organizational members are more likely to persist with entrepreneurial efforts. That is, because failure does not lead to negative emotions anymore, employees are less likely demotivated to try again in future projects. Farson and Keyes (2002) applied intelligent-failure principles to innovation management and came up with the concept of the "failure-tolerant leader," a manager who "through their words and actions, help people overcome their fear of failure, and, in the process, create a culture of intelligent risk taking that leads to sustained innovation" (Farson and Keyes 2002: 4). Normalizing failure leads to reduced fear of failure. For instance, a failure-tolerant leader handles "steps in the innovation process—those that work and those that don't—with less evaluation and more interpretation. They don't praise or penalize; they analyze" (Farson and Keyes 2002: 5). Similarly, "the best coaches take victory or defeat in stride. 'I didn't get consumed by losses,' said the legendary NFL coach Don Shula, 'and I didn't get overwhelmed by successes'" (Farson and Keyes 2002: 5).

Regardless of whether the normalizing failure just happens over time or is intentionally coordinated by the firm, the intelligent-failure method hinges on getting rid of obstacles to generating new knowledge from failures. However, doing so may be challenging. According to Farson and Keyes (2002: 4), "While companies are beginning to accept the value of failure in the abstract—at the level of the corporate policies, processes, and practices—it's an entirely different matter at the personal level. Everyone hates to fail." In the next section, we discuss the challenges associated with normalizing failure in line with an intelligent-failure approach.

The above discussion on normalizing the failure of entrepreneurial projects to eliminate grief *does not take into account* two important implications. First, although normalization is beneficial in lessening negative emotional reactions that can obstruct learning and negatively affect performance after the emotional event, it also lessens the learning-related advantages that such negative emotions can bring about. By changing the failure-related emotions from being strongly negative to neutral (or even somewhat positive), the intelligent-failure strategy may have the same limitations Sitkin (1992) pointed out about Weick's (1984) approach of "small wins." More specifically, emotional neutrality can lead to low attention levels and decreased information search since events with more emotionality are higher priority in individuals' information processing compared to events that are emotionally neutral (Ellis et al. 1971). Furthermore, negative emotional events tend to generate higher levels of attention and information processing than those events that are emotionally positive (Wood et al. 1990). Negative emotions highlight an event's significance and thus guide individuals' attention to actions, beliefs, and events precipitating the negative event to scan for important information (Weick 1979) and encourage adaptation (Lazarus 1993). Similarly, as mentioned, grief occurs when an individual believes he or she has lost something important (Luce et al. 1997). Thus, signals indicating that a failure has happened can encourage change and enhance coping by guiding the individual's attention (Schwarz and Clore 1988) to the circumstances of the event (Pieters and Raaij 1987) and to the achievement of learning outcomes from the failure (Cacioppo et al. 1999).

Second, eliminating negative emotions from project failure may also weaken individuals' commitment to subsequent initiation and advancement of new projects. In other words, because grief is a reaction to the loss of something that is important for individuals' psychological and emotional well-being, eliminating negative emotions entails reducing the project's emotional importance for him or her. In turn, this diminished importance enhances the probability of project failure. Decreased creativity (Amabile 1997; Amabile and Fisher 2000) as well as reduced commitment of the leaders (Song and Parry 1997) and employees (Amabile and Fisher 2000) of the project and team members can all lead to lower performance of the entrepreneurial project.

To illustrate these ideas consider a physician with seriously ill patients, which are roughly analogous to an organizational member and his or her entrepreneurial project. If the physician becomes desensitized to patients' death, he or she will engage in depersonalization. When depersonalization occurs, the physician's interpersonal interaction with patients and their families gets less sensitive, more negative, and perhaps highly detached, ultimately resulting in patient care that is less effective (Peeters and Le

Blanc 2001). Similar to physicians who have faced a considerable number of deaths, employees who have gone through numerous failures can eventually become desensitized to the project's failure and may commit less to subsequent projects.

In the next section, we propose an approach that regulates—instead of normalizing— grief triggered by project failure. We then describe the organizational conditions that will likely lead to superior learning and commitment outcomes using this approach.

COPING ORIENTATIONS AND PROJECT FAILURE

Two approaches exist that researchers believe aid individuals in coping with the emotions caused by loss, and a third approach combining the two: a loss orientation, a restoration orientation, and an orientation of oscillating between loss and restoration orientation (Shepherd 2003; Stroebe and Schut 2001).[2] We now address how each of these orientations impacts learning from project failure as well as their influence on the way employees utilize the time since their last entrepreneurial project has failed to deal with the negative emotions caused by the failure.

When individuals engage in a **loss orientation**, they *work through and process elements of a loss to break the emotional bonds they have to the object lost* (Stroebe and Schut 2001). For this coping orientation, people must concentrate on what happened prior to the failure in order to form a plausible account for the failure event. Thinking about the process and causes of an entrepreneurial project failure can offer opportunities for constructive learning (Corbett et al. 2007; McGrath 1999; Sitkin 1992) if employees compare project performance when failure occurred to expected performance in the initial plans. Negative emotional reactions to the failure indicate how important the lost project has been, which focuses their attention on looking for and evaluating any failure-related information (Clore 1992; Ellis and Chase 1971; Schwarz and Clore 1988). These activities of scanning and comparing provide employees information about the failure and its preceding events. The individuals can then use this information to update their beliefs about the reasons underlying project failures and what can be done to counteract these causes in subsequent projects. Additionally, exploring why the entrepreneurial project did not end as planned can motivate individuals to consider different activities and strategies that could have been initiated (Kim and Miner 2007). Lastly, employees who detect project routines/processes that led to failure and must be altered for following projects may recognize a universal need for more flexibility and change. These individuals may then develop new plans to change routines, strategies, procedures, or actions as needed in subsequent projects (Eisenhardt and Martin 2000).

When employees focus on the loss and develop an account for the failure event, the loss begins to take on new meaning, and the organizational members can finally start resolving their emotional attachment to the entrepreneurial project that has failed. This new plausible failure account triggers an adaptation of how the individuals view themselves and the context in which they act (Archer and Freeman 1999), thus enabling them to control their emotions in a way that stops the failure from causing negative emotions (Gross 1998). Employees with a substantial loss orientation begin grief work right away and start forming a more complete understanding of the project failure. For instance, in our study with a colleague (Shepherd et al. 2011), an aerospace engineering scientist recounted the following: "[After a failure,] I look back. ... It is certainly necessary to make a rational analysis." Yet, working through the loss is draining. After time, individuals begin thinking less about the events preceding the failure and more about the specific event itself and the resulting emotions, which may ultimately cause additional negative emotions (Bonanno 2004). For example, the engineer went on: "I then start asking myself too often 'was this right' and so on ... and I then bedevil myself at points where no concrete conclusion can be drawn ... [and then] only entropy [disorder within the system] is produced." As this example shows, having a strong loss orientation for a long time can result in ruminations; ruminations can lead to a vicious cycle of negative thoughts, emotions, and actions (Nolen-Hoeksema 1991). Moreover, when working through grief entails counterfactual thinking, the individual may have feelings of disappointment, regret, and/or anxiety due to missing opportunities for avoiding the failure overall (cf. Baron 2000, 2004; Roese 1997). Rumination-induced emotions can worsen feelings of loss. Thus, although negative emotions are decreased early on, a loss orientation appears to ultimately lead to even more negative emotions after entrepreneurial project failure.

Next, when individuals engage a **restoration orientation**, they *suppress feelings of loss and proactively attend to loss-related secondary sources of stress* (Stroebe and Schut 2001). As the definition implies, a restoration orientation has two dimensions—avoidance (of the primary stressor, i.e., the failed project) and proactiveness (toward failure-related secondary stressors). None of these dimensions helps individuals learn from project failure, but both help them to "keep a lid on" and/or decrease negative emotions. Avoidance entails distracting oneself to direct attention away from the failed project and the preceding events. For instance, employees may concentrate on dealing with alternative stressors, such as "What is my organizational role now that my project has failed?" and "How can I effectively work with my new project team?" Although dealing with secondary stressors provides employees distraction from the entrepreneurial project failure event and allows them to continue with the their jobs, it offers few learning opportunities as it does not contribute to a more plausible explanation regarding the failure and therefore does not provide insight into the changes and adaptations needed for the next project.

Thus, the likelihood of an association between restoration orientation strength and learning from the failure of an entrepreneurial project is low. However, with a stronger restoration orientation, individuals' negative emotional responses to losing something important are likely to diminish (see Shepherd et al. 2011). That is, by actively avoiding thoughts related to the failure, employees do not consciously acknowledge the failure, and as a result no negative emotional response is triggered (or the response is minimized). Indeed, an individual's focus on non-project-related tasks replaces his or her thoughts and emotions about the failure with other thoughts and emotions. These alternative thoughts, for instance, can include other achievements at work that trigger positive emotions. Moreover, proactively dealing with secondary stressors likely means that when those sources of stress are removed (or reduced), the original loss is no longer as troubling and thus does not cause a significantly strong negative response. Attending to secondary stressors may even generate positive emotions (Ganster 2005). These positive emotions, in turn, can help "undo" the negative emotions (Fredrickson 2001) caused by an entrepreneurial project failure.

Yet, suppressing emotions is usually very draining (Archer and Freeman 1999). As a consequence, suppression may lead to negative psychological (Prigerson et al. 1997) and physical (Gross 1998) issues. In addition, it is often challenging to repress emotions for a longer time period; the negative emotions are likely to come up eventually (Holahan and Moos 1987; Repetti 1992). As a result, more distress and future problems will emerge (Menaghan 1982), which worsen the failure experience overall. Therefore, as with a loss orientation, for a short time after an entrepreneurial project failure, with an increasing restoration orientation, individuals can lessen negative emotions. However, if this orientation persists for a longer time, negative emotions arise, which offsets the benefits of engaging a restoration orientation.

Finally, when individuals engage an **oscillation orientation**, they *move back and forth between a loss orientation and a restoration orientation* (Shepherd 2003; Shepherd et al. 2011; Stroebe and Schut 2001), thus enabling them to realize the advantages of both orientations while reducing the problems associated with engaging in one orientation for too long. Initially experiencing negative emotions from failure activates the autonomous nervous system, focusing a person's attention on what caused the failure (Fineman 1996; Hirshleifer 1993; Weick 1990). Working through the grief they experience, individuals may start ruminating about the failure of their entrepreneurial project and trigger additional negative emotions. These mounting negative emotions may eventually narrow their attention (Derryberry and Tucker 1994; Staw et al. 1981) and hinder the processing of available information (Lyubomirsky and Nolen-Hoeksema 1995; Weick 1990). In other words, the increasing negative emotions caused by a loss orientation that persists for too long can narrow people's attention, diminish their information-processing abilities, and lessen their feelings of control (Carver et al. 1989; Lyubomirsky and Nolen-Hoeksema 1995), all of which are detrimental to effective learning.

Changing to a restoration orientation after a loss orientation can help stop rumination by refocusing a person's attention on activities other than the failure event, including dealing with secondary stressors. After individuals have successfully reduced their negative emotions and increased their capacity to process information (Fredrickson 2001), people with a strong oscillation orientation can revert back into a loss orientation to further understand the failure event. Thus, with a stronger loss orientation, employees are likely to learn more from entrepreneurial project failures as a result of this intensive evaluation of the failure event interwoven with periods of healing and concentrating on addressing secondary stressors. On the other hand, employees with a weaker oscillation orientation are likely to remain in either orientation for too long. If this occurs, the individuals will either become cognitively overwhelmed from thinking about his or her negative emotions (loss orientation) or be unable to adequately form a believable explanation for the failure event (restoration orientation).

Additionally, an oscillation orientation may also improve a person's ability to decrease negative emotions caused by the project failure by harnessing the advantages of both orientations for handling those negative emotions, thus decreasing the cost of staying in either orientation for too long. When a loss orientation helps a person form a more plausible explanation for an entrepreneurial project failure, it may give meaning to the loss and thus reduce negative feelings (Archer and Freeman 1999). As discussed earlier, engaging a loss orientation for too long can activate multiple and diverse negative emotions, leading the individual to recall negative thoughts about him- or herself and their environment (Lyubomirsky and Nolen-Hoeksema 1995; Nolen-Hoeksema 1991). These negative thoughts can in turn initiate a harmful spiral in which negative emotions escalate. When reflecting on the failure event starts to cause negative emotions, employees with a strong oscillation orientation start engaging a restoration orientation, taking initiative to deal with secondary stressors, which can lessen the emotional significance of the project failure. During this time, the individual has the chance to recuperate emotionally, and switching back to a loss orientation after this recuperation (without instantly beginning to ruminate over negative thoughts and emotions) can further diminish the individual's emotional bond with the failed project. Thus, engaging in oscillation orientation can—over time—lessen the negative emotional experience caused by entrepreneurial project failure. However, a limited oscillation orientation is only marginally effective since employees are likely to remain in either orientation for too long.

GRIEF, COPING SELF-EFFICACY, AND SUBSEQUENT ENTREPRENEURIAL PROJECTS

Researchers have recently used social cognitive theory (Bandura 1986) to gain stronger insights into human functioning, with a particular emphasis on self-regulation in individuals coping with trauma (Benight et al. 1999). Similar to failure, trauma involves an event that causes a negative emotional response that may impede people's normal functioning (Janoff-Bulman 1992). Coping entails the thinking and acting individuals utilize to handle the internal and contextual demands of specific stressful circumstances (Lazarus and Folkman 1984a, b). Coping is initiated "in response to the individual's appraisal that important goals have been harmed, lost, or threatened [generating] negative emotions that are often intense" (Folkman and Moskowitz 2004: 747). When the entrepreneurial project represents the loss, it generates grief that is likely to be powerful and internalized. Thus, coping with project failure *involves the thoughts and actions employees utilize to recover from negative emotions experienced in response to project failure.*

A core component of social cognitive theory is that "people tend to avoid activities and situations they believe will exceed their coping capabilities, but they readily undertake challenging activities and pick social environments they judge themselves capable of managing" (Wood and Bandura 1989: 365). This judgment of one's capabilities relates to self-efficacy. Specifically, self-efficacy denotes "beliefs in one's capabilities to mobilize the motivation, cognitive resources, and courses of action needed to meet given situational demands" (Wood and Bandura 1989: 408). Many scholars argue that self-efficacy is specific to a particular task (Bandura 1997). In the specific context of entrepreneurship, self-efficacy has been defined as "the degree to which individuals believe they are capable of performing the tasks associated with new venture management" (Forbes 2005: 628). In the specific case of corporate entrepreneurship, coping self-efficacy "refers to the beliefs in one's capabilities to mobilize the motivation, cognitive resources, and courses of action needed to recover from major setbacks arising from the organization's entrepreneurial activities" (Shepherd et al. 2009a: 593).

Individuals with low coping self-efficacy feel there is a large gap between their coping capabilities and harmful elements of their context. The belief of being unable to cope often intensifies the threat's severity and increases anxiety over other dangers. Someone with low coping self-efficacy in addition believes that he or she is incapable of clearing their minds of invasive thoughts (Bandura 1997; Lazarus and Folkman 1984a, b). People with high coping self-efficacy, on the other hand, believe that they can avoid cognitive overload, have control over intrusive thoughts, and proactively shape situations to make them less threatening (Bandura et al. 1985). For instance, Benight et al. (1999) reported that for Hurricane Opal survivors, perceived coping self-efficacy had a significant mediating effect in explaining who did not have lasting distress from the trauma (Benight et al. 1999).

In addition to helping individuals cope with trauma, self-efficacy also appears to mediate the association between experiencing a substantial loss and recovering from grief. For example, Benight et al. (2001) conducted a study of 102 widows whose husbands had died within the last year, finding that those higher in coping self-efficacy regarding their loss had experienced lower levels of distress and higher overall psychological and physical health (Benight et al. 2001). Recovering from grief enables individuals to continue with their lives and commit to new courses of action (Fisher 2001). As Benight and Bandura (2004: 1133) noted, "a robust sense of coping self-efficacy is accompanied by benign appraisals of potential threats, weaker stress reactions to them, less ruminative preoccupation with them, better behavioral management of threats, and faster recovery of well-being from any experienced distress over them." Thus, coping self-efficacy has an important function in explaining people's reactions to stress, the usefulness of the strategies they employ for coping with hostile circumstances (Bandura 1997), and their persistence when faced with challenges (Bandura 1986).

Building on findings related to coping self-efficacy in the face of traumas caused by the loss of loved ones and natural disasters, my (Dean) colleagues and I (Shepherd et al. 2011) argued that individuals' coping self-efficacy is heterogeneous, which helps explain variation in how effective organizational members are at managing the failure of an entrepreneurial project.

Individuals' thinking, feeling, and acting at work are directly affected by the internal firm context they face (Brief and Weiss 2002). Bereavement scholars have given numerous examples of firms that enable social support by creating rituals and support groups designed to help mourning employees manage their grief (Archer and Freeman 1999). Through these rituals and support groups, firms provide their employees the chance to meet other people who have also experienced a loss. Through interactions with those people who have had similar grief, the employees can mimic coping behaviors and improve their own coping self-efficacy.

With the goal of helping individuals regulate their emotions, support groups are used in numerous contexts, especially in the case of losing a family member. More than 50% of all US hospice providers provide support groups to aid people manage their grief after losing a loved one (Foliart et al. 2001). According to Balk et al. (1993: 432), typical goals of support groups are as follows:

> The goal of the social support group meetings was to facilitate coping with grief and to assist in resolving the difficulties associated with mourning through education regarding adaptive tasks and coping skills pertinent to life crises and through opening channels of communication between groups.

Self-help groups, also called peer or mutual support groups, are the type of social support group that is most frequently used due to their low cost and because participants view such groups as providing high-safety environments (Caserta and Lund 1996). In practice, self-help groups are generally headed by a peer who has previously experienced a substantial loss and coped with it successfully. In the self-help context, leaders are not therapists or counselors but instead organize and facilitate the processes within the self-help support group (Caserta and Lund 1996). For instance, self-help support groups provide members emotional support and a positive environment that encourages information sharing. As a consequence, these groups enable their members to overcome grief more effectively (see Hopmeyer and Werk 1994). Thus, support groups are one example of a social support mechanism firms can use to help failed employees enhance their coping capabilities and (re)build the confidence required to take on future tasks (Caserta and Lund 1993).

Organizations generally have support groups to help participating employees deal with issues from *outside the workplace* that influence performance in their job (e.g., divorce, death of a loved family member) (Kahnweiler and Riordan 1998). Sometimes, organizations also provide support groups to help members cope with *traumatic events* that occur inside the organizational boundaries, such as large-scale corporate changes and downsizing (Esty 1987). Organizational members can further obtain social support from informal relationships they form with colleagues (Riordan and Griffeth 1995). In their study of 816 medical care providers in the Netherlands, Peeters and Le Blanc (2001) found that providers who obtained social support from the coworker could better cope with the emotional challenges of their work without developing insensitivity, indifference, or detachment from the patients' difficult situations; that is, they did not have to rely on depersonalization. Thus, whereas coping self-efficacy represents individuals' beliefs in their ability to cope, organizational social-exchange mechanisms can offer opportunities for employees to support one another and, as such, are important for improving their coping self-efficacy. In other words, social support can be a facilitator: "supporters model coping attitudes and skills, provide incentives for engagement in beneficial activities, and motivate others by showing that difficulties are surmountable by perseverant effort" (Benight and Bandura 2004: 1134). As a facilitator, social support can improve individuals' self-efficacy. In their review of mediation studies across a broad range of situations and samples, Benight and Bandura (2004) established that social support is advantageous only when it enhances individuals' perceived self-efficacy for handling environmental demands. If social support facilitates employees' development of self-efficacy for overcoming grief caused by the failure of an entrepreneurial project, such support is also likely to help members learn from this failure and stay motivated on later projects.

Organizations also create and use rituals to enable organizational members to offer each other social support. Rituals are "standardized, detailed sets of techniques and behaviors that the culture prescribes to manage anxieties and express common identities" (Trice and Beyer 1993: 80).

Advantages derived from funeral rituals, for instance, can go beyond the death of a close family member or friend and be applied to losing something important in the organizational context. After investigating 11 parties, picnics, and dinners taking place in six dying organizations, Harris and Sutton (1986) theorized on parting ceremonies for (former) employees following firm death. They contended that the purpose of parting ceremonies is to offer emotional support for workers and help them learn from their experiences. When firms die, (former) employees tend to mourn over the loss, but they are also likely to benefit from the emotional support offered through parting ceremonies' rituals. These rituals are particularly beneficial as they improve people's coping self-efficacy.

Organizations could utilize a similar process for the emotional challenges associated with entrepreneurial project failures. That is, they could provide some type of funeral or parting ritual when a project fails. In fact, many organizations have already developed rituals to help their members deal with failure (see McCune 1997). For instance, Ore-Ida, a subsidiary of H. J. Heinz, shot off a celebratory cannon whenever a project failure occurred (Peters and Waterman 1982). Similarly, Eli Lilly hosted "perfect failure" parties to honor outstanding scientific achievements that ultimately were associated with the failure of a project (Burton 2004: 1). Shooting off cannons or performing other rituals that signify a project's death can effectively improve learning from failure by helping build employees' coping self-efficacy. Rituals do this by offering a space for social support with regard to the grief-recovery process. When employees know that they will always have social support (because it is a ritual), their confidence in their ability to cope with grief over entrepreneurial project failure will increase.

Social support often results in enhanced well-being, and firms are in the position to create spaces for compassion being received and given (Kanov et al. 2004). This compassion can include empathetic listening to other organizational members' problems (Frost 2003), sympathetic emotions (Carlo et al. 1999), and executing large-scale reactions to unanticipated traumatic events (Dutton et al. 2006). Mostly seen as an important and positive force in firms (Kanov et al. 2004), scholars have explored compassion at numerous levels of analysis; these levels include individuals' compassion for others (Nussbaum 1996), compassion as an interpersonal, people-connecting process (Kanov et al. 2004), and the ways people unite to deliver an organized compassionate organizational response (e.g., compassion organizing (Dutton et al. 2006) and compassion venturing

(Shepherd and Williams 2014; Williams and Shepherd 2016)). Compassion is the manifestation of the instinctive human need to respond to others' suffering in order to ease that suffering. In this context, suffering includes some form of loss or pain that jeopardizes individuals' sense of meaning about their existence (Dutton et al. 2006). Here, compassion represents people's reaction when their self-meaning or psychological health is threatened. Additionally, compassion entails responses to others' suffering, so it is not emotion-based but also involves action (Dutton et al. 2006).

Self-Compassion, Negative Emotions, and Learning from Project Failure

Just like other-directed compassion entails recognizing, feeling, and taking action in response to another individual's suffering (Dutton et al. 2006), **self-compassion** captures *being aware that one is personally experiencing feelings of loss, determining the cause of that feeling (i.e., project failure in this case), and responding by taking action to do something about it* (Shepherd and Cardon 2009). Employees who are self-compassionate are moved by their own negative emotions over project failure, are mindful of their discomfort, and want to ease this suffering by healing themselves instead of avoiding or detaching from the negative emotions' origin (Neff 2003a; Wispe 1991). Unlike other-directed compassion, the relational process of self-compassion (Kanov et al. 2004) happens through the relationships people have with themselves.

We propose that there are three aspects of self-compassion—self-kindness, common humanity, and mindfulness—and we connect them to (1) the strength of individuals' negative emotional responses to project failures and (2) the altering of the association between experiences of negative emotions and people's learning related to the failure event. We make several assumptions with this approach. First, we argue—and empirical evidence shows (Neff 2003b; Shapiro et al. 2005)—that people can learn self-compassion over time. Further, self-compassion is a required (yet insufficient) condition for people to achieve learning outcomes from project failure. Finally, when individuals are self-compassionate, they have less anxiety about negative events and, as a consequence, can better sustain their psychological health (Neff and Davidson 2016).

In this section, we focus on how self-regulation can help individuals handle or counteract threats stemming from project failure and improve their learning from these events. In our theorizing, we suggest that people who are caring toward themselves when evaluating project failure (high levels of self-kindness) view project failure objectively in relation to other individuals (high common humanity), maintain an emotional balance (high mindfulness), have fewer negative emotions from project failure, and are more capable of using the failure as a chance for learning. In the following, we discuss these three aspects of self-compassion that aid employees in self-regulating their negative emotions from project failure in a manner that facilitates learning. We do not provide an exhaustive summary of mechanisms that enhance self-kindness, common humanity, and mindfulness; rather, we simply believe that these mechanisms exist and play a crucial role in explaining variance in people's negative emotional responses to project failure and the extent to which they learn from the experience (based on Shepherd and Cardon 2009).

Self-Kindness, Negative Emotions, and Learning from Project Failure

Self-kindness *refers to being kind to and understanding of oneself instead of extending harsh judgment and self-criticism (Neff* 2003a*: 89) after project failure.* Individuals demonstrate self-kindness—at least partly—when they (1) attempt to understand and have patience with personal traits they do not like, (2) are caring to themselves when suffering from project failure, (3) provide themselves with the tenderness required to handle the difficult aspects of project failure, (4) tolerate their own imperfections and shortcomings potentially having contributed to project failure, and (5) try to be loving toward themselves when they feel negative emotions (Neff 2003b) from project failure.

Self-kindness is unlikely to lessen the emotional significance of the failed entrepreneurial project for those involved; yet, it does help deter individuals from deeming themselves "bad" because of the failure. People who are highly self-kind and go through project failure are less likely to callously be critical of themselves for not being able to achieve optimal project standards (Neff 2003a), which safeguards them against anxiety when they reflect on their weaknesses (Neff et al. 2007). In addition to lower anxiety, self-kindness can keep people from engaging in ruminations, which—as we discussed earlier—can cause increased negative emotions (Nolen-Hoeksema 1991). Thus, having the ability to separate the project failure event from assessments of the self, an employee with high self-kindness can diminish his or her negative emotional response to the failure of a project.

Self-kindness depends on discriminating wisdom, which "clearly evaluates the positive or negative quality of actions but does so with a compassionate understanding of the complex, dynamic situational factors that impact these actions, so that particular performances are not taken as indicators of self-worth" (Neff et al. 2005: 264). We are not suggesting that people overlook such failings or accept them without resistance. Rather, self-kindness facilitates the elimination of failure-related learning obstacles. Only when individuals judge themselves harshly, the ego's protective mechanisms kick in. While these mechanisms conceal inadequacies from individuals' self-awareness to maintain self-esteem (Neff 2003a), they ultimately diminish how much people learn. Self-kindness offers an emotional safety net that enables higher self-awareness by providing an objectively more accurate perception of the project's failure (Shepherd and Cardon 2009). In other words, self-kindness stops people from allowing their subjective reactions to go too far (Neff 2003a), possibly initiating ruminations (Nolen-Hoeksema 1991), and/or worsening negative emotions (Nolen-Hoeksema 1991). This higher level of negative emotions generally obstructs learning (Nolen-Hoeksema 1991; Shepherd 2003) because when individuals concentrate on their negative emotions, they have less capacity to attend to and process information about their failure experience. Furthermore, employees' awareness of their own flaws and mistakes is a crucial input for learning; self-kindness can improve this self-awareness. Thus, having the ability to evaluate entrepreneurial project failure separate from self-worth assessments, those with self-compassion face fewer barriers in their learning process.

Common Humanity and Learning from Project Failure

Common humanity *refers to viewing one's experiences as part of the greater human experience instead of viewing them as separate and isolated* (Neff 2003a: 85). That is, employees with common humanity see their failure experiences in relation to the common human experience in their firm, recognizing that failures are an inevitable element of innovation and that everyone, including themselves, deserves compassion (Shepherd and Cardon 2009). This perspective enables individuals to stay connected to other organizational members. Based on these connections with others in the organizations, the employees can forgive themselves for any of their flaws contributing to project failure.

It is doubtful that mechanisms stressing commonality will lessen the importance of any one entrepreneurial project among employees; rather, when a project fails, they help individuals put their resulting feelings into context. In other words, acknowledging that they share their feelings of grief over project failure with other individuals within the firm helps them be less self-critical (Rubin 1975) and facilitates forgiving themselves for prior shortcomings (Neff 2003a). Thus, these individuals are less likely to perceive project failure as threatening their self-esteem. With decreasing common humanity, on the other hand, employees are more likely to view project failure as threatening since they tend to feel isolated and less related to others, reducing personal well-being. Moreover, individuals perceive the resulting threatening situations negatively, leading to higher anxiety and stress (e.g., Leary et al. 2001).

Higher levels of common humanity will also influence people's ability to learn from entrepreneurial project failure. More specifically, when employees realize that all organizational members experienced the negative emotions caused by the failure, they are more likely to participate in the necessary impartial diagnosis of the failure's cause and provide possible accounts for the failure (Shepherd and Cardon 2009). By blaming themselves less, organizational members will externalize blame attributions less as a means to defend their ego. Externalizing sources of blame is frequently an effective way to protect one's self-esteem (e.g., Brockner and Guare 1983). However, externalizing blame offers few opportunities for learning because there is not much to learn because the individual feels that the failure was due to factors completely outside his or her control (e.g., Diener and Dweck 1980). In this case, common humanity may actually result in a collective desire to determine who or what should be blamed for the failure. Indeed, an employee may ascribe entrepreneurial project failure to numerous causes (e.g., the organizational management or the economic context). Yet, real learning from failure—namely, attempting to understand what went awry and how to avoid similar issues in subsequent projects—requires an impartial and honest evaluation of the failure's primary causes. Leary et al. (2007) called such evaluations impartial attributions as opposed to self-attributions. According to Neff (2003a), self-compassion effectively safeguards employees' personal well-being from negative events irrespective of them causing the event. Further, Leary and colleagues (2007) showed that self-compassionate individuals put forth higher effort to be kind to themselves when they attributed negative events to themselves. In this study, self-compassion was beneficial no matter what the attribution of blame.

Organizational members partly demonstrate common humanity when they try to remind themselves that most people have feelings of inadequacy following entrepreneurial project failure, attempt to see their mistakes as part of the human condition in an organizational environment, remind themselves that there are many employees in their own and other organizations who feel dejected in the case of project failure, and remember that everyone goes through challenging situations (adapted from Neff 2003b). Without connecting to others in this way, people can feel isolated, lessening informal learning and information access as well as decreasing their ability to initiate action (Martinko and Gardner 1982). When employees have higher common humanity, they do not stay connected to the failure of the entrepreneurial project because they have forgiven themselves for any mistakes they contributed to the failure and have also forgiven other project team members who may have been blamed for the failure (Shepherd and Cardon 2009). In turn, this forgiveness deactivates the defensive mechanisms that obstruct learning.

Mindfulness and Learning from Project Failure

Mindful organizational members keep emotions caused by entrepreneurial project failure in check, handle emotions regarding project failure with curiosity and open-mindedness, and maintain a balanced understanding of the failure event by keeping things in perspective (adapted from Neff 2003b). Employees who are less mindful tend to be strongly influenced by personal feelings (Neff 2003a: 88). For instance, when a person concentrates on an entrepreneurial project failure, his or her focus can move away from the failure itself to the negative emotional experiences stemming from the event, thus increasing his or her negative emotions (Nolen-Hoeksema 1991).

We are not suggesting that mindful organizational members do not show emotional reactions to entrepreneurial project failures. Instead, mindful individuals can place these emotions in a larger context and see the significance of these emotions with a broader perspective (Neff 2003a: 89; Teasdale et al. 2000). Because this larger context is unlikely to jeopardize individuals' self-esteem, there are likely few ego-protective obstacles to learning. It appears that mindfulness helps people end the cycle of self-absorption as well as escape ruminations. For instance, Shapiro et al. (2005) showed that an intervention over eight weeks, which was based on mindfulness and aimed at reducing stress, effectively improved health-care professionals' self-compassion and decreased their stress. In the organizational context, mindfulness helps in reducing the significance of the negative results from entrepreneurial project failures and thus reduces individuals' negative emotional reactions to it (Shepherd and Cardon 2009).

Instead of concentrating on the negative thinking and emotions associated with project failure, employees with high mindfulness do not connect project failure to their own self-worth. These employees can accept the event for what it is (i.e., a chance for learning) and become consciously aware of it (Hayes et al. 1996) without severely judging or criticizing themselves. Mindfulness enables individuals to view emotions as a signal that a failure event is an important learning opportunity (Lazarus 1993; Weick 1979) without letting negative emotions overtake their information-processing capacity (Matthews et al. 1990; Wells and Matthews 1994), which would diminish their learning abilities related to the failure. The balancing of emotions in such a way is an essential element of self-regulation and the core aspect of mindfulness. As explained earlier, an individual can balance failure-related negative emotions and improve learning, for example, by oscillating between a loss orientation and a restoration orientation (Shepherd 2003; Stroebe and Schut 2001). Of course, people are heterogeneous to the extent to which they can control their emotions (Tugade and Fredrickson 2004); thus some individuals can better utilize emotion knowledge (i.e., mindfulness) to handle stressful situations (Barrett and Gross 2001).

By keeping ruminations and overidentification under control, mindfulness helps individuals more effectively discern important information regarding project failure and then interpret and learn from that information (Shepherd and Cardon 2009). At one level, mindfulness represents a type of detachment like the non-judgmental perspective therapists take when interacting with clients (Bohart 1993; Neff 2003a). However, it is not independent of evaluation; instead, mindfulness entails separating one's assessment of a particular event from assessments of the self.

Conclusion

In this chapter we have explored the influence of emotions across different stages and tasks of the entrepreneurial process. We illustrate that emotions play a key role in understanding entrepreneurs' opportunity exploitation decisions. Further, we also find that supervisor-managers' emotional displays can impact the motivation of employees to engage in entrepreneurial action. Particularly when entrepreneurial projects within organizations fail, employees often experience substantial negative emotions which diminish motivation and learning from the failure experience. However, we also show that these effects are contingent on the organizational environment normalizing failure, as well as individuals' coping orientations, self-efficacy, and self-compassion.

Notes

1. This notion of excitement is also in line with how we induced excitement using visual stimuli in this study's experimental approach. Although there are likely to be differences in how excited entrepreneurs become when viewing excitement-inducing pictures, a strong research stream has validated that such pictures do induce excitement in observers.
2. These orientations are independent of each other such that a person can concentrate on one orientation but not the other, or be high or low in both orientations. In addition, people who are high in both orientations can be high or low in an oscillation orientation. The analyses that follow demonstrate the independence of these orientations.

References

Ahuja, G. (2000). Collaboration networks, structural holes, and innovation: A longitudinal study. *Administrative Science Quarterly, 45*(3), 425–455.

Allen, R. L. (2001). *The concept of self: A study of black identity and self-esteem.* Detroit: Wayne State, University Press.

Alloy, L. B., & Abramson, L. Y. (1979). Judgment of contingency in depressed and nondepressed students: Sadder but wiser? *Journal of Experimental Psychology: General, 108*(4), 441.

Amabile, T. M. (1997). Entrepreneurial creativity through motivational synergy. *Journal of Creative Behavior, 31*(1), 18–26.

Amabile, T. M., & Fisher, C. M. (2000). Stimulate creativity by fueling passion. In E. Locke (Ed.), *Handbook of principles of organizational behavior* (pp. 331–341). Malden: Blackwell.

Aquino, K., & Douglas, S. (2003). Identity threat and antisocial behavior in organizations: The moderating effects of individual differences, aggressive modeling, and hierarchical status. *Organizational Behavior and Human Decision Processes, 90*(1), 195–208.

Archer, D., & Akert, R. M. (1977). Words and everything else: Verbal and nonverbal cues in social interpretation. *Journal of Personality and Social Psychology, 35*(6), 443.

Archer, J., & Freeman, H. (1999). The nature of grief: The evolution and psychology of reactions to loss. *Nature, 398*(6727), 479–479.

Ashforth, B. E. (2001). *Role transitions in organizational life: An identity-based perspective.* Hillsdale: Erlbaum.
Ashforth, B. E., & Kreiner, G. E. (2002). Normalizing emotion in organizations: Making the extraordinary seem ordinary. *Human Resource Management Review, 12*(2), 215–235.
Averill, J. R. (1975). Semantic atlas of emotional concepts. *JSAS Catalogue of Selected Documents in Psychology, 5,* 330(1103). Amherst: University of Massachusetts.
Balk, D. E., Tyson-Rawson, K., & Colletti-Wetzel, J. (1993). Social support as an intervention with bereaved college students. *Death Studies, 17*(5), 427–450.
Bandura, A. (1986). *Social foundation of thought and action: A social-cognitive view.* Englewood Cliffs: Prentice Hall.
Bandura, A. (1991). Social cognitive theory of self-regulation. *Organizational Behavior and Human Decision Processes, 50*(2), 248–287.
Bandura, A. (1997). *Self-efficacy: The exercise of control.* New York: Freeman.
Bandura, A., Taylor, C. B., Williams, S. L., Mefford, I. N., & Barchas, J. D. (1985). Catecholamine secretion as a function of perceived coping self-efficacy. *Journal of Consulting and Clinical Psychology, 53*(3), 406.
Barbalet, J. M. (1996). Social emotions: Confidence, trust and loyalty. *International Journal of Sociology and Social Policy, 16*(9/10), 75–96.
Barker, J. R., & Tompkins, P. (1994). Identification in the self-managing organization characteristics of target and tenure. *Human Communication Research, 21*(2), 223–240.
Baron, R. A. (2000). Counterfactual thinking and venture formation: The potential effects of thinking about "what might have been". *Journal of Business Venturing, 15*(1), 79–91.
Baron, R. A. (2004). The cognitive perspective: A valuable tool for answering entrepreneurship's basic "why" questions. *Journal of Business Venturing, 19*(2), 221–239.
Baron, R. A. (2008). The role of affect in the entrepreneurial process. *Academy of Management Review, 33*(2), 328–340.
Barrett, L. F., & Gross, J. J. (2001). Emotional intelligence: A process model of emotion representation and regulation. In T. J. Mayne & G. A. Bonanno (Eds.), *Emotions and social behavior. Emotions: Current issues and future directions* (pp. 286–310). New York: Guilford Press.
Baum, J. R., Locke, E. A., & Smith, K. G. (2001). A multidimensional model of venture growth. *Academy of Management Journal, 44*(2), 292–303.
Belk, R. W. (1988). Possessions and the extended self. *Journal of Consumer Research, 15*(2), 139–168.
Benight, C. C., & Bandura, A. (2004). Social cognitive theory of posttraumatic recovery: The role of perceived self-efficacy. *Behaviour Research and Therapy, 42*(10), 1129–1148.

Benight, C., Flores, J., & Tashiro, C. (2001). Bereavement coping self-efficacy in cancer widows. *Death Studies, 25*(2), 97–125.

Benight, C. C., Swift, E., Sanger, J., Smith, A., & Zeppelin, D. (1999). Coping self-efficacy as a mediator of distress following a natural disaster. *Journal of Applied Social Psychology, 29*(12), 2443–2464.

Bharadwaj, S., & Menon, A. (2000). Making innovation happen in organizations: Individual creativity mechanisms, organizational creativity mechanisms or both? *Journal of Product Innovation Management, 17*(6), 424–434.

Blanchard, K. H., Carlos, J. P., & Randolph, W. A. (1995). *The empowerment barometer and action plan.* Escondido: Blanchard Training and Development.

Bohart, A. C. (1993). Emphasizing the future in empathy responses. *Journal of Humanistic Psychology, 33*(2), 12–29.

Bonanno, G. A. (2004). Loss, trauma, and human resilience: have we underestimated the human capacity to thrive after extremely aversive events? *American Psychologist, 59*(1), 20–28.

Borkovec, T. D., Robinson, E., Pruzinsky, T., & DePree, J. A. (1983). Preliminary exploration of worry: Some characteristics and processes. *Behaviour Research and Therapy, 21*, 9–16.

Boyd, D. P., & Gumpert, D. E. (1984). The loneliness of the start up entrepreneur. In J. A. Homaday, F. Tarpley Jr., J. A. Timmons, & K. H. Vesper (Eds.), *Frontiers of entrepreneurship research* (pp. 478–487). Wellesley: Babson College.

Brief, A. P., & Weiss, H. M. (2002). Organizational behavior: Affect in the workplace. *Annual Review of Psychology, 53*(1), 279–307.

Brockner, J., & Guare, J. (1983). Improving the performance of low self-esteem individuals: An attributional approach. *Academy of Management Journal, 26*(4), 642–656.

Brundin, E. (2002). *Emotions in motion: The strategic leader in a radical change process, JIBS dissertation series no. 12.* Jönköping: Jönköping International Business School.

Brundin, E., Patzelt, H., & Shepherd, D. A. (2008). Managers' emotional displays and employees' willingness to act entrepreneurially. *Journal of Business Venturing, 23*(2), 221–243.

Burgelman, R. A., & Välikangas, L. (2005). Managing internal corporate venturing cycles. *MIT Sloan Management Review, 46*(4), 26.

Burton, T. M. (2004, April 21). Flop factor: By learning from failures, Lilly keeps drug pipeline full. *Wall Street Journal*, 1.

Butler, R. (1992). What young people want to know when: Effects of mastery and ability goals on interest in different kinds of social comparisons. *Journal of Personality and Social Psychology, 62*(6), 934–943.

Cacioppo, J. T., Gardner, W. L., & Berntson, G. G. (1999). The affect system has parallel and integrative processing components: Form follows function. *Journal of Personality and Social Psychology, 76*(5), 839–855.

Cardon, M. S., Wincent, J., Singh, J., & Drnovsek, M. (2009). The nature and experience of entrepreneurial passion. *Academy of Management Review, 34*(3), 511–532.

Carlo, G., Allen, J. B., & Buhman, D. C. (1999). Facilitating and disinhibiting prosocial behaviors: The nonlinear interaction of trait perspective taking and trait personal distress on volunteering. *Basic and Applied Social Psychology, 21*(3), 189–197.

Carson, P. P., Carson, K. D., & Roe, C. W. (1993). Social power bases: A meta-analytic examination of interrelationships and outcomes. *Journal of Applied Social Psychology, 23*(14), 1150–1169.

Carver, C. S., & Scheier, M. F. (2001). *On the self-regulation of behavior.* Cambridge: Cambridge University Press.

Carver, C. S., Scheier, M. F., & Weintraub, J. K. (1989). Assessing coping strategies: A theoretically based approach. *Journal of Personality and Social Psychology, 56*(2), 267.

Caserta, M. S., & Lund, D. A. (1993). Intrapersonal resources and the effectiveness of self-help groups for bereaved older adults. *The Gerontologist, 33*(5), 619–629.

Caserta, M. S., & Lund, D. A. (1996). Beyond bereavement support group meetings: Exploring outside social contacts among the members. *Death Studies, 20*(6), 537–556.

Caverley, N., Cunningham, J. B., & MacGregor, J. N. (2007). Sickness presenteeism, sickness absenteeism, and health following restructuring in a public service organization. *Journal of Management Studies, 44*(2), 304–319.

Chandler, A. D., Jr. (1961). *The visible hand: The managerial revolution in American business.* Cambridge, MA: Harvard University Press.

Choi, Y. R., & Shepherd, D. A. (2004). Entrepreneurs' decisions to exploit opportunities. *Journal of Management, 30*(3), 377–395.

Chuang, Y. T., & Baum, J. A. (2003). It's all in the name: Failure-induced learning by multiunit chains. *Administrative Science Quarterly, 48*(1), 33–59.

Clore, G. L. (1992). Cognitive phenomenology: Feelings and the construction of judgment. *Construction of Social Judgments, 10*, 133–163.

Collins, C. (1987). *English language dictionary.* Champaign: Human Kinetics publication.

Corbett, A. C., Neck, H. M., & DeTienne, D. R. (2007). How corporate entrepreneurs learn from fledgling innovation initiatives: Cognition and the development of a termination script. *Entrepreneurship Theory and Practice, 31*(6), 829–852.

Craighead, W. E., Kimball, W. H., & Rehak, P. J. (1979). Mood changes, physiological responses, and self-statements during social rejection imagery. *Journal of Consulting and Clinical Psychology, 47*(2), 385.

Cunningham, G. (2004). *Five cities chosen to compete for the 2012 summer Olympics.* www.citymayors.com/sport/2012olympics_jan04. Accessed 1 Jan 2006.

Dasborough, M. T., & Ashkanasy, N. M. (2002). Emotion and attribution of intentionality in leader–member relationships. *Leadership Quarterly, 13*(5), 615–634.

Deci, E. L., & Ryan, R. M. (2000). The "what" and "why" of goal pursuits: Human needs and the self-determination of behavior. *Psychological Inquiry, 11*(4), 227–268.

Deci, E. L., Connell, J. P., & Ryan, R. M. (1989). Self-determination in a work organization. *Journal of Applied Psychology, 74*(4), 580.

Deeds, D. L., DeCarolis, D., & Coombs, J. (2000). Dynamic capabilities and new product development in high technology ventures: An empirical analysis of new biotechnology firms. *Journal of Business Venturing, 15*(3), 211–229.

DeLongis, A., Folkman, S., & Lazarus, R. S. (1988). The impact of daily stress on health and mood: Psychological and social resources as mediators. *Journal of Personality and Social Psychology, 54*(3), 486.

Denison, D. R., & Sutton, R. I. (1990). Surgical nurses: Issues in the design of a loosely-bounded team. In J. R. Hackman (Ed.), *Groups that work and those that don't: Creation conditions for effective teamwork.* San Francisco: Jossey-Bass.

Derryberry, D., & Tucker, D. M. (1994). Motivating the focus of attention. In P. M. Niedenthal & S. Kitayama (Eds.), *The heart's eye: Emotional influences in perception and attention* (pp. 167–196). San Diego: Academic.

Diener, C. I., & Dweck, C. S. (1980). An analysis of learned helplessness: II. The processing of success. *Journal of Personality and Social Psychology, 39*(5), 940.

Dillon, P. (1998). Failure is just part of the culture of innovation: Accept it and become stronger. *Fast Company, 18*, 1–2.

DiMasi, J. A., Hansen, R. W., & Grabowski, H. G. (2003). The price of innovation: New estimates of drug development costs. *Journal of Health Economics, 22*(2), 151–185.

Dirks, K. T., Cummings, L. L., & Pierce, J. L. (1996). Psychological ownership in organizations: Conditions under which individuals promote and resist change. In W. W. Woodman & W. A. Pasmore (Eds.), *Research in organizational change and development* (pp. 1–23). Greenwich: JAI Press.

Dutton, J. E., Worline, M. C., Frost, P. J., & Lilius, J. (2006). Explaining compassion organizing. *Administrative Science Quarterly, 51*(1), 59–96.

Dweck, C. S. (1986). Motivational processes affecting learning. *American Psychologist, 41*(10), 1040.

Eggen, D., & Witte, G. (2006, August 18). The FBI's upgrade that wasn't. *Washington Post*, A01.

Eisenhardt, K. M., & Martin, J. A. (2000). Dynamic capabilities: What are they? *Strategic Management Journal, 21*(10/11), 1105–1121.

Ekman, P. (1992). Are there basic emotions? *Psychological Review, 99*(3), 550–553.
Ekman, P., & Oster, H. (1979). Facial expressions of emotion. *Annual Review of Psychology, 30*(1), 527–554.
Ellis, S. H., & Chase, W. G. (1971). Parallel processing in item recognition. *Attention, Perception, & Psychophysics, 10*(5), 379–384.
Ellis, N. R., Detterman, D. K., Runcie, D., McCarver, R. B., & Craig, E. M. (1971). Amnesic effects in short-term memory. *Journal of Experimental Psychology, 89*(2), 357.
Esty, H. (1987). The management of change. *Employee Assistance Quarterly, 2*, 89–97.
Farson, R., & Keyes, R. (2002). The failure-tolerant leader. *Harvard Business Review, 80*, 64–71.
Fineman, S. (1996). Emotional subtexts in corporate greening. *Organization Studies, 17*(3), 479–500.
Fineman, S. (2003). *Understanding emotion at work*. London: Sage.
Fisher, J. (2001). Harming and benefiting the dead. *Death Studies, 25*(7), 557–568.
Fisher, C. D. (2003). Why do lay people believe that satisfaction and performance are correlated? Possible sources of a commonsense theory. *Journal of Organizational Behavior, 24*(6), 753–777.
Foliart, E., Clausen, M., & Siljestrom, C. (2001). Bereavement practices among California hospices: Results of a statewide survey. *Death Studies, 25*(5), 461–467.
Folkman, S., & Moskowitz, J. T. (2004). Coping: Pitfalls and promise. *Annual Review of Psychology, 55*, 745–774.
Foo, M. D., Uy, M. A., & Baron, R. A. (2009). How do feelings influence effort? An empirical study of entrepreneurs' affect and venture effort. *Journal of Applied Psychology, 94*(4), 1086–1094.
Forbes, D. P. (2005). Are some entrepreneurs more overconfident than others? *Journal of Business Venturing, 20*(5), 623–640.
Fox, S., & Spector, P. E. (1999). A model of work frustration-aggression. *Journal of Organizational Behavior, 20*, 915–931.
Francis, K., & Dugas, M. J. (2004). Assessing positive beliefs about worry: Validation of a structured interview. *Personality and Individual Differences, 37*(2), 405–415.
Fredrickson, B. L. (1998). What good are positive emotions? *Review of General Psychology, 2*(3), 300–319.
Fredrickson, B. (2001). The role of positive emotion in positive psychology: The broaden-and-build theory of positive emotion. *American Psychologist, 56*, 218–226.
Frijda, N. H. (1986). *The emotions*. Cambridge: Cambridge University Press.

Frost, P. J. (2003). The hidden work of leadership. *Leader to Leader, 30*, 13–18.

Ganster, D. C. (2005). Executive job demands: Suggestions from a stress and decision-making perspective. *Academy of Management Review, 30*(3), 492–502.

Gassmann, O., & Reepmeyer, G. (2005). Organizing pharmaceutical innovation: From science-based knowledge creators to drug-oriented knowledge brokers. *Creativity and Innovation Management, 14*(3), 233–245.

Gilbreath, B., & Benson, P. G. (2004). The contribution of supervisor behaviour to employee psychological well-being. *Work and Stress, 18*, 255–266.

Gist, M. E. (1987). Self-efficacy: Implications for organizational behavior and human resource management. *Academy of Management Review, 12*(3), 472–485.

Gladstein, D. L., & Reilly, N. P. (1985). Group decision making under threat: The tycoon game. *Academy of Management Journal, 28*(3), 613–627.

Gong, Y., Law, K. S., Chang, S., & Xin, K. R. (2009). Human resources management and firm performance: The differential role of managerial affective and continuance commitment. *Journal of Applied Psychology, 94*(1), 263.

Gross, J. J. (1998). Antecedent-and response-focused emotion regulation: Divergent consequences for experience, expression, and physiology. *Journal of Personality and Social Psychology, 74*(1), 224.

Guth, W. D., & Ginsberg, A. (1990). Guest editors' introduction: Corporate entrepreneurship. *Strategic Management Journal, 11*, 5–15.

Hansen, M. T. (1999). The search-transfer problem: The role of weak ties in sharing knowledge across organization subunits. *Administrative Science Quarterly, 44*(1), 82–111.

Harris, S. G., & Sutton, R. I. (1986). Functions of parting ceremonies in dying organizations. *Academy of Management Journal, 29*(1), 5–30.

Hayes, S. C., Wilson, K. G., Gifford, E. V., Follette, V. M., & Strosahl, K. (1996). Experiential avoidance and behavioral disorders: A functional dimensional approach to diagnosis and treatment. *Journal of Consulting and Clinical Psychology, 64*, 1152–1168.

Hirshleifer, J. (1993). The affections and the passions: Their economic logic. *Rationality and Society, 5*(2), 185–202.

Hochschild, A. R. (2012). *The managed heart: Commercialization of human feeling*. Berkeley: University of California Press.

Hogan, N. S., Greenfield, D. B., & Schmidt, L. A. (2001). Development and validation of the Hogan grief reaction checklist. *Death Studies, 25*(1), 1–32.

Holahan, C. J., & Moos, R. H. (1987). Personal and contextual determinants of coping strategies. *Journal of Personality and Social Psychology, 52*(5), 946.

Hopmeyer, E., & Werk, A. (1994). A comparative study of family bereavement groups. *Death Studies, 18*(3), 243–256.

Huber, V. L. (1985). Effects of task difficulty, goal setting, and strategy on performance of a heuristic task. *Journal of Applied Psychology, 70*(3), 492.

Huber, G. P. (1991). Organizational learning: The contributing processes and the literatures. *Organization Science, 2*(1), 88–115.
Humphrey, R. H. (2002). The many faces of emotional leadership. *Leadership Quarterly, 13*(5), 493–504.
Huy, Q. N. (1999). Emotional capability, emotional intelligence, and radical change. *Academy of Management Review, 24*(2), 325–345.
Iacovou, C. L., & Dexter, A. S. (2005). Surviving IT project cancellations. *Communications of the ACM, 48*(4), 83–86.
Ilies, R., & Judge, T. A. (2005). Goal regulation across time: The effects of feedback and affect. *Journal of Applied Psychology, 90*(3), 453–467.
Ireland, R. D., & Hitt, M. A. (1999). Achieving and maintaining strategic competitiveness in the 21st century: The role of strategic leadership. *Academy of Management Executive, 13*(1), 43–57.
Isen, A. M., & Geva, N. (1987). The influence of positive affect on acceptable level of risk: The person with a large canoe has a large worry. *Organizational Behavior and Human Decision Processes, 39*(2), 145–154.
Janoff-Bulman, R. (1992). *Shattered assumptions: Towards a new psychology of trauma.* New York: Free Press.
Kahn, W. A. (1990). Psychological conditions of personal engagement and disengagement at work. *Academy of Management Journal, 33*, 692–724.
Kahnweiler, W. M., & Riordan, R. J. (1998). Job and employee support groups: Past and prologue. *Career Development Quarterly, 47*(2), 173–187.
Kanov, J. M., Maitlis, S., Worline, M. C., Dutton, J. E., Frost, P. J., & Lilius, J. M. (2004). Compassion in organizational life. *American Behavioral Scientist, 47*, 808–827.
Kanter, R. (1968). A study of commitment mechanisms in utopian societies. *American Sociological Review, 33*, 499–517.
Karasek, R. A., Jr. (1979). Job demands, job decision latitude, and mental strain: Implications for job redesign. *Administrative Science Quarterly, 24*(2), 285–308.
Kim, D. H. (1993). The link between individual and organizational learning. *Sloan Management Review, 35*(1), 37–50.
Kim, J. Y. J., & Miner, A. S. (2007). Vicarious learning from the failures and near-failures of others: Evidence from the US commercial banking industry. *Academy of Management Journal, 50*(3), 687–714.
Klaukien, A., Shepherd, D. A., & Patzelt, H. (2013). Passion for work, nonwork-related excitement, and innovation managers' decision to exploit new product opportunities. *Journal of Product Innovation Management, 30*(3), 574–588.
Langlois, F., Freeston, M. H., & Ladouceur, R. (2000). Differences and similarities between obsessive intrusive thoughts and worry in a non-clinical population: Study 1. *Behaviour Research and Therapy, 38*, 157–173.

Lazarus, R. S. (1993). From psychological stress to the emotions: A history of changing outlooks. *Annual Review of Psychology, 44*(1), 1–22.

Lazarus, R. S., & Folkman, S. (1984a). *Stress, appraisal, and coping.* New York: Springer.

Lazarus, R. S., & Folkman, S. (1984b). Coping and adaptation. In W. D. Gentry (Ed.), *The handbook of behavioral medicine* (pp. 282–325). New York: Guilford.

Leary, M. R. (1990). Responses to social exclusion: Social anxiety, jealousy, loneliness, depression, and low self-esteem. *Journal of Social and Clinical Psychology, 9*(2), 221–229.

Leary, M. R., Cottrell, C. A., & Phillips, M. (2001). Deconfounding the effects of dominance and social acceptance on self-esteem. *Journal of Personality and Social Psychology, 81*(5), 898–909.

Leary, M. R., Tate, E. B., Adams, C. E., Batts Allen, A., & Hancock, J. (2007). Self-compassion and reactions to unpleasant self-relevant events: The implications of treating oneself kindly. *Journal of Personality and Social Psychology, 92*(5), 887–904.

Leonard-Barton, D. (1995). *Wellspring of knowledge.* Boston: Harvard Business School Press.

Levinthal, D. A., & March, J. G. (1993). The myopia of learning. *Strategic Management Journal, 14*(S2), 95–112.

Lewis, M. (1998). The development and structure of emotions. In M. F. Mascolo & S. Griffin (Eds.), *What develops in emotional development?* New York: Plenum Press.

Liden, R. C., & Graen, G. (1980). Generalizability of the vertical dyad linkage model of leadership. *Academy of Management Journal, 23*(3), 451–465.

Liden, R. C., & Tewksbury, T. W. (1995). Empowerment and work teams. In G. R. Ferris, S. D. Rosen, & D. T. Barnum (Eds.), *Handbook of human resources management* (pp. 386–403). Oxford: Blackwell.

Liles, P. R. (1976). *New business ventures and the entrepreneur.* Homewood: Irwin.

Lindsley, D. H., Brass, D. J., & Thomas, J. B. (1995). Efficacy-performing spirals: A multilevel perspective. *Academy of Management Review, 20*(3), 645–678.

Logan, M. S., & Ganster, D. C. (2007). The effects of empowerment on attitudes and performance: The role of social support and empowerment beliefs. *Journal of Management Studies, 44*(8), 1523–1550.

Lok, P., Hung, R. Y., Walsh, P., Wang, P., & Crawford, J. (2005). An integrative framework for measuring the extent to which organizational variables influence the success of process improvement programmes. *Journal of Management Studies, 42*(7), 1357–1381.

Luce, M. F., Bettman, J. R., & Payne, J. W. (1997). Choice processing in emotionally difficult decisions. *Journal of Experimental Psychology: Learning, Memory, and Cognition, 23*(2), 384.

Lyubomirsky, S., & Nolen-Hoeksema, S. (1995). Effects of self-focused rumination on negative thinking and interpersonal problem solving. *Journal of Personality and Social Psychology, 69*(1), 176.

Martinko, M. J., & Gardner, W. L. (1982). Learned helplessness: An alternative explanation for performance deficits. *Academy of Management Review, 7*(2), 195–204.

Mathews, A., May, J., Mogg, K., & Eysenck, M. (1990). Attentional bias in anxiety: Selective search or defective filtering? *Journal of Abnormal Psychology, 99*(2), 166–173.

Mayer, J. D., & Salovey, P. (1997). What is emotional intelligence? Implications for educators. In P. Salovey & D. Sluyter (Eds.), *Emotional development, emotional literacy, and emotional intelligence*. New York: Basic Books.

McAdams, D. P. (1985). *Power, intimacy, and the life story*. Homewood: Dorsey.

McAdams, D. P., & Bryant, F. B. (1987). Intimacy motivation and subjective mental health in a nationwide sample. *Journal of Personality, 55*(3), 395–413.

McColl-Kennedy, J. R., & Anderson, R. D. (2002). Impact of leadership style and emotions on subordinate performance. *Leadership Quarterly, 13*(5), 545–559.

McCune, J. C. (1997). Making lemonade. *Management Review, 86*, 49–54.

McFadyen, M. A., & Cannella, A. A. (2004). Social capital and knowledge creation: Diminishing returns of the number and strength of exchange relationships. *Academy of Management Journal, 47*(5), 735–746.

McGrath, R. G. (1999). Falling forward: Real options reasoning and entrepreneurial failure. *Academy of Management Review, 24*(1), 13–30.

McGrath, R. G. (2001). Exploratory learning, innovative capacity, and managerial oversight. *Academy of Management Journal, 44*(1), 118–131.

McGrath, R. G., & MacMillan, I. C. (2000). *The entrepreneurial mindset: Strategies for continuously creating opportunity in an age of uncertainty* (Vol. 284). Cambridge, MA: Harvard Business Press.

McGrath, R. G., Keil, T., & Tukiainen, T. (2006). Extracting value from corporate venturing. *MIT Sloan Management Review, 48*(1), 50–56.

McGraw, K. O., & McCullers, J. C. (1979). Evidence of a detrimental effect of extrinsic incentives on breaking a mental set. *Journal of Experimental Social Psychology, 15*(3), 285–294.

McMullen, J. S., & Shepherd, D. A. (2006). Entrepreneurial action and the role of uncertainty in the theory of the entrepreneur. *Academy of Management Review, 31*(1), 132–152.

Menaghan, E. (1982). Measuring coping effectiveness: A panel analysis of marital problems and coping efforts. *Journal of Health and Social Behavior, 23*(3), 220–234.

Metcalfe, J., & Mischel, W. (1999). A hot/cool-system analysis of delay of gratification: Dynamics of willpower. *Psychological Review, 106*(1), 3–19.

Meyerson, D. (1990). Uncovering socially undesirable emotions. *American Behavioral, 33*(3), 296–307.

Mogg, K., Mathews, A., Bird, C., & Macgregor-Morris, R. (1990). Effects of stress and anxiety on the processing of threat stimuli. *Journal of Personality and Social Psychology, 59*(6), 1230.

Mullins, J. W., & Forlani, D. (2005). Missing the boat or sinking the boat: A study of new venture decision making. *Journal of Business Venturing, 20*(1), 47–69.

Murray, C. A., & Cox, C. B. (1989). *Apollo: The race to the moon.* New York: Simon and Schuster.

Neff, K. D. (2003a). Self-compassion: An alternative conceptualization of a healthy attitude toward oneself. *Self and Identity, 2,* 85–102.

Neff, K. D. (2003b). The development and validation of a scale to measure self-compassion. *Self and Identity, 2,* 223–250.

Neff, K. D., & Davidson, O. (2016). Self-compassion. In I. Ivtzan & T. Lomas (Eds.), *Mindfulness in positive psychology: The science of meditation and wellbeing.* Milton Park: Taylor & Francis.

Neff, K. D., Hsieh, Y. P., & Dejitterat, K. (2005). Self-compassion, achievement goals, and coping with academic failure. *Self and Identity, 4*(3), 263–287.

Neff, K. D., Kirkpatrick, K. L., & Rude, S. S. (2007). Self-compassion and adaptive psychological functioning. *Journal of Research in Personality, 41*(1), 139–154.

Newcombe, M. J., & Ashkanasy, N. M. (2002). The role of affect and affective congruence in perceptions of leaders: An experimental study. *Leadership Quarterly, 13*(5), 601–614.

Nolen-Hoeksema, S. (1991). Responses to depression and their effects on the duration of depressive episodes. *Journal of Abnormal Psychology, 100*(4), 569–582.

Nolen-Hoeksema, S., & Morrow, J. (1991). A prospective study of depression and posttraumatic stress symptoms after a natural disaster: The 1989 Loma Prieta earthquake. *Journal of Personality and Social Psychology, 61*(1), 115–121.

Nussbaum, M. C. (1996). Compassion: The basic social emotion. *Social Philosophy and Policy, 13,* 27–58.

O'Driscoll, M. P., Pierce, J. L., & Coghlan, A. M. (2006). The psychology of ownership. *Group and Organization Management, 31,* 388–416.

O'Reilly, C. A., & Chatman, J. (1986). Organizational commitment and psychological attachment: The effects of compliance, identification, and internalization on prosocial behavior. *Journal of Applied Psychology, 71*(3), 492–499.

Parasuraman, S., & Alutto, J. A. (1984). Sources and outcomes of stress in organizational settings: Toward the development of a structural model. *Academy of Management Journal, 27*(2), 330–350.

Parker, S. K., & Sprigg, C. A. (1999). Minimizing strain and maximizing learning: The role of job demands, job control, and proactive personality. *Journal of Applied Psychology, 84*(6), 925–939.
Patrick, H., Canevello, A., Knee, C. R., & Lonsbary, C. (2007). The role of need fulfillment in relationship functioning and well-being: A self-determination theory perspective. *Journal of Personality and Social Psychology, 92*, 434–457.
Patzelt, H., & Shepherd, D. A. (2011). Negative emotions of an entrepreneurial career: Self-employment and regulatory coping behaviors. *Journal of Business Venturing, 26*(2), 226–238.
Peeters, M. C., & Le Blanc, P. M. (2001). Towards a match between job demands and sources of social support: A study among oncology care providers. *European Journal of Work and Organizational Psychology, 10*(1), 53–72.
Peter, T. J., & Waterman, A. A. (1982). *In search of excellence.* New York: Harper & Row.
Petrovski, H. (1985). *To engineer is human, the role of failure in successful design.* New York: St.Martin's Press.
Pierce, J. L., Kostova, T., & Kirks, K. T. (2001). Toward a theory of psychological ownership in organizations. *Academy of Management Review, 26*, 298–310.
Pieters, R. G. M., & Fred Van Raaij, W. (1987). The role of affect in economic behavior. In W. Fred Van Raaij, G. M. Van Veldhoven, T. M. M. Verhallen, & K. E. Warneryd (Eds.), *Handbook of economic psychology.* Amsterdam: Springer.
Popper, K. R. (1959). *The logic of scientific discovery.* New York: Hutchinson.
Prigerson, H. G., Bierhals, A. J., Kasl, S. V., Reynolds, C. F., Shear, M. K., Day, N., et al. (1997). Traumatic grief as a risk factor for mental and physical morbidity. *American Journal of Psychiatry, 154*, 616–623.
Pugh, S. D. (2001). Service with a smile: Emotional contagion in the service encounter. *Academy of Management Journal, 44*(5), 1018–1027.
Rafaeli, A., & Sutton, R. I. (1987). Expression of emotion as part of the work role. *Academy of Management Review, 12*(1), 23–37.
Rawsthorne, L. J., & Elliot, A. J. (1999). Achievement goals and intrinsic motivation: A meta-analytic review. *Personality and Social Psychology Review, 3*(4), 326–344.
Reed, D. A. 1989. *An orderly world: The social construction of reality within an occupation.* Unpublished Doctoral Dissertation. Bloomington, Indiana University.
Repetti, R. L. (1992). Social withdrawal as a short term coping response to daily stressors. In H. S. Friedman (Ed.), *Hostility, coping, and health* (pp. 151–165). Washington, DC: American Psychological Association.
Richins, M. L. (1997). Measuring emotions in the consumption experience. *Journal of Consumer Research, 24*(2), 127–146.
Richter, A. W., West, M. A., Van Dick, R., & Dawson, J. F. (2006). Boundary spanners' identification, intergroup contact, and effective intergroup relations. *Academy of Management Journal, 49*(6), 1252–1269.

Riordan, C. M., & Griffeth, R. W. (1995). The opportunity for friendship in the workplace: An underexplored construct. *Journal of Business and Psychology, 10*(2), 141–154.

Roese, N. J. (1997). Counterfactual thinking. *Psychological Bulletin, 121*(1), 133–148.

Rubin, T. I. (1975). *Compassion and self-hate: An alternative to despair.* New York: D. McKay.

Russel, J. A. (1980). A circumplex model of affect. *Journal of Personality and Social Psychology, 39*(6), 1161–1178.

Russell, D., Cutrona, C. E., Rose, J., & Yurko, K. (1984). Social and emotional loneliness: An examination of Weiss's typology of loneliness. *Journal of Personality and Social Psychology, 46*(6), 1313.

Ryan, R. M., & Deci, E. L. (2000). Self-determination theory and the facilitation of intrinsic motivation, social development, and well-being. *American Psychologist, 55*(1), 68.

Ryan, R. M., & La Guardia, J. G. (2000). What is being optimized over development?: A self-determination theory perspective on basic psychological needs across the life span. In S. Qualls & R. Abeles (Eds.), *Dialogues on psychology and aging* (pp. 145–172). Washington, DC: American Psychological Association.

Ryan, R. M., Stiller, J. D., & Lynch, J. H. (1994). Representations of relationships to teachers, parents, and friends as predictors of academic motivation and self-esteem. *The Journal of Early Adolescence, 14*(2), 226–249.

Ryff, C. D. (1989). Happiness is everything, or is it? Explorations on the meaning of psychological well-being. *Journal of Personality and Social Psychology, 57*, 1069–1081.

Schindehutte, M., Morris, M., & Allen, J. (2006). Beyond achievement: Entrepreneurship as extreme experience. *Small Business Economics, 27*(4), 349–368.

Schnall, P. L., Landsbergis, P. A., & Baker, D. (1994). Job strain and cardiovascular disease. *Annual Review of Public Health, 15*(1), 381–411.

Schwarz, N., & Clore, G. L. (1983). Mood, misattribution, and judgments of well-being: Informative and directive functions of affective states. *Journal of Personality and Social Psychology, 45*(3), 513.

Schwarz, N., & Clore, G. L. (1988). How do I feel about it? Informative functions of affective states. In K. Fiedler & J. Forgas (Eds.), *Affect, cognition, and social behavior* (pp. 44–62). Toronto: Hogrefe International.

Shane, S., & Venkataraman, S. (2000). The promise of entrepreneurship as a field of research. *Academy of Management Review, 25*(1), 217–226.

Shane, S., Locke, E. A., & Collins, C. J. (2003). Entrepreneurial motivation. *Human Resource Management Review, 13*(2), 257–279.

Shapiro, S. L., Astin, J. A., Bishop, S. R., & Cordova, M. (2005). Mindfulness-based stress reduction for health care professionals: Results from a randomized trial. *International Journal of Stress Management, 12*, 164–176.

Shea, C. M. (1999). The effect of leadership style on performance improvement on a manufacturing task. *Journal of Business, 72*(3), 407–422.

Sheldon, K. M., Ryan, R., & Reis, H. T. (1996). What makes for a good day? Competence and autonomy in the day and in the person. *Personality and Social Psychology Bulletin, 22*(12), 1270–1279.

Shepherd, D. A. (2003). Learning from business failure: Propositions of grief recovery for the self-employed. *Academy of Management Review, 28*(2), 318–328.

Shepherd, D. A., & Cardon, M. S. (2009). Negative emotional reactions to project failure and the self-compassion to learn from the experience. *Journal of Management Studies, 46*(6), 923–949.

Shepherd, D., & Haynie, J. M. (2009). Birds of a feather don't always flock together: Identity management in entrepreneurship. *Journal of Business Venturing, 24*(4), 316–337.

Shepherd, D. A., & Williams, T. A. (2014). Local venturing as compassion organizing in the aftermath of a natural disaster: The role of localness and community in reducing suffering. *Journal of Management Studies, 51*(6), 952–994.

Shepherd, D. A., Covin, J. G., & Kuratko, D. F. (2009a). Project failure from corporate entrepreneurship: Managing the grief process. *Journal of Business Venturing, 24*(6), 588–600.

Shepherd, D. A., Wiklund, J., & Haynie, J. M. (2009b). Moving forward: Balancing the financial and emotional costs of business failure. *Journal of Business Venturing, 24*(2), 134–148.

Shepherd, D. A., Patzelt, H., & Wolfe, M. (2011). Moving forward from project failure: Negative emotions, affective commitment, and learning from the experience. *Academy of Management Journal, 54*(6), 1229–1259.

Shepherd, D. A., Patzelt, H., & Baron, R. A. (2013). "I care about nature, but...": Disengaging values in assessing opportunities that cause harm. *Academy of Management Journal, 56*(5), 1251–1273.

Simon, H. (1957). A behavorial model of rational choice. In *Models of man, social and rational: Mathematical essays on rational human behavior in a social setting.* New York: Wiley.

Sinclair, R. R., Tucker, J. S., Cullen, J. C., & Wright, C. (2005). Performance differences among four organizational commitment profiles. *Journal of Applied Psychology, 90*(6), 1280.

Sitkin, S. B. (1992). Learning through failure: The strategy of small losses. *Research in Organizational Behavior, 14*, 231–266.

Sminia, H. (2003). The failure of the Sport7 TV-channel: Controversies in a business network. *Journal of Management Studies, 40*(7), 1621–1649.

Song, X. M., & Parry, M. E. (1997). A cross-national comparative study of new product development processes: Japan and the United States. *Journal of Marketing, 61*(2), 1–18.

Spreitzer, G., Sutcliffe, K., Dutton, J., Sonenshein, S., & Grant, A. M. (2005). A socially embedded model of thriving at work. *Organization Science, 16*(5), 537–549.

Staw, B. M., Sandelands, L. E., & Dutton, J. E. (1981). Threat rigidity effects in organizational behavior: A multilevel analysis. *Administrative Science Quarterly, 26*, 501–524.

Steele, C. M. (1988). The psychology of self-affirmation: Sustaining the integrity of the self. *Advances in Experimental Psychology, 21*, 261–302.

St Onge, S. (1995). Systematic desensitization. In M. B. Ballou (Ed.), *Psychological interventions: A guide to strategies* (pp. 95–115). London: Praeger.

Stroebe, M. S., & Schut, H. (2001). Models of coping with bereavement: A risk group identified. *Journal of Social Issues, 44*, 375–403.

Sutton, R. I., & D'Aunno, T. (1989). Decreasing organizational size: Untangling the effects of money and people. *Academy of Management Review, 14*(2), 194–212.

Tajfel, H., & Turner, J. C. (1979). An integrative theory of intergroup conflict. In W. Austin & S. Worchel (Eds.), *The social psychology of intergroup relations* (pp. 33–48). Chicago: Nelson-Hall.

Tajfel, H., & Turner, J. C. (1986). The social identity theory of intergroup behavior. In S. Worchel & W. G. Austin (Eds.), *Psychology of intergroup relations*. Chicago: Nelson.

Teasdale, J. D., Segal, Z. V., Williams, J. M., Ridgeway, V. A., Soulsby, J. M., & Lau, M. A. (2000). Prevention of relapse-recurrence in major depression by mindfulness-based cognitive therapy. *Journal of Consulting and Clinical Psychology, 68*, 615–623.

Thompson, C. A., & Prottas, D. J. (2006). Relationships among organizational family support, job autonomy, perceived control, and employee well-being. *Journal of Occupational Health Psychology, 11*, 100–118.

Tice, D. M., & Baumeister, R. F. (1990). Self-Esteem, self-handicapping, and self-presentation: The strategy of inadequate practice. *Journal of Personality, 58*(2), 443–464.

Tjosvold, D., Johnson, D. W., Johnson, R. T., & Sun, H. (2003). Can interpersonal competition be constructive within organizations? *Journal of Psychology, 137*(1), 63–84.

Trice, H. M., & Beyer, J. M. (1993). *The cultures of work organizations*. Englewood Cliffs: Prentice-Hall, Inc.

Tugade, M. M., & Fredrickson, B. L. (2004). Resilient individuals use positive emotions to bounce back from negative emotional experiences. *Journal of Personality and Social Psychology, 86*(2), 320–333.

Vallerand, R. J., & Reid, G. (1984). On the causal effects of perceived competence on intrinsic motivation: A test of cognitive evaluation theory. *Journal of Sport Psychology, 6*(1), 94–102.

Vallerand, R. J., Blanchard, C., Mageau, G. A., Koestner, R., Ratelle, C., Léonard, M., et al. (2003). Les passions de l'ame: On obsessive and harmonious passion. *Journal of Personality and Social Psychology, 85*(4), 756–767.

Vandenberghe, C., Bentein, K., & Stinglhamber, F. (2004). Affective commitment to the organization, supervisor, and work group: Antecedents and outcomes. *Journal of Vocational Behavior, 64*(1), 47–71.

Vince, R., & Broussine, M. (1996). Paradox, defense and attachment: Accessing and working with emotions and relations underlying organizational change. *Organization Studies, 17*(1), 1–21.

Walsh, J. P., & Ungson, G. R. (1991). Organizational memory. *Academy of Management Review, 16*(1), 57–91.

Ward, T. B. (2004). Cognition, creativity, and entrepreneurship. *Journal of Business Venturing, 19*(2), 173–188.

Watson, D., Clark, L. A., & Tellegen, A. (1988). Development and validation of brief measures of positive and negative affect: The PANAS scales. *Journal of Personality and Social Psychology, 54*(6), 1063–1070.

Weick, K. (1979). *The social psychology of organizing*. Reading: Addison-Wesley.

Weick, K. E. (1984). Small wins: Redefining the scale of social problems. *American Psychologist, 39*(1), 40–49.

Weick, K. E. (1990). The vulnerable system: An analysis of the Tenerife air disaster. *Journal of Management, 16*(3), 571–593.

Weick, E. K., & Sutcliffe, M. K. (2007). *Managing the unexpected: Resilient performance in an age of uncertainty* (2nd ed.). San Francisco: Jossey-Boss/Wiley.

Wells, A., & Matthews, G. (1994). Self-consciousness and cognitive failures as predictors of coping in stressful episodes. *Cognition & Emotion, 8*(3), 279–295.

Westermann, R., Stahl, G., & Hesse, F. (1996). Relative effectiveness and validity of mood induction procedures: Analysis. *European Journal of Social Psychology, 26*(4), 557–580.

Williams, T. A., & Shepherd, D. A. (2016). Victim entrepreneurs doing well by doing good: Venture creation and well-being in the aftermath of a resource shock. *Journal of Business Venturing, 31*(4), 365–387.

Wispe, L. (1991). *The psychology of sympathy*. New York: Plenum.

Wood, R., & Bandura, A. (1989). Social cognitive theory of organizational management. *Academy of Management Review, 14*(3), 361–384.

Wood, J. V., Saltzberg, J. A., & Goldsamt, L. A. (1990). Does affect induce self-focused attention? *Journal of Personality and Social Psychology, 58*(5), 899–908.

Yli-Renko, H., Autio, E., & Sapienza, H. J. (2001). Social capital, knowledge acquisition, and knowledge exploitation in young technology-based firms. *Strategic Management Journal, 22*(6–7), 587–613.

Yukl, G. (2006). *Leadership in organizations*. Upper Saddle River: Pearson Education.

Open Access This chapter is licensed under the terms of the Creative Commons Attribution 4.0 International License (http://creativecommons.org/licenses/by/4.0/), which permits use, sharing, adaptation, distribution and reproduction in any medium or format, as long as you give appropriate credit to the original author(s) and the source, provide a link to the Creative Commons license and indicate if changes were made.

The images or other third party material in this chapter are included in the chapter's Creative Commons license, unless indicated otherwise in a credit line to the material. If material is not included in the chapter's Creative Commons license and your intended use is not permitted by statutory regulation or exceeds the permitted use, you will need to obtain permission directly from the copyright holder.

CHAPTER 7

Conclusion

In this book, we summarized important parts of our prior work targeted toward understanding the cognition of entrepreneurs. Specifically, our focus was on the role of knowledge, motivation, attention, identity, and emotions in the entrepreneurial process. Our work has several implications for scholars and practitioners interested in better understanding entrepreneurial cognition.

KNOWLEDGE AND ENTREPRENEURIAL COGNITION

In Chap. 2, we outlined the important role of knowledge for individuals' and teams' recognition of entrepreneurial opportunities. Specifically, we illustrated that individuals are heterogeneous in their knowledge endowments and that this heterogeneity explains, partly, why some recognize specific types of opportunities (e.g., commercial, sustainable, health-related, international) while others do not. We also found that knowledge sources internal and external to the entrepreneur can impact opportunity recognition. Finally, we explored the role of structural alignment as a cognitive process that interacts with prior knowledge in opportunity recognition. Our findings have important implications for scholarship and highlight future research possibilities.

First, entrepreneurship scholars who explore the connection between prior knowledge and opportunity identification should carefully differentiate between types of prior knowledge. For example, prior knowledge can lead individuals to identify more opportunities that are themselves more innovative, but some individuals may become entrenched in mental ruts as they gain more experience. This relationship could be curvilinear such that there is an early rise in the number and innovativeness of opportunities with increasing knowledge followed by a plateau and then a decline. These are just expectations, however; additional research is needed to fully understand these relationships. Moreover, it is likely that the relationship between prior knowledge and opportunity identification is more complicated than a clear-cut main-effect-only explanation. Through our analysis, we argued that the relationship between individuals' prior knowledge of customer problems and their ability to identify an opportunity varies depending on differences in the financial reward they receive for completing the task (Shepherd and DeTienne 2005; see also Csikszentmihalyi 1975, 2000; Maheswaran and Sternthal 1990). While it is valuable to explain why certain individuals (and not others) recognize opportunities based on their prior knowledge, the mechanisms underlying how prior knowledge facilitates opportunity identification remain largely unclear and warrant attention in future research.

Second, we found that entrepreneurial knowledge of the natural or communal environment influences individuals' recognition of opportunities for sustainable development. Specifically, individuals with these knowledge types are more likely than others to recognize opportunities based on changes in the natural and communal environment in which they live. Importantly, we also proposed that the impact these types of knowledge have on opportunity recognition is contingent on entrepreneurial knowledge— that is, knowledge of markets, ways to serve markets, and customer problems (Shane 2000). Specifically, there appears to be a complementary relationship between natural/communal environment knowledge and entrepreneurial knowledge, which implies that interactions between different knowledge types warrant particular attention in future research on the recognition of opportunities that go beyond generating financial gains for entrepreneurs. Interactions between knowledge types in opportunity recognition might also be central to extending businesses from developed economies into developing economies. For example, Hart (2006: 42) argued that "managers, particularly in multinational corporations, are more accustomed to viewing the global market as a single monolithic entity. They focus almost exclusively on the money economy and customers who have achieved a certain level of affluence." Hart (2006: 41) also described the consequences for the lack of economic development in developing countries:

> In the past, ignorance and isolation meant that those in the traditional and market economies were largely unaware of their plight. Today, however, the digital revolution is bringing information—and ideas—to growing number of the world's poor. Such knowledge is potentially empowering, as we will see, creating the potential to reform corrupt regimes, solve environmental problems, and spur more equitable forms of development.

Thus, Hart implied that knowledge about natural and communal problems may interact with knowledge about digital technologies when individuals recognize opportunities for sustainable development. We believe that future research can make important contributions by exploring this proposition. Further, since our theorizing was mainly focused on the formation of the belief that a sustainable development opportunity exists for someone (i.e., third-person opportunity), future research can also explore the role of knowledge about the natural and communal environment (and interactions with entrepreneurial knowledge) in forming the belief that a recognized opportunity can be exploited by the individual who recognized it (i.e., first-person opportunity belief) (McMullen and Shepherd 2006; Shepherd et al. 2007). Finally, it is important to note that little empirical work has tested the proposed (interaction) relationships between knowledge types and sustainable development opportunities. Such studies are urgently needed.

Third, we argued that prior knowledge of health-related problems derived from one's own health problems or the health problems of loved ones can trigger individuals' recognition of opportunities that improve the health of others. However, knowledge of health-related problems can be diverse and captures the medical reason behind the problem, interactions between parts of the problem (e.g., diagnosis, medication, cure plan), and/or the reasons current solutions are insufficient. Future research should go deeper and (potentially empirically) explore how types of health-related knowledge (perhaps interactively) impact opportunity identification. Further, the context of identifying opportunities based on prior knowledge of health-related problems may be interesting for studying the poorly understood phenomenon of user entrepreneurship (Shah and Tripsas 2007). Those who suffer from health-related problems and find insufficient solutions on the market may be particularly attentive to the adoption and improvement of existing products, potentially resulting in the identification of opportunities that not only improve their own health but others' health as well. It appears that future research investigating the user entrepreneurship process in the context of health-related technologies, products, and services can contribute to our understanding of opportunity identification and the role of knowledge therein. Finally, scholars may also investigate how people apply their technological knowledge to a health problem they have not experienced themselves. For example, based on their health-related knowledge, individuals could attend to health problems shared by people worldwide, or to the problems with the greatest financial market potential, or to the problems that are particularly prevalent in their own communities. Perhaps observing a health-related problem only through those suffering from it enables perspective taking in a more distant manner, which facilitates the creativity needed for recognizing health-related opportunities.

Fourth, in the context of international opportunities, Chap. 2 highlighted the importance of considering both internal and external knowledge sources to explain opportunity identification, particularly the contingent relationships between these knowledge sources. Specifically, it appears that entrepreneurs and their management teams with low levels of international knowledge capitalize most on external sources of international knowledge for opportunity recognition in foreign markets. This substitution effect is contrary to findings from absorptive capacity research, which emphasizes the need for knowledge in a particular domain in order to effectively incorporate additional knowledge in that domain (Cohen and Levinthal 1990; Zahra and George 2002). It is also contrary to findings by me (Holger) and my colleague (Domurath and Patzelt 2016), which showed that entrepreneurs who perceive that their venture has higher absorptive capacity for integrating knowledge about foreign markets are more likely to rely on foreign ties (as knowledge sources) when assessing the attractiveness of international opportunities for exploitation. Thus, the findings suggest the need for future research to explore the role of absorptive capacity in individuals' recognition of international opportunities. Further, it is interesting to note that venture capitalists can provide knowledge specific to internationalization to investees and that they seem to gain this knowledge from prior investees outside their domestic market. From an absorptive capacity perspective and related to the earlier discussion, one future research opportunity would be to explore how venture capital managers' own international experience and the experience their venture capital firm has gained through investments abroad interact in triggering future investees' internationalization. Chapter 2 also discussed the potentially important role of proximal firms with international knowledge, arguing that this knowledge might spill over to new ventures and thereby facilitate the recognition of opportunities in foreign markets. Indeed, this situation seems somewhat paradoxical because the most proximal firms trigger the recognition of opportunities in the most distant markets. However, research on knowledge spillover in the context of technological knowledge (Audretsch and Feldman 1996) helps resolve this paradox. It appears that there is further need to extend this notion of knowledge spillover beyond technological domains.

Finally, we elaborated on the role of cognitive processes, particularly the process of structural alignment, in translating entrepreneurial knowledge into the recognition of new business opportunities. While Baron (2006) and Baron and Ensley (2006) pointed out the importance of recognizing patterns for opportunity recognition, structural alignment is a particular cognitive process that describes how such patterns can be recognized. Given the central role of higher-order structural similarities in the process, our arguments explain why pattern recognition that guides opportunity identification is challenging (cf. Dutton 1993; Julian et al. 2008). Specifically, not only do entrepreneurs need to direct attention to environmental signals, but they also must invest cognitive energy to encode and process them at the deep level of structural relationships. It is here that entrepreneurs' prior knowledge comes into play because it facilitates the evaluation of structural relationships based on more developed mental representations of potential opportunities. In recognizing new opportunities, experienced entrepreneurs tend to focus on the causes and effects of difficulties in markets rather than on these markets' superficial features. As Chap. 2 illustrated, the role of knowledge in opportunity recognition goes beyond individuals' idiosyncratic advantages over others (Fiet 1996): prior knowledge serves as an important resource for superior cognitive processing that allows individuals to think of opportunities that have few superficial features in common with the original technology market. Finally, it is important to note that while there is initial evidence about structural-alignment processes in opportunity recognition, the setting of existing studies has been experimental and thus somewhat artificial. It is important that future studies explore, for example, the role of these processes in real-world conditions in terms of entrepreneurs' information overload, work stress, and the team environment typical of young ventures.

Motivation and Entrepreneurial Cognition

Both knowledge and motivation are critical for understanding opportunity beliefs and entrepreneurial action (McMullen and Shepherd 2006). In Chap. 3, we focused on the role of motivation in entrepreneurial cognition.

First, we highlighted how motivation can direct attention toward identifying potential opportunities and toward exploiting those potential opportunities identified. We started this discussion with the promise of financial rewards. Financial rewards provide extrinsic motivation, which in turn enables individuals to generate a greater number of ideas, and these ideas tend to be more innovative. Further, this positive impact of financial rewards is even more positive when entrepreneurs have greater domain knowledge (Shepherd and DeTienne 2005).

Second, people can be passionate about various activities, and we described how individuals can be passionate about entrepreneurial activities, which drive effort, persistence, and hopefully eventual success for the key tasks of the entrepreneurial process. Further, there are different types of entrepreneurial passion. For example, Cardon et al. (2009) described that entrepreneurs can be passionate about innovating, founding, and/or developing a new venture. However, there is little research on how these different types of passion relate to and interact with other motivations. For example, to what extent can financial motivation compensate for the lack of certain types of passion in an entrepreneur's motivation to start or persist with a venture? However, perhaps financial motivation and different passion types are not substitutes but complements. For instance, perhaps an entrepreneur's motivation from passion for developing/growing a venture is even stronger when he or she is also financially motivated. It is important to address these and other questions to better understand the impact of (different types of) passion on entrepreneurs' motivations.

Third, we highlighted how fear of failure is often believed to obstruct entrepreneurial action given the uncertainty (and possibility of failure) inherent in the pursuit of potential opportunities. However, we highlighted the different dimensions of fear of failure and how some may motivate (rather than obstruct) entrepreneurial action. The dimensions of fear of failure are (1) fear of feeling shame and embarrassment, (2) fear of devaluing one's self-estimate, (3) fear of having an uncertain future, (4) fear of losing social influence, and (5) fear of upsetting important others (Conroy 2001; Conroy and Elliot 2004; Conroy et al. 2002). We also explained how passion and fear of failure can interact in determining entrepreneurial action. Again, from these different types of fear of failure, a number of novel research opportunities arise. For example, under what circumstances and for what types of ventures are these fear of failure dimensions most influential in deterring entrepreneurial action? Perhaps entrepreneurs who evaluate opportunities for ventures that will be highly visible in the media may be most influenced by their fear of shame and embarrassment and/or their fear of losing social influence, whereas entrepreneurs with weak personal financial resources might be most influenced by their fear of having an uncertain future when evaluating new business opportunities. Further, going forward, scholars can explore how different fear of failure dimensions interact with other motivational triggers for entrepreneurial action. For example, the impact of prosocial motivation on an entrepreneur's motivation to engage in social entrepreneurship may be diminished when the entrepreneur also has high fear of upsetting others. When a social venture fails, the numerous stakeholders of the venture—including those who are being helped—may become particularly upset, especially if they must return to the miserable situation they were in before the venture started to help them.

Fourth, in the chapter, we discussed how motivation can help explain the identification and exploitation of a special kind of potential opportunity—potential opportunities to preserve nature or sustain communities. We described how an individual's local environment can influence the way he or she "sees" the world, which in turn can motivate the identification and pursuit of potential opportunities to solve social or ecological problems. In exploiting these potential opportunities, entrepreneurs have the chance to generate economic gain for themselves and/or for others. This promise of economic gain for the self and/or others can also motivate the pursuit of potential opportunities for sustainable development (Patzelt and Shepherd 2011; Shepherd and Patzelt 2011). However, to date, we have little empirical evidence of how economic and non-economic gains motivate entrepreneurs' recognition and exploitation of opportunities for sustaining natural and communal environments.

Fifth, individuals are also embedded in environments that can experience or reflect negative health situations—their own or close others—and these experiences can motivate the identification and exploitation of potential opportunities to offer health-related solutions (Shepherd and Patzelt 2015). Moreover, many people with physical or psychological problems are drawn to entrepreneurial careers because these careers provide flexibility, autonomy, and performance-related advantages not available in employment (e.g., Wiklund et al. 2016). However, under what circumstances are those suffering with physical or psychological problems able to adjust their ventures to their needs and therefore maintain motivation over time? For example, some industries may be so dynamic that keeping up with competition requires adaptation that is so fast or has to occur in such a way that it is incompatible with the needs of entrepreneurs with health-related problems. Indeed, in such situations, the competitive pressure faced may actually worsen the entrepreneur's health conditions, causing a downward spiral of diminished health and decreased ability to address the competitive pressure of the venture's environment. The outcome of such a downward spiral for the entrepreneur may not only be decreased motivation for continuing the venture but also bad health. These and related research questions warrant considerable attention to clarify the relationship between entrepreneurs' health and motivation and thereby help those with physical or psychological health problems develop successful entrepreneurial careers.

Finally, motivation can also come from an individual's values. Building on Schwartz (1992; Holland and Shepherd 2013), we discussed the role of the following values in motivating entrepreneurial action: (1) self-enhancement, (2) openness to change, (3) self-transcendence, and (4) conservation. More precisely, we discussed the role of values and other motivational influences in the decision to persist with a particular course of action when the best decision is to stop the action—in this case, terminate the project or business. Entrepreneurs persist with a losing course of action because of (1) personal sunk costs, (2) personal self-interest, (3) lack of other personal opportunities, (4) norms for consistency, (5) previous organizational success, and (6) perceived collective efficacy of organizational members. The impact of these attributes on the decision to persist with a losing course of action depends on the entrepreneur's level of extrinsic motivation (DeTienne et al. 2008). Such persistence can be costly to the entrepreneur and stakeholders if and when the venture eventually fails (Shepherd et al. 2009a, b). Therefore, more motivation is not always an unambiguous blessing in the entrepreneurial context. We encourage further research on the conditions in which entrepreneurial motivation is good or bad for the individual and his or her venture and the ways entrepreneurs can balance both their motivation to start and develop a venture and their ability able to withdraw from the venture when feedback from the environment signals that future success is highly unlikely.

ATTENTION AND ENTREPRENEURIAL COGNITION

In Chap. 4, we discussed the role of attention in the entrepreneurial process. We distinguished between top-down and bottom-up attention allocation and noted how we most often think about entrepreneurial decision making and action arising from a top-down approach. However, we highlighted how bottom-up processes can operate as individuals detect and interpret signals of potential opportunities (Shepherd et al. 2007, 2017). In this situation, the entrepreneur's attention is "free" to be drawn to changes in the external environment and can be focused on interpreting the nature of and the potential opportunities arising from these environmental changes. More research is needed on the role of bottom-up attention-allocation processes in the detection and interpretation of signals of environmental change and how these interpretations impact the formation of opportunity beliefs. We suspect that this future research on attention will involve consideration of entrepreneurs' task demands given that attention allocated to demanding tasks is simultaneously unavailable for scanning the external environment for signals of potential opportunities (i.e., people have limited attentional capacity).

Of course, attention may not be allocated to one task and one potential opportunity. In Chap. 4, we also detailed how the composition of a portfolio of potential opportunities at varying stages of development reflects different firm capabilities for advancing or terminating potential opportunities at specific stages of development in a timely manner. These capabilities to speed opportunity advancement or terminate opportunity pursuit are reflected in the firm's experiences, standard operating procedures, and confidence—all of which direct attention within the organization. In the chapter findings, we also highlighted how engineers were disappointed when the marginal projects they were working on were not terminated—they wanted to be transferred to the next hot project. Indeed, although those who were immediately transferred from a failing project to a new project experienced positive emotions, they did not reflect on the failed project and therefore did not learn from the experience (and neither did the organization). In contrast, those who experienced a delayed termination felt negative emotions but used that time to reflect on, document, and ultimately learn from the failure experience (Shepherd et al. 2014). Future research can, for example, explore how the apparent conflict between experiencing negative emotions and learning can be resolved—that is, under what conditions can team members minimize negative emotions and maximize learning within the project-shutdown period? In addition, perhaps some managerial interventions and support practices can direct employees' attention toward learning in quickly terminated projects (yielding few negative emotions) or minimize the experience of negative emotions in slowly terminated projects (yielding opportunities for learning).

Finally, while much of individuals' attention is automatically allocated to stimuli to inform their decisions, this automaticity can create some problems, especially when thinking about novel tasks and/or working in novel environments. Metacognition is thinking about one's thinking, which enables a more conscious consideration of the current task (similarities and differences) vis-à-vis other decision situations that require one to choose among alternate decision strategies and monitor progress in exploiting that decision strategy. While we speculate that a metacognitive approach is likely to be most useful in novel contexts and when decision speed is not critical, empirical evidence is needed to explore this claim. For example, scholars may explore the potential benefits and downsides of metacognition for entrepreneurs acting in industries with varying degrees of dynamism and technological change.

IDENTITY AND ENTREPRENEURIAL COGNITION

In Chap. 5, we discussed entrepreneurial identity. Identity has a number of important implications in the entrepreneurial context. We described how people who pursue an entrepreneurial career are able to satisfy their need for distinctiveness but also acknowledged that people have the need to belong and that satisfying such a need is both distinctive to and a challenge for entrepreneurs. Indeed, many entrepreneurs report feeling lonely. In Chap. 5, we also discussed how entrepreneurs can develop an identity with the optimal level of distinctiveness by combining their work identity with their non-work identity in a way that maximizes psychological well-being. Of course, we realize (partly from our own experiences) that it is not always easy to "manage" one's work and non-work identities because they conflict at times. Therefore, we discussed alternate identity-management strategies—compartmentalization and integration—and the conditions under which one is more likely to be successful than the other (see Shepherd and Haynie 2009). Going forward, research may explore how entrepreneurs successfully implement these strategies in their daily lives and what aspects of their work- and non-work-related identities they need to manage most actively to resolve identity conflict. Perhaps some industries (e.g., those that are highly competitive) make identity management more challenging than other industries, and perhaps entrepreneurs with some specific personalities are more successful in resolving identity conflict than other entrepreneurs. We believe that there is ample room for research to build on our arguments about entrepreneurs' identity-management strategies.

We also explained how identities are sometimes lost and how the pursuit of a potential opportunity and/or entrepreneurial career can help individuals find, develop, and refine a new work identity. In the case of identity loss from a traumatic event, the first step toward creating a new identity is to build an identity foundation. An identity foundation requires the individual to rebuild fundamental assumptions about the world, humanity, and the self. Without this foundation, identity work will likely fail. Importantly, these individuals (i.e., those who have lost their identity due to a traumatic event) can develop a motivation for an entrepreneurial career (through both pull and push motivations) and can think creatively about how their past career competencies apply to new possible entrepreneurial careers (Haynie and Shepherd 2011). At the same time, these insights open up various future research opportunities. For example, how does the nature of the traumatic event impact the individual's motivation to pursue an entrepreneurial career and the type of venture founded? Also, how does the type and strength of the identity lost by the traumatic event impact entrepreneurial motivation? Perhaps the individual's personality influences to what extent entrepreneurial motivation impacts his or her recovery from trauma through the pursuit of an entrepreneurial career. Understanding these boundary conditions of entrepreneurial motivation as a response to trauma is important not only for building a new theory of entrepreneurial motivation but also for helping traumatized individuals decide whether an entrepreneurial career is an appropriate way to move on in their lives.

We continued this discussion of creating a new identity by exploring the situation of people hitting rock bottom. Rock bottom provides a context for escape. While some escape through identity play, which provides a basis for exploring a range of potential careers and a pathway to recovery, there is a dark side. The dark side involves escape through cognitive deconstruction, which hinders any progress in creating a new identity and stalls recovery (or worse). Individuals who hit rock bottom after losing a career can be helped if they think about the boundary between fantasy and reality, immersed in the present, and engage identity play (Shepherd and Williams 2018). Again, we expect future research to provide valuable insights for both scholars and those who hit rock bottom by building on our work. For example, there are different antecedents and obstacles to engaging in identity play. For example, those who hit rock bottom have a different "psychological space" for identity play (see also Petriglieri and Petriglieri 2010). It would be interesting to study under what conditions entrepreneurs who hit rock bottom have more or less psychological space for identity play and when they are more likely to use this psychological space for identity play as a basis for recovery from hitting rock bottom. In addition, we know little about what tools help people recover with identity play (e.g., scenario planning (Brown and Starkey 2000)). Finally, those who hit rock bottom may create different types of positive identities during recovery. For example, how do different types of identity play as well as different ways of carrying out identity play create new (entrepreneurial) identities, such as those that are positive but may also represent downgrades in some respect (Newman 1988)? Also, what role does culture play in enabling or hindering successful recovery from hitting rock bottom as well as in engaging in identity play?

Furthermore, as discussed in the chapter, an entrepreneur can have multiple identities, and these identities can come into conflict. Such identity conflict is particularly salient in the family business context. Indeed, we discussed the conflict between the family identity and the owner identity in family businesses and the ways this identity conflict can slow entrepreneurial decision making. We also offered some suggestions for how to manage potential identity conflict to speed entrepreneurial decision making. However, we also note here that the nature of both the family and the family business may influence the generation of and escape from identity conflict. These issues warrant further research. For instance, families differ in the extent to which they are involved in the family business. As such, does the conflict between a person's owner and family identities evolve differently if more members of a family are involved in the business? How does conflict among family members (either involved in the business or not) influence the identity conflict that emerges? Further, is this conflict resolved more or less easily (or resolved in a different manner) when the family business has existed for more generations or when it is run by an outside CEO rather than a family CEO? How do non-economic goals often pursued by family members (Chrisman et al. 2014) influence their identity conflict? Future research can make important contributions by exploring these and other questions regarding the family- and business-related factors behind the emergence and resolution of identity conflict for family owner-managers.

EMOTION AND ENTREPRENEURIAL COGNITION

In Chap. 6, we discussed the role of emotion in entrepreneurship. We highlighted that an entrepreneurial career can generate both high positive emotions and high negative emotions. First, we described passion and distinguished between harmonious and obsessive passion and how they influence the decision to exploit a new potential opportunity. We also explained how another positive emotion—excitement—moderates the relationship between passion and the decision to exploit a potential opportunity. However, here, we also note that passion and excitement are only two out of many positive emotions that might play a role in entrepreneurial decision making. For example, Welpe et al. (2012) found that joy can increase the positive impact of opportunity evaluation on exploitation, and Baron (2008) argued that positive emotions generally facilitate opportunity recognition. Therefore, there is good reason to believe that additional positive emotions, such as enthusiasm, happiness, pride, or boldness, might play an important role in opportunity recognition and exploitation. Further, in addition to experiencing these emotions, anticipating such emotions might influence the entrepreneurial process. For example, entrepreneurs who anticipate pride about successfully founding a venture might be more driven toward opportunity recognition and exploitation than those who tend to experience little pride in general. Moreover, a few studies have addressed the issue of negative emotions in the entrepreneurial process. These studies have shown, for example, that entrepreneurs tend to experience fewer negative emotions than non-entrepreneurs (Patzelt and Shepherd 2011), but they have also highlighted the important role of specific negative emotions (e.g., fear and anger) (Welpe et al. 2012; Mitchell and Shepherd 2010) for opportunity evaluation and exploitation. We expect that the study of positive and negative emotions' role in the entrepreneurial process will receive significant scholarly attention in the future.

Second, given that emotions play a key role in an individual's entrepreneurial cognition, we explained how managers' displays of emotions can influence employees' willingness to act entrepreneurially. Specifically, we highlighted our study with a colleague (Brundin et al. 2008) focusing on mangers' confidence, positive emotion of satisfaction, and negative emotions of frustration, worry, bewilderment, and strain and their impact on employees' willingness to act entrepreneurially; employees evaluated all these emotions as being influential for their entrepreneurial motivation. In addition, my (Holger) work with my colleagues (Breugst et al. 2012) found that employees' perceptions of entrepreneurial passion influence their commitment to new ventures but differently for different types of passion: while passion for innovation and venture development increases commitment, passion for founding has a negative effect. These studies reveal considerable potential for contribution when scholars explore not only entrepreneurs' emotions but also how individuals in their environment react to entrepreneurs' emotional displays. Indeed, the literature is almost silent on how employees perceive their work environment within startups, including entrepreneurs' emotional expressions. Further, there is initial evidence that entrepreneurs' passionate displays can trigger investors' funding decisions (Chen et al. 2009), which indicates that a variety of stakeholders (in addition to employees and investors including customers, suppliers, alliance partners) might be influenced by entrepreneurs' emotional displays. Scholars have plenty of opportunities to investigate how entrepreneurs' emotions and emotional displays influence their social environments and thereby ventures' access to resources and—ultimately—success.

We also detailed how employees often become attached to their projects and experience a negative emotional reaction—grief (Shepherd 2003)—when their projects (Shepherd et al. 2009a, 2011) or businesses fail (Byrne and Shepherd 2015; Shepherd 2003, 2009). These entrepreneurs often feel grief because they have lost something important to them—something that satisfied their needs for competence, autonomy, and belonging (Shepherd and Cardon 2009). These negative emotions can obstruct individuals' ability to learn from failure experiences and move on (Shepherd 2003; Shepherd et al. 2011). At the individual level, entrepreneurs (corporate or independent) can oscillate between a loss orientation and a restoration orientation as a means of "managing" negative emotions, which is superior to simply normalizing failure (i.e., taking emotion out of the entrepreneurial process altogether). These individuals can also show themselves self-compassion—self-kindness, common humanity, and mindfulness—which helps stop the escalation of negative emotions and facilitates learning from the experience. We also discussed implications of managing grief over project failure at the organizational level. As such, our work raises interesting questions that future research can explore. For example, how do organizational environment, culture, and leadership facilitate the oscillation between loss and restoration orientations? Further, how do different individuals achieve the best "balance" between these orientations based on their personality characteristics and the nature of their failure experience? We hope that we inspired research along these lines by summarizing what we know about the role of negative emotions in the context of entrepreneurial failure.

Conclusion

In conclusion, entrepreneurial cognition is a fascinating topic that has triggered our curiosity and inspired our research for more than a decade. While scholars have made considerable progress on studying this topic, this final chapter has shown that every research question addressed thus far has opened up more questions that are just as fascinating. The goal of this book was to both summarize what our work has contributed to current knowledge and identify the opportunities for research it has opened up for future scholarship. We hope you enjoyed our book and were able to glean some new insights into entrepreneurial cognition. Even more, we hope we triggered your motivation to join us on the exciting road ahead.

References

Audretsch, D. B., & Feldman, M. P. (1996). R&D spillovers and the geography of innovation and production. *American Economic Review, 86*(3), 630–640.

Baron, R. A. (2006). Opportunity recognition as pattern recognition: How entrepreneurs "connect the dots" to identify new business opportunities. *Academy of Management Perspectives, 20*(1), 104–119.

Baron, R. A. (2008). The role of affect in the entrepreneurial process. *Academy of Management Review, 33*, 328–340.

Baron, R. A., & Ensley, M. D. (2006). Opportunity recognition as the detection of meaningful patterns: Evidence from comparisons of novice and experienced entrepreneurs. *Management Science, 52*(9), 1331–1344.

Breugst, N., Domurath, A., Patzelt, H., & Klaukien, A. (2012). Perceptions of entrepreneurial passion and employees' commitment to entrepreneurial ventures. *Entrepreneurship Theory and Practice, 36*, 171–192.

Brown, A. D., & Starkey, K. (2000). Organizational identity and learning: A psychodynamic perspective. *Academy of Management Review, 25*(1), 102–120.

Brundin, E., Patzelt, H., & Shepherd, D. A. (2008). Managers' emotional displays and employees' willingness to act entrepreneurially. *Journal of Business Venturing, 23*(2), 221–243.

Byrne, O., & Shepherd, D. A. (2015). Different strokes for different folks: Entrepreneurial narratives of emotion, cognition, and making sense of business failure. *Entrepreneurship Theory and Practice, 39*, 375–405.

Cardon, M. S., Wincent, J., Singh, J., & Drnovsek, M. (2009). The nature and experience of entrepreneurial passion. *Academy of Management Review, 34*(3), 511–532.

Chen, X. P., Yao, X., & Kotha, S. (2009). Entrepreneur passion and preparedness in business plan presentations: A persuasion analysis of venture capitalists' funding decisions. *Academy of Management Journal, 52*, 199–214.

Chrisman, J. J., Memili, E., & Misra, K. (2014). Nonfamily managers, family firms, and the winner's curse: The influence of noneconomic goals and bounded rationality. *Entrepreneurship Theory and Practice, 38*(5), 1103–1127.

Cohen, W. M., & Levinthal, D. A. (1990). Absorptive capacity: A new perspective on learning and innovation. *Administrative Science Quarterly, 35*(1), 128–152.

Conroy, D. E. (2001). Progress in the development of a multidimensional measure of fear of failure: The performance failure appraisal inventory (PFAI). *Anxiety, Stress and Coping, 14*(4), 431–452.

Conroy, D. E., & Elliot, A. J. (2004). Fear of failure and achievement goals in sport: Addressing the issue of the chicken and the egg. *Anxiety, Stress and Coping, 17*, 271–285.

Conroy, D. E., Willow, J. P., & Metzler, J. N. (2002). Multidimensional fear of failure measurement: The performance failure appraisal inventory. *Journal of Applied Sport Psychology, 14*(2), 76–90.

Csikszentmihalyi, M. (1975). Play and intrinsic rewards. *Journal of Humanistic Psychology, 15*(3), 41–63.

Csikszentmihalyi, M. (2000). *Beyond boredom and anxiety*. San Francisco: Jossey-Bass.

DeTienne, D. R., Shepherd, D. A., & De Castro, J. O. (2008). The fallacy of "only the strong survive": The effects of extrinsic motivation on the persistence decisions for underperforming firms. *Journal of Business Venturing, 23*(5), 528–546.

Domurath, A., & Patzelt, H. (2016). Entrepreneurs' assessments of early international entry: The role of foreign social ties, venture absorptive capacity, and generalized trust in others. *Entrepreneurship Theory and Practice, 40*(5), 1149–1177.

Dutton, J. E. (1993). Interpretations on automatic: A different view of strategic issue diagnosis. *Journal of Management Studies, 30*(3), 339–357.

Fiet, J. O. (1996). The informational basis of entrepreneurial discovery. *Small Business Economics, 8*(6), 419–430.

Hart, S. L. (2006). Worlds in collision. *Global Business and Organizational Excellence, 25*(3), 13–25.

Haynie, J. M., & Shepherd, D. (2011). Toward a theory of discontinuous career transition: Investigating career transitions necessitated by traumatic life events. *Journal of Applied Psychology, 96*(3), 501.

Holland, D. V., & Shepherd, D. A. (2013). Deciding to persist: Adversity, values, and entrepreneurs' decision policies. *Entrepreneurship Theory and Practice, 37*(2), 331–358.

Julian, S. D., Ofori-Dankwa, J. C., & Justis, R. T. (2008). Understanding strategic responses to interest group pressures. *Strategic Management Journal, 29*(9), 963–984.

Maheswaran, D., & Sternthal, B. (1990). The effects of knowledge, motivation, and type of message on ad processing and product judgments. *Journal of Consumer Research, 17*(1), 66–73.

McMullen, J. S., & Shepherd, D. A. (2006). Entrepreneurial action and the role of uncertainty in the theory of the entrepreneur. *Academy of Management Review, 31*(1), 132–152.

Mitchell, J. R., & Shepherd, D. A. (2010). To thine own self be true: Images of self, images of opportunity, and entrepreneurial action. *Journal of Business Venturing*, 25, 138–154.

Newman, K. S. (1988). *Falling from grace: The experience of downward mobility in the American middle class.* New York: Free Press.

Patzelt, H., & Shepherd, D. A. (2011). Recognizing opportunities for sustainable development. *Entrepreneurship Theory and Practice*, 35(4), 631–652.

Petriglieri, G., & Petriglieri, J. L. (2010). Identity workspaces: The case of business schools. *Academy of Management Learning & Education*, 9(1), 44–60.

Schwartz, S. H. (1992). Universals in the content and structure of values: Theoretical advances and empirical tests in 20 countries. *Advances in Experimental Social Psychology*, 25, 1–65.

Shah, S. K., & Tripsas, M. (2007). The accidental entrepreneur: The emergent and collective process of user entrepreneurship. *Strategic Entrepreneurship Journal*, 1(1–2), 123–140.

Shane, S. (2000). Prior knowledge and the discovery of entrepreneurial opportunities. *Organization Science*, 11(4), 448–469.

Shepherd, D. A. (2003). Learning from business failure: Propositions of grief recovery for the self-employed. *Academy of Management Review*, 28, 318–328.

Shepherd, D. A. (2009). Grief recovery from the loss of a family business: A multi- and meso-level theory. *Journal of Business Venturing*, 24(1), 81–97.

Shepherd, D. A., & Cardon, M. S. (2009). Negative emotional reactions to project failure and the self-compassion to learn from the experience. *Journal of Management Studies*, 46(6), 923–949.

Shepherd, D. A., & DeTienne, D. R. (2005). Prior knowledge, potential financial reward, and opportunity identification. *Entrepreneurship Theory and Practice*, 29(1), 91–112.

Shepherd, D., & Haynie, J. M. (2009). Birds of a feather don't always flock together: Identity management in entrepreneurship. *Journal of Business Venturing*, 24(4), 316–337.

Shepherd, D. A., & Patzelt, H. (2011). The new field of sustainable entrepreneurship: Studying entrepreneurial action linking "what is to be sustained" with "what is to be developed". *Entrepreneurship Theory and Practice*, 35(1), 137–163.

Shepherd, D. A., & Patzelt, H. (2015). Harsh evaluations of entrepreneurs who fail: The role of sexual orientation, use of environmentally friendly technologies, and observers' perspective taking. *Journal of Management Studies*, 52, 253–284.

Shepherd, D., & Williams, T. (2018). Hitting rock bottom after job loss: Bouncing back to create a new positive work identity. *Academy of Management Review*, amr-2015.

Shepherd, D. A., McMullen, J. S., & Jennings, P. D. (2007). The formation of opportunity beliefs: Overcoming ignorance and reducing doubt. *Strategic Entrepreneurship Journal*, 1(1–2), 75–95.

Shepherd, D. A., Covin, J. G., & Kuratko, D. F. (2009a). Project failure from corporate entrepreneurship: Managing the grief process. *Journal of Business Venturing, 24*(6), 588–600.

Shepherd, D. A., Wiklund, J., & Haynie, J. M. (2009b). Moving forward: Balancing the financial and emotional costs of business failure. *Journal of Business Venturing, 24*(2), 134–148.

Shepherd, D. A., Patzelt, H., & Wolfe, M. (2011). Moving forward from project failure: Negative emotions, affective commitment, and learning from the experience. *Academy of Management Journal, 54*, 1229–1259.

Shepherd, D. A., Patzelt, H., Williams, T. A., & Warnecke, D. (2014). How does project termination impact project team members? Rapid termination, 'creeping death', and learning from failure. *Journal of Management Studies, 51*(4), 513–546.

Shepherd, D. A., McMullen, J. S., & Ocasio, W. (2017). Is that an opportunity? An attention model of top managers' opportunity beliefs for strategic action. *Strategic Management Journal, 38*(3), 626–644.

Welpe, I. M., Spörrle, M., Grichnik, D., Michl, T., & Audretsch, D. B. (2012). Emotions and opportunities: The interplay of opportunity evaluation, fear, joy, and anger as antecedent of entrepreneurial exploitation. *Entrepreneurship Theory and Practice, 36*(1), 69–96.

Wiklund, J., Patzelt, H., & Dimov, D. (2016). Entrepreneurship and psychological disorders: How ADHD can be productively harnessed. *Journal of Business Venturing Insights, 6*, 14–20.

Zahra, S. A., & George, G. (2002). Absorptive capacity: A review, reconceptualization, and extension. *Academy of Management Review, 27*(2), 185–203.

Open Access This chapter is licensed under the terms of the Creative Commons Attribution 4.0 International License (http://creativecommons.org/licenses/by/4.0/), which permits use, sharing, adaptation, distribution and reproduction in any medium or format, as long as you give appropriate credit to the original author(s) and the source, provide a link to the Creative Commons license and indicate if changes were made.

The images or other third party material in this chapter are included in the chapter's Creative Commons license, unless indicated otherwise in a credit line to the material. If material is not included in the chapter's Creative Commons license and your intended use is not permitted by statutory regulation or exceeds the permitted use, you will need to obtain permission directly from the copyright holder.

Index[1]

A

Action, 1–3, 13, 14, 16, 17, 26, 27, 29, 52, 55–61, 64, 70, 71, 73, 74, 77–85, 106, 109, 110, 121, 124, 141, 160, 168, 170, 171, 177, 181, 182, 207–210, 212, 216, 224–226, 228, 231, 232, 236, 238, 240, 241, 263–266

Affective commitment, 215–224

Alliance, 18–21, 23, 24, 272

Architectural change, 111, 112

Attention, vii, 3, 4, 8, 9, 12, 13, 24–27, 31–35, 54, 58, 61, 63–67, 73, 105–126, 159, 164, 170, 205, 207, 222, 224, 226, 227, 229, 230, 260, 263, 264, 266–268, 271

Autonomy, 55, 61, 63–65, 67–69, 79, 140, 162, 163, 175, 218–221, 265, 272

B

Belonging, 4, 17, 69, 137–156, 272

Bottom-up, 105–109, 266, 267

C

Career, 4, 14, 53, 67–71, 79, 87, 141, 144, 157–159, 162–166, 169, 170, 185, 210, 217, 265, 266, 268–270

Cognition, viii, 1–4, 7–38, 51–87, 105–126, 141, 164, 168, 169, 185, 201–242, 259–270

Cognitive deconstruction, 167, 168, 269

Common humanity, 236–240, 272

Community, 1, 11, 17, 56, 61–64, 80, 152, 158, 167, 204, 207, 262, 265

Compartmentalization, 147–151, 154, 155, 179, 180, 185, 268

---

[1]Note: Page number followed by 'n' refers to notes.

Compassion, 17, 235, 236, 238
Competence, 55, 61, 62, 64, 65, 69, 74, 81, 163–165, 218–220, 269, 272
Complexity, viii, 1, 25, 107, 111, 112, 145, 212, 213
Confidence, 69, 114, 116, 117, 209, 210, 213, 214, 219, 234, 235, 267, 271
Coping, 4, 63, 158, 161–165, 205, 216, 226–236, 242

D

Decisions, 1, 2, 8, 20, 21, 23, 24, 31, 52, 55, 56, 58–61, 72, 73, 75, 77–85, 106, 109, 110, 112–117, 120–124, 142, 171, 178, 182, 183, 201, 205–208, 216, 220, 223, 241, 266–268, 270–272
Destruction of nature, 72–76
Disasters, 16–18, 233
Disciplined imagination, 172
Discontinuous, 2, 105–109, 111, 158
Disjunctive transitions, 157–159
Distinctiveness, 4, 137–143, 145, 147–156, 268
Divergent, 34–37, 120
Dynamism, 113, 127n2, 209, 268

E

Emotion, vii, viii, 1, 3, 4, 51, 55, 66, 67, 117–120, 123, 138, 139, 141, 159, 161, 168, 170, 171, 176, 185, 201–242, 259, 267, 270–272
Emotional displays, 208–214, 241
Environmental change, 2, 10, 26, 28, 63, 107–109, 111, 112, 121, 122, 126, 267
Escape, 167, 169, 170, 176, 240, 269, 270

Evaluation, 7, 18, 26, 28, 29, 63, 72–74, 76, 77, 106, 113–117, 121, 124, 150, 168, 172, 177, 181–183, 206, 220, 223, 225, 227, 230, 237–239, 241, 263–265, 271
Excitement, 79, 163, 201, 205–207, 271
Experience, 4, 7–10, 12, 13, 15, 16, 18–20, 22–24, 30, 32, 36, 58, 63, 66, 70, 73, 74, 79, 107, 109, 111–126, 142, 143, 158–161, 164–166, 168, 171, 175, 178, 183, 184, 185n3, 201–206, 209–213, 215–224, 229–231, 235–238, 240–242, 260, 262, 265, 267, 268, 271, 272
Experiment, 53, 108, 115, 159, 166, 171, 172, 242n1, 263
Exploitation, 2, 3, 7, 15, 16, 18, 23, 24, 26, 27, 37, 56, 61, 62, 64, 66, 70–76, 84, 105, 113–117, 120, 126, 141, 182–184, 202–205, 207, 241, 261, 262, 264, 265, 268, 270, 271
Exploration, 2, 3, 7, 10, 25, 28, 34, 37, 53, 68, 71, 77–79, 86, 105, 113–117, 125, 137, 141, 148, 151, 154, 158, 159, 162, 163, 166, 169–172, 174, 175, 177, 179, 185, 201, 205, 208, 216, 218, 223, 227, 235, 241, 259, 261–263, 265, 267–272
Extrinsic motivation, 85, 86, 264, 266

F

Failure, 2, 4, 32, 56–62, 72, 84, 87n1, 106, 115–120, 157, 167, 170, 212, 215–231, 233–241, 264, 265, 267, 272
Failure parties, 235

Family, 4, 58, 62, 81, 142, 148, 149, 152, 155, 156, 163, 176–185, 202, 204, 205, 226, 270
Family identity, 152, 155, 156, 177, 179, 182, 183, 270
Fear, 11, 59–61, 63, 81, 158, 225, 264, 265, 271
Financial rewards, 3, 10, 51–55, 79, 86, 260, 264
Flexibility, 67–69, 112, 113, 121, 153, 154, 156, 162, 202, 203, 228, 265

G
Grief, 56, 66, 72, 123, 166, 201, 225–228, 230–236, 239

H
Harmonious passion, 55, 202, 203, 206, 207, 270
Health, 3, 14–16, 61, 63–72, 137, 139, 141, 143–147, 163, 178, 221, 232, 236, 240
Health problems, 15, 16, 65, 68, 70, 72, 261, 262, 266

I
Identification, 2–4, 7–16, 18, 20, 23–37, 51–55, 63–65, 67, 70, 105–112, 138, 139, 152, 157–159, 164, 173, 182, 202, 204, 209, 220, 221, 223, 259–265, 273
Identity, vii, 1, 4, 11, 61, 126, 137–185, 202–204, 218, 219, 221, 222, 234, 268–270
Identity boundaries, 146, 147, 151–157
Identity conflict, vii, 4, 148, 151, 156, 157, 159, 160, 176–185, 268, 270

Identity foundation, 159–164, 269
Identity synergies, 151–157
Incremental, 107–109, 111, 112, 119, 157, 159
Industry munificence, 75–76
Integration, 19, 69, 110, 112, 121, 144, 147–151, 154–157, 185, 268
International, 3, 14, 18–24, 38, 259, 262
Intrinsic motivation, 218

K
Knowledge, vii, 1, 3, 7–38, 53–55, 57, 63–65, 67, 86, 87, 106–109, 111, 112, 115, 116, 121–126, 141, 164, 165, 169, 178, 180, 209, 215–217, 225, 241, 259–264, 273

L
Learning, vii, 4, 8, 12, 26, 30, 79, 113, 115, 117–121, 126, 215–227, 229, 230, 235–242, 267, 272
Loneliness, 69, 70, 139, 142, 143, 221
Loss or Lost, 217, 231, 268
Loss orientation, 227–231, 241, 272

M
Metacognition, 120–126, 267, 268
Micro-identities, 4, 143–157, 185
Mindfulness, 236, 237, 240, 241, 272
Motivation, viii, 2–4, 27, 37, 38, 51–87, 122, 124, 138–141, 162–164, 171, 202, 209, 211–214, 218, 219, 221–223, 232, 241, 242, 259, 263–266, 269, 271, 273

N

Nature (natural environment), 3, 26, 34, 38, 51, 61–64, 70, 109, 112, 120, 122, 124, 125, 146, 151, 158, 171, 178, 184, 185n3, 220, 265, 267, 269, 270, 272
Negative emotions, vii, 4, 117–119, 138, 139, 161, 168, 170, 171, 176, 204, 211–231, 236–241, 267, 270–272
Normalization, 224–227
Notice, 31–33, 35, 58, 66, 107, 120, 212
Novelty, 28–32, 37, 109, 111, 112, 114, 123, 126, 181, 182, 203, 204, 209, 264, 267, 268

O

Obsessive passion, 55, 59–61, 202–205, 207, 270
Opportunity, viii, 1, 8–11, 51, 52, 105–112, 141, 202, 203, 259
Optimal distinctiveness, 4, 140, 143–147
Orientation, 114, 115, 117, 121, 122, 124, 125, 145, 160, 164, 216, 227–231, 241, 242, 272
Oscillation orientation, 216, 230, 231, 242n2

P

Passion, 55, 59–61, 77, 163, 164, 201–203, 205–207, 264, 270, 271
Persistence, 51, 60, 82–86, 106, 225, 233, 264, 266
Perspective taking, 70, 71, 262
Play, vii, 37, 52, 53, 79, 83, 85, 86, 165, 166, 169–176, 214, 237, 241, 263, 269–271

Portfolio, 21, 119, 120, 267
Positive emotions, 4, 55, 139, 171, 201–207, 210, 211, 213, 214, 221, 229, 267, 270, 271
Prosocial motivation, 70, 71, 265
Psychological health (Well being), 63, 65, 67, 69, 139, 141, 143–147, 178, 221, 236, 266
Pull (into entrepreneurship), 53, 59, 162–164, 269
Push (into entrepreneurship), 1, 53, 162, 163, 269

R

Real-time information, 113
Recognition, 3, 4, 7–11, 24–26, 28, 32, 33, 37, 38, 51, 54, 55, 61, 78, 79, 113, 126, 179, 259–263, 265, 271
Recovery, 137, 160, 163, 168, 170, 173, 232, 235, 269, 270
Regulation (regulating), vii, 26
Relatedness, 55, 61, 62, 64, 65, 152, 218, 219, 221, 222
Restoration orientation, 227–231, 241, 272
Rock bottom, 166–171, 176, 269, 270

S

Self, 56, 58, 140, 141, 149, 157–160, 162, 165, 166, 168, 169, 172, 218, 222, 237, 241, 265, 269
Self-compassion, 4, 223, 236–242, 272
Self-efficacy, 73–75, 85, 224, 231–236, 242
Self-help groups, 233
Self-interest, 82, 83, 266
Self-kindness, 236–238, 272
Societal problems, 13
Speed, 8, 113–117, 267, 268, 270

Structural alignment, 3, 25, 26, 28–34, 37, 38, 259, 263
Suffering (and the alleviation of suffering), 16–18, 62, 66–68, 70, 72, 236, 237, 262, 265
Sustainable, 3, 61, 63, 65–67, 259–261, 265

T
Task, viii, 8–10, 14, 18, 28, 30, 52, 54, 57, 59, 69, 73, 74, 81, 85, 105, 108, 110, 111, 115, 116, 118, 120–123, 126, 159, 173, 180, 181, 206, 208, 210, 212, 213, 218, 219, 222, 224, 225, 229, 232–234, 241, 260, 264, 267, 268
Team, vii, viii, 2, 4, 26, 69, 70, 85, 117–119, 142, 143, 146, 148, 152, 175, 202, 207, 210, 212, 214, 217–223, 226, 229, 240, 259, 262, 263, 267

Termination (project), 117–120, 165, 215, 220, 267
Top-down, 105–111, 266
Transient attention, 105–112
Trauma, 158–165, 231, 232, 269

U
Uncertainty, 1, 2, 23, 24, 56–58, 71, 120, 149, 184, 203, 209–214, 264

V
Values, 3, 7, 11, 12, 19, 21, 22, 51, 52, 67, 70, 72–81, 86, 108, 122, 143, 157, 165, 201, 219, 220, 225, 266
Venture capital, 18, 21–23, 38, 262
Venture creation, 70

W
Willingness, 71, 84, 208–214, 271

The manufacturer's authorised representative in the EU is Springer
Nature Customer Service Centre GmbH, Europaplatz 3, 69115 Heidelberg,
Germany. If you have any concerns regarding our products, please
contact ProductSafety@springernature.com

Printed and bound by CPI Group (UK) Ltd, Croydon, CR0 4YY
23/03/2026
02076663-0007